Contents

READINGS

APPENDICES

*Control Your
High Blood Pressure—
Without Drugs!*

Control Your High Blood Pressure— Without Drugs!

CLEAVES M. BENNETT, M.D.
WITH CHARLES CAMERON

Doubleday
NEW YORK LONDON TORONTO SYDNEY

Published by Doubleday, a division of
Bantam Doubleday Dell Publishing Group, Inc.,
666 Fifth Avenue, New York, New York 10103

Doubleday and the portrayal of an anchor with a dolphin
are trademarks of Doubleday, a division of
Bantam Doubleday Dell Publishing Group, Inc.

Library of Congress Cataloging in Publication Data
Bennett, Cleaves M., 1934–
Control your high blood pressure—without drugs!

Bibliography: p. 369
Includes index.
1. Hypertension—Prevention. 2. Hypertension—Diet
therapy. 3. Exercise therapy. 4. Relaxation.
5. Self-care, Health. I. Cameron, Charles. II. Title.
RC685.H8B38 1984   616.1'3206
ISBN   0-385-18927-3
ISBN   0-385-23579 (pbk)
Library of Congress Catalog Card Number 83–45022

To my Mother,
a real winner in my book

Special Thanks

I would like to thank the many people who have contributed to my growth, my thinking, and this book, and specifically to acknowledge: Camille Barton, who read the book in manuscript and offered many helpful suggestions and criticisms; Suzanne Elusorr, for her tireless attention to details; Christine Newport, nutritionist at the INNERHEALTH clinic in Los Angeles and friend, for permission to use her outstanding recipes; Werner Erhard, for helping me to find out what it means to go for it 100 percent; Tim Gallwey, for showing me how to play the Inner Game; the residents I have taught and who have taught me; the patients I have cared for and who have cared for me; and my kids, Geoffrey, Christopher, and Karin, who encouraged me throughout the writing of this book.

Introduction

The doctor of the future will give no medicine, but will interest his patient in the care of the human frame, in diet, and in the cause and prevention of disease.

Thomas Edison

During the last few years I have seen countless people who were suffering from high blood pressure discover they could
- alter their diet,
- lose weight,
- begin regular exercise,
- reduce their stress levels, and
- bring their blood pressure under control,

to the point where their own doctors were able to recommend that they stop taking their medications.

According to recent estimates, as many as 60 million Americans now have blood pressure levels high enough that they run a noticeably greater risk than the rest of us of winding up with a stroke or a heart attack in the not too distant future.

Most of these people are already faced with spending the rest of their lives taking a variety of pills every day, many of which cause a general feeling of apathy and lack of enthusiasm for life, and some of which cause impotence or worse.

But it doesn't have to be that way.

The medicine cabinet doesn't have to be at the center of your life. You can do without those pills. You'd be better off, and feel a whole lot better, if you lived a healthy life without them. But you do need to learn how to live without medications. And that's what this book is about.

Let me put it a little more bluntly. You need to learn how to live without doctors. Listen: I'm a doctor myself, and I feel that doctors are a little like bail bondsmen. You should know they exist, in case you ever need them. You know they serve a purpose in society, you may read about them from time to time in the newspapers or even live next door to one— but you want to be able to live your life without them. They are not a group of people you'd want to do business with all the time.

Don't get me wrong. I am proud to be a doctor. I am glad that modern medicine has spared us smallpox and polio and the plague. My job as a physician is to get you healthy and help keep you that way—and where medications, technology, surgery, or whatever can help me do that, I'm glad to make use of them.

But I don't want to be offering you drugs or surgery or hospital visits when your own body could handle things much better than the best that modern medicine has to offer.

I want you to discover just how much power you have to get healthy, and to stay healthy, and to enjoy it. I want you to know how wonderful life can feel.

For years and years I have sat across the desk from patients with high blood pressure. While making out their prescriptions, I've glanced up and caught their eyes. I've seen a very special kind of sadness.

They knew, and I knew, that the pills I was prescribing might not make them feel better. They knew, and I knew, that we were making the best of a bad job. They suspected, and I suspected, that they would be taking those pills for the rest of their lives.

And now I know it doesn't have to be that way.

Sometimes I'd look at my patients, and I'd know they weren't taking all the medicines I prescribed or that they weren't following the diet I'd recommended. And we'd talk, and they'd tell me about it.

They'd tell me that they felt ashamed or embarrassed that they weren't following their doctor's orders, and that they hadn't intended to let anyone know about it, least of all me. They felt they couldn't tell their wives or their business associates that they'd been out and had a pastrami sandwich or that they weren't taking their pills properly.

They wound up having a whole secret life that they couldn't discuss with anyone. And that's exhausting, debilitating, and depressing. They felt a special kind of isolation, a special loneliness. Most people, if they don't take good care of themselves, feel sort of private about it. And it made my patients feel isolated from the people who really cared about them and from the people who could really help them.

I'm a doctor. But I've had my own problems going to doctors and not wanting to tell them things, because I was worried about what they'd think of me or what they'd find was wrong with me. And I've had my own problems with diets and exercise programs. I understand just how difficult these things can seem.

So I can sympathize with my patients. I've been on their side of the desk myself. But I also feel a lot of confidence, a lot of optimism about myself and about them. I know just how powerful humans really are when it comes to changing things for the better.

Other patients of mine would take their medications regularly enough, and keep to the diet, but they often looked bewildered and hurt, too. Here they were, taking their pills, doing everything they had been told to do, and things still weren't working out.

All too often the medicines just don't work. Or at least they don't work the way they're supposed to, or the way we'd like them to. I would see frustration in my patients' faces and hear it in the things they said to me. "It's not fair. I'm doing what you told me to do. How come I'm not better? How come I still feel so lousy?"

I know now that it doesn't have to be that way.

And then there were the few patients whose faces told me, all too clearly, that life just wasn't much fun anymore. Maybe they thought it was all a normal part of getting older and they were sort of resigned to it. But I could see that it didn't make them happy.

Many people, after taking certain kinds of blood pressure pills for a while, find that their get-up-and-go just got up and went. Their ambition is gone. They just don't have the energy they used to. Often their sex life is a thing of the past, a bunch of memories. And they may think this is all just a part of growing old.

But it's not. Often it's the side effects of the pills that they are feeling. But those side effects may come on so slowly that people don't realize they have anything to do with the pills. That tired feeling just sneaks up on them. They wind up falling asleep in front of the TV every night. And it's not until they get off the pills, and no longer have the side effects, that they realize how bad they used to feel. And they can hardly believe how much better it feels to be off the pills.

And it can be that way for you.

You can keep your blood pressure down, and enjoy life, and not take any pills. I have seen it happen so many, many times. It can happen for you. IF. And it's a big IF. IF you'll read this book carefully, cooperate with your own physician, and have confidence in yourself, and go through the twelve-week program I've outlined here.

In the years since I stopped always prescribing pills for high blood pressure and started treating it with an emphasis on diet and exercise and relaxation, I've seen a very different look on my patients' faces.

I have seen them happier, more assured, and younger-looking. I have seen people coming into my office looking and feeling healthier than they have in years. I have seen that what I am doing has made a difference in their lives. That look in their eyes, if you ask me, is what medicine is all about.

*Control Your
High Blood Pressure—
Without Drugs!*

Do you believe . . .

- that a pinch of salt never did anyone any harm?
- that people who feel okay must be doing okay, even if their blood pressure is a little high?
- that the reason you go to a doctor is to get a prescription?
- that once you start taking blood pressure pills you'll be on them for life?
- that high blood pressure is incurable?
- that you are too young to worry?
- that you are too old to change your ways?

Then read on . . .

1

Myths About Hypertension

> *The only way to keep your health is to eat what you don't want, drink what you don't like, and do what you'd rather not.*
>
> Mark Twain

My mother sailed through life armed with a salt shaker in one hand and a cigarette in the other—a prime candidate for high blood pressure. She survived. She's now eighty-five. And she's doing just fine.

Bettie Bennett's whole life has been devoted to smoking, martinis, armchair activities, and a strict avoidance of exercise. She is very fond of heavily marbled beef and she loves ice cream. In other words, she's been flying in the face of overwhelming scientific odds that she should have expired long ago. As I said, she's eighty-five now and, apart from the fact that she hasn't taken particularly good care of her health, she's in pretty good shape. She goes out every day in her ten-year-old Valiant and beats the pants off anyone who will play her at bridge or gin rummy. If you ask me, I'd say that's fantastic.

My mother has always used a lot of salt in her food. She would add salt to everything before she tasted it. In fact she even used to add salt to her potato chips.

When I graduated from medical school I started to talk to her about the harmful effects of salt. I read up on the subject and told her that salt use seemed to be related to high blood pressure and that it worried me. But genetics were on her side. Even in her fifties and sixties, she didn't have high blood pressure, so she wasn't too ready to listen.

But I now know that if you live long enough, and you eat salt, sooner or later you'll get high blood pressure. It's that simple. And by the time she was seventy-five, sure enough, she had a case of real, live high blood pressure. She didn't feel so good anymore. I didn't know it, because she hid the extent of her symptoms from me. She didn't want some kid doctor to lecture her on how she should lead her own life. Particularly if he was her own kid.

Finally she got to the point where she was so short of breath that going out and playing cards were no longer fun. Then it got to the point where she just couldn't go out at all. And at last she told me she wanted to do something about her blood pressure.

She said to me, "Listen, all my friends take pills. Why don't you give me some pills for my high blood pressure?"

But I had to tell her, "I'm sorry, Mother, it's too late. I don't do that any more. If you'd asked me a few years ago, while I was still a pill pusher, I'd have done it. But now I know it doesn't work. You'll have to go on a diet. You have to come up to the Center and go through our program."

My mother wouldn't hear of that, even though I was the medical director at the Center at that time. She was eighty, she said, and too old to change her life. And she was "not about to go on any damn diet." It was just too late.

So I told her, "I'm not going to give you pills. If you want pills, I'll refer you to another doctor." I contacted a friend and made an appointment for her to see the head cardiologist at a major hospital near her home.

She went to the cardiologist, and he told her just what she wanted to hear. "Well, Mrs. Bennett," he said, "I quite understand you don't want to change your diet, so here's what I'd like to suggest. When it comes to mealtimes, don't use the salt shaker, okay? Just stop adding salt to your food. I'm not telling you you can't use salt in your kitchen. I'm just asking you to stop adding salt to your food when you get to the table."

My mother was already doing that. She had already pretty much stopped adding salt to her food at table. The cardiologist also told her,

"Just take these pills and you'll feel much better." She phoned me the next day to tell me what the doctor had prescribed.

I knew she had a little heart failure by this time, so I said, "Oh, the cardiologist gave you some propranolol? Okay." But I thought to myself, "Wonderful. *He prescribed propranolol for your high blood pressure when you're already in heart failure?*" I knew right away the side effects of the propranolol would likely make her feel even worse. And of course she took the pills and she felt worse.

A few days later she phoned again and said, "Okay, I'll try that damn diet." You know what? Within three days of starting she was out of heart failure, her breathing was 100 percent easier, her blood pressure was down to 130/60, she could walk around, and she couldn't believe it.

One of the biggest thrills of my medical career was that day when she said, "I can't believe it. I can walk down to my car effortlessly. I'm not huffing and puffing. I just can't believe how much better I feel."

Later she told me that when she called up to say she'd give the diet a try she'd really had no trust in it. She didn't phone me because she hoped the diet would do her some good, she said. No, she called me up because she didn't like the thought of my standing over her grave, telling my sister, "If only she'd gone on that diet . . ."

My mother is still going strong. She takes care of her three-hundred-acre grain farm, corn and soybeans, and looks after her stocks. And watch out, she's still a winner at cards.

OUR MYTHS ABOUT HIGH BLOOD PRESSURE

My mother's story gives me a perfect opportunity to discuss some of the myths about high blood pressure that many of us carry around with us. And they are myths. They have no basis in scientific fact.

First off, my mother believed that *salt is harmless.* Many of us do. And it isn't. As Craig Claiborne, a food editor of the New York *Times,* remarked shortly after his own high blood pressure was diagnosed, "They should label salt just as they do cigarettes, saying that it is injurious to your health."

Another myth my mother believed was the one that goes, *As long as I feel okay, I must be okay.* It's a popular idea. But, again, it's a myth. And my mother wouldn't admit what a myth that was until she didn't feel okay anymore; until she was too short of breath to leave the house.

A third myth my mother shared with a large majority of the population is the myth that says, *The reason you go to a doctor is to get some pills.*

Pills may be one aspect of therapy, but the practice of real medicine means a great deal more than acting as a front man for the drug companies.

I'd like to deal with each of these myths in turn. Even though the evidence is against them, they are pretty much taken for granted in our society; and the people who believe them may be setting themselves up for heart attacks and strokes.

THE MYTH THAT SALT IS HARMLESS

The Yanomamo are a tribe of jungle warriors who live in the dense rain forests of northern Brazil and southern Venezuela. They are famous for their warlike nature. During a year and a half spent with the tribe, anthropologist Napoleon Chagnon remembers, one particular village was raided no less than twenty-five times. And by the Yanomamo's own definition, the objective of a raid was "to kill one or more of the enemy and flee." Not surprisingly, Chagnon titled one of his books about them *Yanomamo —The Fierce People.*

William Oliver is another researcher who has spent months living among the Yanomamo. While he was studying the health of the tribe he discovered that not one of five hundred tribespeople he tested had high blood pressure. In fact he also found out that, among the Yanomamo, blood pressure doesn't rise with age. The tribal elders' blood pressure levels were about the same as those of their sons and daughters.

Bear in mind that among every five hundred adult Americans you will usually find between a hundred and a hundred and fifty with high blood pressure. Remember, too, that doctors take it so much for granted that blood pressure rises as you grow older, they often figure the "normal" systolic pressure by the rule of thumb, "one hundred plus your age." You can see why Oliver's finding caused something of a sensation.

You might think the Yanomamo's way of life was an idyllic, pastoral one, with very few of the stresses of modern civilization. Perhaps that's why they have so little hypertension. But remember that the Yanomamo are called the Fierce People, and that one village alone was attacked no less than twenty-five times over a nineteen-month period. Chagnon describes the Yanomamo as living in a state of "chronic warfare." You'd hardly call that a life free of stress.

As Oliver looked around for some other explanation for the Yanomamo's amazing lack of hypertension, he noticed something else unique about them: the Yanomamo have almost no sodium in their urine.

They excrete less than one percent of the amount of sodium that the average American does. And the amount of sodium in the urine is a very accurate reflection of the amount of salt one eats.

The Yanomamo, living on a diet of palm fruits, nuts, bananas, and wild game, consume about three milligrams of sodium a day, compared with an average American diet of three to six thousand milligrams. What's more, they simply don't have any problems with high blood pressure.

Other studies from all over the world have since confirmed that, where salt and other forms of sodium are prominent in the diet, high blood pressure is also widespread. *Time* magazine, in its cover story of March 15, 1982, entitled "Salt, a New Villain?" suggested that, "statistically, the link is clear. In countries where sodium intake is high, so is the frequency of hypertension." But they also commented that, "as with smoking and cancer, cholesterol and heart disease, it is difficult to prove direct cause and effect."

We will get back to this question of proof in a later chapter. For now, let's just say that salt, in the quantities we use every day, is anything but harmless. As *Time* put it,

> One of four Americans suffers from some form of high blood pressure, though many do not know it. The so-called silent killer, it often remains symptomless and undetected for years until it leads to a disabling or deadly heart attack or stroke. For the unaware and unwary, excess salt is all too often its equally stealthy silent accomplice.

THE MYTH THAT IF I FEEL OKAY I MUST BE OKAY

High blood pressure is what is called a *risk factor*. Medical scientists have investigated the types of people who suffer from strokes, heart attacks, and other related ailments, and they have discovered that there are several factors that make it much more likely that a given person will suffer a heart attack. Cigarette smokers, people who have high cholesterol levels in their blood (200 mg/dl and above), people who are overweight, and people with high blood pressure are all more likely to have strokes and heart attacks than people whose lives contain none of these factors.

The more of these risk factors you have, the more likely you are to wind up with a stroke, a heart attack, or whatever.

In the Framingham Study, a classic of its kind, 5,209 women and men between the ages of thirty-five and seventy-four were examined over a twelve-year period by a team of medical researchers. And the conclusions were very clear.

In the New England city of Framingham, Massachusetts, where the study took place, people with high blood pressure were found to be three times as likely to suffer heart attacks as their neighbors with normal levels. They were six times more prone to congestive heart failure. And seven times as likely to have a stroke.

When you consider that, according to the National Heart, Lung, and Blood Institute, one American in six has high blood pressure, it's not hard to figure out why hypertension, either directly or indirectly, disables and kills more Americans than any other medical condition you might care to name.

And that figure of one in six is a conservative estimate, using a measure for high blood pressure that suggests 35 million Americans have the disease. A later report suggested that the situation may be a lot more serious. The 1980 Report of the Joint National Committee on Detection, Evaluation, and Treatment of High Blood Pressure stated that 54 million, not 35 million, Americans have blood pressure high enough to put them "among the potential beneficiaries of therapy." More recent reports put the figure even higher—up to 60 million (or one in every four of us).

Sixty million Americans, whether they know it or not, are up to seven times more likely to have a stroke than their fellows—simply because their blood pressure is higher.

One recent estimate suggested that "only one-third of the people who have high blood pressure are being treated, and only half of those being treated follow their physicians' recommendations rigorously enough to bring their blood pressure under control."

The National High Blood Pressure Education Program was established in 1971, in an attempt to make Americans more aware of the risk that high blood pressure adds to their lives. This massive public education program has been very successful in persuading people to have their blood pressure checked and in convincing those whose blood pressure is high that, even if they feel okay, they are actually at risk.

Largely as a result of this campaign, in the period between 1973 and 1977 the number of deaths due to stroke in the country dropped by almost seventeen percent, while the deaths due to various types of heart disease were down eight percent. The number of lives saved in this period alone has been estimated at 300,000.

In some ways, however, the campaign has not gone far enough. The campaign's theme was expressed in the phrase, "High blood pressure—the silent killer." That phrase neatly emphasizes the point that high blood pressure can creep up on one unnoticed. A stroke or a heart attack is often the first signal many people get that their high blood pressure could kill them.

By the time you suffer a heart attack or stroke you are already involved in serious and costly medical care. Nor is that all. Roughly forty percent of the people who recover from strokes will need special nursing attention for the rest of their lives. As many as ten percent will spend the rest of their lives in hospitals.

Is hypertension really so silent?

It's certainly quiet enough that not many of us notice it until we are very far along in the disease. But someone who was listening very carefully to his or her body could hear it many, many years before a stroke or a heart attack. It's just that our society is so distracting, so demanding, that we rarely take any time to listen and to find out what's really going on with ourselves.

Hypertension isn't really silent at all. It's just that in its early stages it's too subtle for most of us to detect.

Thus the education program has raised public consciousness about the disease, and it has probably saved many thousands of lives. But in a sense it has also misdirected us. It has sent people to doctors and pharmacists in search of treatment; it hasn't made them look at themselves. It hasn't moved on to the next step, which I call the medicine of the eighties. It hasn't faced the fact that drugs are not really a good answer for many chronic ailments and that high blood pressure can and should be controlled by good nutrition, exercise, and stress reduction.

Of course it's better to treat high blood pressure with drugs than not to treat it at all. It's better to be aware you have high blood pressure, and to do something about it, than to let it slide. But it's better still to avoid the pills, with their side effects, and to concentrate instead on living a healthy life. The best health care of all is seeking good health.

THE MYTH THAT YOU GO TO A DOCTOR FOR PILLS

Which brings us to the last of the myths that my mother's story illustrates. And it is a complete myth. Yet so many of us—physicians and patients both—have come to believe it that we have turned it into a reality.

It goes like this: *If I have high blood pressure, I should get a prescription from my doctor, right?*

So many patients feel they haven't received treatment if they don't walk out of the doctor's office with a prescription, and so many doctors know just how much more likely a stroke or heart attack is for hypertensives who do nothing to bring down their blood pressure, that an agreement is reached.

And the agreement says, Take these pills. You don't have to look after yourself. Let the pills do it.

The trouble is, the pills won't cure high blood pressure. They may lower it for as long as you keep on taking them. But they won't cure it. And they may also have side effects that range all the way from mild drowsiness to impotence.

Yet current medical practice encourages everyone who has high blood pressure to take these drugs, although high blood pressure itself is only a risk factor. That is, it may predispose many of the people who have it to eventual heart attack, stroke, and the rest. But many of the people who have high blood pressure will never have a stroke or a heart attack. And they too are invited to spend the rest of their lives taking medicines with known, harmful side effects.

As Michael Oliver recently suggested in the pages of the prestigious *New England Journal of Medicine* (1982), "The risks involved in correcting risk must be compared with the risk of the disease in question."

In fact the whole philosophy of drug prescription for the degenerative diseases is coming in for a great deal of discussion and questioning at this time. As Dr. Richard Cabot wrote, "The patient has learned to expect a medicine for every symptom. He was not born with that expectation. . . . It is we physicians who are responsible for perpetuating false ideas about disease and its cure."

A MEDICINE FOR THE EIGHTIES

Sir William Osler once observed that "it is much more important to know what sort of patient has a disease than what sort of disease a patient has."

In recent years more and more doctors have come to feel that the relationship between doctor and patient has been going astray. "We have lost something in the areas of human relations, compassion, and communication," says Max Parrott, past president of the American Medical Association (quoted in Ogle 1979). And the equation that says medicine equals pills is a symptom of this loss.

In my view the medicine of the eighties and nineties will turn away from the giving of pills to relieve symptoms. It will see the physician not as some high authority figure but as a learned friend of the patient, encouraging him or her in those practices that lead to health.

In my treatment of hypertensives I do not recommend pills. Let me stress that *this does not mean that I recommend that anyone stop taking medicines that have been prescribed for him or her, without the supervision and approval of a physician.* But when a patient comes to me who is already taking hypertensive medication, I do everything in my power to bring the blood pressure down by such natural methods as exercise, dietary change, and stress management. And when the blood pressure drops, as it almost always does, I am able to recommend that the medications be tapered, and in most cases eventually stopped completely.

Perhaps the most hopeful and important side of the new approach to medicine is its emphasis on the patient's contribution to his own care and cure.

As Norman Cousins expressed it in his "Letter to a Patient" in the New York *Times:*

> You own a body that has been beautifully honed by at least a million years of experience in coping with all sorts of disorders. This built-in cellular wisdom goes by the name of the immunological system. I have no loss in pride in admitting that I know far less about you than your own body does. My job is to put that natural knowledge fully to work when anything goes wrong. I am not the healer. You are.

In this book, as well as in my own practice as a physician, the emphasis is on you, the patient, as the one who can truly heal yourself.

2

Further Myths

> The only reason I'd take up jogging is
> because I'd want to hear heavy breath-
> ing again.
>
> Erma Bombeck

If you're quite sure that there's nothing you can do about your high blood pressure except take the medicines, you won't spend much time looking for ways to cure it. Am I right? Because you'll have a belief about it, and your belief will get in your way.

But you can lower your blood pressure without those medicines if you read this book and work at it with your doctor—just as long as your beliefs and assumptions don't tell you it's impossible from the start.

Let's talk about beliefs for a moment: how powerful they can be, and how they can get in the way of our learning new ways to do things.

Beliefs are sort of like colored glasses. Our assumptions and beliefs "color" the way we see life in just the same way that colored glasses do. Let me give you an example.

I'm sure we all know some pessimistic people. No matter what happens, they always see the darker side of things. A pessimist is like a little kid who gets an electric train set for Christmas. But he's afraid to play with it too much, because he's scared it's going to break—and then he'll really be unhappy.

And we all know some optimists. People who look on the bright side, even when things aren't going so well. An optimist is like a kid who comes into his room one day and finds it an inch deep in horse manure—and starts jumping up and down, shouting, "Hooray, Mommy bought me a pony!" We even have expressions to describe people like that. We say they see life through rose-colored glasses—the French call it *la vie en rose.*

I'm not going to tell you that optimism is good and pessimism is bad. But I am going to ask you to read these chapters on myths carefully, because I want to give you a new set of glasses that are clear and transparent and colorless—so you can really see what's going on with you. I don't want you looking at your high blood pressure with dark glasses and deciding it's incurable, when in fact you can beat it. Or looking at it through rose-tinted glasses, and telling yourself it's just fine the way it is, when it's not.

So let's look at some more beliefs, assumptions, and just plain old myths that many people have about high blood pressure. And let's clear up some of them.

When my doctor told me I had high blood pressure, he said it was incurable[1] and that I'd be on pills for the rest of my life.

That's certainly the message you receive from most doctors and most books on the subject. Once you have high blood pressure, you always have high blood pressure, and you'll have to take medicines. Even if your blood pressure comes down when you take the medicines, it would go right back up if you ever stopped taking them. So you had better get used to the idea that you'll be taking them for the rest of your life.

It doesn't have to be that way at all!

It's certainly true that if you just stop taking the pills you may be even worse off than you were before you started taking them. There's plenty of scientific evidence for that. It's also true that if you find out the one or

---

[1] In the course of this book, we have used the male form ("he," "him," "his") in referring to individuals of unspecified gender. We feel that the use of such recently proposed pronoun forms as "s/he" and "hir" would tend to distract readers, as would extensive use of phrases such as "him or her," "she or he," etc. We would like to express the hope that our choice in this matter will not be understood to reflect beliefs concerning the appropriateness of gender roles.

more causes of your high blood pressure—working closely with your own doctor—and begin to correct them, you can probably get the problem licked. Then your doctor will be able to taper you off the pills, carefully and appropriately.

The medicines must be okay. After all, my doctor prescribed them, my pharmacist filled the prescription, and the FDA must have tested them for years before they allowed them onto the market.

I have no quarrel with your doctor and your pharmacist. They are my colleagues and I respect them; but I am more than a little worried about the quality and quantity of the testing that happens before a new drug is allowed onto the market.

For sure, the Food and Drug Administration makes certain the drug companies conduct tests. However, it's not until a drug comes out on the market and is heavily promoted—which it always is—that we find out whether or not it's really safe. People have to take it for a while, perhaps months or even years, before we find out all the side effects.

Recently a new diuretic came onto the market with a lot of favorable publicity. It was called Selacryn. It did what a diuretic is supposed to do—reduce the body's retention of sodium. But, more than that, it got around a common side effect of diuretics, namely, raising the blood uric acid levels, thus increasing the risk of gouty arthritis. In fact it actually reduced the blood uric acid.

Now that was a major breakthrough. Unfortunately, Selacryn turned out to have some toxic side effects, and within a short time it had to be taken off the market.

Not so long ago a new drug for arthritis, called Oraflex, came out. Again, it was heavily touted as some kind of breakthrough. People who saw it on television (my mother among them) went to their doctors and asked for it. It sounded so good.

A short time after it was released on the market it too had to be withdrawn. It was too toxic. Some people who took it were actually dying from it. The FDA screening tests had somehow let it slip through. It wasn't until the drug was in widespread use that we discovered how dangerous it was.

The *British Medical Journal* (1982), in its report on a similar experience with the drug in England, severely criticized the current "explosive" marketing policies of the major British pharmaceutical companies.

So, yes, I know the FDA screens drugs before they are allowed on the market. But I also know that a million or more people taking the drug for a couple of years often turn up problems that the FDA studies missed. The FDA is made up of humans, like the rest of us. They make mistakes. And they're a relatively small agency, keeping track of a great many giant companies. The scary thing is that the present administration in Washington, by shortening and "streamlining" the FDA drug review process, is making it easier for drugs to get on the market, not harder.

I'm not too happy about that.

I asked my doctor about other treatments for high blood pressure, like diet change and relaxation, and he told me they weren't proven yet and that he couldn't recommend them until they were.

When we try to research diseases like high blood pressure or coronary heart disease, we are looking at problems that have a number of different causes that interact with each other, sometimes in a highly complex kind of way. Sorting out all the strands can take a very long time indeed.

John W. Farquhar, M.D., in his book *The American Way of Life Need Not Be Hazardous to Your Health*, comments that medical researchers often have what he calls a "let's wait for complete proof" attitude. He labels it *scientific conservatism*.

Do we really need to wait for conclusive proof before taking common-sense action to improve health? Dr. Farquhar's conclusion is that we "should continue to support basic research while *simultaneously* implementing our best efforts for appropriate preventive measures, rather than sit passively and wait for the basic research to yield conclusive findings on *all* facets of the complex puzzle." (Italics his.)

A recent paper by members of the Nutritional Committee of the American Heart Association takes the same line. The paper "Diet and Coronary Heart Disease," published in the *New England Journal of Medicine* (1978), suggests that physicians often must make decisions "in the absence of absolutely conclusive scientific proof." Open heart surgeons do it every day. Nothing wishy-washy about them.

So I tell my patients, "Look, I'm convinced. I've seen the evidence, I've seen the results—and I've changed my own diet. I've changed the way I live my life. I know there are some doctors out there who aren't convinced. But you've come to me, and this is my honest opinion, based on my reading of the evidence."

We've taken a look at some assumptions, beliefs and myths that have to do with the medications used to correct high blood pressure. Now let's take a look at some assumptions that have to do with the disease process itself.

My doctor tells me I have hypertension. That means I'm very tense, right?

Not exactly. Or not always.

Hypertension literally means *high tension* or pressure in the arteries. It's the scientific name for high blood pressure. It doesn't mean tension in the sense of stress. All the same, many people who have a high level of stress in their lives do suffer from hypertension. Many don't. And some people who rarely worry and wouldn't think of themselves as leading very stressful lives have hypertension.

We'll deal with the subject of stress more fully later on in this book.

I always thought that if you had hypertension you would have head-aches or nosebleeds or blurred vision. I don't have any of those things, so why is my doctor so concerned that my blood pressure is a little high?

When I was in medical school we were taught that people with the disease called hypertension had symptoms. So if one of our patients didn't have any symptoms we didn't worry so much about the blood pressure being high. But things have changed since then. We've learned a lot.

We now know that people with high blood pressure often have symptoms that are so subtle, they get confused with the normal process of getting older. Nosebleeds and dizziness are the exception, not the rule. In fact most of the damage goes on inside you—inside your arteries, inside your kidneys, even inside your eyes—where you can't feel it.

You may not know that even mild hypertension interferes in a subtle way with your mental processes, your thinking or cognitive abilities, and your memory. Drs. M. Franceschi, A. P. Shapiro, and colleagues showed this in a series of elegant studies of hypertensive and normal people pub-lished in *Hypertension* (1982). Really marked personality changes may occur in people whose blood pressure problem is severe.

Your doctor is concerned that you have high blood pressure because he knows it can lead to other serious problems if left untreated, whether it causes symptoms or not.

If you faithfully follow the program in this book, and manage to bring your blood pressure back down, as I know you will, you'll find you really did have symptoms all the time—you just hadn't noticed them. I think you'll find yourself feeling a whole lot better, a whole lot more energetic, a whole lot more alive.

My doctor just told me I have hypertension. I can't understand it. I never had it before! Where did it come from so suddenly? What did I do?

We tend to think of diseases as things we "catch"—perhaps from eating something disagreeable, or from standing out in the rain, or coming in contact with someone else who has them. Hypertension isn't like that. It's not something you just suddenly get one day.

In fact it takes many years to "catch" it. Usually you have to live a certain way, behave in a certain way, and eat certain kinds of food for a long, long time before you get high blood pressure. It's the result of the way you've been living. It's sort of like having a red warning light go on on the dashboard of your car. It's just a way for your body to tell you that some of the things you're doing don't work.

If hypertension is a disease you've "caught," you've been running after it for a while.

I've had high blood pressure so long, I'm beginning to think it's just my "normal" blood pressure and not something I should worry about.

I see a lot of patients who have had high blood pressure for years, often whether or not they take their medicines, and little or nothing has happened to them. Some of them begin to feel that high blood pressure is somehow normal in their case. After all, we are all unique, aren't we? Some people even tell me they feel much better when their blood pressure is high, and not so good when the drugs bring it back down again.

But it isn't that way. There is not one single person in whom high blood pressure is "normal." Granted, you can feel okay for a long time with high blood pressure (that's why it's known as the "silent killer"), but the damage is going on inside you, silently, inevitably, inexorably. High pressure just pounds away, pounds away, and pounds away at your insides. You may not feel it, you may not even know about it, until something catastrophic occurs—such as a stroke or a heart attack.

When my patients tell me they feel better without the drugs, that doesn't surprise me. That's not because high blood pressure is okay for them—or you. It may be because the drugs they are taking are making them feel tired and listless.

High blood pressure runs in my family. I guess there's nothing I can do about it.

I have some good news for you. High blood pressure itself isn't hereditary. Sensitivity to the causes of high blood pressure is hereditary, but high blood pressure itself isn't.

Some people are naturally very resistant to stress, dietary salt, and being overweight, the principal factors that cause high blood pressure—let's call them the environmental factors. Others are very sensitive to them. It seems to depend on your genetic predisposition. This genetic or inherited tendency can't possibly cause high blood pressure all by itself; it can only determine how quickly you'll get it if you expose yourself to all those environmental factors.

Drs. F. C. Luft, Clarence Grim, and their colleagues have studied this susceptibility or predisposition *(American Journal of Medicine,* 1982) and have shown that it can be inherited or acquired. Those who are real sensitive may get high blood pressure when they're eighteen or nineteen, and those who are real resistant may not get it until they're in their eighties. But most of us will get high blood pressure eventually if we're exposed to the environmental factors. On the other hand, no matter how many people in your family have high blood pressure, if you keep away from those environmental factors—if you exercise, and relax, and have a healthy diet, with very little sodium—you won't get high blood pressure.

High blood pressure isn't inevitable. Not if you get rid of the factors that cause it.

I've had kidney disease for quite a few years, Dr. Bennett, and my doctor says everyone with kidney disease has high blood pressure and that I'd just better learn to accept that and live with the pills. There's really nothing else I can do about it, right?

Wrong, I'm happy to say. There is something you can do about it. About five percent of the people with high blood pressure have some kind of kidney disease, such as Bright's disease or nephritis, that probably triggered their high blood pressure, or at least greatly contributed to it. And since there's no cure for such diseases of the kidney, they're told they'll have high blood pressure for the rest of their lives.

It is true that having a disease of the kidney usually makes you extremely susceptible to the other causes of high blood pressure. In this it resembles the genetic or hereditary predisposition described above. But, like the genetic factor, kidney disease is something we can work around. If you can handle the other factors you may be able to have normal or close to normal blood pressure, even with kidney disease.

I would like to warn you, though, that if you have kidney disease you will need to be very careful indeed about all the other factors. You really will need to live an exemplary life. There's just very little room for error in your case.

My doctor told me I had essential hypertension, and he said that meant we didn't know what caused it in my case.

Hypertension is called "essential" because, about forty years ago, some doctors thought it might be essential to the health of people who were growing older. It isn't. Unless you have kidney disease, your kind of high blood pressure will still be called essential hypertension for some time to come.

As for the cause of hypertension being unknown, that's a myth we might look into.

Infectious diseases always have a specific *cause*—some bacterium or virus or whatever. The way medical science proves that it has established the cause of a disease is by a rigorous scientific proof that shows the disease is always associated with this cause and never occurs without it. If you take away this causative factor, the disease simply vanishes.

This approach works very well with infectious diseases, such as tuberculosis. But it doesn't work so well with the so-called degenerative diseases, such as high blood pressure. We know the causes of high blood pressure. We can reproduce them in laboratory animals. We can even identify them in individual patients and choose an appropriate therapy for each patient, based on our knowledge of those causes.

Dr. John Laragh of Cornell is the most eloquent and persistent advocate of this sensible approach—each patient is an individual; individual specific mechanisms of disease can be found; and the patient can be given treatment accordingly.

Dr. Laragh has tirelessly educated the medical profession about this approach, in scores of scientific articles and in his book, *Topics in Hypertension.*

So, as I was saying above, we know the causes of high blood pressure. We don't know, and we will never know, the single cause. Because there isn't one single cause. And because there isn't one single cause the medical profession still tends to think of hypertension as something mysterious. Because that single cause hasn't been isolated yet.

It won't be. It doesn't exist. But high blood pressure isn't mysterious. It isn't inevitable. It just doesn't happen to be like an infectious disease.

The last group of myths, beliefs, and assumptions I'd like to expose have to do with reasons for not taking care of oneself. These are assumptions that very easily turn into excuses.

Several times in the past few years my doctor has told me my blood pressure was up a little. But I feel good, I'm doing fine—in fact, I'm having a lot of fun. I just don't believe this high blood pressure is anything to worry about. I'm young. I've got all the time in the world.

Oh, so you're too young to worry? That's a pity, because you've fallen for the myth of indestructibility. None of us are indestructible. In fact we are building our futures right now, block by block. What we do or don't do right now will matter very much, a little further down the line.

You may be twenty-five or thirty, you may not know anyone in your age group, or even close to it, who has had a heart attack or a stroke. Perhaps you feel cardiovascular disease is a little like Saudi Arabia. You know it exists, you think it's pretty important—but it all seems so remote and foreign to you that you can't relate to it.

High blood pressure pounds away at you as surely and silently as inflation eats away at your money in the bank. If you had the chance, you'd wipe out inflation. High blood pressure you can wipe out. Now. While it's still in its early stages.

I'm sure everything you say may be true, Doctor. But I'm too old now to change my ways—even if I wanted to.

High blood pressure in older people often contributes to heart attack and stroke. So it's not a benign or harmless condition at all. We need to handle it just as aggressively as we would in someone younger.

That shortness of breath that stops you when you walk, or wakes you at night, is another sign of blood pressure out of control. Doctors call it "congestive heart failure." When a doctor tells you that you have heart failure, you may tell yourself, "Oh, it's my heart, something's wrong with my heart." Often it's not something wrong with your heart, it's something wrong with what you're eating, or the lack of exercise, or with the amount of stress in your life. So let's not always blame your heart.

If you have high blood pressure you probably have a good heart. It's just that the way you're living is asking too much of it, and that's something we can change—whether you're sixty, or seventy, or even eighty.

You're never too old to change. In my experience, there's always a tremendous impact when one of my older patients brings his or her blood pressure down without using drugs. It dramatically reduces human suffering. It improves the quality of their lives enormously. It can make an incredible difference. So don't, please, ever think you're too old to change.

Listen, Doc, I'm okay. I can handle it. I deal with stress real well. In fact I actually like it. I do my best when the pressure's on. So don't you worry about me. This blood pressure thing isn't going to get me down.

A lot of people have a hard time admitting that stress is getting to them. Maybe they're worried that if it looks as though they're having a problem they'll lose their jobs or some of their friends won't think so much of them. Some people feel that to admit to stress is a sign of weakness. And this is particularly true of men who want to have that tough, macho image.

Some of my executive patients have come to me from quite a distance, because they don't want people at work to know they've been to see a doctor. I can understand their reluctance. Hey, it's a tough, competitive world out there. But I can't feel very happy about it. If the situation in your world doesn't allow you to acknowledge problems and stresses, and to deal with them appropriately, you could be in big trouble.

It takes courage to come out into the open and admit that the stresses of life are getting to you—and that the pressures you are under are showing up in your blood pressure. But you've got that kind of courage. It's no sign of weakness to admit it: life is stressful, and it's worth your while to make sure you hang around a little longer.

I've always been this way. I'm a worrier. It's the way I am, and I guess it's the way I'm always going to be. And if there's nothing I can do about it, why bother?

If you have a lot of stress in your life, or a lot of worries, or if you're living in the fast lane, you may feel there's not a whole lot you can do about it.

You may think you'd have to change your circumstances drastically—get a divorce, throw out your teenage son, get rid of your boss, or move somewhere where you don't have to ride the crowded freeways every day—in order to lower your blood pressure. For most people, these kinds of changes are out of the question.

Maybe you've tried a few things already—changed jobs or moved to a different neighborhood—and decided that, since nothing improved, you must be the kind of person who gets tense and upset no matter where you are. I hear a lot of people talking like this. "I guess I'm just naturally tense. . . . It's the way I am. . . . I just don't have any willpower. . . . I have a bad temper, that's just me. . . . I'm stubborn. . . . I am the way I am, Doc, and nothing's going to change it."

But in fact all the ways we are, all the things we do—the nice things, the crazy things, the angry things, the stupid things—are just the ways we are and the things we do. And whatever we do, we learned it. We learned to do it that way. *It isn't us.* It's just something we've learned to do—and if it doesn't work we don't *have* to do it that way any more.

Most of us are so closely identified with our own behavior that we think it's who we are. We imagine it's as unchangeable as the number of toes on our feet or the color of our eyes. But it isn't. You can change your behavior —because you aren't your behavior, you're you!

So if you've discovered that the real key to your high blood pressure has something to do with the way you live, the way you behave, the way you react to things, you don't have to feel it's hopeless. You're the one who's in control of all that. You can change it.

"Now wait just a minute," you may be thinking.

When it comes to medical subjects—the dangers of medications, say, or the way the kidney works—you'll probably rely on my authority, my credentials, my degrees, and my experience. After all, I'm the doctor. But when I start talking personal, when I get down to you, your habits, your weaknesses, and your very own personality—hey, that's a different matter. How do I know what you can and can't do? How do I know whether you can change your behavior?

I know because you're a human being. And my experience of human beings tells me they can learn *anything.* At any age you can see for yourself that a particular behavior isn't working and change it. Just like that. Oh, it'll *seem* hard, just before you do it, and maybe while you're doing it, too. But later, when you have that smug look on your face, you'll tell people, "Oh no, it wasn't that bad at all."

I know you want to eat ice cream and salted crackers, and smoke cigarettes, and watch horror movies until your blood pressure doubles.

I also know that you want to be healthy and feel good. My experience tells me that human beings want to be healthy a lot. That it's a very deep and strong motive, stronger and deeper than those other cravings. All I have to do is put you in touch with that motivation to tap into that power and remind you that that's what you really want.

You'll do the rest.

Let's take a look at one last assumption. Because it's a real important one. It has to do with a very important issue: the quality of life. And it goes something like this:

Listen, I've only got one life to live and I might as well enjoy it. And if you start telling me I've got to stop eating all the things I like, and start jogging or something ridiculous like that—forget it! That's where I draw the line. I think you guys want to take all the fun out of life, and I for one am not going to go along with it.

Hey, my friend, I'm as concerned about this as you are. I don't want to take the fun out of anyone's life. I want you to stay around long enough to enjoy the fun, and I want you to be healthy enough to get a heck of a lot more out of it.

I spoke at a men's club a while back, and the president, to set me up for the group, told the joke about a man who asked his doctor, "Hey, Doc, if I quit smoking and drinking and eating too much, and running around with women all the time, will I live to be a hundred?" And the doctor replied, "No, but it'll seem like it!"

So when you tell me you really enjoy eating bacon, eggs, french fries, corned beef and cabbage, and smoking cigarettes, and going to brunches on Sunday and filling your plate four or five times, I understand. I've done that myself. But I also know that eating all that stuff may taste good at the time but it's often not really quite so neat afterward. Remember?

Taking care of yourself, eating healthfully, getting a reasonable amount of exercise, and relaxing properly feels great too. And you don't get a hangover, or a queasy stomach, or a taste like sandpaper in your mouth afterward. In fact it's a whole lot more enjoyable. What we're talking about in this book is having more fun, not less.

And not the least of it is that, if you get off the drugs, you'll certainly feel better. Taking drugs every day for the rest of your life, more than once a day, is no fun at all. Particularly if the drugs cause impotence, or drowsiness, or cramps.

Well, there are some myths, beliefs, and questions that I run up against in patient after patient. I don't want you to feel you have to agree completely with everything I've said in this chapter. You don't have to believe every word. If you still hold some of the beliefs that I've been talking about, I do ask that you set them aside while you read the rest of this book and do the program.

You don't have to be totally convinced that high blood pressure is curable and that the program will work before you start. You just have to be open to the possibility. So that's what I'm talking about: being open, keeping an open mind about this whole thing. That's all I need.

I've been doing this thing a long time. I've seen success after success after success. And most of my successes have come with people who didn't believe it to begin with. They were willing to try, however; they were open, and they kept coming back. They stuck with the program even when it didn't seem to be working, even when there seemed to be some reversals, even when I tried to take them off some medicine and it turned out to be a little too soon. Eventually the program worked.

I guess the bottom line is this: I want you to be willing to have it work for you. If you still have some beliefs and ideas that are in the way, I'd just like you to be ready to set them aside while you find out for yourself whether or not I'm right about all this.

Because so much is at stake.

Because this program will work for you if you let it.

Because it's your life, and you deserve the best.

3

What Is Blood Pressure?

> *Each of us is a mobile museum. The fluid in our bodies is a perfect replica of that ancient sea in which we grew to fruition following our liberation from the clay.*
>
> Lyall Watson

Stephen Hales was the first man ever to measure blood pressure. Although he was a Church of England clergyman, he was fascinated by scientific experiment. In 1711 he measured the blood pressure in the carotid artery of a horse—using a brass needle and a hollow glass tube nearly thirteen feet long.

To the amazement of the crowd that had gathered around him, the horse's blood rose up the tube to a height of over eight feet.

It was the first measurement of blood pressure—and also the first demonstration of the effect that stress has on blood pressure. Initially, the horse was frightened and in pain. But as it became calmer its pressure settled down to about five feet, which is closer to what we now know is normal for a horse.

What exactly is blood pressure?

Pressure is defined by the dictionary as "the force exerted by one body on another." The bodies, of course, may be fluid or gaseous, as well as solid. The pressure in your tires is the force that the air pumped into them exerts on the walls. Water pressure is the force that pushes water along the pipes in your house and out through the faucet. If your water pressure is low, all you get when you turn on your shower is a trickle.

Your blood pressure is the pressure inside the blood vessels, which builds up, and then slackens a little, and then builds up again, every time your heart pumps. This pressure moves the blood along the vessels (or pipes) in your body, from the heart to tissues and organs and back again.

The heart is an amazing organ. It starts pumping blood before you're born, when you're still only a few inches long. And it grows as you do, adapting in size to handle whatever work your body needs it to do.

Although your heart is only the size of your fist, it pumps some 40,000 gallons of blood through your body each day, along 60,000 miles of blood vessels. Unbelievable! And it manages all this by beating 100,000 times a day, for as much as eighty or ninety years at a stretch. The finest pumps that engineers have designed simply don't measure up to it. It's phenomenal.

When your heart beats, it pumps blood out through the *aorta*, an artery about the size of a garden hose. Smaller and smaller *arteries* branch out from the aorta and carry the blood to all parts of the body. The smallest branch arteries, which are called *arterioles*, are about a thousandth of an inch wide. You'd need a microscope to see them. And there are millions of them in every organ and tissue of your body.

From the arterioles, the blood passes into even more microscopic vessels, the *capillaries*. Here an exchange takes place between blood and tissue, the blood passing oxygen and nutrients to the tissues of the body, and the tissues unloading carbon dioxide and wastes into the blood.

The blood then returns to the heart via the *veins*, and the cycle begins again.

All this movement of blood through your blood vessels is accomplished by pressure that is generated by your heartbeat. The pressure in the blood is highest at the aorta, and the entire system of aorta, branch arteries, and arterioles through which the blood is pumped all over the body is a high pressure system.

The network of capillaries, and the veins which bring the blood back to the heart, are low pressure systems.

Now here is the really ingenious part—the control system for your circulation. The purpose is to provide adequate blood flow to every organ and tissue in the body, recognizing that their needs change fairly often. The heart, in order to respond to changing needs, can beat slower or faster and can pump more or less blood with each beat. In the tissues and organs, each of those millions and millions of tiny arterioles has a muscle in it, so it can open up or close down slightly. These tiny muscles are all under the control of your endocrine and nervous systems, making it possible to redirect the flow and send more blood wherever it is needed.

Your endocrine and nervous systems get the message that more blood is needed in the kidneys. They will signal the arterioles in the kidneys to open up, maybe close down the arterioles in the spleen a bit, and send some extra blood to the stomach. That sort of supply and demand is going on all the time—delicate and precise adjustments to tissue and organ blood flow, to keep everything working smoothly. It's a beautiful system! It's marvelous, in the sense of something to be marveled at and appreciated. Your wonderful body!

There is one other aspect of the system you need to know about. This is a reflex protective action in the arterioles themselves that opens them up as the overall blood pressure falls and closes them down (or constricts them) as the pressure goes up too high. This process is called the *myogenic reflex,* meaning that it originates in the muscles themselves. Nowhere is it more vigorously operative than in the brain and retinal circulation.

As the blood pressure rises in hypertension, the microcirculation is closed down; that is, the arterioles constrict all over the body, especially in the brain and eyes. Your doctor can actually see this constriction when he looks inside your eyes using an ophthalmoscope (the instrument with a bright light and a magnifying glass). This is a homeostatic reflex—that is, it tends to keep the organ and tissue blood flow constant, in spite of fluctuations or changes in the pressure.

The little arterioles control the runoff from the major arteries. Thus their tiny muscles play an important part in regulating your circulation— and in controlling blood pressure.

But of course it is your heart that causes the pressure, because it's the pressure generated by your heart pumping that sends the blood to its destination. No heartbeat, no pressure. Weak heartbeat, low blood pressure. So high blood pressure actually implies a strong heartbeat. Remember that. We'll talk more about it later.

Let's see how the heart and the arterioles work together to maintain the circulation and the blood pressure.

When the heart gets filled with blood, it beats. And each beat forces approximately two or three ounces of blood out of the heart and into the arteries. That extra amount of blood, added to what is already there, affects the arteries the way water coming into a hose affects the hose. There's a sudden increase in pressure.

Most people, particularly young people whose bodies are still in pretty good shape, have fairly elastic arteries. When that extra blood comes in, the larger arteries all expand a little, and the pressure doesn't rise quite as much as it would if the arteries were like the stiff pipes in your house. You can feel that expansion at your neck or wrist—it's your pulse.

Many older people who suffer from arteriosclerosis (the medical name for hardening of the arterial wall) have less flexible, less elastic, less expandable major arteries. And when the heart empties blood into them the pressure rises much more than it does in younger people—because there is less elasticity, less slack to take it up. But whatever the state of your arteries, the blood pressure always goes up when the heart beats.

Now during the short period of time in which the heart is beating, the blood is draining from the little arterioles into the capillaries and veins. As the heart relaxes and begins to fill again, the blood is still draining out of the arterioles, so the pressure in the arteries (blood pressure) falls rapidly, and keeps on falling until the next beat of the heart drives it back up. So the pressure in your arteries is always fluctuating, rising and then falling, rising and falling again like a wave.

HOW DO WE MEASURE BLOOD PRESSURE?

When we measure your blood pressure we obtain two figures. We measure the pressure at its highest and at its lowest—at the top of the wave and at the bottom.

The higher figure, which gives the pressure just after the heartbeat, is called your *systolic pressure*. And the lower figure, when the heart has relaxed, filled, and is nearly ready to beat again, is called your *diastolic pressure*. These two figures are usually written together (120/80) and both of them are important.

The original method for measuring blood pressure that Stephen Hales invented was obviously too cumbersome and awkward for busy physicians to use on a regular basis. Imagine trying to fit that thirteen-foot-long glass tube into a black bag! And who would want the doctor sticking needles into the carotid artery anyway?

Better techniques and equipment needed to be developed before the measurement of blood pressure could catch on with doctors and their patients. Scipione Riva-Rocci invented the equipment, and N. C. Koratkoff first used it, and so, since the turn of the century, we have measured blood pressure indirectly.

This is done with a device known as a *sphygmomanometer*, or blood pressure cuff. Basically, the sphygmomanometer consists of an inflatable cuff (in practice, a flat rubber bladder inside a cloth cover), with a small bulb to inflate it, and a dial or column of mercury with calibrations on it, which show how much air pressure is in the cuff at any given time. Accurate digital readouts are also available now.

We place this inflatable rubber cuff around the upper arm and inflate it until the pressure in the cuff is greater than the pressure in the artery in the arm. The cuff is now too tight to allow any blood to pass through the artery.

Using a stethoscope to listen to the artery just below the cuff, we begin to let air out of the cuff slowly. At first no blood is flowing through the artery, so there is nothing to hear. But as the pressure in the cuff drops just below the systolic pressure in the artery, a very little blood begins to make its way past the cuff for a short time during each heartbeat, and the noise can be heard in the stethoscope. At this point, when the sound of the blood flow first appears, we read the dial on the sphygmomanometer and obtain the *systolic* reading.

As the pressure in the cuff continues to drop, we continue to hear the sound of the artery opening and closing, as the artery pressure rises and falls during each heartbeat.

Eventually we reach a point where the pressure in the cuff equals the lowest pressure found at the end of the relaxation or filling phase of the heartbeat. Below this point, blood is passing through the artery without obstruction at all times—and once again we are unable to hear it with the stethoscope. Our second reading is taken at the point where the blood flow again becomes inaudible—giving us the *diastolic* pressure.

Thus we measure the blood pressure indirectly, by measuring the pressures in the cuff that correspond to both the systolic (highest) and the diastolic (lowest) pressures in the artery. The figures given are expressed in terms of millimeters of mercury (mm Hg for short). For example, a systolic pressure of 120 is the pressure needed to raise a column of mercury 120 millimeters up a tube.

Dr. Koratkoff first used this device in St. Petersburg (now Leningrad), Russia, in 1905, and the sounds we hear when we take your blood pressure are known to this day as Koratkoff sounds.

RESTING BLOOD PRESSURE

How much pressure should there be in the arteries? What really is normal blood pressure—and I don't mean normal in the sense of average, I mean healthy, A-okay for humans, optimal?

Is 120/80 (that's the number most of us learned in medical school) really the answer?

I think these questions require a little explanation.

Basically, we need just enough pressure to keep the blood circulating to all parts of the body. And what that really means is that we need enough pressure to make sure the blood reaches the highest point—the brain.

Getting the blood to circulate to the rest of the body doesn't require much pressure at all—since gravity would do most of it anyway. There's no problem getting blood to your feet—unless, of course, you're standing on your head!

So the circulatory system is really designed to run at a fairly low pressure, about 80/40 or 90/50 mm Hg. In certain cultures (on the Solomon Islands, the Cook Islands, and in central New Guinea, for example) it stays about that level throughout people's lives. No need for 120/80. No need for "essential" hypertension as you grow older. There's absolutely nothing essential about it.

Young children in our culture usually start with a blood pressure around 80/40, but it rises progressively with increasing age. Yet for most of us there's certainly no need for this increase. It's not optimal. It just happens.

If we were giraffes, of course, things would be different. Giraffes actually need to have high blood pressure, at least enough to lift the blood all the way from the heart, up all that long neck, to the brain. But unless you're a giraffe you can probably get by just fine with a blood pressure of 80/40 or 90/50, and you certainly don't need a systolic pressure that's higher than 100 at rest.

I've reassured a lot of patients about their new "low" blood pressure. When you're on an excellent low-salt, low-fat diet, exercising daily, losing weight, and relaxing—really taking care of yourself—your early morning blood pressure might be 85/52, or 90/56, something like that. "Are you sure it's okay, Doc? My pressure's never been that low," my patients say. I smile and tell them, "You're standing up, aren't you? Not feeling faint? Don't worry, that's the blood pressure you're supposed to have!"

So when we know a little bit about blood pressure we see that 120/80 isn't all that great, really. It's just a pretty darn good pressure for most of us, about as low as you usually see it in an adult living the "good" American life. But we'll talk more about your life style and what it does to blood pressure later.

By the time we try to define what *high* blood pressure is, or what qualifies as the disease of *hypertension*, we're really just picking numbers. Most all the experts agree that the lower your blood pressure is the better off you are.

The only reason to pick out a pair of numbers and say that anyone with blood pressure above them has "hypertension" is to know at what point to start giving medicines. If you don't have to give any medicines, then the lower the pressure the better.

And by the way—low blood pressure doesn't produce a tired or run-down feeling. In the chapters on exercise, when we get into the program itself, we'll find out the real reason why so many people think they need Geritol!

If you can learn to get your blood pressure to be less than 100/50, great —because you're probably better off than if it's 110/60 or 120/80. But nobody would be willing to start you on medicines to get your pressure that low, that's for sure.

Most doctors now would call anything above 140/90 hypertension. That's the figure the American Heart Association uses, and it's the most common definition. However, you should know that a recent study showed that there was a higher risk of vascular disease associated with a diastolic pressure of 90 than with one of 80, and certainly if my own systolic pressure was consistently above 130 or 135, I'd want to do something about it.

The real truth is that the lower your blood pressure the better off you are.

NON-RESTING BLOOD PRESSURE

So far we've been talking about blood pressure at rest. Rest—think about what that means. The dictionary puts it this way. Rest: to cease from effort or activity for a time. To be at peace, to be tranquil. It's an unusual state for modern man or woman, this state of rest, don't you agree?

What happens to your blood pressure when you're not at rest?

There are, of course, a number of circumstances in which it's appropriate for your blood pressure to go up when you're not at rest. When the body has to meet some challenge or stress, the emergency or sympathetic nervous system turns on. For a small stress (the toast is burned) it may turn on a little; for a big challenge (your son wrecked your new car) it turns on a lot. Your heart beats more rapidly and forcefully on these occasions, delivering more blood into the arteries, and the blood pressure rises. This happens whenever you get even a little bit excited or angry or tense. And it also happens when you exercise.

In a normal, healthy person who is exercising vigorously, the systolic pressure may go as high as 180 or even 200. This increase is due to the fact that, when you exercise, the heart fills up more fully and also empties more completely. When you're exercising extremely hard, your heart may be pumping out seventy-five to eighty percent or more of the blood it can hold with every stroke, whereas at rest the fraction is nearer fifty percent.

Not only that, the venous reservoirs in your body deliver more blood into the active circulation, and more blood is returned rapidly to the heart. Cardiac output (the amount of blood pumped by your heart in one minute) can rise tenfold in these ways. Diastolic pressure, which might be driven up by the rise in systolic pressure and cardiac output, actually falls because the arterioles in the vascular beds in muscle and skin open up so completely.

Psychological stress can also raise the blood pressure.

When the emergency (sympathetic) nervous system switches on to enable you to handle a stressful situation, your body prepares itself for one of two reactions: fight or flight. In fact, the stress response is often known as the *fight or flight response*.

What does this mean? For thousands of years the main threats to human beings were predators—wolves, tigers, other humans, or whatever. And the best ways to deal with them were either by fighting them or getting away fast. Usually the latter!

Both these ways of dealing with unpleasant situations call for drastic action—and so the body prepares itself by partially shutting down the blood flow to such organs as the stomach, bowels, and liver, shifting some blood stored in reservoirs on the venous or low pressure side into the heart and arteries, and getting ready to send an enormous amount of blood to the muscles. Adrenalin and other hormones pour into the bloodstream to give us strength and energy to deal with the crisis. And the heart beats more forcibly and rapidly.

When you feel threatened, it's not often a tiger that's bothering you. It may be a problem at the office or a run-in with your teenage son who won't cut his hair. And fighting the office problem—or the son—or running away from them at top speed—just isn't going to help.

The body is all prepared for fight or flight—and there's nowhere to go. Nothing physical is happening, or likely to happen. Oh, there may be some yelling if it's your son, but that doesn't use enough muscles to burn up all the energy you have ready to go. As a result, all the extra blood that's been readied for use by the muscles isn't in fact needed. Meanwhile, the hormones are still in the bloodstream, stirring things up—and there you are, cooking! Right?

In situations like this your blood pressure remains high because your heart continues to beat more forcefully and rapidly, and the extra blood's still there . . . and that's the effect of stress on blood pressure.

What is stress?

Of course we all know that when people or things or situations push us or bump into us too much we get upset—and that's stress. Usually we associate stress with upset—anger, fear, unpleasant emotions. And most of us put the blame on someone or something outside us. It's the job, it's my mother or my husband. Or the neighbors, or their kids.

For people with hypertension, however, the emergency nervous system is on a good deal more than they're aware of it. It's on even when they are not upset.

I remember a lawyer in his fifties from Miami. Just coming in my office sent his pressure up 30 to 40 mm Hg. And he liked me! That's the amazing part. He enjoyed our visits. He had absolutely no feeling of apprehension, anxiety or upset when he came to see me. Nothing telling him, "Look out! Emergency! Emergency! Get ready to fight or flee!" No alarms going off in his head. He was totally unaware of the reaction that was going on in his own body.

Do you notice the reaction that takes place in you when you do mental arithmetic? Drive fast on the freeway? Watch a football game? Or an exciting movie? Try noticing in your own life how often you are provoked, or excited, or turned on, or annoyed.

In some especially sensitive people the emergency nervous system goes on at almost every interaction they have with other people, indeed at most every kind of sensory input, unless it's very, very soothing and mellow.

And it doesn't happen only with other people. Man versus machine can have the same effect. It's not just the vacuum cleaner or your automobile anymore—we've got some real creative annoyances in our lives right now. The computer! Ever try to close a bank account and have the computer keep billing you service charges for a year? With compound interest running at twenty percent? And how about answering machines? I know my blood pressure goes up when I ring someone up and one of those damn machines comes on the line!

It's all very simple and straightforward. None of these processes are mysterious. You know that when you're walking or running your blood pressure is going to go up, and come down again when you relax. And you know that when you're upset at the boss (or the telephone) your blood pressure goes up, and once again, it will come down again if you can relax.

That's the trick, isn't it?

Letting go of the upset. Completely.

And the main difference between these two kinds of stress is that running may well help your blood pressure in the long run, and getting mad at the boss is more likely to make things worse. Physically and economically.

4

What Is High Blood Pressure?

*To administer medicines once disease
has taken hold is like forging your sword
when the battle already rages around
you.*

Chinese proverb

If you have a lot of stress in your life, so that your arterioles are constricting all the time, this can go one stage further. You can wind up with a permanent or fixed partial constriction of the arterioles, which will again make the blood flow slower, reducing the fall in pressure when the heart relaxes—and giving you a permanently high diastolic pressure.

People who have a lot of stress in their lives over long periods of time end up with hearts that are pumping more forcefully to push blood through the closed-down or constricted arterioles, a greater volume of blood in the system, and both high systolic and diastolic pressures.

The thing that really makes high blood pressure stay around, that sustains it and makes it chronic, is having a very particular abnormality, a very special problem with the kidneys. That's the key to most forms of hypertension.

Most people who have high blood pressure have kidneys that work just fine handling calcium, phosphorus, urea, amino acids, glucose, potassium, and most of the rest. And your doctor will likely tell you, on the basis of the tests that he runs, that your kidneys are just fine. There's only one thing wrong.

If you have hypertension, or a family history of hypertension, it probably means that you have inherited a pair of kidneys that can't handle the amount of salt that's in the foods you eat. Don't get me wrong. You may have perfectly fine kidneys in all other respects. They're just not adapted to the amount of salt in the typical Western diet.

By the time we are adults, most of us are eating ten to twelve grams of sodium chloride—salt—a day. That's a huge amount! The kidneys were designed to deal with maybe a tenth of that amount. Remember that early man grew up in Central Africa, where salt is rare and fresh food is available year round!

The quantities of salt we actually eat are a great burden on our systems. It's so destructive. As we eat more salt than the kidneys can readily excrete, over a long period of time, many years, salt builds up in the body. Now salt is so toxic that, in order for the body to tolerate it, it must be diluted in water. So the body begins to retain water as well, also in the kidneys.

When we say you're holding on to excess salt, what we really mean is that you're holding on to water as well. By the time you're an adult you may be walking around with five or ten pounds of extra water on your person, water that's only there to keep that salt diluted.

What does all this have to do with blood pressure?

Well, it turns out that pressure is a very powerful diuretic (force or substance that increases sodium excretion by the kidneys), perhaps the most powerful one of all.

When we are young and eat excess salt, our body fluids increase, and they suppress those factors that tend to cause sodium retention and enhance those factors that tend to cause sodium excretion. So we dump the salt pretty easily.

As we grow older this mechanism works less and less well, presumably because the kidneys become injured or altered in some way. Maximally suppressed sodium-retaining factors and enhanced sodium-excreting factors no longer do the job. So to stabilize the situation, and make it possible once again to excrete completely a high-sodium dietary intake, our blood pressure rises.

The body's way to get rid of more of that salt and water is to push it out through the kidneys by raising the blood pressure.

Do you realize that nearly every bit of salt you eat every day is excreted by the kidneys? If your kidneys were able to handle all that salt easily, your body wouldn't have to go to the trouble of raising your blood pressure to get rid of it. But the kidneys weren't designed to handle that much salt, so the blood pressure goes up. And that's why diuretic drugs bring the blood pressure down in some cases—they force the kidneys to excrete more salt and water, and the blood pressure drops because the diuretics are now doing the trick.

I'll let you in on a secret: eating less salt is a much simpler way of going about it.

If you have hypertension, your kidneys are probably the kind that have trouble excreting salt. Maybe you inherited this tendency. Or you injured them by eating too much salt or protein. They may get that way as a result of some kidney disease such as nephritis or Bright's disease. Or you may have simply lost one of your kidneys, perhaps by donating it to a relative for transplantation.

We used to think that anyone who didn't already show signs of having high blood pressure could safely donate a kidney to someone who needed one. But it doesn't look quite that safe anymore. We are beginning to realize that over time most everyone's kidneys become unable to cope with large amounts of salt—and that people who have only one kidney are simply hurrying that process up.

Let's put it this way: if you eat the amount of salt that most of us do for long enough, your kidneys will probably lose their ability to excrete it normally. There's at least a two out of three chance that it will eventually happen. Some people just don't reach that point as fast as others. With a favorable family history and no kidney-related problems, you might not get high blood pressure till you are seventy or eighty. But with kidney disease, or a family history of high blood pressure, it may happen a lot sooner.

It happens to children. It happens to adolescents. It happens to young adults. It happens to most of us, sooner or later. If we eat salt.

WEIGHT AND HIGH BLOOD PRESSURE

No doubt about it, there's a close relationship between being over-weight and having high blood pressure. Not everyone by any means, but most obese people have higher blood pressures than they would if they weren't obese—and obese people are more likely to have hypertension (blood pressure of 140/90 or above). And this relationship between weight/obesity and blood pressure starts in childhood.

One explanation is that it takes more pressure to pump blood through that extra fatty tissue. The basal metabolic rate of people who are over-weight is higher because they have more cells and more tissue that need oxygen—so their heart rates are faster, and their heat production and cardiac output are greater, than those of other people; yet their blood vessels are about the same size. Thus an increased flow through their vessels may require a higher pressure to accomplish it.

Such people also have a higher level of sympathetic (emergency) ner-vous system hormones—the material is presented in a paper in *Hyperten-sion* (1982)—and these hormones may also cause a rise in blood pressure.

Probably both these reasons contribute to the relationship between obesity and high blood pressure—but, for whatever reasons, your blood pressure will sure get better when you lose those extra pounds!

ESTROGENS

There's another way of setting yourself up for high blood pressure that I'd like to mention. And, again, it has to do with the kidneys, and it's preventable.

If you take birth control pills or the estrogens that are prescribed to relieve the symptoms of menopause, you are stimulating the liver to make a substance that an enzyme (renin) made by the kidneys works on to produce a hormone (angiotensin) that raises blood pressure. Not only that, angiotensin also reduces the flow of blood in the kidney, making it harder for you to excrete the salt you eat. You might say that taking those pills was equivalent to giving yourself the kidney factor.

Dr. Norman Hollenberg wrote the classic paper on this, in *Circulation Research* (1976). He studied women who were being considered as possi-ble kidney donors for transplants, and he found that kidney blood flow in the women who were using birth control pills was significantly lower than in those who were not.

Nearly everyone who takes birth control pills will experience a rise in blood pressure if she takes them long enough. Some women will get hypertension, some of them severe hypertension, some of them malignant hypertension. But everyone will experience some rise in blood pressure. It's that simple. The relevant papers are by Dr. N. M. Kaplan, in the *Annual Review of Medicine* (1978), and Drs. I. R. Fisch and J. Frank, in the *Journal of the American Medical Association* (1977).

Millions upon millions of women started taking these pills in the late fifties and early sixties, and it takes twenty to thirty years to find out just how severe this problem will be. So we will be finding out soon enough.

RARE CAUSES OF HYPERTENSION

About one in a thousand people may get a blockage in the artery leading to the kidneys at some point in their lives, and that can cause high blood pressure too. The problem is very rare and can be dealt with pretty easily when it crops up. A few people have tumors of the kidney or the adrenal glands, which can also cause high blood pressure. But these problems are usually pretty obvious to the doctor taking care of you.

OVERVIEW

To sum up: ninety-five percent of people who have high blood pressure have it for one or more of five causes: salt, chronic stress, excess weight, loss of the kidneys' ability to handle salt, and time.

And salt is the worst of these.

With or without hereditary disposition, salt will get you in the long run. And with or without that same hereditary factor, a salt-free diet will work wonders.

Isn't it worth it?

I've heard that the lower your blood pressure the better off you are. Is that true? I take medicine, but my diastolic pressure doesn't get below 90. Should I take more medications, the way my doctor wants me to?

I agree with your doctor that a diastolic pressure of 80 is better than one of 90. It means you're less likely to suffer from cardiovascular disease—heart attack or stroke—and I'm all for that. So I'd like to get your diastolic pressure down below 90 too. The question is, how do we do it?

Basically, drugs don't seem to be the way to go. Dr. Norman Kaplan, the noted author and chief of the Hypertension Divison at the University of Texas in Dallas, puts it this way: "The wider acceptance of a more cautious, conservative approach toward drug therapy in general seems warranted, even though it will fly in the face of current dogma and practice."

Writing in the *Journal of the American Medical Association* (1983), Dr. Kaplan reviewed the evidence for and against treating the 30 to 40 million people in the United States who have mild hypertension with drugs. Acknowledging that hypertension "experts" and pharmaceutical advertisements have been pushing hard for "early and aggressive" drug treatment of mild hypertension, he injected a word of caution.

Because he is such a leader in the field, and a scientist whose opinion most physicians would respect, I want to share with you some of his recommendations, which are similar to my own.

After suggesting that everyone with high blood pressure should be carefully monitored, he went on to talk about people who, in addition to elevated blood pressure, have other heart disease risk factors—such as smoking, obesity, blood cholesterol greater than 200, high stress, positive family history, sedentary life style, and physical deconditioning.

Dr. Kaplan suggested that these risk factors should all be attended to and that aggressive treatment of high blood pressure was warranted in the case of this group—to bring the blood pressure down by any means available.

And he concluded, "All patients, regardless of risk status, should be offered and strongly encouraged to follow non-drug therapies that are likely to help—weight reduction for the obese, moderate sodium restriction for all, and one or other relaxation techniques for those willing to use them."

Every time I go see my doctor, whether I've been taking my pills or not, my blood pressure seems to be high, and he seems to worry about it. I just can't believe it's that high all the time. I even checked it at home a few times, and it wasn't that high. It's getting where I'm worried every time I go see him. I'm afraid he's going to shake his head at me and write out another prescription.

I know exactly what you mean. A lot of my patients tell me the same thing. And I tell them not to worry so much. Round-the-clock blood pressure measurements have shown that people's blood pressure is often higher when they go to see their doctors. And in some cases the differences can be extreme. If you or your doctor want to read the details, there are articles about this in the *Journal of the American Medical Association* (1982 and 1983) and the *Lancet* (1981).

Your pressure can vary a lot just as a result of how you feel about having it measured—and who's doing the measuring. It's not uncommon, for instance, for patients to feel that doctors are authoritative and a little menacing, while nurses are more sympathetic, more "on their side." For myself, I almost always take my patients' pressure once, say, "That's not bad," or something reassuring of the sort, and then take the pressure again. And it's usually lower the second time around!

Joanne and I go back several years. She was already on a good diet, worked out at a gym, practiced TM (Transcendental Meditation)—what more was there to do?

Well, I couldn't get her to take a look at her own blood pressure. She'd even miss appointments, just so she wouldn't have to find out what her blood pressure was. She couldn't face all that worry building up inside, before I told her, "It's not so bad, 180/105," or something like that. In fact she actually stayed away a whole year at one point. She kept on taking her medicines. But she just didn't want to get her blood pressure checked.

Finally she relented. She came back and started taking her pressures at home this time—and turned the whole thing around. She's off medicines completely now. And I know that what finally solved the problem for her was her own willingness to take responsibility for her blood pressure and her body.

5

The Conventional Treatment

*The desire to take medicines is perhaps
the greatest feature which distinguishes
man from the animals.*

Sir William Osler

Breathe a sigh of relief. Because even if you show up in a doctor's office
today with severe high blood pressure the chances are nobody's going to
recommend the use of surgery.

As little as thirty years ago a surgical procedure known as *sympathectomy* was commonly used in the treatment of severe high blood pressure.
It involved cutting all the nerves of the sympathetic nervous system along
both sides of the spine. It was a pretty drastic procedure. But it was the
best option we knew about in some cases. It probably even saved lives. If
you're a medical nostalgia buff you can read about it in the *Journal of the
American Medical Association* (1949).

But the practice of medicine has come a long way since the decade
following the Second World War, and the current treatment of hypertension is very different from what it was back then. Medical science is still
making progress. And it's the medicine of the eighties and nineties—the

drug-free health care approach—that I want you to have, right now, to-day. That's what this program is all about.

In the meantime I would like you to know something about the way the medical profession currently handles hypertension. As an informed citizen, you have every right to know. And, as a patient, it's in your own best interests to keep informed.

Doctors aren't infallible, and the stakes are high. Your life expectancy, the quality of your life, and large sums of your money are all at risk here. So you need to have as clear an understanding of what's going on as you can. Your doctor is a highly skilled professional, and he can help you a great deal. But you need to have some input into the kind of relationship you're going to have with him. Don't go into his office completely blind.

When you go to see your doctor, and he finds out that you have high blood pressure, there are two things he'll want to do. He'll want to give you a diagnostic workup or evaluation, and find out what your life is like, what kinds of symptoms you have, and so on. And he'll want to prescribe some form of treatment.

THE DIAGNOSTIC WORKUP

The first thing your doctor ought to do is to ask you a lot of questions about your life. Some of them may be personal. He needs to know what kinds of foods you eat, how active you are, and what kinds of stresses and strains you have to face, both on the job and at home—and he needs to find out what symptoms you have.

Do you get headaches? Is your vision blurred some of the time? Does your stomach ache a lot? Do you get up at night to urinate? Do you have chest pains, or dizziness, or maybe heart palpitations? Have you been having any difficulty breathing at night? Is your sexual function normal? When you walk, do you find yourself getting winded very easily?

Do you have any problems in your life that might be affecting your health? Are you under a lot of stress?

A while ago a patient showed up at the Hypertension Clinic that I run in Los Angeles. Here's a man who's about twenty-four years old, who had worked as an assembler for General Motors. He has a very strong family history of high blood pressure—his brother and his father both have it. He has a wife and two kids. And he's on welfare at the moment, because he was laid off a few months ago and his unemployment benefits have run out. You know what's been happening to the auto industry, so none of that's too surprising.

To cope with his situation, he's been drinking a little too much. He eats mostly convenience, "junk" foods. And he doesn't get much in the way of exercise. Worrying just doesn't qualify as an aerobic workout.

By the time I've found out about all this, I know why he has high blood pressure. He's under an enormous amount of stress. His diet's terrible, he's eating a lot of salt, and he's drinking too much. He doesn't exercise. And he has a strong genetic predisposition to get high blood pressure.

And it was really important for me to know all that. If I didn't know it, I might think he was pretty young to have a blood pressure of 180/115 and start ordering a lot of expensive X rays and tests, to find out whether he has a tumor of the adrenal gland or the kidneys, or some other kind of special problem.

But when I know about his family situation, and what's been happening since he was laid off, and what kinds of food he eats, the explanation for his problem is a lot more straightforward. It's not likely that he has a tumor of the adrenals—very, very few people have them. The cause of his high blood pressure is much more obvious than that. And I don't need to order all those expensive and uncomfortable X rays and other tests.

That's why it's very important for your doctor to ask you all those questions. He needs to understand what's been happening to you, to find out why your blood pressure is up.

The most important adverse effect of elevated blood pressure is that it worsens atherosclerosis, and so raises your risk of coronary artery closure and heart attacks. So your doctor will want to ask you about other aspects of your life style, to see if you have any habits that also contribute to this risk.

Do you smoke? And if so, how much do you smoke, and how long have you been doing it? Are you sedentary or active, a desk worker or a heavy laborer? How much alcohol and coffee do you drink? What kind of diet are you on, and what's been happening to your weight?

Of course, your family history is important too. We sometimes learn unhealthy habits from our parents and sometimes inherit a sensitivity to unhealthy life practices from them as well. If they're obese, we probably will be too. If they smoke, we're much more likely to than if they don't. These two problems seem to be learned from, rather than inherited from, our parents. But there are other problems, notably the kidney factor that we discussed in Chapter 4, which we inherit. And we probably inherit the likelihood of having coronary artery disease as well.

Then your doctor needs to give you a careful physical examination. He will want to check your eyes and ears, and listen to your heart, your lungs, and your stomach. Do you have any lumps that shouldn't be there? Are any of your organs more sensitive than they should be? When he uses his stethoscope, can he hear any noises in your lungs or belly that mean that something's wrong?

He'll be looking for any possible cause of high blood pressure; and he'll also be on the lookout for any damage your high blood pressure may have caused already.

The most important place to check for damage is in the back of your eyes. Your doctor will use an ophthalmoscope to shine a light on the tiny arterioles in the back of your eyes while he examines them. He will be looking to see whether the arterioles have become narrowed (which is called *spasm*), or have burst *(hemorrhaging)*, or closed down completely so there's no more blood flowing through them and part of the retina has died *(infarction*—an infarction of the retina looks like a small ball of cotton or wool, so it's also called a cotton-wool spot). And to see if, because of the hypertension, the protective mechanisms have broken down and allowed a high blood flow and pressure inside the eyes and the brain, and in the fluid that surrounds the brain *(edema)*.

He also needs to listen to your heart, to hear if it is beating normally. Sometimes he may be able to put his hand on your chest and feel the heart beating too forcefully. This happens if your emergency nervous system is stimulating the heart excessively. When you're sitting on the exam table your heart doesn't need to pump blood as if you were walking up-stairs two steps at a time! But that's exactly what can happen to some people with hypertension; their hearts behave as if they were running, even when they're at rest.

If this excessive stimulation goes on long enough, and especially if the blood pressure is raised a lot of the time, the heart muscle gets bigger, just the same way that the biceps (the muscles on the inside of your upper arm) get bigger if you lift weights every day. This process is called *hyper-trophy*, and it usually involves only the left ventricle.

Your doctor can feel this as a larger and more forceful impulse of the heart beating, near the left nipple in men, or just under the left breast in women. Everyone with chronic hypertension has some degree of left ven-tricle hypertrophy (LVH for short) although the severity varies a lot from patient to patient. In mild cases, your doctor won't be able to detect it during his physical exam.

If stimulation and hypertrophy don't provide enough energy for the heart to do its job, then the heart may *enlarge*, that is, the chamber size may get bigger. The muscle fibers in the heart wall are then stretched more as the heart fills, and thus they can contract and shorten more powerfully, producing a stronger heartbeat. Your doctor can detect this enlargement quite easily when he examines your heart by *percussion*, or thumping your chest with his finger. And it shows up in your chest X ray, too.

When the heart is enlarged, the valves sometimes begin to leak, and he can hear the leaking as a heart murmur.

If your doctor hears a *gallop* rhythm—that is, the heartbeat doesn't sound like a simple *lub-dub*, but like *ba-lub-dub*, a triple or gallop rhythm —that's another fairly common sign of hypertension.

At other times the heart can get so overloaded that blood backs up into your lungs, and you may find yourself very short of breath when lying down or sitting quietly. Your doctor will test you for this possibility by listening to your lungs, to see if he can hear the sound of *rales*—excess fluid in the lungs. In some cases the blood can back up not only into the lungs but into the rest of your body as well. Your doctor may check for this possibility by seeing whether your ankles are swollen, whether your neck veins are full when you are sitting, or checking to see if your liver is oversized and sensitive.

This careful physical exam is an important part of your workup.

Then your doctor will need to do some blood tests. He'll want to find out whether there's anything in your tests that points to a specific cause of your high blood pressure, and whether the tests indicate any damage that the hypertension may have caused already, for example to the kidneys; and he'll also be checking to find out whether you have some of the other risk factors for stroke or heart attack—which he'll do by measuring your fats and cholesterol levels and blood uric acid.

He'll need to run a routine urinalysis, to see whether any signs of damage to the kidney have shown up. The kidney factor that makes it difficult to excrete salt won't show up in this test, but other kidney problems can cause high blood pressure (Bright's disease or nephritis), or result from it (the kidneys may leak some protein and red blood cells into the urine). A urinalysis will let your doctor know whether you are having any of these problems.

Then you will need a chest X ray, to see whether there are any signs of heart enlargement or fluid in the lungs. And you will need an electrocardiogram, to see whether your heartbeat is regular, and whether your heart muscle has grown larger and stronger *(hypertrophied)* or shows any signs of injury from lack of oxygen.

I think everyone who has been diagnosed as having high blood pressure should have a chest X ray and an electrocardiogram, at least once.

There are two other tests that are sometimes given by doctors today, which most experts agree are unnecessary. The first is a urine test called a VMA. It checks for a tumor of the adrenal glands. It goes by other names as well (a metanephrine or catecholamine test), but the disease being looked for is the same.

The test is not completely accurate. And in any case fewer than one in ten thousand people with high blood pressure have adrenal tumors. So the test leaves us little wiser than we were before it, and costs us time and money. Few experts recommend routinely measuring the VMA in a urine sample any more.

Another test that's fairly common is a kidney X ray, known as an IVP *(intravenous pyelogram)*. This test involves injecting a dye into your vein (you'll feel flushed and a little sick), and then taking a lot of X rays to see whether one of the arteries to your kidneys is blocked, or whether you have any other kidney abnormalities.

Once again, it's an expensive test that's only marginally accurate, and the disease we're looking for is pretty rare. IVPs are expensive and a little dangerous, and a total waste of time for most patients.

There are circumstances in which I would be more inclined to recommend looking for these rare causes of hypertension. If you are very young —under the age of twenty or twenty-five—with no family history of high blood pressure. Or if you are over the age of fifty-five or sixty and your high blood pressure has suddenly come on like gangbusters. In this kind of situation I would want to look very closely to see whether the sudden rise was caused by a tumor, or a blocked artery to the kidney, or something like that. But for most people these tests that look for rare causes of hypertension just aren't worth bothering about.

All right. Let's assume that your doctor has talked to you about your life and diet and so on, and examined you, and, other than your high blood pressure, there's really nothing out of the ordinary—except that, like most Americans, you're a little overweight, you don't exercise enough, your diet's terrible, and you have a lot of stress.

What usually happens next is that your doctor talks to you a little. He says, "Well, George, better cut down on the salt. Drink a little less coffee. I advise you to stop smoking, lose some weight—and maybe you should take some time off from work occasionally and not push yourself so hard. Don't worry so much. Try to relax."

That was your doctor's way of telling you to take better care of yourself, his two-minute crash course in preventive medicine.

But he's not through yet. He reaches in his drawer and pulls out a prescription pad. "What I want you to do," he says, "is take these pills."

If you want to know how the conventional, current treatment of hypertension continues from there—what those drugs your doctor is writing you a prescription for are called, what effects they have, and what side effects —you can turn to the back of the book and read Chapters 21 through 23.

But I have a different prescription. I am going to prescribe the medicine of the eighties—a twelve-week program to control your high blood pressure without the use of those drugs.

The Program

6

The Program That Works

> *It should be the function of medicine to
> have people die young as late as possi-
> ble.*
>
> Ernst L. Wynder, M.D.

The first thing people noticed about Ollie was his size. Ollie was a trucker, a big, strong man with tanned arms and face. He had too much of a potbelly—but it only made him look all the more imposing. I'd already tried three or four medicines, and his blood pressure was still up.

"Damn," I thought. "What am I going to tell him now—take another pill?"

"You're in a jam, Ollie," I told him, "and it's going to get worse. What you're doing to yourself is far stronger than what I'm doing with these drugs. The things you eat and the way you live have such a powerful effect on your blood pressure, they make my pills seem like water."

He looked a little scared at this; he knew exactly what I was saying. "I know you don't like these pills," I went on, "and I can't blame you. But the next group of drugs have even worse side effects. I just hate to do this to you."

We just sat there looking at each other for a minute, and the room got real quiet. Finally I said, "Look—let's turn this thing around, now, you and me. Let's get you working with me instead of against me. Okay?"

You mean there's something I can do?

Let's face it: taking drugs for the rest of our lives—especially some of the most powerful and unpleasant drugs on the market today—isn't something that any of us would look forward to. And when I tell my patients that *what they do really counts*, they sit up and take notice.

This program tells you what you can do that will really make the difference. It's a complete and successful program for controlling high blood pressure without the use of drugs.

According to Dr. Robert Levy, director of the National Heart, Lung, and Blood Institute, some *60 million Americans* have high blood pressure. And top medical authorities are throwing up their hands in despair at the prospect of so many people taking blood pressure medications indefinitely.

"Risks of Correcting the Risks of Coronary Disease and Stroke with Drugs" is the title of a recent (1982) article in the *New England Journal of Medicine*. The article discussed the "increasing number of unexpected adverse effects" of drugs given over many years to control high blood pressure.

A note in the *Journal of the American Medical Association* (1981) stated that there is "mounting evidence that many antihypertensive drugs . . . may actually increase the risk of coronary artery disease."

Drs. R. P. Ames and P. Hill, writing in *Circulation* (1982), demonstrated that patients who are taken off hypertension medications actually show improvement in glucose (sugar) tolerance, as well as lowering of lipid (fat) concentration in the blood—and both of these effects tend to diminish the likelihood of heart attack.

Let me emphasize here, right at the start, that I am not suggesting that you should stop taking your blood pressure medications *without a physician's supervision*.

What I am suggesting is that you and your doctor should team up. Working together, following the program I describe in this book, you can beat high blood pressure and avoid those costly and unpleasant drugs. I have seen it happen time and again.

Believe me, your doctor will be more than happy to have your cooperation. He's concerned about your welfare—and he knows he's done a good
job when he sees you looking and feeling well.

WHY THIS PROGRAM WORKS

The program works because it's *specific* and because it's *comprehensive*.
The only other approach specifically tailored for people with high blood
pressure is the one the drug companies are pushing. And they are pushing.
In fact they are even advertising in popular magazines these days.

And why not? A Wall Street analyst was quoted in *Fortune* magazine
(1981) as estimating that sales of just one new blood pressure pill might
run as high as half a billion dollars a year.

So let's suppose you'd rather control your blood pressure without the
use of drugs. The three most important skills you'll need to learn are:
 • safe and appropriate exercise;
 • proper nutrition;
 • and effective stress management.
But that's just for starters.

You'll also need to know enough about how your body works and what
you've been doing to yourself that has contributed to your high blood
pressure.

Look, I know you're real busy. People, places, and things crowd you all
the time. So you'll need to know how to take what you've learned about
yourself, and about exercise, nutrition, and stress management, and effectively integrate it into your life.

And you'll need to get motivated—and learn how to keep your motivation going, so that your newfound interest and enthusiasm don't just run
down after a few days or weeks or months.

This program teaches you all of that. It *educates* you about high blood
pressure. It explains what's going wrong and what you need to do about it.
It *motivates* you. And step by step, through the twelve weeks of the
program, it *teaches you the techniques*—all the techniques you need—to
bring your blood pressure under control, safely and very successfully. It's a
comprehensive and specific approach. And that's why it works so well.

THE PROGRAM THAT PUTS YOUR EDUCATION AND MOTIVATION TO WORK

First of all, you need to work with a professional who can take care of you. I know there are books on the market about how to avoid probate and how to get your own divorce. This is not that kind of book. This is a book about becoming a partner with your doctor and helping him look after you. Because you are with you all the time, and your doctor isn't.

Your doctor is still the one who has to order the tests and decide about the prescriptions. But you can learn a lot about the drugs you're taking. And you can learn to take your blood pressure at home—the *American Heart Journal* (1979) reported a study showing that forty-three percent of people with high blood pressure experienced an improvement of ten or more points after they learned to do just that.

Your doctor can only do so much, however. After all, he's not the one who sits down to that breakfast of ham and eggs. He's not the one who ate that dinner of corned beef and cabbage, or went out to a Chinese restaurant and poured soy sauce over everything. You're the one who can and must learn the skills needed to take better care of yourself.

Your doctor can't exactly get up in the morning to do your exercise for you or bring your blood pressure down by remaining calm while you're in the middle of a traffic jam—but you can.

THE THREE THINGS YOU CAN DO

This program will teach you all you need to know about *nutrition*—specifically as it applies to high blood pressure—and will help you to improve your own diet.

We've known for forty years or more that diet plays a significant role in causing high blood pressure—but only recently have we once again started taking nutrition seriously as a means of controlling it.

Take salt, for example. *Time* magazine (March 15, 1982) termed dietary salt the "stealthy silent accomplice" of hypertension—the silent killer. And an editorial in the *Lancet* suggested that high blood pressure could be considered a form of "salt poisoning." The *Medical Letter for Drugs and Therapeutics* (1980), a kind of *Consumer Reports* for doctors, recently stated that "many studies have shown that changes in sodium [salt] intake may be associated with parallel changes in blood pressure."

As a result of the mounting evidence that salt intake plays a primary role in much hypertension, Dr. Arthur Hull Hayes, Jr., commissioner of the U. S. Food and Drug Administration, recently stated that patients on drug therapy respond better to their medication, and may need fewer drugs or lower doses, if they lower the amount of sodium in their diets *(American Medical News,* 1982). Indeed, the American Medical Association and the Food and Drug Administration are now working together to limit the sodium in foods *(American Medical News,* 1982).

This program will also teach you about losing weight. Two articles in the *New England Journal of Medicine* emphasize the importance of weight loss in the treatment of hypertension. Dr. E. Reisin and others (1978) showed that weight loss by itself has a beneficial effect on blood pressure in overweight patients—independent of the effects of salt restriction. And researchers from the UCLA School of Medicine (1981) found a significant decrease in blood pressure to the normal range in all their patients after a twelve-week reducing diet.

You will discover how caffeine stimulates the emergency nervous system, how sugar increases the bad effects of stress, and why dietary fat is such a risk factor.

Teaching good nutrition is the biggest gun in my arsenal—and when I see someone with really bad high blood pressure, that's when I know diet is most important.

You will feel much better eating an appropriate diet. Your blood pressure will begin to drop. And maybe your doctor will be able to taper you off some of those pills.

This program will teach you all you need to know about *exercise.*

A lot of people do calisthenics or other forms of exercise that involve push-ups and stretching and so on. But that kind of exercise has little or no beneficial effect on blood pressure. In fact weight lifting, and other types of exercise that make you grunt and strain and stress, can actually make your blood pressure go up a lot. So it's important to know the kind of exercise that helps.

Aerobic exercise is the kind in which your muscles are moving freely and generating heat. You get warm, you sweat, you get flushed. That's the kind of exercise you need—and you must learn to do it safely.

You need to be careful about it, because your blood pressure may go up a lot at the time you're actually doing this kind of exercise—and if you are taking hypertension drugs your body may not tolerate this type of exercise very well.

However, Dr. Robert Cade, of the University of Florida (quoted by

Eileen Mazer in *Prevention*, 1982), reported that ninety-six percent of hypertensives he tested showed a ten- to fifty-point improvement after three months of aerobic exercise.

This program will introduce you to aerobics safely—and again, your blood pressure will drop and you'll feel much better.

This program will teach you what you need to know to manage *stress*.

First off, it will encourage you to avoid unnecessary stress. Recently David, one of my patients, told me he'd made a breakthrough. He was incredibly proud of himself—he'd been in one of those situations with a teenage son that are always cropping up, and instead of yelling at his son and spoiling the whole evening for everyone—which is what he always used to do—he just stayed calm and didn't yell. He avoided unnecessary stress. He felt so much better. And his blood pressure stayed down too.

You will also learn Rational Emotive Therapy—which is a fancy name for a certain kind of common sense.

You will learn to play. That's right, you will need to set aside some time each week for play—and for humor. You may find yourself taking in a movie by the Marx brothers, or even Richard Pryor—on doctor's orders!

You will learn assertiveness techniques, so that your friends won't be able to bully you into that second helping of something you'd rather not eat.

You will learn nonjudgmental awareness—how to avoid constantly judging yourself—so that you will no longer get even more upset about being upset, or angrier at yourself because you're feeling angry.

You will learn about Progressive Muscle Relaxation, biofeedback, and meditation. The evidence is there—these techniques work.

Drs. D. A. Kristt and B. T. Engel reported in *Circulation* (1975) on patients who had learned to control their blood pressure through biofeedback techniques. And the *British Medical Journal* (1976) discussed several studies of the effects on blood pressure of meditation and relaxation techniques. The article, entitled "Meditation or Methyldopa?" concluded that some well-motivated hypertensives might be able to control their blood pressure without using drugs, using these methods alone.

The *Lancet* (1980), in an article entitled "Lowering Blood Pressure Without Drugs," concluded ". . . there is now evidence from randomized controlled trials that a variety of techniques of meditation and relaxation lead to a fall in blood pressure in the longer term."

These various techniques of muscular relaxation, biofeedback, and med-

itation are stress reduction techniques that you can learn, and then practice on your own.

A HIGH BLOOD PRESSURE PROGRAM
FOR THE EIGHTIES

Dr. Levy, director of the National Heart, Lung, and Blood Institute, in
an article in *Circulation* (1982), accepts the effectiveness of conventional
modes of therapy but adds that few of us "would take comfort in con-
signing 40 million or more Americans to a lifetime of drug therapy if
something better is available. . . ." He goes on to say that we should
"look to nonpharmacologic means that may achieve adequate blood pressure control."

Dr. Jeremiah Stammler, who has made enormous contributions to the
prevention of heart disease, has been doing just that. He reports on the
"Prevention and Control of Hypertension by Nutritional-Hygienic
Means" in the *Journal of the American Medical Association* (1980) and
terms his findings "highly encouraging in regard to the potential of safe,
nonpharmacologic nutritional approaches" to the prevention and control
of high blood pressure.

If you want to control your blood pressure without drugs—you can. But
it means you'll probably have to do some things a little differently in
future.

Few of us like to change too much, but it can be done. And there's even
scientific evidence to prove it! Some recent research that was reported in
Circulation (1982) showed that it is possible for us to change even very
stubborn personality traits, when they constitute a major risk factor in
heart disease. The idea that we can't change is just another myth. We *can*
change—and it can make all the difference in the world.

I remember Harvey, a patient of mine who had been going to the
racetrack for years, and driving his blood pressure sky-high betting. One
day he quit going. Just like that. And this is what he told me: "Listen, I
don't need that aggravation. I'd rather feel good, and have my blood
pressure under control, and not have to take pills, than go out and get all
upset about whether I was winning or losing on the ponies."

If you've ever sat in the waiting room of your doctor's office, worried
about your blood pressure and wondering whether he's going to prescribe

yet another pill, if you've ever asked yourself if there isn't some other possibility, some other way to go—this program is for you.

It offers you a successful, drug-free way to control your blood pressure. In fact it's the program we've all been waiting for.

7

Getting Ready

If we do not change our direction, we are likely to end up where we are headed.

Chinese proverb

Do you remember the first day in school each year when you were a kid? The anticipation was so thick, you could hardly finish your breakfast. Do you remember putting on the clothes you'd specially chosen the night before, and then waiting for the bus, or walking over to the school? And seeing your friends, including some who lived so far away that you hadn't seen them all summer? Finding your classroom, seeing which teacher you got, and discovering who else was in your class?

After all that excitement, the teacher spent at least the whole of the first morning passing out books, telling you how she specifically wanted the headings put on all your papers, and giving you all her ground rules for the rest of the year. Suddenly you remember just what school was like, it was so incredibly boring!

I don't know why my teachers never spent that first morning telling us about all the really interesting things we were going to learn. Things like,

"This year we'll be learning to read and write cursive script, so that when you come across notes written by adults you can read them." Or "This year we'll be learning about the explorers who discovered the north and south poles, and what those are." Or, "We'll learn the kinds of math you'd need to make change if you were collecting for a paper route—because this is the first year you'll be old enough to apply for one."

So here we are, getting ready to start the program—"how to control your high blood pressure without drugs"—and we'd like to tell you about some of the neat things that will be going on during the twelve weeks of the program—and about the graduation party you'll be having when the twelve weeks are up. We'll try to keep it interesting.

This is the time to make your preparations. It's a chance for you to get acquainted with the program and to see how it all fits together.

We'll be focusing in on four areas: nutrition—what you eat; exercise—how physically active you are; stress—because we all have some stress in our lives; and medical care—how you can work in real partnership with your doctor to turn your blood pressure around.

And first of all I'd like to suggest we take a look at the directions we'll be moving in, so that you get a clear idea of what needs to be done. Later on we'll be setting some goals. But for the moment just getting a feel for the kinds of things we're aiming for will do.

As you start this program, what direction are you headed in as far as nutrition is concerned? Is this some kind of diet, or what?

No, this isn't a diet—at least, not in the usual sense. Nobody's going to tell you just what you must or mustn't eat. But we will be telling you about the kinds of food that most of us eat, and you'll begin to realize that the average American diet is none too healthy—particularly if you already have hypertension.

The average American diet has gotten pretty far removed from the diet that is natural and ideal for the human body. As a consequence, a lot of people in our society are unnecessarily sick. It may take a long time for the food we eat to make us sick enough to sit up and take notice, but millions of people in Europe, the United States, and other "developed" countries are beginning to recognize the problem.

So, as far as nutrition is concerned, our program is based on a diet that's healthier and more natural for the human body. It'll likely have less salt, fat, cholesterol, and protein in it, and it will obviously have less calories, if excess weight is a problem. You're headed toward a diet that's lower in sugar and caffeine, and somewhat limited in terms of alcohol. But it's also a diet that's more naturally nutritious, more adapted to your actual needs, and so more delicious.

We want you to discover how to be more aware of what you eat and when you really want to eat it—and, just by themselves, these two skills will add immensely to your enjoyment of food. You will no longer be so easily swayed by the commercials on TV, by habit, or by your friends. You'll discover a whole new range of choices are open to you, and you'll find these choices make a whole lot of sense, too.

We'll also be showing you how to integrate this new way of eating into your everyday routine. We'll show you how to adapt recipes (and teach you some delicious new ones), and how to order healthy food in restaurants and on airplanes. In every case, we'll be showing you how to fit this new approach into your life. Ultimately, you'll wind up on a diet you really like that really works for you.

As you go through this program you'll be finding out for yourself, from your own experience, that how you feel depends importantly on how you eat; that there's a direct connection between what you eat and how healthy you are. You'll learn about this by trying a healthier diet under no compulsion at all, and discovering how much better you feel as a result. We'll be giving you lots of guidelines, for sure; but the idea is for you to find out what works for you.

It's as simple as that.

One thing I'd like to stress here—and it applies to the rest of the program as well as to your diet—is that you'll likely make mistakes, and really that's just fine. It's normal. It's to be expected. In fact the mistakes you make in choosing your diet and changing your style of eating will likely turn out to be as important as anything else.

Mistakes are what we all learn from, right? They can actually be some of the best friends we have. Besides, nutrition's one area where you can make almost any kind of mistake, as long as you learn from it. It's not likely to be fatal in the short term—unless of course you go eating some strange new kind of mushroom that nobody's heard of before.

So admit your mistakes and learn from them; please don't cover them up, or lie to yourself about them, or punish yourself.

What about exercise?

First of all, we're not talking about push-ups and pull-ups and weights and that kind of thing. We're talking about aerobic exercise—and your goal is going to be to find out how that can fit into your life.

I know you're busy—as C. Northcote Parkinson once said, "Work expands so as to fill the time available." But I also know you'll want to find a way to fit regular aerobics into your life. Because you want to get the job done right. You want to be able to throw away those pills.

What kinds of exercise are aerobic? We'll be learning more about that over the twelve weeks of the program—but for the moment let's just say things like running, walking, swimming, cycling, and dancing.

And you'll be learning how to exercise safely, and get the most out of it, and enjoy it. Yes, I said *enjoy*. In time you'll find aerobic exercise is a powerful tool for relaxation, for feeling more energetic, lowering your blood pressure, and reducing your risk of heart disease. And the bonus? It firms you up, makes you look better, reduces your weight—and makes you feel like a million bucks.

Ultimately you'll choose exercise because you know how wonderful it makes you feel—and you won't feel you always have to lecture yourself, always have to push yourself into it. That'll be a relief, won't it? How good you feel will be pretty good, too.

Stress.

We all have stress. I don't know anyone who doesn't—no matter what income we have, what age we are, or what our circumstances may be. No one escapes it. Even the people most of us would envy tremendously, who seem to have everything going for them, are experiencing stress too. Believe me, we all are. Even if we don't know it.

And it's funny, but it turns out that reducing stress usually has very little to do with changing circumstances, or changing your situation. It seems as though it would, until you change your situation, change your circumstances, make the money and get the job you're sure will make the difference—only to discover that the stress is still there, just as it always was.

Sometimes it's useful to change the circumstances around us, but mostly stress results from what we do and how we see the world we live in. It's mostly a matter of attitude—our own!

The goal here will be to discover, in yourself, the ability to relax, no matter what the circumstances are. You can only worry so much—and it really doesn't do any good anyway, does it? You'll learn to leave off worrying for a little while, take a vacation from it, and relax, and you'll still be able to go back to your battleground any time you want to.

We'll be teaching you quite a fascinating variety of stress reduction techniques, from muscle relaxation, meditation, and visualization (some people call it imaging, or imagining) to being more assertive, and from going fishing (and unwinding that way) to going to the movies (and laughing away your tensions with Groucho Marx or Chevy Chase or Mel Brooks).

The last thing we'll be emphasizing is working in close partnership with your own physician. This is really important, particularly if you're already on pills.

We've talked about doctors—what they have to offer you, what their limitations are (they can't eat your breakfast, remember?) and what you can do to help your own doctor.

You'll be learning about the drugs, what they have to offer, and what their limitations are. So that you don't have to wander around thinking, "Let's see, I take that blue pill. What does that do? And then I'm supposed to take one of the pink ones three times a day. I wonder what they're for?" Or, "Do you suppose these pills have anything to do with how tired I've been feeling lately?" It's time you took the responsibility for knowing about your drugs.

You will become an informed and intelligent partner with your physician—and you and he will decide together which drugs you need and which drugs you don't. Maybe, if you really follow this program completely, if you really get into it, you and your doctor will decide you don't need any drugs at all. That's what we're going for. That's why we've called this book CONTROL YOUR HIGH BLOOD PRESSURE—WITHOUT DRUGS!

That's what all the fuss is about.

GOING SHOPPING AND GETTING READY

You need to get yourself a notebook—the kind you can make columns and lists in, with plenty of pages, because you're going to be using it a lot. You're going to make notes and observations about yourself and this program—and you're going to learn a lot by making those notes.

You're also going to need a marking pen (red or yellow)—the kind you can use to highlight printed material: they're sometimes called "highlighters."

One of the important things you're going to do in this program is learn how to take your own blood pressure at home. Which means you'll need to buy a blood pressure measuring device soon. The device is called a sphygmomanometer; don't let that name bother you: just ask about a "blood pressure cuff." Most drugstores in America have them; but you can also get one from a medical supply house or a department store such as Sears. They range from $25 on up. If your doctor prescribes the cuff for you, this is a tax-deductible expense—or you may be able to get your insurance company to pay for it.

You could ask about cuffs in your local drugstore, or at a department store like Sears, or you could try at a medical supply house. Or you could read up on the subject in the *Consumer Reports Buying Guide* (1980–81). It's probably in your local library.

But don't buy one this week; I want you to talk it over with your doctor when you see him and decide between the two of you which is the best kind of cuff for you.

That brings us to the one other thing you'll need to do before you start. You need to set up an appointment to see your doctor—because the week you see him will be Week One of your program and you'll need some very important tests. These tests will measure the amount of potassium in your blood, the amount of uric acid, hemoglobin, your triglyceride levels, cholesterol level, and fasting blood sugar level. They are best taken at a time when you haven't eaten or drunk anything except water for a period of twelve to fourteen hours. So try to arrange for an appointment fairly early in the morning.

THE PROGRAM OVERVIEW

Here is a quick rundown of what will be happening to you, week by week, for the twelve weeks of the program. I'd like you to read this section carefully, because when we're through we're going to be doing some scheduling, and it'll be easier for you to do it if you've got a general idea of how the whole program works.

On Sunday, the day before you begin Week One, you're going to set some goals for yourself—health goals, personal goals, and career goals. You're going to prepare your notebook for the first week. You're going to talk to your family and get their support. And you'll be signing a contract with yourself. To really follow this program.

During Week One you're going to find out a lot about yourself—what you eat, what your food tastes like, how your body feels afterward, and so forth. You'll be measuring your weight, your blood pressure, and your early morning pulse every day. You'll be getting a better idea of what the drugs you're taking are doing to you. You'll be talking about this program with your friends and colleagues and getting their support. And you'll be visiting your doctor for a discussion and a few tests.

In Week Two you'll be finding out more about the drugs you're taking. You'll read about the various drugs that are used to treat hypertension and you'll learn what they can and can't do.

You'll go back to your doctor to get the results of your tests and discuss your situation with him, talk to him about the drugs you are taking now, and see which ones you really need to take. From that point on you'll take your medicines faithfully for as long as you're on this program—unless your doctor says you can decrease them.

You'll also be paying more attention to the food you eat and the effect it has on how you feel. You'll tidy up any details that were left over from Week One.

Finally, you'll construct a Coronary Artery Disease Risk Profile, based on the information your doctor gives you and your own observations. By the end of Week Two you'll have a pretty good idea of where you're starting from.

In Week Three you'll learn about proper nutrition and you'll begin the first phase of building a healthy diet. You'll start involving your family in what you're learning about nutrition and about the effects different kinds of food have on you (and them), so that they can become your partners in this venture.

This week (and for the rest of the program), you'll be monitoring your blood pressure and keeping track of it, and watching your weight. As you begin to show signs of improvement you'll begin to feel pride in your accomplishments and will be able to keep your doctor informed about what's happening.

During Week Four you'll begin your exercise program. You'll begin to look at the things you do for recreation and find out whether they actually relax and refresh you or just run you ragged. And you'll be starting to notice more and more the effects the drugs have on you. Because this will be the second week of your nutritional program, you'll really begin to feel a whole lot better.

In Week Five you'll learn what you need to know about stress and your body, and you'll be starting your personalized stress management program.

By now, if you've really been following the program, some of the drugs you've been taking may be too much for you. So you will need to call your doctor and set up an appointment for Week Six or Seven, to check your progress, your blood tests and blood pressure.

In Week Six you'll tidy up anything that's left over from the first five weeks and make sure you understand all we've explained about drugs, nutrition, exercise, and stress. And you'll move to phase two of your nutritional program.

At the end of this week you'll want to see your physician. If you've been making progress in terms of lowering your blood pressure and losing weight, thereby convincing him that you're really serious about completing this program, you can talk to him about decreasing your drugs.

In Week Seven you'll switch to phase two of your exercise program, and you'll choose some recreational activities that really relax you (and thus tend to lower your blood pressure).

This week you should see your physician, if you didn't do so in Week Six. By now you ought to be in full swing and should be able to see quite a few positive effects of the program. Your doctor is going to be delighted. Make an appointment to see him again in three or four weeks. And whatever you and he have decided about the drugs—you need to take them faithfully until next time you talk to him.

Week Eight will introduce you to phase two of your stress reduction program. You will learn some more simple and effective techniques for turning off your emergency nervous system. And, as in other weeks, you'll catch up on any tasks left over from previous weeks.

By now you'll be feeling the benefits of your relaxation and exercise programs and finding it easier to fit them into your life.

In Week Nine you'll move to phase three of your nutrition program. Recreation will now be a regular part of your life—two hours a week, at least, of enjoyable and relaxing activities. Because once you've really learned to relax you can do stimulating things too. If the "old" you spent most of your leisure time getting excited and upset (over a pesky golf match, for example), by now the "new" you will be feeling the difference in your body—it'll literally be breathing a sigh of relief.

During Week Ten you'll begin phase three of your exercise program. And this may be a good time to really try some extreme (but temporary) dietary measures, to see what's the maximum benefit you can get out of good nutrition in terms of your blood pressure. Because this week (or early next week), you should see your physician again and discuss whether you can cut back on the drugs again and, if so, how fast.

Week Eleven brings you into phase three of your stress management program. And if you've been following the program faithfully, by now you should really be seeing a whole lot of results. You'll be so pleased that you won't be able to resist talking about the program (and this book, I hope) to other people you know with high blood pressure.

Week Twelve should find you going full steam ahead on all aspects of the program. And this is where you'll make some more observations about yourself and compare them with the ones you made in Week One. You'll really be able to appreciate how much progress you've made.

And then it will be time for graduation! You're going to have a party. We have some delicious recipes for you. You're going to see your doctor again. He's liable to hug you and jump up and down. You're going to jump up and down too. And your family and friends and colleagues are going to be thrilled.

But not half as thrilled as you are!

THE TIMELINE

Okay, that's the overview.

Now you need to look at the chart on pages 68–69 and use it as a basis for making yourself a timeline. The idea is to make a sort of calendar for the twelve weeks of the program. You'll see we've built in the parts of the program for each week. And we've also left some spaces for you to fill in, so that you can warn yourself in advance about vacations and business trips and social obligations and guests. You'll seldom find a twelve-week period that's free of all those things, but if you know they're coming up you'll be able to work around them.

Make several copies of your timeline and keep them in the office, in the kitchen, and in other places—so they'll always be up there to remind you what's happening next.

Timeline: photocopy this chart, and keep copies at home and at your office

Week	'	1	'	2	'	3	'	4	'	5	'

Date

Phases:

Diet					phase 1 ....
Exercise						phase 1 ....
Stress							phase 1 ....

M.D. visits	initial testing	follow-up (results)			

Reading	chapters	drugs 21–24	nutrition 25	exercise 26–27	stress 28–30

Other:

Holidays

Vacations

Trips

Visitors

Conflicts

Obligations

6	′	7	′	8	′	9	′	10	′	11	′	12	′

---

phase 2 . . . . phase 3 . . . .

. . . . phase 2 . . . . phase 3 . . . .

. . . . phase 2 . . . . phase 3 . . . .

---

check K$^+$
? reduce medications

check K$^+$
? reduce medications

Graduation: Celebration
M.D. visit, check lipids, ? reduce medications

The other thing you'll need to do at this time is to work out how you're gradually going to fit the various activities of this program into your regular schedule. If your wife or secretary usually does your scheduling for you, go over the timeline with her and ask her to set aside the appropriate times in your appointments book.

It's important to start scheduling time for this program now, because this is an important learning program that you're going to be involved in. It's a home study program, but it will take some time, and to do it justice you need to begin planning now.

Sure, I know you're busy. So am I. But if you don't take the time now you'll just have to do it later, when everything's worse. And meantime you'll still be taking those *!*! drugs.

FINDING A PARTNER

It's difficult for human beings to manage much of anything when they're doing it completely without support. We all need support, we all need warmth, we all need encouragement from time to time—on a daily basis, if we can work it out. We wouldn't be human if we didn't.

So whether it's moral support, or physical support, or advice, or counseling, or financial aid or whatever, to get things done, we need other people on our side. We need to ask for support. And we need to know where to go to get it.

Most people seem to have some kind of natural tendency to want to help others, too. I guess we're built that way. So I think you should consider finding yourself a buddy or a partner to go through this program with you.

Let me say right away that I don't want you *not* to do this program because you don't have a buddy, can't find a buddy, are too embarrassed to ask anyone to be your buddy, or don't think you need a buddy in the first place.

You can do this program just fine without a partner. But the best way to do this program is to do it *with* one.

Your partner needs to be fairly accessible—someone you can easily see two or three times a week, someone at work, or someone you play golf with, perhaps. Your partner needs to be someone who will encourage you and not criticize you. And, ideally, you both want to go through the program together, so that you can support each other all the way to success. That's the ideal.

So why don't you put the book down for a moment and think about a few people who might like to do this with you. And if the right name occurs to you, or the right face just pops into your head—pick up the phone!

8

The Sunday Before You Start Week One

> *That which we are, we are, and if we are ever to be any better, now is the time to begin.*
>
> Tennyson

There are five things I want you to do this Sunday, before your first week begins. (If Sunday just doesn't fit with your schedule, you can do them some other day, but the closer to your starting day you can manage the better.)

First, perhaps sometime in the afternoon, I want you to take stock of your life.

I want you to spend an hour or two alone, somewhere private, where you won't find yourself being interrupted or disturbed. Tell the other people in your house that you need some time to yourself, take the telephone off the hook, and sit down somewhere comfortable, with your notebook and a pencil.

On the top of the first page of the notebook I want you to write, *My*

Health Goals. On the second page you should put, *My Personal Goals.* And on the top of the third page, *My Career Goals.*

Now I want you to begin to list all the things you want. The things you want to have happen, the things you want to have or get, and the things you want to accomplish. List as many of them as you can under each of the three headings. First let's look at your health goals.

What do you want in the way of health? What would you really like? Do you just want to wait around while things get worse? Or do you want to make a real difference now in your health?

If you want to make a difference, if you want to help your health improve, write it down on that first page. "I want to take the steps that are necessary to live a healthier life. I want my health to improve."

Put it in your own words. But write it down. The clearer you are about your own goals, the easier it will be for you to attain them.

Are you reconciled to the idea, "Well, I'm getting older, and I'm not so interested in sex, in hiking, or going out dancing any more . . ."? Do you really feel that way? If the truth is that you would still like to do something but it just doesn't seem possible anymore, write it down. "I'd like my health to improve enough that I can go out backpacking with the kids again this year."

Some of us find we spend a lot of time excusing ourselves from things we'd really like to be a part of. "I'm getting older, I'm not feeling so good." "I didn't sleep too well last night." "I've had a tough week this last week." Or, "I've got the flu."

That last one, "I've got the flu," covers up an awful lot. It's a wonderful excuse. "I've got the flu, so I can't be expected to do whatever you are going to do, or what you'd like me to do." "Come outside and play with me, Grandpa." "Well, I'd like to, but I've got a touch of arthritis here . . ."

Dr. Alex Comfort tells the wonderful story of a hundred-and-four-year-old man who came to his doctor with a touch of stiffness in one of his knees, and his doctor told him, "You're a hundred and four years old; you can't expect to be quite so agile at your age as you were when you were twenty." But the old man just didn't buy it. He told his doctor, "I've had my other knee for a hundred and four years, too, and it's not stiff at all. . . ."

A lot depends on your attitude. Arthritis is a fine excuse if you want an excuse. But if you'd genuinely rather not have arthritis and would like to be able to play outside with your grandchildren instead, write that down.

"I'd like to be able to play with my grandchildren instead of staying indoors on sunny days because I've got a touch of arthritis."

What are your health goals? Are you content to have your medicine cabinet fill up with more and more of those ridiculous little bottles that you can't get the tops off? The ones that are supposed to be childproof and turn out to be almost adultproof too? Do you want to spend your days wrestling with the tops of those bottles? Do you want to have to invent all sorts of games and strategies so that you won't forget to take your pills? Do you want your wife or husband or children to have to keep reminding you to take your medicine? Or would you rather taper down your medicines? Would you rather get well enough that your doctor tells you you don't need to take so many pills, or that you can cut them out entirely?

Write it down. "I'd like to get healthy enough that my doctor cuts down on the number of pills he thinks I need. I'd love it if I got so healthy that he took me off them entirely."

Remember: your doctor prescribed the pills in the first place because he diagnosed a condition that called for them. *You shouldn't stop taking them without his advice and close supervision.* But if you can show him that your blood pressure is notably lower than it was he'll be glad to hear it. You will be one of the few patients who really help him do his job. If there's any way he can cut down on your medications appropriately, he will.

Your doctor will be delighted to see you taking more of the responsibility for your health. Do you really think he's the one who should take all the responsibility? He's a nice guy, and he's had a whole lot of training because he has to take responsibility for the health of so many people who don't look after themselves. But he can't possibly know you as well as you know yourself. He doesn't live where you live. He doesn't really know the people you live with or what you do all the time. He can't possibly. Do you want him to be the one who's responsible for how you feel? Or would you rather take the responsibility yourself? If you would, then write it down. "I want to take responsibility for my health."

Do you want to be what your doctor calls "just okay" or do you want to feel better than that? Do you want him to check you over and say, "You're okay, don't worry about it, your blood pressure's just a little bit off, just a little bit abnormal, but it's nothing to be concerned about"; and meanwhile he's thinking to himself, "Most of the people who come to my office are this way; their blood pressure is up a bit, their hearts are a little enlarged, their kidney function is down some, they're overweight, there's a little stress there . . ."? Is that what you want? To be like the rest of the people who come to his office?

Do you want to be the kind of person who has a lot of complaints, and a medicine for every complaint? Or would you rather be fit and energetic?

Do you want people to say, "Hey, he really looks great for his age," or, "Imagine that, he's playing eighteen holes of golf three times a week . . ."? Or, "She can dance and dance, and wear everyone else out"? Would you like people to talk about you in a way that's a little envious, a little admiring?

If you'd like that, write it down.

"I'd like my old 'get-up-and-go' to get up and come back."

Now let's turn to your personal goals.

You want to list those too. What kinds of things do you want? Do you want a boat, or an airplane, or a fancy car, or a house at the beach, or a cabin in the woods? A new fishing rod? Or a stamp collection? Or do you want to take a long vacation? Have a girlfriend, or a boyfriend, or a husband, wife, kids, grandkids? Or have you already got a girlfriend, or husband, or grandkids, but you just never seem to find the time to be with them? What do you want to do? What would you like to do? What are your dreams made of?

You should ask yourself these questions as honestly as you can. Because if you can identify what the things are that you really want, and if you want them badly enough, you can really have them.

So think about it, and write down the things you want the most. You are using a technique that no competent businessman would be without— you are practicing the art of goal clarification.

And now turn to the third page and begin to list your career goals. Do you want a raise, do you want a better job than the one you have now, or a different kind of job? Do you want to be vice-president of your company, or head foreman, or chief mechanic, or president? Do you want to move to a job that's nearer your son's house or your daughter's college? Do you want to make fifty thousand dollars a year?

Do you want to make a lot of money? Or have a good time? Maybe you'd like both?

Once again, think about all this very carefully. List the things that seem most important to you in this area. Don't be shy about it. And remember, no one need look at these lists except you.

All right. You have thought about things for a while and made out your lists. Now read through them, slowly, and get a detailed picture of what you want.

The reason it's so important for you to make these lists is that they actually put something out there in black and white for you to walk toward. And that's often more than half the battle. If you can see something out there that you can walk toward you can probably get there. The wonderful thing about human beings is that if they have some direction to go in, and some idea of how far they have to go, they can get there. It's almost always possible, as long as you know what you really want.

The second thing to do on the Sunday before your program begins is to get the rest of your notebook ready, so that you can use it as a program diary in the weeks ahead. I'll be explaining the way I want you to use the diary in more detail as we get into the program. For the moment, I'd just like you to set it up.

During the first week of the program I shall want you to record in your diary: what kinds of food you are eating; how much exercise you are getting; what kinds of stress you come up against in your life; and how you handle it. Your record of these things will need to last for seven days, and you will need at least a page each day for each of the three sections: Diet, Exercise, and Stress.

Food and Drink
Tuesday

Time	Meal	Foods	Comments
6:30 P.M.	dinner	cereal and fruit cup split pea soup	soup too salty

Take your notebook and mark the next seven pages with the days of the week and the word *Diet*. *Nutrition* will do, if that makes you feel more comfortable. Or even *Food and Drink*. (See chart above.)

You will need four columns on each page. The first column is where you note the time of day; and you make an entry in your diary every time you eat. The second column tells you whether this was a meal or a snack. The third column, which will be the largest, is for making a list of the things you eat. And the fourth is for comments.

The next seven pages of your diary are for you to keep track of the exercise you get during the first week. Once again, put the days of the week at the top of the next seven pages, together with the word *Exercise*. Then make a column for the time at which you did any physical activity, and a column telling you what the activity was, and a column for you to make any additional notes. (See chart below.)

Exercise
Tuesday

Time	Activity	Comments
8 A.M.	walked the dog 3 blocks	sunny and clear but cold

You should mark the next seven pages of your diary with the days of the week, and label them *Stress*. These pages need to be divided into five columns. In the first column you are going to note down the time at which a stressful event occurred. In the second column you will record the external event that triggered the upset. In the third you will make a note of any attitudes and emotions that were involved in the stressful situation. The fourth column is for describing your physical sensations. The fifth column will be for your own comments. (See chart on page 78.)

We'll be using the diary for various things in the coming weeks, but Week One is the only week when you'll be keeping such a close track on your nutrition, exercise, and stress management.

I'd like you now to turn to another page and label it *Measurements*. You can simply divide this page down the middle and write *Week One* at the top of the left-hand column and *Graduation* at the top of the column on the right.

On a new page, put down the heading *Weight*. You'll need room on this page to record your weight once a day for the first week of the program, and once a week after that.

The next left-hand page should be headed *Week One: Blood Pressure*,

Stress
Tuesday

Time	Event	Emotion	Sensation	Comments
1 P.M.	phone call from boss	anger and fear	flushed, then headache	lasted more than an hour, then ate 2 candy bars

and the page opposite, *Week One, Pulse*. And the pages following should be headed in the same way for Weeks Two through Twelve.

That's it. Your diary is now ready.

The third thing I want you to do is to bring your family together and tell them you're going to be spending the next twelve weeks on a program to lower your blood pressure and increase your overall health, and ask them for their support.

This is extremely important.

Tell your family that you have read this book and that this twelve-week program is going to transform your life totally. Tell them it will undoubtedly reduce, and perhaps even eliminate, your need for blood pressure medications altogether. Explain to them that it will make you feel a lot better, allow you to enjoy your life a whole lot more, help you to appreciate them and your friends more, and even improve your productivity at work. There are going to be a great many positive changes, and all the people in your life will benefit. Ask them for their support!

When I talk about support, I don't mean to suggest that anyone has to stand next to you and hold you up. I mean that your family should know what you want to do and be willing to support and encourage you in doing it, even at times when you forget. This also means that they are not going to tempt you or try to persuade you to eat things that you have chosen not to eat anymore. It means that they are not going to try to talk you out of doing things that you know you want to do and should do. Nor will they try to talk you into doing things you don't want to do and shouldn't do.

They have to support you. This is very important. Your family's support is a critical part of this program. We humans often have a foolish notion that we can "do it on our own," that it is somehow embarrassing to admit that we need support and help. But it's not like that. We all feel best when we help one another. Your family's support will bring you all closer together. It will give all your family members a share in your effort and a share in your success.

It will encourage them, too, to take responsibility for their own health, because they will see the remarkable impact the program has on the life of someone who is very important to them.

The fourth thing I want you to do today is to make a commitment to follow through on this program.

One of the things I have learned over the years is that people have a lot of integrity. When they make themselves a promise they usually keep it. So the last thing I want you to do on this Sunday is to sign a contract with yourself, promising that you are going to do this program: that you are going to see it all the way through to the end.

I want you to make sure that you do this, because no matter how good the program itself is, and no matter how strong your intentions are when you start, by the time you are a few weeks into the program, something is likely to get in your way. That's the way the world is.

Maybe one new client with an early deadline will mean you have to do a lot more work. Maybe your wife will want you to take her on a vacation. It could be anything. You may just not feel up to it; you may tell yourself you have the flu. A lot of different things are going to happen that will get in the way of your following the program. It's hard in this day and age to imagine anyone having a clear twelve-week stretch in which nothing happens to interfere with a program like this. That's particularly true for those of us who have jobs, families, and the responsibilities that go with them.

I'd like you to admit to yourself, up front, that obstacles are likely to come up. I'd like you to acknowledge it and make your determination now to press right on through to the end. Half a program can be worse in some ways than no program at all, because it can leave the taste of failure in your mouth. So this contract is very important.

The contract itself can be quite simple. All that it needs to say is, "I am going to do the complete twelve-week course, starting tomorrow, and not stopping until the twelve weeks are over." You should date it. And you should sign it.

Okay. You've made your commitment. You've signed the contract. That brings us to the fifth and final thing for you to do today. I'd like you to read Chapter 9, which deals with the first week of the program, so that you'll know a bit more about what's coming up this next week. Then I'd like you to read Chapter 19, "The White Lab Coat," in the Readings section at the end of the book. It's a way for me to introduce myself to you as we start out on this program together.

That's it. We're on our way.

9

The First Week

*Whatever you can do, or dream you
can, begin it. Boldness. has genius,
power, and magic in it.*

Goethe

Let's get it rolling.

Tomorrow is the first morning of the first week, and you have a note-book/diary, right? It will go most everywhere with you this week. Its purpose is to let you know the point that you are starting from as you begin the program. It's extremely important that you should understand this. The program can only work if you have a clear, unbiased picture of your starting point. If you wanted to go to New York, you'd have to know where you were starting from or you wouldn't know which direction to take.

Wherever you are right now, it's totally okay for you to be there. It's just your starting point. You need to be very clear about this. You need to know in some detail how you are right now, and during the course of this week you will be finding out.

How much are you eating these days? How much exercise are you taking? How much do you talk about exercise, without doing it? How well are you taking care of yourself right now? How do you feel about the way you are taking care of yourself? What are your thoughts about all this? What do you notice about yourself?

The important thing about all these questions is that you need accurate, truthful answers. It doesn't matter that you may not be taking as much exercise as you think you should, or as you think your doctor thinks you should, or as you think anyone else thinks you should. *What matters is how you are actually doing.* There's no right or wrong about it, absolutely nothing to be ashamed about, and no need to tell yourself any flattering lies. The important thing is to get a clear idea of what's happening now.

So I'm going to ask you to keep track of these things in your diary for a week.

The things I want you to record in your diary deal with how you are actually doing at the moment. I want you to record in your diary: what kinds of food you are eating; how much exercise you are getting; what kinds of stress you come up against in your life; and how you handle it.

Let's deal with diet first. Turn to the pages in your diary that are set aside for Diet. The first column is where you note the time of day; I want you to make an entry there every time you eat. In the second column, I'd like you to note down whether this was a meal or a snack.

In the third column I'd like you to list the things you eat. The list should be as detailed as you can make it. You should include the names of foods, brand names if that's appropriate, and the approximate quantity you eat. You should be careful to include the kinds of seasonings you put on your food—salt, or some kind of sauce or dressing, or whatever condiments you use.

You should write down everything you eat and the time you eat it. Remember to list what you drink, too.

Never mind if you think some of the things you eat are not good for you. Put them all down. No one except you need ever see this diary. And the only way you'll ever know what to do about your diet is to begin by finding out what your diet is now.

This week I'd also like you to become more aware of the taste of salt in your food. Some foods are very salty; some are not salty at all; and some have a slightly salty taste. As you are eating your food, make a mental note of just how salty it is. Rate each food that you eat for saltiness, on a scale of 1 to 5. You can note the ratings in your diary under "Comments," in column four.

At the same time I'd like you to become aware of how much oil and fat there is in your food. For example, many of the red meats are very fatty and greasy, and they are often served with gravies that are the same way. If you eat out, the food you are served will often be swimming in oil and grease. Don't stop eating what you normally eat. All I ask this first week is that you begin to notice the fat, become more aware of it in your diet, and make a note of it.

So you'll have a little mental game that's going on with every meal. You will be rating the saltiness and the greasiness of the foods you eat, and writing your evaluations in the Comments column of your diary.

The next pages of your diary are for you to keep track of the exercise you get. Again, don't worry about it not being "enough." You are the only one who needs to see this diary. And you already know what you do and don't do.

During the course of the week I want you to make a note in your diary every time you are physically active. This might include walking the dog, walking up a flight of stairs, going for a walk, jogging, going to a health club, taking an aerobic dance class—whatever. I'd like you to note down the time and the nature of the activity.

I'd also like you to note any times you thought of taking some exercise and didn't. In the third column, under Comments, you should note down all the reasons you gave yourself for not exercising: it was raining; you were too stiff; you'd just eaten; it was too late; you were too busy; you needed to spend some time with the kids; you were just plain lazy; or reruns of "Dallas" were on TV.

You don't have to make your diary a masterpiece of literature—just short notes to yourself will do, so long as you can understand them. By the end of the week you will be able to look back and get a fair idea of what's going on between you and exercise. You need to be clear about that before we get down to work.

Now let's turn to the pages headed Stress. In the first column you are going to note down the time at which a stressful event occurred. You should note down any time you felt ill at ease or uncomfortable as a result of any event, emotion, thought or feeling, any upsets; any time you felt angry, any worries, any fretting, any anxieties.

In the second column you should record the event that triggered the anger, the worry, the upset.

In the third column you should make a note of any beliefs, attitudes, ideas, and emotions that you recognized during the stressful situation.

In the fourth column describe your physical sensations. Do you get a headache? Do you have sweaty palms? Do you get indigestion or an upset stomach? Does your ulcer act up? Do you begin to breathe faster? Does your heart palpitate? Just note down the physical sensations that you can discover in connection with each stressful episode.

And in the fifth column you can note down any other comments.

Keeping a diary will help you get better acquainted with yourself. It's a good beginning. We'll be using the diary for various things in the coming weeks, but this week is the only one when you'll be keeping such close track of your nutrition, exercise, and stress management. And at the end of the program you will be able to look back at this week and see how much progress you've made.

There are some other things I'd like you to do this first week, though— and some of them involve taking a few more notes in your diary.

Sometime in the early part of the week I'd like you to take about twenty minutes to look at yourself in the mirror.

I'd like you to do this with no clothes on, or just the bare minimum of clothing. Simply study yourself. Study your body, not with the idea that it is bad or good; but just so that you become better acquainted with it. Notice the curves and the straight parts, the lumps and the bumps, everything.

You don't need to rate your body; you don't have to evaluate it. Just become aware of it. See whether you can look at your body without automatically criticizing it. See if you can't quiet any criticism that comes into your mind, or any pride, for that matter. Just put your body in front of a mirror and study it for about twenty minutes.

And I'd like you to measure yourself around your thighs, hips, stomach, chest, and upper arms—and make a note of the measurements on the page you've set aside for this in your diary. We'll be looking at your measurements again later in the program—but not until then.

I would also like you to get hold of a camera and take a photo of yourself in a bathing suit. You can either take a picture of yourself in the mirror or you can get someone such as your husband or wife to take a picture of you. If someone else is going to take the picture, you could ask him or her to take several shots, several different views. And you should just take the photos, remove the film from the camera, and keep it in a safe place with your diary. Don't develop the film yet. If you are using a Polaroid, you should simply file the pictures away in an envelope without looking at them.

Another thing you need to do is weigh yourself. You should weigh yourself every day this first week, so you can get an idea of your weight range over the course of a week. On different days your weight will fluctuate; and it's good for you to keep track of that. Weigh yourself at the same time every morning, preferably before you eat breakfast, and after you have emptied your bladder and bowels. Record those weights in your diary too. You'll be weighing yourself once a week throughout the program, so you should leave some room on the page.

I'd also like you, during the course of this week, to tell your friends, the people at work, and your doctor that you are going to be doing this program for the next twelve weeks and that you'd appreciate their support. You will need their understanding and help, particularly during these twelve weeks while you are learning a whole set of new skills and ways of doing things.

That's about it. The only thing left is your appointment to see your doctor.

When the day for you to see him comes round, you should tell him in a little more detail what you are going to be doing and ask him for his support. If he hasn't seen it already, you should certainly ask him to read Chapter 20, "Letter to a Physician." It will help you make sure that he doesn't think you are going to do anything foolish, inappropriate, or abrupt.

You need to let him know that you are serious about improving your health; that you are not going to make any sudden and capricious moves on your own; that you are just going to learn how to take better care of yourself, so he can take better care of you too; that you are going to work with him and find out whether what you do can reduce your need for medications.

He ought to be delighted.

On this visit, remember that you are scheduled for some blood tests if you have not had them recently. These are the tests that measure the amount of potassium in your blood, the amount of uric acid, hemoglobin, your triglyceride levels, cholesterol level, and fasting blood sugar level (see list on page 86).

You need these tests now, because the results will be important to you in Week Two, when we come to the point of calculating your Coronary Artery Disease Risk Profile, which tells you what likelihood you have of developing a heart attack or stroke.

1. Standard blood chemistry screening panel, to include
     Sodium (Na)
     Potassium (K)
     Uric acid
     Fasting serum glucose (blood sugar)
     Cholesterol
     Triglycerides (be fasting for twelve to fourteen hours)
     Creatinine or BUN (blood urea nitrogen, serum urea nitrogen)[1]
2. Hemoglobin
3. Urinalysis[1]
4. Electrocardiogram (EKG or ECG) at rest.
5. Treadmill stress test or other exercise test with EKG and blood pressure checks.
5. Estimation of body fat or other estimate of how much you are above ideal lean weight.
6. Prescription for blood pressure cuff.

[1] The urinalysis and creatinine or BUN tests measure your kidney function. If your values on these tests are abnormal and you have high blood pressure, it probably means that your kidneys are very strongly sodium-retaining. If this is so, in order to get your body fluid volumes anywhere near normal you will need to limit your salt intake very strictly—and you may not be able to eliminate the use of a diuretic completely, although with care you may need it only once or twice a week. Ask your doctor about this.

Please remember to talk to your doctor about the blood pressure cuff we discussed in Chapter 7. Ask him whether he recommends any specific kind and whether he will write you a prescription for one. You will need a pressure cuff to measure your own blood pressure at home.

You'll also want to ask him whether you need a cardiogram (EKG) if you haven't had one recently. You need to find out if you have any heart damage as a result of your high blood pressure.

And the other thing you want to do during this visit to your physician is to discuss with him the possibility of your doing some kind of exercise test to find out what happens to your heart and your blood pressure when you exercise.

Many people (and, among them, some physicians) do not know that someone who has only a mild elevation of blood pressure while at rest may have blood pressure that rises to an alarming degree with even a small amount of exercise. The only way for you to find out whether this applies to you is for you to get your blood pressure measured while you exercise. The very best way to do this is to get a *treadmill stress test,* or TMST. You should ask your doctor where you can get this test in your area.

All that the test involves is walking on a treadmill, a looped belt that moves around at a certain speed. Sometimes it's done on a stationary exercise cycle instead of a treadmill. And that's just as good. There will be a doctor there, and a technician who runs the equipment. They'll monitor your electrocardiogram, your pulse rate, and your blood pressure and watch to see how well you handle exercise. They will want to know if you feel stiff or sore, if you have any pain in your legs or chest, any dizzy feelings, or any other symptoms.

They'll bring you up to the maximum level of exercise that you can do without problems, and then, when you're tired, or something begins to change on your electrocardiogram, or your blood pressure begins to go up too much, they'll tell you to stop.

Or you may reach your *Predicted Maximum Heart Rate* (PMHR), which the technician can look up in a chart. (Your PMHR can be roughly calculated at 205 minus one half your age (men) or 220 minus your age (women)—so if you are a forty-year-old woman your PMHR would be approximately 180.) When you reach your PMHR the test is over, and the technician will slow the treadmill and let you cool down for a few minutes.

When you've taken a treadmill test, the doctor or technician will be able to advise you about what level of exercise is safe and appropriate for you, and what level of exercise you will get the most benefit from.

YMCAs often have cardiac rehabilitation programs where you can get a stress test with a minimum of fuss and bother—without your having to get a referral to visit a cardiologist, who asks you whether you have heart disease and may wonder why you are bothering him if you don't. And they will often give you an exercise prescription, too.

Before you start to change your exercise patterns in the course of this program, the important thing is to find out what level of exercise is safe for you. So *some form of test is important.* If you can't get a treadmill stress test, because it's not available, or it's too bothersome, or you simply can't afford it, you should ask your doctor if he or his nurse could monitor your blood pressure during exercise. You will need to exercise with a blood pressure cuff in place on your arm and get your blood pressure checked as soon as you stop your exercise, to find out whether it has gone up an alarming amount in the meantime.

Before you leave the doctor's office, be sure to make an appointment to see him again next week, to get your blood test results. If your doctor has also scheduled you for a cardiogram or a TMST, be sure to note those appointments in your diary as well.

So that's it for this doctor visit.

From now on you and your doctor are working as a team. And I'd like you to take whatever medications he's prescribed *faithfully* from here on in—until you and he decide together that it's safe and appropriate to cut them down.

Now that you've seen your doctor and discussed blood pressure cuffs with him, I'd like you to buy one. I'd like you to measure your blood pressure under a variety of conditions over the course of the week: first thing in the morning when you open your eyes; during or right after an argument with your wife or husband or your teenage son; after you've had a couple of martinis or a couple of glasses of wine; immediately after driving back from the office, fighting the traffic all the way home. That kind of thing. If you take regular exercise, check your blood pressure about fifteen minutes after the end of the exercise. And keep a record of your blood pressures in your diary.

Begin to find out what happens to your blood pressure at different times of day and under varied circumstances. You may be surprised to find out that, even if you are taking blood pressure pills, your blood pressure may vary as much as twenty or thirty points, depending on the activity you have just been doing. For some people, the difference can be even greater.

You may find your blood pressure is actually highest when you go to see your doctor. Going to a doctor and having him measure your blood pressure, and tell you that things are going well, or not so well, and that you do, or don't, need to increase the number of pills you must take can certainly have an effect. All that expectation and worry and concern is enough to raise anyone's blood pressure!

HOW TO USE YOUR BLOOD PRESSURE CUFF

1. Be sure that the cuff is snug around the upper arm just above the elbow. Keep your arm relaxed and still while checking blood pressure. The rubber bladder inside the cuff must be over the artery, whose pulse can be

felt on the inside of the arm, at the elbow joint, on the side closest to the body.

2. Pump up to around 200, or above the systolic pressure, and let the pressure down fairly rapidly to find approximate values for the systolic pressure (when the sound can first be heard) and the diastolic (when the sound disappears again). Then pump up again and let the air out more slowly (down 10 mm/Hg per five to ten seconds). Pause just before the estimated systolic reading and again just before the diastolic, so they can be recorded accurately. Most nurses let the pressure in the cuff fall too rapidly, so after the nurse has taught you, do it more slowly when you are on your own.

3. Repeat the process until you get a stable reading (i.e., a reading that is within five points of the previous reading). This may require repeating the procedure three or four times.

4. Your diastolic pressure is measured at the point when the sound disappears. It may have become muffled, or very low-pitched, or hard to hear, ten to twenty millimeters above this point. But let pressure out slowly while you listen very carefully for the sound to disappear completely.

5. There may be some faint background noise—such as the noise of your heart beating even when the cuff is not inflated. Listen for this so you will not be fooled into reading your diastolic pressure much lower than it really is. This is especially a problem if your heart is beating vigorously— for example, just after exercise.

Another part of your self-testing program will be to monitor your pulse rate first thing in the morning, before you even get out of bed. So, before you go to bed at night, you'll want to get a watch or clock with a second hand and put it beside your bed. And when you first open your eyes in the morning you should measure your pulse: count how many times your heart beats in fifteen seconds, then multiply by four to find out your pulse rate for a minute.

Record this waking pulse in your diary too, along with your blood pressure. It doesn't matter what your pulse rate is at other times during the day. You can check it if you feel like it—but it's not that important.

And that's it. For next week I'll be asking you to read Chapter 10 (the chapter for Week Two) and some of the material in Chapters 21 to 24 at the back of the book. In Weeks Three through Five, as we begin to explore nutrition, exercise, and stress management, you'll have several chapters to read each week. And from Week Six on, there'll just be one short chapter a week for you to read.

THE SUNDAY AT THE END OF WEEK ONE

At the end of each week of the program from now on, I'd like you to set aside Sunday evening (or some other convenient time), so you can run a quick check on what's already happened, look over the next week's business, and make sure that everything's going as planned. You'll find these Sunday evening sessions will really help you keep to the program.

Each week, at the end of the chapter for the week, you'll find two checklists. One will list the things we had hoped to accomplish over the course of the previous week. On Sunday evening, then, I'd like you to go through this checklist and make certain that none of the things on the list still need to be done. Then I'd like you to take a look at the other list, which talks about what the next week has in store for you. I'd like you to schedule your week so that you can not only catch up with anything that's left over from the week before but also fit in the appointments, exercise times, and so forth that you'll be needing over the course of the upcoming week.

CHECKLIST: WEEK ONE

This last week, have you:

Kept your week's diary of nutrition, exercise, and stress?

Weighed yourself each day for a week and recorded the weights in your diary?

Taken your own blood pressure at different times of the day and noted it?

Taken your early morning pulse?

Told your friends about this program? And asked for their cooperation and support?

Told the people at work?

Seen your doctor to get your blood tests taken?

Made an appointment to see him next week, to pick up the results?

Talked with him about the program and asked him to read "Letter to a Physician"?

Asked him about cardiograms, exercise testing, and blood pressure cuffs?

Bought a blood pressure cuff?
Studied yourself in the mirror?
Measured yourself and recorded the measurements in your diary?
Taken a photo of yourself?

This past week's checklist is probably one of the longest, so don't let it daunt you. Next week you can tidy up whatever parts of this first week's program didn't get finished. But don't put them off any longer or you'll fall too far behind.

You have gathered a lot of support this week, from your family, your friends, the people you work with, and your physician. You have begun to find out a great deal about yourself. You now have a pretty fair idea of where you're starting from. Your doctor is probably pleased to hear you'll be taking better care of yourself.

CHECKLIST: WEEK TWO

Now (Sunday night before Week Two):

Read Chapter 10 through completely.
Make a list in your notebook of all the drugs you were recently or are currently taking.
Read those parts of Chapters 21 to 24 that describe the kinds of drugs you are taking.
Fill in your stress analysis questionnaires (see pages 98–107).

Monday to Sunday:

Check your blood pressure once or twice a day and note in your diary.
Take your early morning pulse and note in your diary.

Sometime this week:

Visit your doctor and pick up your results.
Take your list of medicines with you so you can discuss the medicines you are taking.
Find out from your doctor whether you're low on potassium.
Obtain and take a potassium supplement if your doctor thinks you need one.
Ask your doctor for the specific information you need to fill in your Coronary Artery Disease Risk Profile (see page 109).

Take a treadmill stress test or ask your doctor to measure your blood pressure while exercising.

Discuss your exercise test with your doctor and find out your maximum heart rate.

Fill in your Coronary Artery Disease Risk Profile.

Use your red marker to mark the foods in the fridge and cabinet that have sugar or sodium in them.

Weigh yourself and note your weight in your diary.

See your partner (if you have one) and compare notes.

Over the weekend:

Read next week's checklists and chapters, etc.

That's it. We are ready to start Week Two in the morning.

10

The Second Week

*You are never given a wish without also
being given the power to make it true.
You may have to work for it, however.*

Richard Bach

We've started! We're on our way. The first thing you need to do this week is to tidy up any details of the program that are left over from Week One.

I'd like you to check your blood pressure once or twice every day this week. I'd like you to take your early morning pulse every day. And I'd like you to weigh yourself at least once this week. And keep a record of all these things in your diary.

Although we're not going to be suggesting anything about what you do and don't eat this week, I would like you to continue to be a little more aware of what you do eat, when you eat it, and what it tastes like. In fact I'd like to recommend you eat a little more slowly and begin to get used to savoring your food.

I'd particularly like you to continue to taste the salt in the foods you eat, and also, this time, the sugar. And I'd like you to keep tasting the fats and oils too. I'm not saying these things are good or bad, and I'm not in any way asking you to feel guilty about them. I'm not even asking you to take notes in your diary this week. I'm just asking you to notice how foods taste when they have these things in them.

You know, you're probably pretty good at tasting things and expressing your opinion. You notice garlic all right, don't you? So just direct some of that skill and attention into tasting the salt, sugar, and fat.

I'd also like you to begin to notice the effect that caffeine has on your system. If you're a heavy coffee or tea drinker, or if you drink a lot of soft drinks of the cola variety, I'd like you to notice what the caffeine does to you.

WIELDING YOUR RED MARKER

I'd also like you to go to your cupboard, your refrigerator, and your freezer, look inside them, and begin to be aware of what foods are there and what's in them. I'd like you to take that red or yellow marker you bought a while back and mark on the labels wherever you see sodium or sugar.

And remember that salt and sugar often crop up on food labels under a lot of different names. The label may say brown sugar, corn syrup, honey or molasses—but it's all sugar. And "sea salt" still means salt. It's all the same stuff—salt is salt is salt. And you'll want to mark any other kinds of sodium salts the foods may contain, too, such as sodium bicarbonate, monosodium glutamate (MSG), sodium nitrate, and sodium nitrite.

Remember, these substances are listed on food packages in order of quantity—so a package with sugar listed first or second has a lot of sugar in it. But a package that has sugar listed third and fourth and sixth, under different names each time, may have just as much.

So all that sugar and salt may be quite well hidden. But with a little detective work you'll be able to find it.

VISITING YOUR DOCTOR AGAIN

Last week you went to see your doctor, and he ran some tests on you, and you made an appointment to see him again this week to get the results. So one of the most important things you'll be doing this week is getting those results. When you see your physician this time I'd like you to be able to discuss with him in detail the medicines you're taking now, and whether you really need to be taking all of them, or whether you can stop any of them. In fact that's going to be a major focus for this week.

Before you go to see your doctor I'd like you to make a list in your notebook of all the drugs you are currently taking (including medications that are not for high blood pressure), and their doses.

Then I'd like you to read the chapters at the back of this book that deal with the various drugs on this list. You don't necessarily have to read all of the material in those chapters, but do be sure to read the chapters that apply to the kinds of drugs you are currently taking.

For example, do you take Inderal? Do you know why? What exactly does it do? Do you experience any side effects from taking it? You need to be an intelligent, informed consumer. Don't just swallow those pills without knowing what they are for, what they are, and what they do.

If you want to learn even more about these drugs you can go to a bookstore or your local library and get hold of a book that gives you the names of all the prescription drugs, with a list of their effects and side effects. And you could look up all the medicines you are taking and become familiar with what they do and what their side effects are.

The People's Pharmacy by Joe Graedon is very good. *The Good Housekeeping Family Guide to Medications,* by Judith K. Jones, would also do. Both are probably available at the library, or you could find them at the bookstore. The *Physicians' Desk Reference* is the standard heavyweight book in this area. But the others are written in a style that's a lot more readable.

Okay, you've read the chapters in the back, and maybe you've gone out and read up on those drugs in even more detail.

This week you're going to go back and see your doctor. I want you to get your blood test results back. And I'd like you to discuss with him the drugs you're taking. So I want you to take that list of drugs in your notebook with you.

One of the important bits of information you need to make sure you get from your physician, if you've been on a diuretic, is whether or not you're low on potassium in the blood. Because that is a good indicator that your entire body stores of potassium are depleted.

And during this week, and for the rest of the program, it's very important that you replenish your body's potassium stores, if they're low, by taking whatever forms of potassium your doctor prescribes—on a regular basis.

Not only will this make you feel better and stronger—simply replacing lost body potassium will tend to lower your blood pressure.

Now that your blood test results are back, you need to discuss the various drugs you're taking and come to a complete agreement with your doctor about them. It's likely, in fact it's almost certain, that as you go through this program your need for drugs will diminish. But right now you and your doctor need to decide what to do—and then you need to do it. Because that's the only way your doctor can tell what effect the drugs are having on you.

So there shouldn't be any secrets.

From this point on, until you talk to your doctor again, I'd like you to take the medicines you and he decided you should be on. It's very, very important.

While you're at your doctor's this week I'd also like you to get the information you need from him to calculate your Coronary Artery Disease Risk Profile. You'll find what you need in the way of information from the Coronary Artery Disease Risk Profile on page 109. You can copy it out of the book or just take the book with you.

If you're going to have a treadmill stress test, this week's the week to do it—or to ask your doctor to measure your blood pressure while he puts you through a series of exercises.

When you discuss the results of your exercise test with your doctor there are three things you'll need to know.

Was your test normal—no sign of coronary artery blockage—*or was it abnormal?* If your test is abnormal, it adds a lot of points to your Coronary Artery Disease Risk Profile, and your doctor will have some pretty strong opinions about how you should conduct your exercise program.

Did your blood pressure rise a lot while you were exercising? If so, at least early on in your exercise program you're going to be doing things very carefully and slowly.

What was your Maximum Heart Rate achieved just before you quit (or before some trouble developed)? Write it down in your notebook, because you'll be using your Maximum Heart Rate in calculating your Training Heart Rate for exercise in Week Four.

Those are the bits of information you'll be needing. And your doctor or exercise physiologist may or may not give you an exercise prescription at this point.

My doctor was surprised to find that my treadmill test was abnormal. There were some changes on the electrocardiogram that worried him, so he stopped the test even though I felt fine and could have gone on longer. What does this mean? Will I still be able to exercise aerobically?

The changes may indicate that you have a partially blocked, hardened coronary artery. At high heart rates, when your heart needs more oxygen, a blockage like that can prevent the increase in blood flow and oxygen delivery that the heart needs. And so it shows signs of heart muscle lack of oxygen (called *myocardial ischemia*).

Usually people with ischemia have a tightness or discomfort in the chest—right in the middle. This is called *angina*, or more completely *angina pectoris* (literally, a squeezing sensation in the chest). People who have the electrocardiogram changes but no chest pain may or may not have a blocked artery; more sophisticated tests are required to find out.

Your exercise prescription should allow you to exercise at a lower level of intensity, where these changes don't occur. To be on the safe side, you may want to see a cardiologist—ask your own doctor—and enter a cardiac rehabilitation program, where they can monitor you carefully for a few months while you are learning to exercise.

YOUR STRESS ANALYSIS

Since we'll soon be calculating your Coronary Artery Disease Risk Profile, you'll need to do the simple four-part stress analysis that follows.

The first part of your stress analysis lets you see how many things are going on in your life right now that most people would find stressful. And those things generally involve change.

If you're about to change your job, or your kid went off to college a month or two ago, or you just moved house—it's likely to be stressful. Those changes, those kinds of instability in your life, tend to affect your nervous system in a pretty predictable way—and the result is stress.

Rate the amount of unsettling change in your life according to the instructions in the following test.

RECENT EXPERIENCES AND STRESS[1]

If one of the events listed below has happened to you during the last year, or perhaps happened a couple of years ago yet still worries you a lot, or is very likely to happen in the next few months, copy the number in the impact column into your score column. If you feel the impact of an event has already diminished, estimate a smaller impact score. Double your score for events that have occurred more than once. Estimate impact scores for any other stressful events and list them under "Other" at the bottom of this test.

Event	Impact	Score
Death of a spouse	100	_____
Divorce	73	_____
Marital separation from spouse	65	_____
Sentenced to time in jail	63	_____
Death of close family member other than spouse	63	_____
Major personal injury or illness	53	_____
Marriage	50	_____
Being fired from your work	47	_____
Marital reconciliation with mate	45	_____
Retirement from work	45	_____
Major change in health or behavior of close family member (e.g., teenager on drugs)	44	_____
Pregnancy	40	_____
Major readjustment in business	39	_____
Gaining a new family member (includes adoption, older family member joining household)	39	_____
Sexual difficulties, worries, concerns	39	_____
Major change in finances (a lot better off or worse off than usual)	38	_____
Death of a close friend	37	_____
Changing to a new line of work	36	_____
An increase in the number of arguments with your spouse	35	_____

[1] Adapted from the Holmes-Rahe Life Changes Scale, *Journal of Psychosomatic Research* (1967).

Taking on a large debt or mortgage (purchasing a home, business, etc.)	31	_____
Foreclosure on a mortgage or loan	30	_____
Troubles with your in-laws	29	_____
Large promotion, demotion, or change of work responsibilities	29	_____
Son or daughter leaving home (e.g., marriage)	29	_____
Outstanding personal achievement	28	_____
Beginning or finishing formal schooling	26	_____
Spouse beginning or ceasing work away from home	26	_____
Major change in living situation	25	_____
Major change in personal habits (dress, hairdo, manners, friends, etc.)	24	_____
Increased trouble with boss	23	_____
Changing schools	20	_____
Major change in working hours or conditions	20	_____
Moving (changing residence)	20	_____
Major change in religious or spiritual activities	19	_____
Major change in usual type or amount of recreation	19	_____
Major change in social activity (dancing, movies, clubs, etc.)	18	_____
Taking on a smaller mortgage or debt (buying a freezer, TV, etc.)	17	_____
Major change in sleeping habits (including time, length, quality)	16	_____
Change in number of family get-togethers	15	_____
Major change in eating habits	15	_____
Major vacation	13	_____
Minor infractions of the law (traffic tickets, jaywalking, etc.)	11	_____
Other	—	_____
	—	_____
	—	_____
	—	_____
	—	_____
	TOTAL:	_____

JOB-RELATED STRESS FACTORS[2]

Now we are going to look at the job-related factors that usually trigger a stressful response in ordinary people like you and me.

It's a sad fact that many companies and institutions tend to use people in ways that leave them burned out. You need to take a good long look at your work situation and see just how stressful it really is. I'm not suggesting here that you should change jobs—just that you should teach yourself to relax and stay calm, even in an adverse and stressful environment.

Score one point for each of the following factors that you think is present for you in your work situation. It doesn't matter whether an "impartial observer" would agree with you or not—so don't be concerned with the absolute truth of the matter, just record what you think is happening at your place of work.

1. Time constraints, need to work fast, many deadlines   _____
2. Frequent work overloads; you or "they" keep piling it
   on   _____
3. Uncertainty about role at worksite; your role conflicts
   with others   _____
4. Inadequate information and/or communication
   (about products, services, the company, activities
   elsewhere in the company), feeling that you are kept
   in the dark   _____
5. Vague objectives and goals   _____
6. Job dissatisfaction, personal and among your
   colleagues   _____
7. Responsibility for other people and their performance   _____
8. Lack of job security   _____
9. Too little responsibility   _____
10. Feeling of obsolescence or growing uselessness   _____
11. Poor relationships with boss or colleagues   _____
12. New supervisor or subordinates   _____
13. Under- or overpromoted in past year   _____

[2] Adapted from L. Galton, *Coping with Executive Stress* (New York: McGraw-Hill, 1983).

14. Frequent performance evaluations _____
15. Competition, not cooperation, at place of work _____
16. Poor quality of life at worksite (noisy, crowded, dirty, etc.) _____
17. Management by crisis _____
18. At career capacity, no upward mobility possible _____
19. Sociopolitical constraints such as racial prejudice, sexual harassment, etc. _____
20. Inability to delegate _____

TOTAL: _____

PHYSICAL SYMPTOMS OF STRESS

Next we'll be looking for physical symptoms and problems that commonly show up when people are under stress. Most of the problems listed here are stress-related. A few of them may not be. Some of them may occur as a result of an external circumstance or condition (such as an extremely high concentration of ragweed pollen in the air, or heavy exposure to a "cold" virus from your children who are in school, etc.).

Look carefully to see which symptoms or problems you have (not including exceptions such as those just mentioned), and give yourself one point for each one.

1. Frequent accidents or mistakes _____
2. Skin rashes without an obvious cause, hives, itching skin _____
3. Frequent colds or other infections _____
4. Allergies acting up without obvious cause _____
5. Headaches, migraines _____
6. Neck and back pain with stiffness, bursitis, muscle tension _____
7. Chest pains _____
8. Teeth grinding, pain associated with the TMJ (temporal mandibular joint) _____
9. Rhythmically tapping thumb and fingers together, tapping feet or fingers on floor or table _____
10. Frequent distortion of facial expression, grimacing, tics _____
11. Sleeping more, feeling less rested, chronic fatigue _____

12. Heartburn, indigestion, peptic ulcer, difficulty
    swallowing   _____
13. Change in appetite (increase or decrease), frequent
    snacks   _____
14. Loss of sex drive, frigidity, or impotence   _____
15. Breathing trouble, including wheezing or asthma   _____
16. Increased smoking or alcohol use   _____
17. Anxiety attacks, depression   _____
18. Nightmares, insomnia, restlessness at night   _____
19. Finger chewing, nail biting   _____
20. Cold hands and feet in a warm room   _____
21. Frequent use of tranquilizers, sleeping pills   _____
22. Constipation, diarrhea, very noisy stomach, gas,
    bloating, colitis   _____
23. Pacing, restlessness, can't relax   _____
24. Irritability with family, friends, coworkers   _____
25. Sweating and flushed in cool room   _____
26. Decrease in memory, difficulty concentrating   _____
27. Thyroid problems   _____
28. High blood pressure   _____
29. Palpitations, pounding heart   _____
30. Can't stand to be alone   _____

                                      TOTAL: _____

TYPE A OR B PERSONALITY SCALE[3]

Finally, you need to look at how you react to the ordinary, everyday things that go on in your life. Your job. The traffic between your work and home. The people you bump into from day to day—store clerks, policemen, your kids' teachers, your fellow employees, your neighbors.

How do you react to people and things? Are you Type A, the dynamic type, or Type B, more easygoing? This test will help to identify which you are.

Some people are really mellow about things, really calm, some people have an average response, and some people tend to be easily upset. And you need to be quite objective as you're assessing yourself. Because these questions will help you to understand your own reaction to stress.

[3] Adapted from the Glazer Questionnaire, in L. Galton, *Coping with Executive Stress*, p. 62.

In fact I'd like you to get a second opinion about your behavior and personality. When you've taken this test and rated yourself on it, I'd like you to ask your spouse (or someone else who's around you a lot and knows how you act) to take this test too, answering the questions as they apply to you.

When you've got two scores, one that you calculated yourself and one calculated by your spouse or friend, I'd like you to use the higher of the two scores in making your calculation—because it's likely to be the more accurate.

To take the test, you just need to rate yourself honestly from 0 to 5 on the scale for each of these pairs of values. Rate yourself the way you really are, not the way you think you should be or would like to be. If you find the statement in the column on the left describes you pretty accurately, circle the number 0; if the right-hand column is very much your style, circle the 5; and if you feel that you're somewhere in between, circle one of the numbers between 1 and 4 as appropriate.

The primary purpose of this test is to observe your own behavior and to recognize that there is a whole spectrum of possible reactions available in every kind of life situation.

doesn't mind leaving tasks unfinished if it is time to go home	0 1 2 3 4 5	keen to complete tasks once started as soon as possible
calm and unhurried about appointments, sometimes late, sometimes runs over allotted time	0 1 2 3 4 5	punctual about appointments, seldom runs over allotted time, sometimes impatient with others
competitive when appropriate, but loses gracefully	0 1 2 3 4 5	highly competitive, determined to win, disturbed when losing
careful listener, waits for others to finish before starting to speak, attentive to the ideas of others	0 1 2 3 4 5	prepares the next point while others are still speaking, interrupts, finishes sentences for others

calm and relaxed under pressure, rarely looks or feels hurried	0 1 2 3 4 5	high sense of time urgency, under almost continuous deadlines
able to wait in lines, able to greet others who are late calmly	0 1 2 3 4 5	takes work or reading material along to occupy time in case of wait, ruffled if kept waiting
relaxed, easygoing, slows down to enjoy things	0 1 2 3 4 5	hard-driving, always going full speed to get more things accomplished in less time
seldom combines activities, devotes full attention to current activity	0 1 2 3 4 5	often combines activities, i.e., reading and eating, dictation and driving
slow, deliberate, thoughtful speech	0 1 2 3 4 5	rapid, vigorous speech, with forceful gestures
concerned with satisfying self, less concerned with what others think	0 1 2 3 4 5	concerned to receive appropriate praise and recognition from others
expresses feelings openly, admits negative emotions (sadness, anger, etc.)	0 1 2 3 4 5	keeps feelings to self, seldom admits weaknesses
has varied interests, recreation is important, rarely brings work home	0 1 2 3 4 5	brings work home often, few interests and pleasures outside of work
seldom sets deadlines or quotas for self	0 1 2 3 4 5	sets deadlines or quotas for self, concerned with own productivity

high degree of satisfaction in job and personal life most of the time	0 1 2 3 4 5	highly ambitious, rarely completely satisfied, always striving for greater accomplishments
feels personally responsible for own tasks, able to delegate easily	0 1 2 3 4 5	takes personal responsibility for all details, reluctant to delegate anything of importance
precise and exact only when necessary, can also approximate when appropriate	0 1 2 3 4 5	extremely precise in attention to detail at all times
approaches tasks slowly and with appreciation, enjoys work as it progresses	0 1 2 3 4 5	acts with panache and vigor, interested in end product, not process
flexible, easygoing, adapts well to inconveniences, etc.	0 1 2 3 4 5	unexpected problems are inconvenient, upsetting
tends to calm and relax people in the same office or household, patient and understanding	0 1 2 3 4 5	high standards, demanding and critical of colleagues, friends, and family
usually finds time for simple tasks such as shopping for clothes, etc.	0 1 2 3 4 5	seldom has time for trivial tasks such as shopping for socks

Add up your scores, and remember, when you've finished giving yourself this test, to ask someone who knows you well to go through it a second time, scoring you on it as he or she sees you. Then use the higher of the two scores to tell whether you have more of an A Type or B Type personality.

Scores of 0–20 represent an extreme B Type;
21– 40	B Type
41– 60	average
61– 80	A Type
81–100	extreme A Type personality

If you have an A Type personality, you may well be very successful in your work—but you should know that your personality type predisposes you to cardiac risk and is often known as the "cardiac-prone" personality type.

Good stress management is particularly important in your case.

YOUR TOTAL STRESS SCORE

Using your scores on the four types of test you've just taken, we are going to obtain an average stress score that will be an index of how you react to stress. We will be using this average score in just a moment, as we calculate your Coronary Artery Disease Risk Profile.

Recent Experiences and Stress

0– 80	very low
81–160	low
161–240	moderate
241–320	high
320–above	very high

Job-related Stress Factors

0– 1	very low
2– 3	low
4– 6	moderate
7– 8	high
9–above	very high

Physical Symptoms of Stress

0– 1	very low
2– 3	low
4– 6	moderate

        7- 8   high
        9–above   very high

Type A or B Personality Scale

        0– 20   very low
        21– 40   low
        41– 60   moderate
        61– 80   high
        81–above   very high

OVERALL STRESS SCORE

Score 1 for each very low, 2 for each low, 3 for each moderate, 4 for each high, and 5 for each very high you scored. Add these total scores together and divide by the number of tests you took, then round off to the nearest whole number to obtain your overall stress score.

Example:

Recent Experiences and Stress	high	4
Job-related Stress Factors	moderate	3
Physical Symptoms of Stress	high	4
Type A or B Personality Scale	high	4
	Total:	15

divide by number of tests taken: $15 \div 4 = 3.75$
round off to whole number: 4
overall stress score 4, rating high

Your Score:

Recent Experiences and Stress	_____	_____
Job-related Stress Factors	_____	_____
Physical Symptoms of Stress	_____	_____
Type A or B Personality Scale	_____	_____
	Total:	_____

divide by number of tests taken: _____ $\div$ _____ = _____
round off to whole number: _____
overall stress score _____, rating _____

ABOUT CORONARY ARTERY DISEASE RISK PROFILES

The purpose of a Coronary Artery Disease Risk Profile is for you to see how you measure up compared to other people who are also living in America in the 1980s, those who are at high and those who are at low risk.

Modern medical science can now predict the likelihood of heart disease with a high level of accuracy. Despite what the newspapers would have you believe, there is very little controversy nowadays about how people can get (or avoid) heart attacks. Countless committees of experts have come to the same conclusions. Yet another distinguished committee of scientists and physicians, this time appointed by the World Health Organization, and headed by Geoffrey Rose, M.D., of London, recently reported *(Circulation,* 1983) that coronary artery disease (CAD) prevention is a program of the highest priority and has issued a call for action at all levels of the world community. Their recommendations basically encourage people to reduce their overall risk of CAD by attacking the very risk factors listed in this chart.

Risk factor analysis is not a new and untested theory. It is backed up by an immense volume of research. And it is an idea whose time has come.

YOUR CORONARY ARTERY DISEASE RISK PROFILE[4]

To create your own Coronary Artery Disease Risk Profile, you should first fill in the column "your values" in the chart on page 109, using the data obtained from your blood tests, treadmill or exercise test, etc.

Then, in each of the nine categories, find which of the ratings your value corresponds with. If you have quit smoking, for instance, your rating would be low (1), and you would score 1 point, which you should then note in the column headed "your points." Notice that you score 0 each time your rating corresponds with the very low (0) column, 1 for the low (1), 2 for the moderate (2), etc. Note also:

a You can use an estimate of your excess weight in pounds if you haven't received a measure of your percentage body weight as fat from

[4] This CAD Risk Profile is based on the work of Dr. Kenneth Cooper at the Cooper Clinic in Dallas, Texas, and Dr. John Farquhar at the Stanford Heart Disease Prevention Program in Palo Alto, California.

CORONARY ARTERY DISEASE RISK PROFILE   Date: / /

risk factor / your values	very low (0)	low (1)	moderate (2)	high (3)	very high (4)	your points
your age	0 – 29	30 – 39	40 – 49	50 – 59	60 +	
family history of heart disease	none	developed over the age of 50 (2)		developed under the age of 50 (4)		
body weight	near ideal weight	up to 10 lbs. excess	11-20 lbs. excess	21-30 lbs. excess	30 + lbs. excess	
or: % body weight as fat (see note a)	less than 20%	20 – 24%	25 – 29%	30 – 35%	more than 35%	
smoking	never	quit	1 – 10 day	11 – 30 day	more than 30 day	
stress factors	very low	low	moderate	high	very high	
fitness level in METS women	more than 10	8.7-10	7.4-8.6	6.0-7.3	less than 6	
men	more than 12	10.7-12	9.4-10.6	8.0-9.3	less than 8	
or: physical activity (see note b)	vigorous exercise 20-30min. 4 + x a week	vigorous exercise 20-30min. 2-3 x a week	vigorous exercise 20-30min. 1-2 x a week	occasional vigorous exercise	rarely exercise	
systolic blood pressure	less than 110	110 – 120	120 – 130	130 – 140	more than 140	
diastolic blood pressure	less than 70	70 – 80	80– 90	90 – 100	more than 100	
serum cholesterol	less than 150	150 – 180	180 – 215	215 – 250	more than 250	
or: usual dietary intake of saturated fats and cholesterol	nearly vegetarian rare egg dairy or lean meat	several meatless days/wk no butter egg yolk only lean meat non fat dairy	mostly lean meat some eggs & dairy (low fat)	USA average diet meat or eggs or cheese every meal	lot of red meat shell fish liver eggs whole fat dairy 3 + x/day	

subtotal: _____

extra points (notes d – l): _____

total: _____

your doctor (see chart on page 111). If you are overweight or obese, you can estimate how many pounds overweight you are by using the chart and a ruler.

You should keep the right side of the ruler at your height in the right column, and move the left side downward or upward until the ruler is at the center of the acceptable range for your sex, in the middle column. Now note the weight indicated where the ruler crosses the left column. Then subtract this weight from your present weight and use the difference in calculating your coronary risk.

b If you haven't received a measure of your maximum work capacity in METS (METS are a unit of work on a treadmill or exercycle) as part of your exercise prescription, you may use your frequency of exercise instead.

c If you haven't received a measure of your (blood) serum cholesterol level, you can use your dietary intake instead.

When you have rated yourself on all nine areas, add up your subtotal.

Now read notes (d) through (l) following, to find out how many extra points you should add to (or subtract from) your subtotal:

d Add 2 points if you are under thirty years of age, and subtract 2 points if you are over the age of sixty.

e Add 1 point if your early morning resting pulse is usually greater than 75, and subtract 1 point if it is usually less than 60.

f Add 3 points if your fasting triglycerides level is greater than 150 (women) or 230 (men).

g Add 3 points if your uric acid level is greater than 6 (women) or 8 (men).

h Add 1 point if your hemoglobin is greater than 15 gms/dl.

i Add 3 points if your fasting (blood) serum glucose is more than 120.

j Add 2 points if your resting ECG is abnormal.

k Add 8 points if your exercise ECG during treadmill stress test was abnormal and showed a lack of blood and oxygen to the heart.

l Add 8 points if you've ever had a heart attack (documented myocardial infarct).

You should then add (or subtract) these extra points to (from) your subtotal, to obtain your total score. Your risk of developing coronary artery disease (angina, heart attack, or sudden death) in the next five to ten years is as follows:

Total Score:	Risk:
0– 4	very low
5–12	low

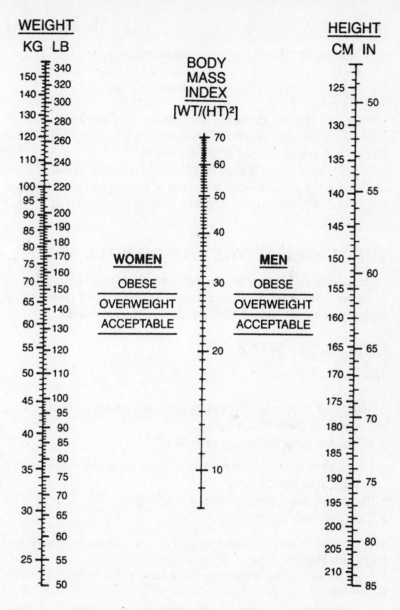

George A. Bray, *International Journal of Obesity*, 2:1 (1978).

13–23	moderate
23–34	high
above 35	dangerously high

Please note that this Coronary Artery Disease Risk Profile is an approximate one, designed to be self-administered. Your doctor may have a more detailed and precise method of risk assessment.

Your Coronary Artery Disease Risk Profile gives you an idea of how you are doing at the moment—and at the end of the program you'll be calculating your CADRP again and will be able to see how much progress you've made.

THE SUNDAY AT THE END OF WEEK TWO

Once again I'd like you to take some time out on Sunday evening (or whenever's convenient) to go over these checklists, making plans for next week so you'll have time to fit all the parts of the program in.

CHECKLIST: WEEK TWO

This last week, did you:

Make a list in your notebook of all the drugs you are currently taking, and read about them in this book?

Fill in your stress analysis questionnaires?

Use your red marker to mark the foods in the fridge and cupboards that have sugar or sodium in them?

Check your blood pressure once or twice a day?

Take your early morning pulse?

Go to your doctor's appointment, pick up your results, and discuss your drugs with him?

Come to an agreement with him about them and stick faithfully to the agreement?

Find out from your doctor whether you're low on potassium, and obtain and take a potassium supplement if your doctor thought you needed one?

Ask your doctor for the information you needed to fill in your Coronary Artery Disease Risk Profile?

Take a treadmill stress test or ask your doctor to measure your blood pressure while exercising? Discuss your exercise test with your doctor and find out your maximum heart rate?

Fill out your Coronary Artery Disease Risk Profile?

Weigh yourself once during the week?

Keep notes of these measurements in your diary?

And see your partner (if you have one) and compare notes?

Apart from reading two new chapters of the book, and meeting once with your partner, there's not a lot you need to schedule for next week.

CHECKLIST: WEEK THREE

You'll need to:

Now (Sunday night):

Complete any tasks left over on your checklist for this week, such as reading, filling out your Coronary Artery Disease Risk Profile, marking the labels in your fridge, etc.

Read the Chapter 25, "Nutrition," and then read Chapter 11, the chapter for the week.

Monday to Sunday:

Begin your nutritional program, phase one.

Begin to avoid salty foods at home and when you eat out.

Begin to decrease your intake of fats and oils.

Begin to decrease your intake of caffeine.

Keep an eye out for the cues that start you eating.

Begin to share your discoveries about food with your family.

Check your blood pressure and waking pulse, and keep track of them in your diary.

Keep taking potassium supplements.

Keep taking the medicines you agreed to take.

Sometime this week:

Weigh yourself once and record your weight.

Meet with your partner to compare notes.

Over the Weekend:

Read next week's checklists and chapters, etc.

11

The Third Week

*Never go to a doctor whose office plants
have died.*

Erma Bombeck

This week we're going to concentrate on nutrition.

So by Monday morning you should have read this week's chapter on
nutrition (Chapter 25). That's your reading for the week. Because I want
to make sure you've found out all you need to know about salt, protein,
fat, carbohydrates, and the rest. And then you can start making some
experiments with what you eat.

Now one thing I really don't want you doing is telling yourself, "Oh,
I've got to go on a diet." I don't believe in diets. I've seen too many
people go on diets and take off any number of pounds, then come off the
diets and put the same number of pounds back on.

And the pounds they put back on were pure fat.

We're going to be trying out some different strategies in terms of food
and nutrition. Over the next few weeks you'll be trying different kinds of

food and different ways of eating, until you find out what works best for you.

So the whole purpose here is not to deny yourself. It's to explore and experiment. Because there is a diet that you'll enjoy, that will nourish your body properly and make it possible for you to live without high blood pressure and without taking pills. But you probably don't know what it is yet, and neither do I. It's something we'll be finding out over the course of this program.

So, as much as possible, I'd like you to go into phase one of your nutritional program with a real sense of adventure and exploration. I want you to discover what works best for you. Because that's the thing you'll also enjoy the most.

NUTRITIONAL PROGRAM PHASE ONE

The first thing I'm going to ask you to try this week, and for the next few weeks, is not to add sodium (salt, sea salt, seasoned salt, garlic salt, or any other kind of sodium salt) to your food at table. (Potassium salt, or salt substitute, or No Salt are okay. But potassium is bitter, so you should use it very sparingly!)

If you're doing the cooking, I'd like your family to support you in not adding any in the kitchen, either, when you eat at home. And when you go out to eat, I'd like you to ask the restaurant not to add any salt to your food.

Of course that may or may not be possible. But it's probably a whole lot more possible than you'd think. And you may need to use a little assertiveness when you ask.

I'd also like you to avoid obviously salty foods like pretzels, potato chips, and crackers, unless they specifically say "no salt added" on the label. (The good news is that more and more foods marked "no salt added" are available in regular supermarkets these days.) I'd like you to avoid things like ham, bacon, and processed meats that are heavily salted during processing. As much as possible, I'd like you to cut back on your intake of cheeses, because most of them are heavily salted. And to stay away from canned and preseasoned frozen foods.

There's a list of common foods with a lot of salt in them (that doesn't always appear on the label) on pages 116–18.

The idea is to avoid salty foods as much as possible.

I'd like you to begin to decrease your intake of fat, oil, grease, butter, and lard as well.

This isn't necessarily a permanent thing. But I think that as you go through this program your desire for these high-fat foods will diminish. If you're drinking whole milk, you can gradually phase down to low-fat, and finally to skim milk. If you use high-fat cheeses, you can switch to the lower-fat varieties. If you eat very heavily marbled tender red meat, you can begin to move away from it to the leaner cuts. And remember that fried foods and processed meats are all high in fat.

You want to try to make as much progress in this area as possible, starting this week.

And notice how you feel.

FOODS THAT ARE HIGH IN SODIUM (BUT DON'T NECESSARILY TASTE THAT WAY)

One portion of one of these foods blows a third to a half or more of your whole day's sodium allotment (1,000 to 1,500 milligrams [mg]).

Cheeses and Dairy Products	*mg*
1 oz. blue cheese	500
1 oz. cheese spread	460
1 oz. Parmesan	450
1/2 cup lowfat cottage cheese	450
1 oz. Roquefort	460
1 oz. processed Swiss cheese	330
1 qt. milk	500
1 qt. buttermilk	1120

Cereals	
2 oz. Cheerios	650
2 oz. cornflakes	640
2 oz. Wheaties	710
2/3 cup rice cooked with salt in water	400

Canned Foods	
11 oz. New England-style clam chowder	1500
1/2 cup peas and onions	440

4 oz. green beans	470
7.5 oz. cheese ravioli in sauce	975
6.5 oz. tuna	1200
1 cup mushroom chow mein	1160
1 cup baked beans	1000
6 oz. tomato juice	650

Frozen Foods

Entrees:

12 oz. fried chicken	1540
9 oz. turkey	1340
tuna pie	1000

Dinners:

12 oz. chicken dinner	2270
9 oz. lemon sole	1180
8 oz. chicken pot pie	950

Vegetables with Sauces:

1/2 cup peas with sauce	400
3.3 oz. baby limas in sauce	440
3 oz. broccoli	500

Meats

1.3 oz. bologna	400
4 oz. corned beef	2000
1.6 oz. hot dogs	500

Sauces and Dressings

2 tbs. catsup	500
1/4 cup taco sauce	450
1 tbs. Italian dressing	200–400
1 tbs. Thousand Island dressing	200–350

Desserts

1 piece mince pie	700
1/2 cup Jell-o chocolate pudding	470
1 piece apple pie	450
4.5 oz. Sara Lee apple coffee cake	500

1 piece chocolate fudge cake	450
6 Oreo cookies	480

Fast Foods

Big Mac	1510
Whopper	910
3 pieces Kentucky Fried Chicken	2300
1 fillet fried fish	850
1/2 small pizza	1500
McDonald's apple pie	1035

Snacks

3 green olives	380
kosher dill pickle	600–1000

As much as possible, you should avoid caffeine, which is in coffee, tea, chocolate, and cola drinks.

And I'd like you to begin to keep an eye out for the cues that start you eating. Do you eat because it's lunchtime? Or because your stomach's hungry? Or because you're going out with a bunch of friends and everybody's eating?

I'd like you to start to notice how much of the time you're really eating out of boredom, or because of stress, because you're unhappy, or want to go along with the crowd, and how much of the time you're eating because you've listened to your body and your body wants you to eat.

This week I'd also like you to begin sharing some of your discoveries about food with your family. Let them know what you've learned about how things taste with more or less salt in them, and with more or less fat. Because the better your family can understand what you're doing, and the more interested they can become in the program, the more they're liable to support you, all the way through.

You'll notice I said begin to share your discoveries about food with them. Go easy on them. Don't hog the entire conversation. They want to enjoy their meals too!

What else?

I'd like you to keep on checking your blood pressure and your waking pulse every day, and recording them in your diary. I'd like you to weigh yourself once this week and make a note of your weight. I'd like you to keep on taking potassium supplements if that's something you agreed with your doctor that you'd do. (Be sure to tell your doctor if you're using a potassium-based salt substitute.) And I'd like you to keep taking whatever medicines you've agreed upon, faithfully.

If you're going through this program with a partner, you'll want to spend some time together this week, encouraging each other.

That's enough to be going on with. You've started your nutrition program, phase one.

THE SUNDAY AT THE END OF WEEK THREE

Once again, I'd like you to read the checklists and prepare for next week.

CHECKLIST: WEEK THREE

This past week, have you:

Read Chapter 25, "Nutrition," at the back of the book?

Begun your nutritional program, phase one?

Begun to share your discoveries about food with your family?

Checked your blood pressure and waking pulse daily, and kept track of them in your diary?

Kept taking the potassium supplements and other medicines you agreed to take?

Weighed yourself once and recorded your weight?

Met with your partner to compare notes?

CHECKLIST: WEEK FOUR

This next week you'll need to:

Now (Sunday night):

Complete any tasks left over on your checklist for the previous week.

Read Chapters 26 and 27 (on aerobic exercise), and then Chapter 12, the chapter for the week.

Monday to Sunday:

Start your exercise program, phase one.

Set aside roughly an hour to do your stretching and aerobics and take a shower, three to five times this week.

Set aside the time and take one or two slow walks this week, on days when you aren't doing your aerobic workout.

Make sure you have a complete rest on at least one day this week.

Set aside at least two hours, sometime this week, for recreation and play.

Carry on with phase one of your nutritional program.

Notice the effects your drugs are having on you.

Check your blood pressure and waking pulse and keep track of them in your diary.

Keep on taking your potassium supplements and the other medicines you agreed to take.

Sometime this week:

Weigh yourself once and record your weight.

Meet with your partner to compare notes.

Over the Weekend:

Read next week's checklists and chapters, etc.

And that's it for Week Three.

12

The Fourth Week

*No greater popular fallacy exists about
medicine than that a drug is like an ar-
row that can be shot at a particular target. Its actual effect is like a shower of
porcupine quills.*

Norman Cousins

You've read the two chapters (26 and 27) that describe aerobic exercise
and its benefits. Let's start in on your exercise program, phase one, right
away.

It's very important that *when you start out* on an exercise program you
do it in a noncompetitive way. You're not trying to prove anything to
anyone. You're not meant to be shooting for the Olympics quite yet.
You're just beginning something. That means that, if I ask you to do
something and you can't manage it as yet, don't be embarrassed about it. I
don't want you to overdo it, to overexert yourself, or get exhausted or
discouraged, or hurt yourself.

The important thing is to make a start that you can feel comfortable with.

Phase one of your exercise program involves a sequence of exercises which you'll be doing for thirty to forty minutes, three to five times a week. The sequence is outlined in the chart on pages 122–23.

First you'll do some stretching exercises. Then you'll warm up for about five minutes, using a slow version of whatever form of aerobic exercise you've decided to do. This might mean walking slowly or slowly riding a bicycle. And then you'll do your actual aerobic exercise—aiming to remain at your Training Heart Rate (THR) for about twenty to thirty minutes.

By now you should either have had a treadmill test and have been given an exercise prescription, or you have worked out your THR by means of the formula we gave in Chapter 26 (roughly, eighty percent of 220 minus your age). If you haven't been given an exercise prescription, remember that one way to make sure your exercise is of the right intensity is by means of the talking test. You should be able to talk during exercise—though you may be experiencing a little shortness of breath; and you'll probably be sweating a bit.

You'll be trying to keep at your THR for twenty to thirty minutes a day, three to five times a week. But for the first week or two you may not be able to go that long. That's not a problem. Just make it your goal to work your way gently but surely up to the point where you can. If you've been fairly inactive these last few years, that may be quite an achievement in itself.

When you're done with the aerobic phase you need to cool down again, by keeping on doing whatever you're doing for about another five minutes, but more slowly.

And after the cool-down period you'll want to do some more stretching again.

AEROBIC SEQUENCE

1. Stretching for 5–10 minutes.
2. Warm up: easy aerobics—at a slower pace for 5 minutes.
3. Aerobic exercise to Training Heart Rate (THR) or talk test.
   Work up toward 25–30 minutes at THR in phase one;
   Stay at THR for 25–30 minutes in phase two, and
               30–35 minutes in phase three.

4. Cool down: easy aerobics, again at a slower pace, 5 minutes.
5. Easy stretching.
   Repeat the exercises in number 1. Be careful, don't overdo it.
   Remember, if it hurts, it's too much.

In addition to going through that sequence three to five times a week, I'd like you to take one or two slow walks a week, on the days you don't exercise. The idea is to take some form of exercise five or six days a week if you can.

And leave one or two days for complete rest, so that your muscles and bones can recover.

You may be stiff and sore for a while as you start up, and a little of that is okay. It means your muscles are going to get stronger. Just keep on stretching, *gently*, and listening to your body. And remember—if the soreness gets better when you walk or run or whatever, keep exercising. But if it gets worse you'd better see your doctor or a sports medicine expert.

Well, that's phase one of your exercise program.

I'd like you to keep on checking your blood pressure and your early morning pulse rate every day, and to weigh yourself once during the week.

And I'd like you to start making sure you spend about two hours a week in recreation or play. Maybe that's something you already do—and then again, maybe it's not. So, for starters, I'd like you to notice what kinds of recreation you have.

Do you basically sit and watch other people do something in the movies or on TV? Is it a passive, spectator sort of recreation? Or do you do things yourself? Is it active and involved? Is the kind of recreation you do relaxing to you? Or is it stimulating? Does it excite you and get you all riled up, or does it relax you and calm you down?

This is your second week on phase one of your nutritional program, too, and I want you to begin to notice how many times and in what ways you deviate from your diet, and to see what happens when you do.

Remember, your mistakes can be your biggest allies, if you'll let yourself learn from them. So this is no time for feeling guilty. This is a time to pay attention and to learn as much about yourself as you can. Without judgment. All right?

What happens when you eat salty food? What happens when you eat more fat than your nutritional needs call for? What happens to your blood pressure after you drink a cup or two of coffee? Measure it. I'm sure you'll notice the difference. How does it make you feel?

You've been on your nutritional program for over a week now, and I want you to begin to notice the effects of the drugs you're on, too. About now, if you've been following the diet pretty faithfully, you'll probably be more sensitive to the effects of the drugs than you were before. You may notice some sort of feeling you get when you take the drugs. Or, since you're now monitoring your blood pressure, you may (or may not) notice a change in the blood pressure reading whenever you take the pills.

So it's very, very important, this week, to notice how the drugs are treating you. And to make notes in your diary. How do they make you feel? What effect do they have on your blood pressure? It's important, because very soon you'll need to talk to your doctor about all this.

If by any chance the nutritional program is beginning to have a very big impact on you, and the drugs are getting to be too strong for you, you should call your doctor and discuss with him whether you need to start decreasing your drugs right now.

To be honest with you, if you're on any of the blockers, but especially the central-acting ones—methyldopa (Aldomet), clonidine (Catapres), and guanabenz (Wytensin)—you may not even know you're slowed down and lazy and sleepy—because you may have forgotten what it's like to be energetic.

The point is, you may need to reduce the dose just to get alert enough to know that the drugs are making you dopey! But ask your doctor about tapering your dose—*don't stop the drugs suddenly on your own.* You may have a big rebound, with blood pressure going sky high, if you do.

I recently saw an elderly woman who had been brought into the clinic by her daughter-in-law. She'd had hypertension for a long time, and I noticed her chart mentioned a diagnosis of organic brain disease—senility, slowness, loss of memory, apathy, that sort of thing.

Obviously this was creating a problem for the family—this woman was just sitting around in her son's house waiting to die. She didn't do anything or go anywhere. And they didn't understand why.

I shook the big bottle of methyldopa pills and said to the daughter-in-law, "If you or I took 500 mg of this four times a day, we wouldn't be able to get out of bed in the morning, let alone get anything done all day. You want to know why she's so lazy and slow? It's the pills. We've got to get her off of them. Older people just don't tolerate these drugs."

And that's why so many people stop going to their doctors with high blood pressure. It's a survival instinct. And that's why so many people want to find a better way.

THE SUNDAY AT THE END OF WEEK FOUR

CHECKLIST: WEEK FOUR

This past week, did you:

Read Chapters 26 and 27 on aerobic exercise in the Readings section at the back of the book?

Start your exercise program, phase one?
Set aside roughly an hour to do your stretching and aerobics, and take a shower, three to five times this week?
Set aside the time, and take one or two slow walks this week, on days when you weren't doing your aerobic workout?
Carry on with phase two of your nutritional program?
Notice the effects your drugs are having on you?
Check your blood pressure and waking pulse, and keep track of them in your diary?
Keep taking your potassium supplements?
Keep taking the medicines you agreed to take?

Make sure you had a complete rest on at least one day this week?
Set aside at least two hours, sometime this week, for recreation and play?
Weigh yourself once and record your weight?
Meet with your partner to compare notes?

CHECKLIST: WEEK FIVE

This coming week, you'll need to:

Now (Sunday night):

Complete any tasks left over on your checklist for this week.
Read Chapters 28–30 (on stress and stress management), and then Chapter 13, the chapter for the week.

Monday to Sunday:

Start your stress management program, phase one.
Keep on with your exercise program, exercising to Training Heart Rate three to five days a week, and taking one or two slow walks on the off days.

Check your blood pressure and waking pulse and keep track of them in your diary.

Keep taking the potassium supplements and medicines you agreed to take.

Sometime this week:

Set aside the time to record for yourself a cassette tape for relaxation tape, then spend twenty minutes every day relaxing with the tape.

Call your doctor and make an appointment to see him in Week Six or Seven.

Spend two hours in recreation.

Weigh yourself once and record your weight.

Meet with your partner to compare notes.

Over the Weekend:

Read next week's checklists and chapter.

And that's it for Week Four. Keep going—this program's going to work for you.

13

The Fifth Week

*Rule #1 is, don't sweat the small stuff.
Rule #2 is, it's all small stuff. And if
you can't fight and you can't flee, flow.*

Robert Eliot, M.D.

This is such a beautiful week. It's beautiful because this is the week you start your personal stress management program. By now you should have read through the three chapters (28–30) on stress and stress management. Stress management could well turn out to be what has the biggest impact on the quality of your life, in the shortest amount of time. Not to mention that good stress management will make things a lot easier in your nutrition and exercise programs, too.

Now—if you haven't done so already—I'd like you to take the four stress analysis tests in Chapter 10 (Week Two). It's very important to know where you are starting from, so you can really appreciate the progress you make. And if you've already taken these tests I'd like you to look over your results again carefully.

Most of us are real stress addicts. I can't tell you how many people I've seen who are stressed at the office and have problems at home. . . . And what do they do on the weekends, when the choice is up to them? They go out and play golf or tennis and get all upset there too. I don't mean excited and having fun, I mean upset and frustrated and angry.

We're continually overstimulating and exciting ourselves one way or another, even though we walk around complaining about how stressful life is. "My God, I can't stand it a moment longer," we say. "I really need a break. What's on at the movies? *Revenge of the Barbershop Vampires?* Great. Let's go." More stress! We do it again and again and again.

It's not surprising that we are this way. After all, we all want to feel alive and well and excited about life. But when we get so continuously excited that the emergency nervous system is almost always on, it's tiring, it's unpleasant, and, if we have high blood pressure, we wind up taking pills that cut that precious excitement right back out of life again.

This program isn't intended to take away the fun and the excitement— just the opposite. It's intended to make you relaxed, refreshed, and all-round healthy enough to enjoy the exciting things of life. More—not less —is our goal!

AVOIDANCE

One of the things I'd like you to do in this first phase of your stress management program is to see how much unnecessary stress there is in your life—and then avoid it.

It's natural that avoidance will be the first step in any stress management program, because if you can avoid being in the stressful situation in the first place you won't need any other stress management techniques to cope with it!

I'd like you to look at some of the things you do in your life that make you feel worried or upset or angry or just plain frazzled. Until you've learned how to sit back and let go of your worries and irritations a little better, and really relax, I'd like you to avoid those things that bother you. If you want to go back to worrying or getting furious (or watching vampire revenge movies) after you've learned to relax, that's entirely up to you.

Take a look at the stress list below and notice how many things there are that can switch on anyone's emergency nervous system and send blood pressure rising. Maybe you can add a few items of your own to the list. Take out your diary and, in one of the spare pages at the back, jot down your own version of this list.

SOME EXCITEMENTS YOU COULD STAND TO MISS

1. *Caffeine, nicotine, alcohol, and sugar tend to excite the emergency nervous system.*

Caffeine, nicotine, and sugar are stimulants. Their chemical effect on the body is to stimulate the stress response and switch on the emergency nervous system. And alcohol is a depressant, but it has a rebound effect when it wears off. So these four things all tend to make us unnecessarily stressed.

2. *Certain sorts of recreation tend to do the same.*

Whether your recreation is the active kind, playing tennis, maybe, or golf, or whether it's the more passive sort like watching football or basketball or baseball games, or the races—if you get real excited and upset over it, ask yourself whether you need that extra stress. And remember, gambling on the outcome only makes these things more stressful.

3. *Starting in on new projects can be stressful.*

Most of us have a hard time saying no to anything. So when a new project comes across your desk at work, or a friend suggests that you might like to get in on a little business scheme he's cooking up . . . ask yourself whether you really have the time and the energy to deal with it right now. You're already starting a new nutrition program and an exercise program and a stress program, and they all take up some of your time. So don't just think to yourself, "I'll fit this new project in somehow," and then go crazy when you find you can't.

4. *Arguments and fights don't help either.*

Listen, you're still going to have arguments and fights. But why not at least try to avoid the most predictable ones? You can always say, "I just don't want to play that game for a while." "I'm just not going to call Alice for a while, because I *know* if I call my ex-wife we're going to get into a scene."

5. *Illicit affairs cause a great deal of stress.*

When doctors counsel people who have had heart attacks about how they can resume a normal sexual life, one of the things they tell them is to avoid adulterous affairs—because they're so stressful. Patients with a history of heart disease can literally sometimes die of them. And if illicit affairs are stressful enough to be a medical risk for coronary care patients, they are stressful enough to raise your blood pressure too.

6. *Unnecessary entertaining can put considerable strain on you.*

Some entertaining may be necessary, and some entertaining is a pleasure. But if you're the kind of person who takes on big dinner parties and then frets about every little detail you'd probably do well—while you're following this program and learning to handle stress—to cut out as much unnecessary and stressful entertaining as you can.

7. *Traffic jams, too.*

The English magazine *Punch* had a cartoon a few years back about a driving school that taught its pupils that traffic jams were "a chance for our students to sit back and enjoy the landscape." It's not a bad attitude if you can manage it—but few of us can. And if the traffic patterns on your way to work every day get you frustrated, find out if there is an alternative route to work, and avoid the rush hours if at all possible.

8. *Bad news is bad news.*

If you listed all the news stories you read in the papers or heard on the radio or TV over the next few days, you might be surprised to find out just how many of them were bad news. Now you may think you're immune to bad news and that it doesn't affect you. But when you read about an overturned school bus a thousand miles away, to a certain extent your body mimics the terror you would feel if that bus had your children on it. You're really not immune, and bad news does take its toll on your health. So, while you're learning stress reduction, avoid exposing yourself to bad news if you can.

9. *And you should avoid horror and violence in entertainment.*

You certainly have a choice about whether or not to go to a horror movie or watch the violence on TV. And I'd like you to find out what watching scenes of horror and violence does to you—how it affects your nervous system—and then see if you can stop doing it over the course of this program. Because it's like grabbing a live wire and giving yourself a nasty jolt.

10. *Excessive noise can be a problem—and that includes music.*

Researchers have found that you can raise someone's blood pressure just by adding noise to their environment. So I'd advise you to avoid noisy situations. And while you're learning to relax you'd do well to avoid loud and exciting music.

11. *Overscheduled trips and vacations are stressful.*

There was a film out not so long ago called *If It's Tuesday This Must Be Belgium.* It was about one of those vacations during which you visit ten different countries in seven days. And of course no one had a real vacation, everyone got completely stressed. We tend to do that. We want to see everything and do everything, and so that's the way many tours are set up.

But if you're going to go on vacation during the three months of this program—let it be a real vacation. Just go to France, or New England, or wherever, and relax and enjoy yourself. Do yourself a favor.

12. *Roller coasters are not recommended for people with high blood pressure—at least while they're learning to control it.*
Life's enough of a roller coaster as it is. So try to avoid roller coasters and sky diving. And whatever you do, don't go over Niagara Falls in a barrel.

13. *And please, please avoid getting yourself into messes.*
You know the sort of thing I mean. You've borrowed money and find you can't pay the loan. Or you've loaned it, and need it, and can't get it back. Or other situations in which you wind up telling lies or being lied to. You want to try to keep your relationships with other people real simple and clean for a while.

The idea is for you to begin to see how you can avoid unnecessary emergency nervous system arousal for the next few months—until your relaxation program begins to really work for you.

As you learn to avoid unnecessary stresses and strains you'll be creating the kind of nurturing environment in which the rest of the learning that needs to take place these coming weeks can happen more easily.

RATIONAL EMOTIVE THERAPY

The next skill you'll need to learn as part of phase one of your stress management program is really just plain old common sense. Only there are books out about it, and in psychological jargon it's called Rational Emotive or Cognitive Therapy.

What it all boils down to is this. When you get upset you need to bring some simple common sense to bear on the problem.

The driver who just cut in ahead of you on the freeway may have been rude, but he didn't even come close to crashing into you or killing you. I know you feel like honking your horn at him, but what harm did he actually do? If you look at the whole thing calmly and rationally, I think you'll find that the worst thing that happened is that he may have made you about a fifth of a second later in reaching your destination. How much upset do you suppose that fifth of a second is worth? How high do you think your blood pressure goes when you sit on your horn?

If you tend to get highly emotional at the drop of a hat, and common sense flies out the window every time, you might like to find out some more about Rational Emotive Therapy. In which case, I'd recommend a

book by Dr. Albert Ellis and R. Harper, *A Guide to Rational Living,* or
D. S. Goodman's *Emotional Well-Being Through Rational Behavior.*

I have included a list of twelve irrational beliefs that human beings
commonly hold.

We learn these beliefs as small children, and they are frequently rein-
forced or reintroduced as we grow into adult life. They may become more
than just beliefs and turn into a system, a way of looking at our world and
all that happens in it.

When these beliefs are stated as openly as they are in this list, most of
us can recognize how irrational they are. And thus we can begin to see we
don't need to act them out in our lives.

Remember: when your friends tell you "you don't need to get so excited
or upset," they're probably right at least some of the time. And they're
trying to give you a chance to calm down and practice a little informal
Rational Emotive Therapy!

TWELVE COMMONLY FOUND IRRATIONAL BELIEFS[1]

1. *It is an absolute necessity for an adult to have approval from peers, family, and friends.*
In fact it is impossible to please all the people in your life. Even those who
basically like and approve of you will be turned off by some qualities and
kinds of behavior. This irrational belief is probably the single greatest
cause of unhappiness.

2. *You must be unfailingly competent and almost perfect in all you undertake.*
The results of believing you must behave perfectly are self-blame for inevitable failure, lowered self-esteem, perfectionist standards applied to mate
and friends, and paralysis and fear at attempting anything.

3. *Certain people are evil, wicked, and villainous and should be pun-ished.*
A more realistic position is that they are behaving in ways that are antiso-
cial or inappropriate. They are perhaps stupid, ignorant, or neurotic, and it
would be well if their behavior could be changed.

4. *It is horrible when people and things are not the way you would like them to be.*

---

[1] Based on the work of Dr. Ellis and adapted from M. Davis et al., *The Relaxation and Stress Workbook* (Richmond, Calif.: New Harbinger Publications, 1980).

This might be described as the *spoiled child syndrome*. As soon as the tire goes flat the self-talk starts: "Why does this happen to me? Damn, I can't take this. It's awful, I'll get all filthy." Any inconvenience, problem, or failure to get your way is likely to be met with such "awfulizing" self-statements. The result is intense irritation and stress.

5. *External events cause most human misery—people simply react as events trigger their emotions.*
A logical extension of this belief is that you must control the external events in order to create happiness or avoid sorrow. Since such control has limitations and we are at a loss to manipulate completely the wills of others, there results a sense of helplessness and chronic anxiety.

Ascribing unhappiness to events is a way of avoiding reality. Self-statements *interpreting* the event caused the unhappiness. While you have only limited control over others, you have enormous control over your emotions.

6. *You should feel fear or anxiety about anything that is unknown, uncertain, or potentially dangerous.*
Many describe this as "a little bell that goes off, and I think I ought to start worrying." They begin to rehearse their scenarios of catastrophe. Increasing the fear or anxiety in the face of uncertainty makes coping more difficult and adds to stress. *Saving the fear response* for actual perceived danger allows you to enjoy uncertainty as a novel and exciting experience.

7. *It is easier to avoid than to face life's difficulties and responsibilities.*
There are many ways of ducking responsibilities: "I should tell him or her I'm no longer interested—but not tonight. . . . I'd like to get another job, but I'm just too tired on my days off to look. . . . A leaky faucet won't hurt anything. . . . We could shop today, but the car is making a sort of funny sound."

8. *You need something other or stronger or greater than yourself to rely on.*
This belief becomes a psychological trap in which your independent judgment and the awareness of your particular needs are undermined by a reliance on higher authority.

9. *The past has a lot to do with determining the present.*
Just because you were once strongly affected by something, that does not mean that you must *continue the habits you formed* to cope with the original situation.

Those old patterns and ways of responding are just decisions made so many times that they have become nearly automatic. You can identify those old decisions and start changing them *right now*. You can learn from past experience, but you don't have to be overly attached to it.

10. *You are helpless and have no control over what you experience or feel.*

This belief is at the heart of much depression and anxiety. The truth is, we not only exercise considerable control over interpersonal situations, *we control how we interpret and emotionally respond* to each life event.

11. *You shouldn't have to feel pain; you are entitled to a good life.*

The realistic position is that pain is an inevitable part of human life. It frequently accompanies tough, healthy decisions and the process of growth. Life is not fair, and sometimes you will suffer no matter what you do.

12. *Your worth as a person depends on how much you achieve and produce.*

A more rational assessment of your real worth would depend on such things as your *capacity to be fully alive*, feeling everything it means to be human.

AWARENESS TRAINING

The third thing I'd like you to do as part of your stress management program, phase one, is to begin to increase your awareness of your body when you feel stress coming on. It's really helpful to be aware as early as possible of your emergency nervous system turning on. Because when you can feel stress coming on you can begin to control it.

Learning to relax is like learning to ride a bicycle. It's not like memorizing French irregular verbs or the multiplication tables. Nor is it like solving a math or physics problem. It is experiential—you and your body have to go through the process repeatedly, together, in order to learn it.

It's like learning to ride a bicycle. You go out there and get on the bicycle, and you fall down. So you get back on the bicycle and fall off again. But each time you begin to fall, you're learning to feel the difference between being in balance and out of it. And so you can catch yourself beginning to go out of balance earlier and earlier. And then the moment comes when you catch yourself early enough to be able to stay in balance. And you can ride!

When you can feel your stress reaction turning on really early in the game, it won't be able to get you off balance so easily. And you can learn to become very sensitive to your body's stress reaction—as sensitive as you are to your sense of physical balance.

So just becoming aware of your stress is a very powerful tool in learning how to cope with it.

QUITTING SMOKING

I know I mentioned this under the heading of *avoidance*. But I'd like to emphasize just how important a stress management technique this is.

Nicotine really is a powerful stimulant. It's incredibly powerful. And you'll be so much better off without it.

Becoming an Ex-Smoker, by Brian Danaher and Edward Lichtenstein, is a good book to read when you're ready to give up smoking.

And if you feel you can't stop smoking on your own, get some help. Call the American Cancer Society and say, "I want to stop smoking. What should I do?" And they'll tell you. They have a whole list of programs, some of which cost money and some of which are free.

PROGRESSIVE MUSCLE RELAXATION

The fifth stress reduction technique I'd like you to learn this week is muscle relaxation.

Most of us carry quite a bit of tension in our bodies, all the time. And sometimes we just forget about it. We don't notice it anymore. Some people carry their tension in the stomach. Some people carry it in the back. Or the shoulders. Or the neck. Or the forehead, which is where I tend to carry mine. And this tension we carry around with us gets to be so chronic, so persistent, that we don't know how to relax it.

So the principle of progressive muscle relaxation is to tense those muscles on purpose, even more—to really tense them a lot. And then, after a minute or so, when they're exhausted, relax them.

(Yawning is an instantaneous tensing and relaxing of muscles that you can practice anywhere, anytime. You could try it right now—almost all of us have a few stifled yawns hidden away somewhere, so just sit back and let yourself . . . yawn!)

If you turn to the back of the book you'll find a script there for a comprehensive progressive muscle relaxation session. I'd like you to read that script, very slowly, into a tape recorder. And then, for twenty minutes a day, I'd like you to sit down somewhere comfortable, where you won't be interrupted—and play yourself that tape and practice progressive muscle relaxation.

After a while you'll get used to relaxing, and you probably won't need to tense your muscles up before you relax them. You'll just be able to focus your attention on your muscles when you're tense, and let the tension drain right out of them.

But for the moment, make yourself a tape of the PMR script at the back of the book and allow yourself those twenty minutes of relaxation every day.

Well, that takes care of phase one of your stress management program. I expect you're really hitting your stride by now in your nutrition program, making less mistakes and learning from the mistakes you do make.

And you'll have been exercising for a week. By now you may be finding that you're a bit sore. I'm sorry, but that's the way it is at the beginning. You're supposed to be a little sore, your muscles are supposed to hurt a bit.

But I'd like you to remember a simple rule of thumb about this. If you're stiff or sore, but when you start stretching, warming up, and doing your exercise, the stiffness goes away, then you're doing fine. But if the stiffness and soreness get worse when you exercise, if you get any kind of really sore legs, knees, or hips, that's when you need to talk to a professional about your situation.

That's the time to go see your doctor. Or if your doctor doesn't exercise himself, you might want to talk to some runners, or ask around at a health spa, to make an appointment to see someone who practices sports medicine. This may be a podiatrist, or an orthopedist, someone in family practice, or even a chiropractor.

I'd still like you to be checking your blood pressure and waking pulse daily, and keeping track of them, and checking your weight once a week. And on the average you shouldn't be losing more than two to three pounds a week, even if you're a bit overweight.

And if you're not overweight, then you don't want to be losing weight at all.

Pretty soon, one effect of your exercise program may be that you'll be losing more bulk than pounds. Because your muscles and bones will be getting stronger and heavier while that low-fat, low-calorie diet will be taking off the fat. And muscles and bones are much less bulky than fat, so you'll be losing inches and trimming up, without necessarily losing so many pounds.

Another thing.

Now that you're on the third week of your nutrition program, you'll want to make sure that the medicines you're taking aren't too much for you. One of the things that could happen, if you're really managing to restrict your sodium intake pretty well, is that you may find the diuretic you're on is just too much.

So if your mouth is dry all the time, or you're getting dizzy, or your skin is suddenly getting wrinkled, or you feel a little dehydrated—call your doctor, and do something about it right away.

And in any case I'd like you to call your doctor this week and make an appointment to see him at the end of Week Six or sometime early in Week Seven—to have your blood potassium checked again, and to discuss with him how the program's been going, and to talk about whether it's time to reduce your drugs. He'll need to see your diary of blood pressure recordings to decide about this, so be faithful and accurate in keeping your record up to date.

And the last thing I'd like you to do this week is to pay really close attention to what kind of recreation you have—what you do with your leisure time and whether it's stimulating or relaxing.

Try to find out how well you can actually sense the stimulation or relaxation that occurs during your leisure hours.

THE SUNDAY AT THE END OF WEEK FIVE

CHECKLIST: WEEK FIVE

This past week, did you:

Read the three chapters on stress and stress management (Chapters 28–30)?

Start your stress management program, phase one?

Start practicing avoidance, Rational Emotive Therapy, awareness training?

Quit smoking?

Exercise three to five times this week, take one or two slow walks on the other days, and rest completely at least one day?

Check your blood pressure and waking pulse daily, and keep track of them in your diary?

Keep taking your potassium supplements and the medicines you agreed to take?

Set aside the time to make yourself a progressive muscle relaxation tape (see Appendices), and spend twenty minutes every day relaxing with the tape?

Call your doctor and make an appointment to see him in Week Six or Seven?

Spend two hours at least in recreation and play?

Weigh yourself once and record your weight?

Meet with your partner to compare notes?

CHECKLIST: WEEK SIX

This week, you'll need to:

Now (Sunday night):

Complete any tasks left over on your checklist for this week.

Read the first half of Chapter 14 (the part that deals with Week Six).

Monday to Sunday:

Start phase two of your nutritional program.

Continue to exercise three to five times a week, take one or two slow walks on days when you're not doing aerobics, and rest one day this week.

Continue to use your relaxation tape every day.

Check your blood pressure and waking pulse daily, and keep track of them in your diary.

Keep taking your potassium supplements and the medicines you agreed to take.

Sometime this week:

Go see your doctor, if you made an appointment earlier.

Continue to spend two hours a week in recreation.

Weigh yourself once and record your weight.

Meet with your partner to compare notes.

Over the weekend:

Read next week's checklists and chapter.

Listen, I know this all sounds very time consuming—the exercise, and the new kinds of cooking to learn, and the tapes . . . And it is. And it isn't.

It's a matter of learning to fit a lot of new things into your life. And at first there's probably some resistance from the other things that are already there. They don't want to be pushed aside or become less important to you. So there's this battle going on.

But don't give up.

Learning to get rid of your blood pressure problem and off the pills is intruding into every part of your life. It's unsettling and sometimes, frankly, it's a damn nuisance! Like learning to speak French or Swedish from Berlitz—they want you to talk it all the time, and you're thinking, "Give me a break, will you?"

But they know what works. And so do I. If you want to learn, you've got to put up with the nuisance for a few more weeks.

And thanks. Thanks for doing this. We all appreciate it. Your family. Your friends and colleagues.

And especially your own body.

14

The Sixth and Seventh Weeks

> *Flexibility, adaptability, and sensitivity to personal needs characterize the art of medicine, which must constantly temper and complement the technology of medicine.*
>
> Max Parrott, M.D.,
> past president of the AMA

It's Week Six already, and by now you're well launched into all aspects of the program. Once again, I'd like you to make sure you've completed any tasks that are left over from previous weeks—and particularly the reading of the various chapters on nutrition, exercise, and stress reduction.

This week you'll be starting on phase two of your nutrition program, continuing to eat a low-sodium, low-fat, low-meat, and low-dairy-product diet, that is, restricting your intake of those substances as much as possible.

When you do eat meat, try to avoid the red meats, which are so full of animal fats, and instead stick with white meats—chicken and turkey—and white fish.

It's particularly important for you to limit your intake of very high cholesterol foods such as egg yolks, shrimp, lobster, and organ meats, and foods that are exceptionally high in animal fats, such as butter, whole milk, whole cheese, and ice cream. When you eat a diet that's low in these foods you will also be reducing your intake of calories.

As much as possible, you will also want to avoid sugar and limit your intake of alcohol. If you do drink, watch very carefully to see what alcohol actually does to you. If you have a glass of wine or two, or a couple of beers, notice what happens to your blood pressure afterward—and what happens to it the next day.

If you are a calorie counter there are a number of diet plans that make a lot of sense. They help you limit your calories while eating good, nutritious food. Check out the cookbook section in your local bookstore and you'll find a number of low-salt, low-fat cookbooks. Pick out one or two that look interesting. They'll help you lose weight and lower your blood pressure. While you are learning to limit your calories, it's important for you to break out of some of those old eating habits. I was talking to a doctor friend the other day who had lost about twenty-five pounds over the last year, and he told me that one of the most important things he'd learned was *not to clean his plate*. That can be a pretty important habit to break. Another is the habit of eating *because it's lunchtime* or *because the people you're with are eating.*

This week I'd like you to begin to listen to your body. It can tell you *when* it wants to eat and *what* it wants to eat. And that may well turn out to be different from what you imagined you wanted or what your habits would usually dictate.

It's been proven scientifically—there's lots of evidence—that if you can just become more sensitive to what your body actually wants you won't be so overweight, and you'll wind up eating a splendid diet that contains all the essential nutrients in just the right amounts for you.

So this week I'd like you to begin to pay more attention to what your body is telling you. To do that, you need to pay less attention to some important sources of misinformation, such as commercials.

The last episode of *M.A.S.H.* was on TV not so long ago, and a phenomenal number of millions of people tuned in and watched it. Now a lot of the commercials during that program were for food. Those commercials cost $15,000 a second. That's $450,000 for a thirty-second spot. And you know the psychologists who work for the people who bought those spots designed their commercials so that they were effective. If you sit in front of a television and expose yourself to commercials like that, of course your behavior will be influenced. Someone paid *$15,000 a second* to make sure it would be.

The truth is, we're so overwhelmed with commercial messages about food that it's hard to block them out. So it may be a good idea to start *avoiding food commercials*—because they do work. This week I want you to be able to hear what your body's advice about eating is—not the advice of the most successful advertising companies in New York.

I also feel it's important that you don't leave what you're going to eat to chance. For example, some people have a problem with their lunches, because where they work there may only be a greasy spoon restaurant, a fast food hamburger stand, or a place that serves fish and chips to choose from. If that's all there is, you'd better start taking your lunch to work. It's time to brown-bag it!

You can get a thermos with a wide mouth and put some low-salt vegetable soup into it. But don't give yourself one of those excuses that go, "I can't help it. The lunch wagon rolls up and the guy doesn't have anything that's healthy, so there's nothing I can do about it." Take better care of yourself than that: take snacks. Think of it as a picnic. Throw yourself a low-calorie, high-spirited party.

If you're the kind of person who goes down to the coffeepot on your midmorning break, and you know someone's likely to have brought some doughnuts, and that you're going to be tempted, stay away while you're learning to know what your body wants. Take along an apple instead. Or some fresh strawberries. These will not only help to satisfy your appetite, but all the vegetables and fruits you eat will help to replenish your potassium stores. Fruits and vegetables are rich in potassium—and also mercifully low in sodium, particularly if they're fresh.

The final thing I'd like to say this week on the subject of nutrition is this: I want you to eat three square meals a day. Oh, they may be small ones. But let's get away from that line that goes, "I never eat breakfast and hardly ever eat lunch, I just sort of grab a bite here and there, and then at eight o'clock at night when I finally have time I really pork out."

That's a pattern I'd like you to break. When you go for a real long drive in your car, you fill it with gasoline at regular intervals, right? You should eat three small meals a day for the same reason. You know that if you put leaded gasoline into a car that's supposed to run on unleaded you'll mess up the engine, right? So you want to make sure your body gets the right kind of food too.

Your body needs the right kind of food on a regular basis—and this week I'd like you to make sure it gets it. And, just by itself, that will be a major relief and an important step toward stress reduction.

I'd like you to find the time to play your new progressive muscular relaxation tape every day for twenty minutes, so that you learn to relax those muscles.

It's like learning to play the piano. You can't learn to play Chopin nocturnes unless you practice. You can't learn to relax your muscles unless you practice, either. Soon you won't need to practice with the tape anymore. You'll be able to relax just by putting your awareness on the muscles that are tense.

So at least four times a week, and preferably every day, I'd like you to spend twenty minutes listening to that cassette and relaxing. You could take the cassette to your office, or play it in your car during lunch break, or find the time to do it at home. But do it.

This week I'd also like you to notice how often you laugh. Laughter is very good for your blood pressure. Think about buying some humorous records, or joke books, or going to funny movies (I don't mean strange films, I mean films that are genuinely funny). Or watching comedy shows on TV. Or telling jokes.

And while we're on the subject, let me tell you one I heard recently. If you've already heard this one, just forgive me, and go on to the next page.

There was this guy who went into a singles bar to pick up a girl, you see. But although he was an attractive enough fellow he was really quite shy. So he downed a couple of drinks and was looking at all the girls. And finally he got enough alcohol (and courage) into him that he went over to one girl and said, "Hi, my name's George, and I'd really like to buy you a drink."

The girl looked at him in a fairly indignant way and said, in a loud voice that made everyone in the bar turn around and stare at him, "A motel? I wouldn't be seen dead in a motel with you! Buzz off, you jerk!"

Well, the poor guy was pretty embarrassed, and began to blush, and whispered to her, "No, no. I didn't ask you to go to a motel. You must have misheard me. I just offered to buy you a drink."

And she yelled at him again, "I'm not about to go to a motel with you, so why don't you go away! Just leave me alone!"

That was enough. The guy went back to his table, tipped back the rest of his drink in one gulp, and was getting ready to leave—when the girl came over to his table.

Well, by this time the fuss had died down and no one was paying any attention to him or the girl anymore. So the girl said to him, very quietly, "My name is Susan, and I want to apologize to you. I'm taking a psych course this term at the university, and our instructor gave us the assignment to go to some public place and humiliate someone, and then take notes of the reaction. So I'd really like to apologize to you for what I must have put you through just now."

And the guy turned to her and said, in a loud and scornful voice, "*A hundred dollars?!!*"

Okay. I'd like you to keep on checking your blood pressure and early morning pulse each day, and weighing yourself at least once a week. And at the end of this week or the beginning of Week Seven I'd like you to go see your doctor again, to talk to him about the drugs you're on and to ask him about reducing or stopping them if that's appropriate. If you're taking potassium, you may need your blood potassium checked to see what's happening to it.

You're going to take him your diary of blood pressures and early morning pulse rates, and show him what's been happening to you in terms of your weight. You'll be telling him how you feel better, how you've lost your headaches, how your digestion is improving, how your bowels are more regular, and how you've been sleeping a lot better, or whatever.

Your doctor is going to be real pleased to see how well you've been following the program, because there's nothing like a partner who keeps his end of a bargain. You're a delight for him to work with.

You may also want to ask him to check your twenty-four-hour urine sodium excretion, because that will give both of you a very good idea of how much salt you're still eating.

I know that by now you're not using your salt shaker, and you're not using salt in your cooking, and you may even be up to the point where you're managing to eat low-salt food when you're out at a restaurant. But there's probably still a lot of salt in some of the foods you eat that you simply don't know about. And a twenty-four-hour urine sodium test is a real good way to find out.

If your doctor agrees, you should ask him to order a specimen bottle for you. You collect every bit of urine you excrete over a twenty-four-hour period (it's probably best to do this over the weekend), and then a laboratory analyzes it.

Ideally, you should be excreting less than 50 millimoles of sodium a day. Certainly you should be under 100 millimoles by now (the average American excretes 150–200, or about 9 to 12 grams of salt). And if you're not under 100, you should begin to look a lot closer, to see where the extra sodium is coming from.

One source of sodium you might look into is your drinking water. Talk with your doctor about that, or phone the water company and ask them how their water tests for sodium. Particularly if you live somewhere where the water is softened, you may have found your answer. Softened water is salty—and the harder the water was to begin with the saltier it'll be when it's softened.

So if you live somewhere where they soften the water, or if the water is softened in your house, you may need to use some kind of filter, or you may need to buy distilled water to drink.

THE SUNDAY AT THE END OF WEEK SIX

CHECKLIST: WEEK SIX

This last week, did you:

Start phase two of your nutritional program?

Continue to use your relaxation tape every day?

Exercise three to five times this week, take one or two slow walks, and rest completely at least one day?

Check your blood pressure and waking pulse daily and keep track of them in your diary?

Keep taking your potassium supplements and the medicines you agreed to take?

Go see your doctor, if you made an appointment earlier?

Spend two hours at least in recreation and play?

Weigh yourself once and record your weight?

Meet with your partner to compare notes?

CHECKLIST: WEEK SEVEN

This coming week, you'll need to:

Now (Sunday night):

Complete any tasks left over on your checklist for this week.
Read the second half of this chapter, which deals with Week Seven.

Monday to Sunday:

Move into phase two of your exercise program, exercising four to five times a week, taking one or two slow walks on days when you're not doing aerobics, and resting one day.
Check your blood pressure and waking pulse daily, and keep track of them in your diary.
Keep on taking your potassium supplements and the medicines you agreed to take.

Sometime this next week:

See your doctor, if you didn't do it this week.
Continue to spend two hours a week in recreation.
Weigh yourself once and record your weight.
Meet with your partner to compare notes.

Over the Weekend:

Read next week's checklist and chapter.

And that's all for Week Six. We're at the halfway point already. Congratulations!

THE SEVENTH WEEK

This week you move up into phase two of your aerobic exercise program.
Basically, what this involves is simply continuing with the program as before. Stretching, and warm-up, and then whatever aerobic exercise you've chosen—whether it's running or swimming or cycling—then a period of cooling down, and then some more stretching.

And by now I'm hoping that you'll be going through your actual aerobics for about twenty-five to thirty-five minutes, and doing it four or five times a week. Doing it this often benefits your heart and blood vessels, burns up unsightly fat stores, and is an excellent stress reducer as well. On the sixth day you'll be taking a casual, slow walk of some kind that lasts about forty-five minutes. And on the seventh you'll rest those poor tired feet and let those muscles and bones and cartilages heal and get stronger.

You may find you want to do some stretching on the day you rest, however, so that you'll be able to start up again the next day without so much discomfort. And if you're finding you've been having muscle cramps at night, which you may have been, one of the ways to handle that is to do your stretching exercises just before you go to bed.

A lot of people take quinine pills because they have charley horses or muscle cramps at night that get them up. But you can do without the quinine pills if you just do the stretching exercises before you lie down at night.

And remember, if it hurts when you start out exercising, listen to your body. It may just be saying, "Please start slowly, give me a chance to warm up and I'll be okay." Or it may be telling you, "Forget it, I have a tear in my lateral crural ligament, and I want to be taken to the doctor right away." You'll know soon enough. Because if it starts feeling better as you warm up, everything is fine. And if it hurts worse, you'll know to go home early and phone your physician.

By now you're in your fourth week of exercise, and you should be able to go further and faster than you did when you started, unless you started out in pretty good shape. If you started out in less than good shape, by now you should be noticing that it takes more exercise to fatigue you. That you may have to go a little faster than you used to, to keep yourself at your Training Heart Rate.

And that's fine.

The important things to watch are your Training Heart Rate—don't go above your THR yet—and the duration of your exercise, keeping it up for about a half an hour or so.

Try not to get impatient. Some people tell themselves, "Well, instead of running for thirty minutes at my Training Heart Rate, I'm going to run a bit above it for twenty minutes and save some time, because I've got a lot of work to do today." Believe me, that's the way to hurt yourself.

When you push yourself much beyond your Training Heart Rate, your blood pressure may go up. So remember what I told you several weeks ago? *Don't try to push too hard.* Don't try to increase your distance or your speed more than about ten percent every two weeks. That's very important if you're going to avoid injury.

But it is okay to push yourself a bit. If you've been given a Training Heart *Range*, by now you can push yourself up toward the upper end of the range.

So that's your exercise program, phase two.

By now you should be able to follow your exercise prescription, whatever it is. And you'll be feeling the benefits.

You'll be seeing your doctor this week, if you didn't do it at the end of last week, so I'd like you to turn back to the chapter on Week Six and make sure you understand what this visit's about.

It's to make sure your potassium levels are okay, and to show your doctor the notes you've been taking on your weight and pulse and blood pressure, and to discuss whether or not now's the time to cut back on those drugs. But I'd like you to read the section about this doctor visit in Week Six anyway (page 144), to make sure we understand each other.

And you'll need to make another appointment to see your doctor in Week Ten.

Whatever you and he agree to do about the drugs this time, I'd still like you to do it faithfully. And if you feel *at any time* that they're getting too much for you, your blood pressure's too low, you're feeling dizzy or dehydrated, call your doctor. Set up an appointment. This is true any week, any time you feel the drugs are getting to be too much for you. Always check with your doctor.

This week (and in the coming two or three months) it's particularly important, as you're learning to relax, to avoid as far as possible the kinds of leisure-time activities that really jazz you up or upset you. Try to pick some forms of recreation that you find really relaxing and not so competitive or demanding.

I know, we're all creatures of habit, and you may still be drinking cups of regular coffee, or you may find yourself watching the fights on TV. And if you do catch yourself doing those things, do us a favor—notice what happens, feel what happens to your body as a result. See if you can feel your emergency nervous system switching on.

Simply becoming aware of your reactions can teach you more about stress reduction than any number of lectures from me!

I've included on pages 149–50 a "Prescription for an Ulcer"—or for high blood pressure, for that matter. It's just a little bit whimsical, but it's close enough to home that it really pokes a little fun at all of us. Of course, by now you're so into this program that nothing about this description of a hard-driving executive applies to you anymore—right?

You'll be keeping on with phase two of your nutritional program, and you'll be finding time to listen to your relaxation tapes and really letting that tension go.

Talk to your partner if you have one, and your family, and let them know what's happening, so they can acknowledge your efforts and your successes. There's nothing like getting a few pats on the back in the middle of the program.

PRESCRIPTION FOR AN ULCER[1]

Writing in the *Medical Annals of the District of Columbia* some time ago, Dr. William T. Gibb had some advice on getting an ulcer—the executive's "wound stripe." We summarize it here:

- Forget everything but your job. It comes first and your family understands why you have no time for them and appreciates what you are doing.
- Weekends and holidays are excellent times for work at the office. The family members can go to the beach by themselves.
- Carry your briefcase with you always. Thus, you can review all problems and worries of the day.
- Never turn down any request that might even remotely further your career. Grab all invitations to meetings, dinners, and committees.
- Recreation is a waste of time unless it's with customers or business associates. Time spent at the nineteenth hole is the best of all.
- Don't delegate responsibility. You can do it best. Carry the whole load.
- If you have to travel, work all day and drive or fly all night to the next appointment. Take a few "uppers" so you can be fresh the next morning.

[1] Quoted by permission from L. Galton, *Coping with Executive Stress.*

- Be a joiner. Always seek office. It may add a few customers.
- A couple or three quick martinis before dinner is fine for the appetite. No need to relax and chat with the family for half an hour.
- A quick drink before a conference or deal clears your mind and adds to your alertness. Drink along with your luncheon companions; maybe one of them will get a little tight and sign a bigger order.
- Eat only when you are hungry; it's what healthy wild animals do. Lots of gravy and rich desserts are what an active executive needs.
- Never mind doctors; they just want to turn you into a sissy. You're strong as an ox; those height-weight charts do not apply to you.
- Crack the whip constantly on your subordinates. That will keep them alert and make them admire you.
- Take a pep pill or two during the day for extra energy and a good sedative before bed because you're all keyed up by the day's events.

If you have followed these suggestions, observed Dr. Gibb, you may already have your ulcer—and maybe high blood pressure as well.

THE SUNDAY OF WEEK SEVEN

CHECKLIST: WEEK SEVEN

This past week, did you:

Move into phase two of your exercise program, exercising four to five times this week, and taking one or two slow walks on the other days?

Keep taking your potassium supplements and the medicines you agreed to take?

Check your blood pressure and waking pulse daily, and keep track of them in your diary?

See your doctor, if you didn't do it last week?
Spend two hours at least in recreation and play?
Weigh yourself once and record your weight?
Meet with your partner to compare notes?

CHECKLIST: WEEK EIGHT

This coming week, you'll need to:

Now (Sunday night):

Complete any tasks left over on your checklist for this week.
Read the first half of Chapter 15.

Monday to Sunday:

Begin phase two of your stress reduction program.
Continue to exercise four to five times a week, and take one or two slow walks on days when you're not doing aerobics.
Check your blood pressure and waking pulse daily, and keep track of them in your diary.
Keep on taking your potassium supplements and the medicines you agreed to take.

Sometime this week:

Take the time to record your visualization tape, and continue to listen to one or other of your relaxation tapes daily.
Set aside at least two hours this week for laughter, and read jokes or see a funny film.
Continue to spend two hours a week in recreation.
Weigh yourself once and record your weight.
Meet with your partner to compare notes.

Over the Weekend:

Read next week's checklists and chapter.

And that's it again, until Week Eight.

15

The Eighth and Ninth Weeks

The art of medicine consists of amusing the patient while nature cures the disease.

Voltaire

This week you begin phase two of your stress reduction program. Keep on avoiding the things that tend to make you feel stressful. Now that you are getting better at recognizing the early signs of stress you can begin to avoid some stresses as they arise. Of course there will be stressful situations that you can't avoid—but you should learn to be as relaxed as possible while you are dealing with them.

LOOKING ON THE BRIGHT SIDE

In addition, this week I'd like you to practice a technique that's the flip side of avoidance. Actively seek out things that are pleasing to you, that are actually relaxing. The resources we all need to restore and repair our battered bodies and souls can be found all around us.

One of the first things I'd like to suggest is that you actively seek out *good news.* Look in your morning paper and find three items of good news every day. Look for them. Seek them out. Then read those items real carefully. Four thousand auto workers have been rehired. Three children who were missing have been found and their mother is very happy. The kind of news that does your heart good. Seek out the good news as well as avoiding the bad.

Music soothes not only the savage breast but the stressful one as well. Discover some music that you find calming and restful. You may be able to find a station on the FM band of your radio. PBS may be broadcasting a concert on TV. Your public library may have a collection of classical music or a jazz collection. Check out their records and tapes for a week or two. You may find some real treasures and decide you'd like to buy your own recording of this or that piece.

Your car radio is wonderful for listening to music. You can also buy a cassette player, and then you won't be so dependent on what's on FM. Some soothing music sure makes it easier to get through the morning traffic and helps you get through your day.

Keep on the lookout for all the *beauty* that's around you. We're all surrounded by a lot of noise and ugliness and other nonsense. But we're also surrounded by beauty—and you can choose to focus on the ugliness or you can choose to focus on the beauty. Look for the flowers. Look for the sunset. Look for the trees. Look for the rainbow. Wherever you are, look for the beauty. It's your choice.

Look for the *positive.* Try to see the best in people. Actively seek out the best in people who usually irritate you. We all have good points as well as bad ones. See if you can't find something to like about them for a change. Try to see the best in situations. Find something positive to be happy about—don't let things get you down, okay?

And look for *humor;* it's all around us too. Make sure you read the funnies at the back of your paper—they're better news for you than the disasters on page one. As you go about your day, actively seek out the humorous side of things—and enjoy it.

RECREATION

I'd like you to make sure that, from this week on, you spend at least two hours a week in some form of noncompetitive, truly relaxing recreation.

Recreation is a very important part of human existence. So for the rest of this program, and the rest of your life, it's very important for you to be a little bit self-indulgent as far as recreation is concerned. Don't always try to combine recreation with work. Sometimes it does make paperwork a little more bearable if you take it out to the poolside, but don't think that that's recreation. It may have made the work more bearable, but it isn't recreation. You need a complete break from your normal routine!

So I want you to spend two hours a week, *minimum*, in some kind of recreational activity that's pleasurable, noncompetitive, and relaxing. I've made some suggestions on pages 154–55, and no doubt you have some ideas of your own.

If in the past you've been the sort of person who rewards yourself with food or alcohol or tobacco, begin now to reward yourself with some kind of recreation instead. Rewards are important. I want you to enjoy yourself thoroughly.

I'd also like to make sure you understand that you need this recreation *whether or not* you feel you deserve a reward. We all deserve a reward for something—but even if you're the kind of person who never thinks you deserve anything, look for the beauty in yourself—and reward it.

Take a look at the list of suggested recreations and use your imagination to come up with a few others that are your special favorites—and then make sure you spend at least two hours a week in pleasurable and relaxed recreation.

RECREATIONAL ACTIVITIES YOU MIGHT CONSIDER

1. Fly a kite.
There are shops now that sell nothing but kites, so you can find some real beauties.
2. Go skating.
3. Putter about in the garden.
Smell the roses. Take cuttings from the geraniums.
4. Try some cabinetmaking or other woodworking projects.
5. Build model airplanes or ships.
6. Get some watercolors or oils and try your hand at painting.
7. Play a musical instrument.
8. Go fishing.
In our culture, fishing is traditionally a man's business; but it's no secret that what fishing is really about isn't catching fish—it's unwinding and

relaxing in beautiful surroundings, with the gentle sounds of water all about you. And that's something we can all benefit from.

9. Visit a museum.

10. Go to the botanical gardens.

11. Get yourself a massage or a facial.

12. Shop for some fun piece of clothing or other goody.

13. Have a picnic.

14. Go boating.

15. Do a jigsaw puzzle.

16. Sit in a sauna, or a hot tub, or a Jacuzzi.

Or get some bath salts or bath oils and just soak in your own bath at home.

17. Read a book.

18. Play cards.

But here's a warning. You should only choose this one if you can manage to do it noncompetitively.

19. Go for a walk in the park.

Or you could drive out of the city to a place where there are no more buildings—and take a ramble in the woods.

20. Try some needlework.

You remember what I said about fishing? Needlework is the women's traditional method of relaxing in our culture. They know how important it is, and they don't kid themselves they do needlework for the sake of a chair cover. Needlework is a wonderfully calming and focusing activity. And the men who have tried it generally seem to feel they've discovered one of the women's open secrets.

WORRYING ON PURPOSE

I've been trying to get you to avoid worrisome things and to look on the bright side, but you probably still worry from time to time. Well, if you do, I'd at least like you to do it on purpose. So instead of worrying in a haphazard way, scattering it off and on throughout the day, I'd like you to take control of this thing. Set aside ten or fifteen minutes once or twice a day for worrying, and really worry in a creative and imaginative way.

Focus on something that has been bothering you, and worry about it the way a dog worries at a bone. Get to the meat of it. Find out what's the worst that could possibly happen. Then imagine something even worse. Now push the problem around creatively and see if you can't come up with some solutions. And make up solutions that couldn't possibly happen, that would be real examples of miracles if they did.

I think you'll find that if you really take the time to worry in a focussed and deliberate way, or in an exaggerated and humorous one, it will lighten up the problem, which in turn will lighten up the rest of your day.

LAUGHING

I can't tell you how important laughing is. Last night I went to a comedy club in Los Angeles and laughed for two and a half hours straight. And today I feel terrific.

Laughter really is healing. There are plenty of scientific studies to prove it—and Norman Cousins wrote a wonderful book recently, *Anatomy of an Illness,* in which he documented his own experience of the healing power of laughter.

So read Norman Cousins' book. Pick up some copies of the *Reader's Digest,* and read the jokes in "Laughter, the Best Medicine." Because that's exactly what laughter is. Go to a funny movie. Watch comedies on TV. Support your local comedians. And laugh along with life.

I'm going to prescribe for you a minimum of one or two hours a week of laughter. You can take it in small doses, ten minutes at a time, trading jokes around the water cooler, for instance, or all at once on Friday night at a funny movie.

VISUALIZATION

And there's one other, very important stress reduction technique that you should learn this week.

As I pointed out in the chapters on stress, in some ways your emergency nervous system is dumb. It can't tell the difference between imaginary danger and real danger. It switches on for both. So if you imagine something really scary is going on, your ENS is going to react, and you'll be in the middle of a fight or flight response.

But the opposite is true too. If you imagine something that's pleasant, calming, restful, and fun, your emergency nervous system is going to switch itself right back off.

So, with this idea in mind, once or twice a day take twenty minutes or so and *imagine* something pleasurable and relaxing: your favorite hideaway; a lake in the mountains; waves on the ocean; a sun-swept beach; or a cool, green forest glen. Imagine yourself there with the people you like most—or by yourself, if that's what you'd prefer. And you'll be able to take a vacation in the middle of your busy day.

I've provided you with a *visualization script* in the Appendices, and I'd like you to record it, just as you did the muscle relaxation script. Then settle down in a comfortable place where you won't be disturbed, once or twice a day for twenty minutes, and play yourself a tape.

Some days, play the muscle relaxation tape, and others, play this one. See which one works best for you. And if you want to use our script as a model for writing your own—with your own special details—go right ahead. You'll find the instructions for recording the tape in the Appendices.

As you listen to your tape, your emergency nervous system will turn off and you'll relax beautifully. And when you do that once or twice a day, the benefit lasts all day long. It's amazing. But it's true.

Well, that's phase two of your stress reduction program, and everything in it is designed for your enjoyment. We're meant to enjoy life, and these techniques really help.

You'll be continuing with phase two of your nutritional program this week. Make certain you're getting those three meals a day, and brown-bagging your lunch if you can't find the proper foods.

By now you should be losing weight if that's been a problem. If you're not losing weight, and you're really avoiding fat, and your diet is low in meat, dairy foods, salt, and sugar, then what's probably happening is that you're getting too much of the high-calorie items (the grains, the pastas, the bread, rice, potatoes, and beans) and not enough of the vegetables, the salads, soups, and fruits.

You may need to make some adjustments, and eat more vegetables and fruits and less of the other high-calorie foods. For the rest of this program (and the rest of your life), keep on making adjustments until you get the kind of results you want. If you try one particular food and it doesn't work, make some adjustments. Trial, error, correction, and success—that's the formula you need, and no fixed set of dietary rules will ever work without it.

By this time, I hope you're asking for the foods you need in restaurants, in other people's homes, and on airplanes (call the airline twenty-four hours ahead), and not just passively accepting whatever people put in front of you. You do need to speak up. You do need to be reasonably assertive. You do need to eat the kind of food that's suited to your health and well-being.

In restaurants, remember, you're the customer. Your money is paying for this meal, and the management wants to serve you and please you. I've found that when I ask for food without salt, or fat, or sauces, or boiled instead of fried, I can usually have it the way I want it. And so can you.

You'll also be continuing with phase two of your exercise program. And this week I'd just like you to watch your tendency to come up with excuses. If you want this program to work you've got to go out there and do it. So I'd like to give you a lot of encouragement this week to do what you've already said you'll do. Go out and get it done. Without pushing yourself beyond your Training Heart Rate, do the best possible job of exercising that you can.

You'll still be checking your blood pressure and waking pulse every day, and weighing yourself once during the week. And you'll be noticing what excites and upsets you, and what relaxes and calms you. Pay attention to the earliest point at which you can sense stress coming on. Keep track of these things in your diary—and avoid unnecessary worries and upsets and excitements.

And now for a joke.

An elderly man came home from the office one day, looking pretty upset. So his wife asked him what the problem was. "Oh, I haven't been feeling too well recently," he said, "so I went to our doctor today, and he gave me some tests. He told me I had an incurable illness. In fact, he only gave me a few more hours to live. He told me he was pretty sure I wouldn't live through the night."

His wife came over and put her arms around his neck. "He wanted to send me to the hospital," the man continued, "but I told him to forget it —I'd like to spend my last few hours at home with my wife."

They cried on each other's shoulders for a while, and finally she said, "Well, what do you want to do?"

"I'd just like to have a wonderful evening at home," he said.

After they had dinner by candlelight, they went upstairs and made love for the last time. It was wonderful, and pretty soon they fell asleep. But after a while he woke up, still feeling okay, and he nudged his wife and said, "Honey, let's make love one more time." His wife grumbled some sort of reply, but she didn't open her eyes. So he nudged her a few more times.

At last she rolled over and looked at him, groggy-eyed, and said, "Listen, I have to go to work in the morning. You don't."

THE SUNDAY OF WEEK EIGHT

CHECKLIST: WEEK EIGHT

This past week, did you:

Begin phase two of your stress reduction program?

Continue to exercise four to five times a week and take one or two slow walks on the other days?

Check your blood pressure and waking pulse daily, and keep track of them in your diary?

Keep taking your potassium supplements and the medicines you agreed to take?

Set aside at least two hours this week for laughter, and read jokes or see a funny film?

Spend two hours at least in recreation and play?

Take the time to record your visualization tape and continue to listen to one or other of your relaxation tapes daily?

Weigh yourself once and record your weight?

Meet with your partner to compare notes?

CHECKLIST: WEEK NINE

This coming week, you'll need to:

Now (Sunday night):

Complete any tasks left over on your checklist for this week.

Read the second half of this chapter.

Monday to Sunday:

Move into phase three of your nutritional program.

Continue to exercise four to five times a week and take one or two slow walks on days when you're not doing aerobics.

Keep listening to your relaxation tapes.

Check your blood pressure and waking pulse daily, and keep track of them in your diary.

Keep on taking your potassium supplements and the medicines you agreed to take.

Continue to spend two hours a week in recreation, and the same doing something that makes you laugh.

Weigh yourself once and record your weight.

Meet with your partner to compare notes.

And that's the plan for Week Nine.

THE NINTH WEEK

Week Nine is here, and your program's really moving along.

The main thing this week is to move into phase three of your nutritional program, which is really just a matter of doing what you've been doing more carefully, more precisely, more consistently.

By now your diet should be making you feel a lot lighter and healthier and happier. So what you need to do is keep it up, and adjust things where they aren't working yet.

Emphasize a lighter diet, with more whole grains and vegetables and fresh fruits, and cut back on those rich sauces and seasonings. Keep on avoiding the fat and the cholesterol, and those heavy meats and dairy foods that you've probably found by now are not so essential after all.

This week I'd like you to make sure you're emphasizing fiber, which you can principally get from whole wheat, whole brown rice, and whole fruits and vegetables.

As we continue to learn about nutrition and your body is healing and getting stronger, I'd like you more and more to avoid the processed foods and eat raw vegetables and fruits rather than cooked ones.

Make sure you're getting enough calcium in your diet, particularly if your dairy-food intake is lower than it was. The way to make sure you get enough calcium is to eat plenty of whole grains, like whole wheat and brown rice, and leafy vegetables, like broccoli, cauliflower, spinach, and chard.

We've really been brainwashed into thinking we need a lot of milk to get enough calcium in our diet. I know I was brainwashed into thinking that if I didn't drink enough milk all the time my teeth would fall out! But it simply isn't true.

Most of the people who have ever lived on this planet drank a whole lot less milk than the average American—and did just fine. And in fact humans are the *only* mammals that still drink milk into adult life. As far as the rest of the mammals are concerned, milk is strictly for babies!

And many people don't even have the proper enzymes to digest lactose, or milk sugar. So if you're drinking milk at all it should be the nonfat kind by now, and if you're eating yogurt or cottage cheese, it should be the low-fat or nonfat sort. If you are over forty and particularly if you are a woman, your doctor may advise calcium supplements to prevent osteoporosis (thin bones) in later life.

If you still need to lose weight, keep checking to see that your nutritional program is working. If you're not losing weight and you think you should be, you're probably eating just enough to stay in calorie balance—whereas, in order to lose weight, you need to be several thousand calories below the balance point each week. That means you have to burn several thousand calories more than you eat.

It may be that you have such a habit about eating that you're not really giving yourself enough flexibility—just not allowing yourself to change your habits when you need to.

Maybe you should eat more often, and less at each meal. You may need to pay more attention to your hunger and less to the clock or what your friends are doing. It may mean that you should just order an appetizer instead of a whole meal at that business lunch. Or split an entree with your friend or spouse when you go out to dinner. Do whatever you can to be more flexible about your habits—and you'll be able to lose weight more easily.

If you're restricting your calories, you should be taking one of the multivitamin pills, to make sure you get all the necessary vitamins and minerals.

This is the time for you to begin to adapt your favorite recipes, if you haven't done it already. If someone else does the cooking, your wife, husband, friend, this is the time to talk to them about adapting some of their recipes to your needs.

You'll find you can usually rewrite a recipe without the salt and fat and cholesterol, and still make it delicious. And there are plenty of recipes that can be cooked without a high fat content. Often just leaving out the salt entirely is no problem at all.

Here are a few specific ways you can adapt recipes to avoid the foods you want to avoid, and at the same time enhance the flavor of your cooking:

RECIPE ADAPTATION

Salt

Salt is the biggest no-no. Leave the salt out of all items that call for boiling in salted water (rice, pasta, potatoes, vegetables, etc.). Don't add it to anything. In fact, don't even have it in the house. You can use a salt substitute if you wish, but remember to use a much smaller quantity than you would of sodium-based salt, so as to avoid the bitter taste.

You'll find you won't miss it for long. Someone has even proved scientifically *(Annals of Internal Medicine,* Supplement, 1983) what you may already be discovering—that the less salt you eat the less you want. Your poor old tongue is only too happy to recover from the caustic burning it's received all these years. And you'll be decreasing your risk of stomach cancer, too *(Preventive Medicine,* 1983). We've known since 1964 that salt was a causative factor in stomach cancer.

Salt, salt, salt. It's a very effective rat poison, but not really something humans should eat.

Oils, Fat, Grease, Lard, Butter

Your car needs oil—but you don't.

Nonstick cookware is a must if you are to avoid cooking with oil. Sauté in a little water or stock instead of butter or oil.

Where oil is used to flavor, try to leave it out entirely or replace it with a watery liquid. Very flavorful oils, such as olive or sesame seed oil, can be added in small amounts—one or two teaspoonfuls—without harm if that flavor is needed.

Many oil-free salad dressings are available—be careful, they may contain lots of salt. Make your own with the very flavorful vinegars—rice vinegar, raspberry vinegar, etc.—that are increasingly available. Then add your spices.

Try hot-oven baking instead of frying—french fries, tortilla chips, etc. —on a nonstick cookie sheet. Take care you don't burn them!

Dairy Foods

Use nonfat (skim) milk where the recipe calls for milk. Or use evaporated *skim* milk (in a can) in recipes where evaporated whole milk is called for. Use frozen low-fat yogurt for ice cream. Use nonfat (or low-fat) yogurt in place of sour cream, cream, or mayonnaise. Look for low-sodium, low-fat cheeses—hoop cheese is actually made from skim milk, for example.

Eggs

Throw out the yolks and shells, and double the number of eggs called for, to replace lost yolks. Or try one of the egg replacers in cooking (but be sure to pick a sodium-free product). I use the Ener-G Foods brand out of Seattle, Washington. It replaces the egg function but doesn't taste like eggs. So don't try to scramble it!

Meat, Poultry, and Fish

Avoid the red meats as much as possible, they are so high in fat. Marinate flank steaks and the tougher (leaner) cuts to make them more delicious and tender. Use the white meat of poultry as a substitute for beef in chili, tacos, meatballs, etc. Many entrees, such as lasagna and other pasta dishes, are delicious when simply cooked without meat.

I find that after a while many people don't miss eating so much meat—and feel much better for it.

Sugar, honey, syrup, etc.

Most sweetened dishes are too sweet—once you've been using less sweetener for a while, you'll find you don't need so much. In fact you may be surprised to find out how much of a sugar junkie you've been!

Add half as much sugar (to taste) as recipes recommend, or use honey or fructose—which are sweeter than sugar, and thus can be used in even smaller quantities. Or try sweetening with fresh or dried fruit, right in the dish.

So that's phase three of your nutritional program.

You'll be carrying on with phase two of your exercise and stress reduction programs, checking your blood pressure and waking pulse daily, and weighing yourself once during the week.

And this is a good week to measure inches.

As I told you before, when you go on a program of diet and exercise, you not only *lose* weight in fat, you also *build up* heavier muscles and bones. You may notice there's more of a difference in the number of inches you've trimmed off than in the actual number of pounds lost.

So this is a good week to measure the inches you've lost around your thighs, hips, stomach, chest, or upper arms—wherever you've noticed that you're getting thinner. Check those inches and make a note about them in your notebook.

I'd like you to rate your level of stress a few times this week, on a scale of 0 to 10. 0 means that you are totally calm, with no stress at all, and 10 is how you'd feel if three guard dogs had gotten loose and were coming after you, and your shoes seemed to be made of lead!

STRESS SCALE

Where we go when
we're late for an
important meeting
with the boss.

****

0   1   2   3   4   5   6   7   8   9   10

****

Where most of us
live every day—
are you ever
carefree anymore?

0–1.   You're three years old, your tummy is full (your bowels and bladder are empty), you're a little sleepy, you are riding home in the back seat of the car with your parents after seeing your favorite grandmother, who gave you a new picture book to read. Remember being that carefree?

9–10.   Don't even think about it! A worse fright than the worst you ever had.

Rate yourself on this scale under different sorts of circumstances—after an exhausting workout, and driving down the freeway, and first thing in the morning, at work, at a party, at home, that kind of thing. You don't have to do anything special about it, just notice where you are on that scale of 0 to 10.

And rate yourself before and after listening to your relaxation or visualization tape.

Biofeedback is coming of age. There are certified biofeedback technicians in many cities to whom your doctor can refer you. They can show you how to use biofeedback machines that allow you to see (as measured on their dials or gauges) just how active your emergency nervous system is at any moment—and to learn to control it.

Until now, though, the usual biofeedback approach to treating high blood pressure was indirect. That is to say, the machines monitored some related phenomena such as your skin temperature or perspiration, not the blood pressure itself.

If you use biofeedback and learn to control your skin temperature, you're actually learning to control the emergency nervous system's command of the small arterioles that supply blood to the skin. For some people, that's direct enough, and their blood pressure comes down *(British Medical Journal,* 1981).

Now James Lynch of the University of Maryland has developed a computer-assisted direct visual display of the blood pressure itself—and the biofeedback is more direct. Although it's new, this technology appears very promising *(Journal of the American Medical Association,* 1982), so much so that I'm gearing up to use it in my clinic.

If the idea of biofeedback appeals to you, ask your doctor about it. For some people, it makes a lot of difference. Biofeedback training sessions can certainly be used to supplement your stress reduction program if you and your doctor think you would benefit from them.

Continue to notice the effects your drugs are having on you, and to make notes about them, so you can tell your doctor about them when you see him next. Now's the time to set up another appointment with your doctor. You'll be wanting to see him at the end of Week Ten or at the beginning of Week Eleven.

President Reagan, Henry Kissinger, a bishop, and a boy scout were (for some reason connected with this joke) flying in a small aircraft over the Colorado Rockies one day, when the pilot announced that he was bailing out.

"There are three parachutes in the passenger section," he announced, "so you'll have to work it out among yourselves. I'm hitting the button on my ejector seat." And whuumpf! off he went.

President Reagan spoke first. "As President of this nation," he said, "I feel I have a duty to survive." He picked up a chute and jumped.

Dr. Kissinger was the second to go. "As the brightest man on earth," he said, "I, too, am indispensable."

The bishop turned to the boy scout and said. "You take the last parachute. I've had my hard times and my doubts, but all in all it's been a good life, and I'm not afraid of where I'll be going. And besides, you're young. You still have your whole life ahead of you."

"Thanks anyway, Father," said the boy scout, "but we're both going to be okay. The brightest man on earth just picked up my backpack and jumped out of the plane."

THE SUNDAY AT THE END OF WEEK NINE

CHECKLIST: WEEK NINE

This last week, did you:

Move into phase three of your nutritional program?
Continue to exercise four to five times a week, take a slow walk on one of the other days, and rest completely one day of the week?
Continue to listen to your relaxation tapes?
Check your blood pressure and waking pulse daily, and keep track of them in your diary?
Keep taking your potassium supplements and the medicines you agreed to take?

Continue to spend two hours a week in recreation, and the same doing something that made you laugh?
Set up an appointment to see your doctor?
Weigh yourself once and record your weight?
Meet with your partner to compare notes?

CHECKLIST: WEEK TEN

This coming week, you'll need to:

Now (Sunday night):

Complete any tasks left over on your checklist for this week.
Read the first half of Chapter 16.

Monday to Sunday:

Start your exercise program, phase three: exercise four to five times a week, take a slow walk on a day when you're not doing aerobics, and rest completely for one day during the week.
Continue to use your relaxation tapes daily.

Check your blood pressure and waking pulse daily, and keep track of them in your diary.

Keep on taking your potassium supplements and the medicines you agreed to take.

Sometime this week:

Continue to spend two hours (at least) a week in recreation, and the same doing something that makes you laugh.

Weigh yourself once and record your weight.

See your doctor, if you made an appointment.

Meet with your partner to compare notes.

And that's the plan for Week Ten.

16

The Tenth and Eleventh Weeks

*Illegitimis non carborundum (don't let
the bastards grind you down).*

Anon.

Fantastic.

It's Week Ten, you're into double figures—and if you ask my opinion, that means you're doing great.

This week you're still in phase three of your nutritional program. If you're still on medicines, or if your blood pressure is still up there higher than you'd like it to be, I'd like to suggest you try one of the most powerful approaches there is to lowering your blood pressure by diet.

It's based on the work of a Dr. W. Kempner of Duke University, and he discovered it back in the thirties, when the drug treatment for hypertension was even more unsatisfactory than it is now. In the forties, others followed his lead.

Dr. Kempner showed that his approach to diet was incredibly effective for reducing blood pressure, for the improvement or cure of diabetes, and for weight loss. And both Dr. Kempner and his approach to diet are still going strong.

What I'd like you to try is very simple. It's called the rice-fruit diet, and it's a diet of brown rice and potatoes, and any kinds of fruits and vegetables. Just enough to satisfy your hunger. And that's all. That's all you eat. No meat, no dairy foods, no processed foods. That's all there is to it.

THE "DON'T WORRY, IT'S ONLY TEMPORARY" RICE AND FRUIT DIET[1]:

For the time being, please restrict yourself to the foods, beverages, and condiments listed below:

Grains (all grains and grain products should be *whole grain.*)

Rice	Wheat	Rye	Pasta (noodles, spaghetti, etc.)
Millet	Oats	Bran	Corn tortillas
Barley			Crackers (unsalted)

Flour

Cornmeal	Arrowroot	Whole wheat	Rye flour

Starchy vegetables

Dried beans	Corn	Popcorn (air popped, no salt)
Peas	Parsnips	Potatoes (white, sweet, etc.)
Lentils		

Vegetables

Artichokes	Cucumber	Alfalfa sprouts
Okra	Eggplant	Tomato products (unsalted)
Onions	Endive	Bean sprouts (not mung)
Pea pods	Beets	Green beans
Peppers	Broccoli	Water chestnuts
Radishes	Jicama	Brussels sprouts
Zucchini	Cabbage	Green onions
Rutabaga	Kale	Squash

[1] By permission of Janet Segal, R.D.

| Cauliflower | Lettuce | String beans |
| Chard | Mushrooms | Tomatoes |

Fruits

Apples*	Dates	Melons	Plums
Applesauce	Figs	Nectarines	Prunes*
Apricots	Grapes*	Oranges*	Raisins
Bananas	Grapefruit*	Papayas	Raspberries
Berries	Guavas	Peaches	Strawberries
Cantaloupe	Mangos	Pears	Tangerines
Cherries		Pineapple*	

Beverages

Fruit juices of fruits listed (*) above
Herb tea   Decaffeinated coffee
Water   Low-sodium tomato or V-8 juice

Condiments

Vinegar   Limes   Lemons
Herbs and spices (salt free)

This diet is so low in fat and sugar and salt that your body's health begins to improve immediately. Try it for a day, a few days, or even a whole week. You'll notice a difference right away. Your need for medicines, especially diuretics, will probably decrease. And this diet tends to shut off the emergency nervous system, too.

I'm not suggesting you should stay on this diet for the rest of your life. But try it for a week to see just how well your body responds to it, and you'll always have it in reserve. Whenever you find your regular diet is getting a little out of hand, try another few days of the rice-fruit diet and work yourself a little miracle.

In the short term, it's one of the healthiest diets there is.

Warning: your need for blood pressure pills, particularly diuretic (water) pills, may drastically decrease while you are on this diet. If you take insulin or diabetic pills, they may need to be stopped or decreased. Please consult your doctor.

You'll be switching into phase three of your exercise program this week, which means making sure you're doing your aerobic exercises for thirty to thirty-five minutes at Training Heart Rate, four or five times a week. (Don't forget to walk one day and rest one day as well.) And you should still be stretching and warming up before your aerobics, and cooling down and stretching again after them.

By now you may have reached a sort of plateau, where you discover that your miles (or laps) and your times are staying pretty constant. And, if you have, I'd like to introduce you to *interval training*.

Basically, this involves exercising at a somewhat more intense level for a short period of time during your regular aerobic exercise.

For example, if your Training Heart Rate is 22–24, you would work at a slightly higher heart rate for two, three, or even five minutes in the middle of your aerobic workout, by running, jogging, walking, or swimming a bit faster. You will likely get to the point where you are breathing a little harder than usual, and maybe sweating a bit more.

You can do this once, or even twice, for up to five minutes, in each workout. That's interval training, and after a while you'll find you're moving off your plateau and are able to go further in your workout and still keep at Training Heart Rate.

But you need to be careful about this. If you have coronary heart disease, interval training may not be appropriate. You should certainly ask your doctor about it before you try it. If he thinks interval training is okay for you, so much the better. But take care. And please don't push yourself further than you and your doctor feel happy about.

You've been doing your aerobics for some time now, and you may have been concentrating on one particular form of aerobics, such as jogging. If you have, and if you're finding it's getting a bit boring as time goes on, you might like to try a little more variety. Sometimes jog, sometimes cycle outside, sometimes use the Exercycle, and sometimes swim or square dance, or go to a jazz exercise workout.

You might even feel like doing some very lightweight muscle training, to keep your upper body fit and to make it more attractive. But the weights should be fairly light. We don't want you doing any severe straining—because that will send your blood pressure up.

And that's exercise, phase three.

You're still in phase two of your stress program, and you should be listening to your relaxation and visualization tapes once or twice a day for twenty minutes, and spending a minimum of two hours a week at some form of enjoyable and relaxing recreation or hobby.

Keep on checking your blood pressure and waking pulse daily, and measuring your weight once a week. At the end of this week or the beginning of Week Eleven, you'll be seeing your doctor. He's going to see the improvement you've been making, and your growing self-confidence, and he'll take a look at the blood pressure records you've been keeping.

Both of you are going to feel very good about what's happening. And you can talk to him about reducing your drugs again. Particularly if you've been on the rice-fruit diet, your need for the drugs may have declined very noticeably.

By now things are shaping up very well for you; not only are you feeling better because of your nutritional program, and the exercise, and the stress reduction techniques you've been using, but likely you'll be feeling healthier from here on in because you'll be taking less of those damn drugs.

Great!

A businessman dies. He goes immediately to the angel who guards the pearly gates and presents his business card. "Ah, yes, Mr. Hampton," the angel says. "Perhaps you could wait a minute while I consult our computer."

The angel returns in a moment with a sheaf of notes. "I'm afraid we don't seem to have a record of your performing any good deeds, Mr. Hampton. But I'm sure that a man of your reputation and integrity must have done *something* . . ."

Mr. Hampton wishes his executive secretary was there. He racks his brains to think of some good deed that he can recount. "Yes, let me see. . . . I believe I gave a beggar a dime once. And I threw fifteen cents in the Salvation Army kettle last Christmas."

The angel excuses himself again and places a brief telex to the throne. The answer comes back at once.

"I'm afraid we can't help you, Mr. Hampton," says the angel, "now or ever. The boss's words were, 'Give the guy back his quarter—and tell him to go to hell.'"

THE SUNDAY OF WEEK TEN

CHECKLIST: WEEK TEN

This last week, did you:

Start your exercise program, phase three, and continue to exercise four to five times a week, take a slow walk on days when you weren't doing aerobics, and rest from exercise completely for one day during the week?

Continue to use your relaxation tapes daily?

Check your blood pressure and waking pulse, and keep track of them in your diary?

Keep on taking your potassium supplements and the medicines you agreed to take?

Continue to spend at least two hours a week in recreation, and the same doing something that made you laugh?

Weigh yourself once and record your weight?

See your doctor, if you made an appointment to do so?

Meet with your partner to compare notes?

CHECKLIST: WEEK ELEVEN

This coming week, you'll need to:

Now (Sunday night):

Complete any tasks left over on your checklist for this week.

Read the rest of this chapter.

Monday to Sunday:

Begin phase three of your stress reduction program.

Continue to exercise four to five times a week, take a slow walk one or two days when you're not doing aerobics, and rest one day.

Check your blood pressure and waking pulse daily, and keep track of them in your diary.

Keep taking your potassium supplements and the medicines you agreed to take.

Sometime this week:

Take the time to record a meditation tape and an affirmation tape, and to use one of your relaxation tapes daily.

Continue to spend two hours a week in recreation, and the same doing something that makes you laugh.

Weigh yourself once and record your weight.

See your doctor if you didn't see him last week.

Meet with your partner to compare notes.

Over the weekend:

Read the checklists and the chapter for next week.

And that's it for Week Ten.

THE ELEVENTH WEEK

This is the week in which you start phase three of your stress reduction program, and what a beauty it is! Because this week you'll be learning about meditation.

Meditation is simple. Just about anyone can do it. And it's wonderful. It feels wonderful and it does wonderful things for you.

The idea of meditation is to learn to pay less attention to your thoughts, your worries, your duties and schemes and plans, your failures and your successes—and to focus instead on something that's calming and relaxing.

Dr. Herbert Benson showed just how effective this form of relaxed, focused concentration can be in his book, *The Relaxation Response* (New York: Morrow, 1975), which you can read if you want to know more about it.

The rules are very simple:

You need to be in a quiet environment, with your eyes shut.

You need to be sitting or reclining comfortably, so that you won't need to move your body for about twenty minutes and you won't fall asleep.

You need some mental device that you can use as a focus of internal attention.

And you need to have an accepting, quiet attitude to the whole process, so that you ignore distracting thoughts and bring your attention back to your point of focus.

That's the Relaxation Response as Dr. Benson defines it.

The focus of meditation we'd like you to use is your breath. At the back of the book, along with the muscular relaxation and visualization scripts, you probably noticed a script for meditation. I'd like you to record the Relaxation Response script this week and use it.

It's very, very simple to do. You'll be paying attention to your breathing. And as you breathe in you'll say the word "in." And as you breathe out you'll say the word "out." And if you'd like, you can slowly open and close your hands at the same time.

As you begin to focus on your breathing you'll tend to pay less attention to your thoughts and worries and concerns. And your emergency nervous system will quiet down and switch off. And you'll experience a simple, deep sense of peace.

As I said before, anyone can do this, but almost everyone, while doing it, thinks, "I don't think I'm doing this right," or, "I don't think it's working for me."

So be forewarned. You're very likely to think those thoughts—and others too. But they're just thoughts, and you're supposed to focus on your breathing and let the thoughts go. You *are* doing it all right, and it *is* working for you, and it's really very simple, and satisfying, too. The satisfaction may take longer, but just hang in there anyway.

By the time you've recorded your Relaxation Response tape you'll have a choice of three tapes to play—progressive muscle relaxation, visualization, and Relaxation Response. And I'd like you to play one or other of those tapes every day, once or twice a day. But feel free to choose among them. Give yourself some variety and find out which one works best for you at different times.

I'm also going to ask you to record the affirmations script, in the same appendix, sometime this week or next—and you can use it in the same way. So, by the time you've recorded the script for your affirmations as well, you'll have four choices.

Affirmations are just good things that you tell yourself and that your body responds to. Every time we criticize ourselves the emergency nervous system switches on—and whenever we say nice things about ourselves it switches off.

So this affirmations script will give you a chance to say some wonderful things about yourself in a very complimentary, sincere way. And your body will respond positively. And the affirmations will become truer and truer as you grow into them in this way.

This week or next, I'd also like you to look into time management. Are you making the most effective use of your time? Do you know how to set priorities? How to keep lists so that you do all the things you need to do? How and when to delegate your authority?

There are a number of good books on time management, and some excellent courses and workshops. Look into them—and try to make sure that you learn to use time well.

By now I hope you've pretty much stopped using Valium, sleeping pills, or alcohol as a crutch. And that you've quit smoking. There's nothing more difficult than trying to handle stress if you keep on smoking. So, if you haven't stopped smoking, phone the American Cancer Society and find out what programs are available locally. Or read Brian Danaher's book (see page 135).

You're on phase three of your nutritional program and may be trying out the rice-fruit diet. And you're on phase three of your exercise program, too.

Do your exercise on a really regular basis now, and make fewer and fewer excuses to yourself. If you're jogging, take your jogging shoes with you when you go on trips. If you're swimming, take your bathing suit.

As before, I'd like you to spend two hours this week in relaxed, enjoyable recreation. Keep checking your blood pressure and waking pulse rate daily, and weigh yourself once during the course of the week. If you didn't see your doctor last week, see him this week.

Take in your notes so he can see the progress you've been making. By now you're going to be looking better, feeling better, and feeling more confident. Your blood pressure is going to be improved, too. This is a good week to let your physician really see how well you're doing—and to ask him about reducing your medications.

A Catholic priest, a Dominican, once walked into London's Farm Street Jesuit Church and found one of his Jesuit friends kneeling in prayer, smoking a cigarette.

"How do you get away with it?" the Dominican muttered. "I asked my father confessor if I could smoke while I was praying, and he absolutely forbade it."

"No wonder," said the Jesuit. "I inquired if I could *pray* while I was *smoking*, and my confessor said, 'Of course, old boy, feel free. . . . I don't believe you should ever stop praying.' "

THE SUNDAY OF WEEK ELEVEN

CHECKLIST: WEEK ELEVEN

This last week, did you:

Begin phase three of your stress reduction program?

Exercise three to five times this week, take one or two slow walks on the other days, and rest completely at least one day?

Check your blood pressure and waking pulse daily, and keep track of them in your diary?

Keep taking your potassium supplements and the medicines you agreed to take?

Take the time to record a meditation tape and an affirmation tape, and use one of your relaxation tapes daily?

Spend two hours this week in recreation, and the same doing something that made you laugh?

Weigh yourself once and record your weight?

See your doctor if you didn't see him last week?

Meet with your partner to compare notes?

CHECKLIST: WEEK TWELVE

This next week, you'll need to:

Now (Sunday evening):

Complete any tasks left over on your checklist for this week.

Read Chapter 17.

Monday to Sunday:

Continue to exercise four or five times a week, take one or two slow walks on days when you're not doing aerobics, and rest completely one day.

Continue to use your relaxation tapes daily.

Check your blood pressure and waking pulse daily, and keep track of them in your diary.

Keep on taking your potassium supplements and the medicines you agreed to take.

Sometime this Week:

Spend two hours in recreation and the same doing something that makes you laugh.

Weigh yourself once and record your weight.

Meet with your partner to compare notes.

That's it for this week. Great! Only one more week to go!

17

Week Twelve—The Final Week

> *The will to live is a window on the future. It opens the individual to such help as the outside world has to offer, and it connects that help to the body's own capability for fighting disease. It enables the human body to make the most of itself.*
>
> Norman Cousins

I realized that in Week Twelve I should discuss one of the most powerful stress reduction techniques of all—forgiveness. In a way, I suppose I've been saving the best for last. And I say "the best" because forgiveness is both a beautiful and a very powerful technique.

When I talk about forgiveness I'm talking about giving again, giving *anew*—your love, and your affection, to someone you've been angry or disappointed with. Even if the resentment has been around a long time. And it's not the kind of thing that depends on whether the person deserves it or not.

That shouldn't even be an issue.

And forgiveness really isn't something that in any way encourages that person to do the same thing that disappointed or annoyed or angered you in the first place, either. Whether you stay mad or forgive him or her will make a whole lot more difference to *you* and the quality of *your* life than it will to the other person.

When you forgive someone, you give up holding the "thing" against that someone—whatever it was, however you were hurt. No more "remember when's"—you just let go of it as completely as you can.

One of my favorite stories is about two Japanese Zen Buddhist monks named Tanzan and Ekido, who as part of their spiritual vows had renounced the world[1]:

> Tanzan and Ekido were once traveling together down a muddy road. A heavy rain was still falling.
>
> Coming around a bend, they met a lovely girl in a silk kimono and sash, unable to cross the intersection.
>
> "Come on, girl," said Tanzan at once. Lifting her in his arms, he carried her over the mud.
>
> Ekido did not speak again until that night when they reached a lodging temple. Then he no longer could restrain himself. "We monks don't go near females," he told Tanzan, "especially not young and lovely ones. It is dangerous. Why did you do that?"
>
> "I left the girl there," said Tanzan. "Are you still carrying her?"

Forgiveness means leaving your complaint behind you, like Tanzan, not carrying it around with you the way Ekido carried his memory of the girl.

I know some of you may feel that whatever happened to you is just too big for you to let go of it completely. And to you I'd say, try it a little bit at a time. Even make it a temporary thing.

I know I do that sometimes. Most of the time I forgive my ex-wife, and I'm sure my blood pressure's lower because of it. And sometimes I slip up and start rehashing past indignities in my head and get upset. But then I can go back again into the forgiving state—and boy, does it feel better!

So try it for an hour at a time. And if you want to, pick something small to start with. You don't necessarily have to start out with a big one, the way Otis did.

Let me tell you about him.

Otis was lying in the Coronary Care Unit, a little drugged and dopey,

---

[1] This story comes from Paul Reps's delightful book, *Zen Flesh, Zen Bones*.

his blood pressure coming down from about 240/150. He must have been wondering what had happened to him.

One minute he was at home, the next in an ambulance with sirens screaming, and now here he was in the hospital—before he could say Blue-Cross-Blue-Shield.

He told me he'd gotten upset with his son-in-law over something and then, next thing he knew, his chest was hurting real bad, his head ached, and someone called the paramedics. It turned out that he hadn't spoken to his son-in-law for two and a half years. There had been a little misunderstanding, then another and another—and now there was a wall of silence between them. Impenetrable. And at sixty-one, when you haven't spoken to your son-in-law in two years, you're probably not going to be too keen about changing your mind.

But you never can tell. And a lot was at stake. Otis was a Catholic, so I told him to talk to his priest about it. I figured priests are pretty knowledgeable about forgiveness. And that was my prescription: see your priest, and learn to forgive your son-in-law. "Never mind whether the SOB deserves it. You deserve it," I said. Oh, I gave him some medicines, too. But I knew they wouldn't have much effect if this business with his son-in-law was still eating away at him.

Well, I saw Otis four weeks later, standing up on the treadmill, ready to start our cardiac rehabilitation program. He deadpanned beautifully, but I could sense his excitement. "How are things at home?" I asked. He let a little smile through. It turned out he'd seen the priest, he was talking to his son-in-law again, he'd mended some of the fences, he felt better—and his blood pressure was down quite a bit. Of course it was! When you unclench your fist you can relax. And that's what was happening to Otis for the first time in two and a half years.

He told me he was going around now to all the other people he'd held grudges against, and cleaning things up. And he was pretty happy about it, too, I can tell you.

And that's what makes my day brighter—hearing a story like that, and knowing that someone has turned his life around.

This week you'll be continuing with phase three of your nutrition, exercise, and stress management programs, and they'll all be working together for you—in fact the total effect will be greater than the sum of its parts.

From time to time you'll make mistakes. That's okay. All I ask you to do is to learn from them. When you make a mistake, see the mistake for what it is, but don't spend a lot of time criticizing yourself. Just make the necessary corrections. You may be having various problems, but you'll have the capacity to solve them, if you only pay attention. Don't buy your own excuses. Keep at it. And keep going for it.

It's very doubtful that you'll have lived up to your own highest ideas and expectations. We rarely do anything quite as well as we'd like to. But that doesn't have to be a problem.

So this week I'd like you to give yourself some real, warm praise. I'd like you to acknowledge to yourself just how far you *have* gone, and how many weeks you *have* hung in there, and come bouncing back when things didn't work out quite so well as you would have liked them to.

This week I'd like you to record your affirmations tape, if you didn't already do it last week, and play it several times. It's okay to like yourself—don't be like Groucho Marx, who is supposed to have said, "I'd never want to belong to a club whose standards of membership were so low they'd invite me to join."

And I'd also like you to check out all the coping mechanisms we have for stress—the ones that don't really help, and the ones that do. I've listed a great many of them on pages 182–84, and I'd just like you to be aware of them—because your own awareness and motivation will be enough to do the rest.

DESTRUCTIVE STRESS MANAGEMENT TECHNIQUES

1. Thinking overtime.

And that includes planning and scheming and worrying and resenting and regretting.

2. Using Valium or other tranquilizers.
3. Eating snacks all day and night, or just plain old overeating.
4. Excessive and inappropriate use of alcohol.
5. Planning some kind of revenge, or getting even.
6. Gossiping.

And recruiting other people to be on your side in disputes.

7. Excessive partying.

Look in the mirror, you'll know what I mean.

8. Stimulating and highly competitive play.

I mean the kind of play in which winning is the most important thing.

9. Using coffee or other caffeinated drinks excessively, to stay alert.
10. Becoming a workaholic.

Working at home in the evenings and on weekends.
Working as a way to distract yourself.
  11. Very intense passive distractions.
Such as loud music, horror movies, etc. These are the kinds of distraction
that upset and excite you rather than calm you.
  12. Cigarettes and other kinds of smoking.
  13. Sexual affairs.
  14. Finger-tapping, foot-tapping, nail-biting, teeth-grinding.
  15. Excessive sleep, and the use of hypnotics to get to sleep.
  16. Gambling.
  17. Excessive and inappropriate shopping, or even shoplifting.
And you can add your own. . . .
  18.
  19.
  20.

HELPFUL STRESS MANAGEMENT TECHNIQUES

  1. Assertiveness training.
  2. Acknowledging yourself and listening to affirmations.
  3. Exercise, particularly aerobics.
  4. Meditation and deep breathing.
  5. Muscular relaxation.
  6. Visualization.
  7. Calming types of recreation.
  8. Time management seminars or workshops.
  9. Humor.
  10. Awareness.
  11. Acceptance and common sense (Rational Emotive Therapy).
  12. Forgiveness.
  13. Seeking out the beauty around us.
  14. Avoiding upsetting circumstances.
  15. Creating a nurturing environment for ourselves.
  16. Receiving support from others, and delegating authority and responsibility.
  17. Trainings, seminars and workshops.

The kind that help you discover the real, wonderful, capable you.

18. Vacations.
19. Apologizing.
20. Hugging.
21. A pet you can play with and love.
22. Ceremonies and traditions.
23. Prayer.
24. Detached awareness.

And once again, you can add your own. . . .

25.
26.
27.

Okay, that's it for stress, and if you'll just keep these things in mind you'll find ways to reduce stress as easily as you used to find ways to increase it.

I'd like you to look in a mirror this week, just as you did in Week One, and simply acknowledge what you see now. And I'd like you to take another photo of yourself and compare this second photo with the one you took in Week One to really see how much progress you have made.

Look back in your notebook to Week One, read the goals you set for yourself at the beginning of the program—especially the health goals— and see how far you've come in realizing them.

Keep on taking your blood pressure and waking pulse, and weigh yourself again this week. And make sure you have an appointment to see your doctor next week, because you'll need some more blood tests and a complete reevaluation, so that he can see how far you've come these past twelve weeks.

And maybe take you off those drugs.

The joke for the week:

Back in the old homesteading days, a Kansas parson once sold a horse to a member of his congregation. "She's a fine animal," he said, "but there are two things you have to remember. She's been well trained. When you want her to get going, say, 'Praise the Lord'—and at 'Amen,' she'll stop."

The proud new owner saddled her up to ride her home, and when they got out of town she broke into a gallop. Nothing he tried could slow her down; she kept right on going until they were racing toward the edge of a cliff.

At last he remembered what he'd been told, and screamed out, "Amen, Amen," in the nick of time. The horse came to a stop not two feet from the ravine.

"Praise the Lord," said the thankful horseman.

So that's the joke for Week Twelve.

This week you don't have any checklists to check. The only thing you need to do is to make sure you get an appointment to see your doctor and get your blood tests run again. And when you get your tests back it will be time for you to have your graduation party—so don't stop now!

18

The Results, Your Graduation Party, and Life

> *Snatching the eternal out of the desperately fleeting is the great magic trick of human existence.*
>
> Tennessee Williams

Congratulations. You've made it. For twelve weeks you've hung in there. There may have been times every day when it felt a bit as though you and gravity were having a tug-of-war. You were working against the pull of old habits, old patterns, old viewpoints. And I know it was hard.

But you've been accelerating out of the pull of that gravity for twelve weeks now and you've made it. You're in free space now, just traveling. So a lot of congratulations are in order—from yourself, from your buddy, from all the people who have supported you through the program, and from me.

Sometime in the next couple of weeks you'll be throwing a party to celebrate—with all the people who've been a part of this with you.

The week the program ends, you should go to see your doctor again. Take your blood pressure records. Take your new, slimmer body. Get your blood checked again and set up an appointment for next week, to go back and get your results. Enjoy having him tell you that your blood tests look better; that your cholesterol is down; that your triglycerides and blood sugar are down too, if they were out of line before.

If you'd like to, talk to your doctor about having another treadmill stress test. It's up to you, but maybe you'd like to see some "hard proof" about how far you've come with exercise. The test will show you how much longer and faster and higher on the treadmill you can go before you poop out, or before you reach your maximum heart rate.

After you get your test results from your doctor next week, you'll be able to collect all the information you need to make out another Coronary Artery Disease Risk Profile (see Chapter 10 for instructions). There's a blank one in this chapter for you to work with. Enter the data, and compare it with the one you did back in Week Two. See how much your Coronary Artery Disease Risk Profile has changed. I know that if you've followed this program faithfully your Risk Profile will have dropped substantially, particularly if it was pretty high the first time.

Maybe your doctor's going to get you off pills completely now. I'll tell you my way of thinking about it. See if you can get yourself down to either having normal blood pressure or only mild high blood pressure (with a diastolic under 100 or 105, and a systolic under 160 or 170). If you can manage that without taking the pills, then there's very little reason for you to take them.

The growing feeling among the experts is that it doesn't make a lot of sense to treat mild hypertension with pills, particularly if the person is doing something about reducing the other risk factors for heart disease. So if you've stopped smoking, and you've lost some weight, and you exercise regularly, without fail, and you've changed to a healthy diet, then it's not worth it to use pills to try to lower mild high blood pressure into the normal range. There are times when the usual treatment for something simply isn't justified: the beneficial results are just too small.

There are scientific references to back up what I'm saying here in Chapter 20, "Letter to a Physician." You and your doctor should talk it over. And stay in touch with him. Every three to six months, check back with him. Let him know how you're doing. I'm sure that in the coming years the very aggressive drug treatment of mild hypertension that we sometimes see now is going to become a thing of the past.

CORONARY ARTERY DISEASE RISK PROFILE Date: / /

risk factor	your values	very low (0)	low (1)	moderate (2)	high (3)	very high (4)	your points
your age		0 – 29	30 – 39	40 – 49	50 – 59	60 +	
family history of heart disease		none	developed over the age of 50 (2)		developed under the age of 50 (4)		
body weight		near ideal weight	up to 10 lbs. excess	11-20 lbs. excess	21-30 lbs. excess	30 + lbs. excess	
or:							
% body weight as fat (see note a)		less than 20%	20 – 24%	25 – 29%	30 – 35%	more than 35%	
smoking		never	quit	1 – 10 day	11 – 30 day	more than 30 day	
stress factors		very low	low	moderate	high	very high	
fitness level in METS — women		more than 10	8.7-10	7.4-8.6	6.0-7.3	less than 6	
fitness level in METS — men		more than 12	10.7-12	9.4-10.6	8.0-9.3	less than 8	
or:							
physical activity (see note b)		vigorous exercise 20-30min. 4 + x a week	vigorous exercise 20-30min. 2-3 x a week	vigorous exercise 20-30min. 1-2 x a week	occasional vigorous exercise	rarely exercise	
systolic blood pressure		less than 110	110 – 120	120 – 130	130 – 140	more than 140	
diastolic blood pressure		less than 70	70 – 80	80– 90	90 – 100	more than 100	
serum cholesterol		less than 150	150 – 180	180 – 215	215 – 250	more than 250	
or:							
usual dietary intake of saturated fats and cholesterol		nearly vegetarian rare egg dairy or lean meat	several meatless days/wk no butter egg yolk only lean meat non fat dairy	mostly lean meat some eggs & dairy (low fat)	USA average diet meat or eggs or cheese every meal	lot of red meat shell fish liver eggs whole fat dairy 3 + x/day	

subtotal: _____

extra points (notes d – l): _____

total: _____

YOUR PARTY

When you get your test results back from your doctor it will be time to start preparing for your graduation party.

Pick a time for it, call everybody up. Invite them. Your partner. Your family. Your friends and neighbors. The people you see at work every day. Tell them how much their support has meant to you, that you're having a celebration, and that you'd like them to be there to share it with you. Don't forget to invite your doctor. I'll bet he's nearly as delighted with you as you are. And if I'm in town, invite me. I'd love to come to your party.

In case you're wondering what to serve at the party, I've included a number of suggestions, with all the recipes you'll need. And when you go shopping for the food, buy a couple of rolls of crepe paper streamers too. Twist them up, string them across your ceiling—and have a wonderful party!

Here are my suggestions for your celebration menu:

APPETIZERS:
angeled eggs*
hummus*
French onion yogurt dip*
salsa sabrosa*
creamy guacamole dip*
pita bread
bread plate with:
    sourdough,
    whole rye, or
    whole wheat breads
raw vegetable plate with:
    broccoli tops
    cauliflower tops
    carrots
    celery
    cherry tomatoes
    green pepper strips
corn tortillas

COLD SALADS:
Greek island salad*

pasta primavera*
delicious chicken salad*
German potato salad*

ENTREES:
ratatouille*
celebration rice*
meatballs in Middle Eastern sauce*
Indian curried chicken and vegetables*

DESSERTS:
fresh fruit salad*
poached fresh pears with raspberry mint sauce*
banana date bread pudding flambé*

Sounds delicious, doesn't it?

If you prepare the recipes that follow, and serve the menu above, you should have enough food for ten to twelve people. If that's too much, you should cut down on some of the cold foods, since they can't be kept very long, whereas leftover entrees can be frozen.

And remember: you don't need to tell your guests right away that these are "healthy" foods—let them enjoy themselves before you spring that news on them. Encourage them to taste the food, to spend a little time on it and savor it. They'll be surprised that anything this good is also healthy!

Well then, let's move right along to the starred recipes.

ANGELED EGGS

12 large eggs
2 large white potatoes
    or several small red potatoes, boiled
1/4 cup finely chopped onion
1/4 cup minced fresh parsley
1/4 cup finely chopped celery
2–3 tablespoons hot, spicy mustard (to taste)
saffron or curry powder for coloring
paprika for garnishing
dash of red wine vinegar

Hard-boil the eggs and cool quickly. Slice in half lengthwise and scoop out the yolks.

Discard—that's right, discard—the yolks and rinse the egg white halves to remove all traces of yolk. Remember, one egg yolk has 250 mg of cholesterol.

Mash the boiled potatoes and combine them in a bowl with the remaining ingredients.

Fill egg whites with the mixture, garnish with paprika, chill, and serve in nests of alfalfa sprouts.

HUMMUS

Hummus is a Middle Eastern dish with a very distinctive taste. It goes especially well with whole wheat pita bread or Ak-Mak crackers.

> *defatted, unsalted chicken stock (see note)*
> *1/2 onion, chopped*
> *1/4 cup finely chopped parsley*
> *1 tablespoon basil*
> *1 tablespoon oregano*
> *2 tablespoons curry powder, or to taste*
> *1 small clove garlic, minced*
> *juice of 1 lemon*
> *2 tablespoons toasted sesame seeds, crushed*
> *3 cups freshly cooked (not canned)*
>   *garbanzo beans, puréed*

Sauté the onion until transparent in a little chicken stock, using a non-stick frying pan. Add all the remaining ingredients except the garbanzo beans and continue to sauté just until the parsley is soft. Remove from heat, add mixture to puréed garbanzos, and mix well.

Chill well before serving as a dip for raw vegetables or crackers.

Note: Unsalted chicken stock may be purchased in cans in many grocery stores now. Or you can make your own by simmering chicken parts in enough water to cover for about 2 hours. Add onions, carrots, bay leaves, or garlic for more flavor.

To defat stock, chill in refrigerator overnight and spoon the congealed fat from the surface. Leftover stock can be frozen for later use.

FRENCH ONION YOGURT DIP

> *1/4 cup dried minced onion flakes*
> *1 clove garlic, minced*
> *1 teaspoon Parmesan cheese*
> *1 teaspoon Veg-It (low-sodium seasoning)*

freshly ground black pepper, to taste
2 cups nonfat plain yogurt

In a nonstick frying pan, brown the onion flakes. Add the flakes and other seasonings to the yogurt. Fold in well. Return dip to refrigerator and allow it to sit at least overnight for the flavors to blend fully.

Serve next to a plate of celery, carrots, cauliflower and broccoli tops, cherry tomatoes, and green pepper strips.

SALSA SABROSA

4 large tomatoes, chopped
1 medium onion, cut into large pieces
2 canned green chilis or one fresh jalapeño pepper
1 tablespoon red wine vinegar
1 tablespoon fresh cilantro, if available

Combine ingredients in blender or food processor, *very briefly*, just until blended but not homogenized. The salsa should be chunky. Refrigerate and allow to marinate for an hour before serving. Makes about 2 cups.

Serve with homemade toasted corn chips, freshly steamed corn tortillas, or vegetable sticks.

CREAMY GUACAMOLE DIP

2 cups nonfat yogurt
1 ripe avocado (1/2 cup)
2 scallions, whole stalk
1 clove garlic
juice of 1 lemon
chili powder to taste
cumin to taste

Combine all ingredients in a blender and blend until smooth. Chill.

You can serve this as a dip with unsalted crackers or toasted wedges of corn tortillas. To prepare the tortillas, cut them into wedges and spread them out on a cookie sheet. Bake them at 400°, checking them every 2 minutes, until they are lightly browned. Fresh vegetable sticks also make delicious scoopers for this dip.

GREEK ISLAND SALAD

Put a little Greek folk music on the record player while you're doing the cooking for your party and enjoy its tremendous vitality.

> *1 large firm tomato*
> *1 cucumber*
> *1 red onion*
> *3/4 cup freshly cooked (not canned) garbanzo*
> *   beans, chilled*
> *1 small clove garlic*
> *1 tablespoon fresh basil*
> *1 tablespoon fresh oregano*
> *1/2 cup red wine vinegar*
> *1 tablespoon frozen apple juice concentrate*
> *1/2 cup hoop or other nonfat, unsalted cheese*
> *   (optional, if available in your area)*

Cut tomato into wedges. Peel cucumber, slice in half lengthwise, scoop out the seeds, and slice. Slice onion. Put vegetables in a salad bowl, press garlic on top, add herbs, vinegar, and apple juice concentrate. If you use dried herbs, use only 1/2 tablespoon of each. Mix thoroughly. Add cheese cut into small pieces. Allow to marinate at least 2 to 3 hours.

PASTA PRIMAVERA

> *1/2 pound spinach pasta, your choice of shape*
> *1/2 cup broccoli flowerets (tops only)*
> *1 pound frozen baby green peas*
> *2 scallions, finely chopped*
> *1 small jar pimientos (brand without salt)*
> *   or 1/2 fresh red pepper*
> *1/4 cup nonfat yogurt*
> *2 teaspoons red wine vinegar with garlic*
> *1 clove garlic, pressed*
> *1 teaspoon low-sodium stone-ground mustard*
> *1 teaspoon honey*
> *1 teaspoon fresh basil or fresh dill*

Cook the pasta in unsalted water, drain, and rinse.
Lightly steam the broccoli until bright green, about 2 minutes. Cool

quickly to retain color by running it under cold water. Place pasta, broccoli, and thawed peas (raw) in serving dish.

Combine remaining ingredients to make a marinade. Pour over the pasta, broccoli and peas, toss, and chill.

DELICIOUS CHICKEN SALAD

Such surprising flavor contrasts. You may want to save a little out, hiding it for your lunch tomorrow!

> 3 chicken breasts, cooked, skinned, and diced
> 2 red delicious apples, diced
> 2 stalks celery, diced
> 1/4 cup sunflower seeds
> 1/4 cup diced onion
> 1/2 teaspoon poultry seasoning (use a brand,
>   such as Schilling, that contains no salt)
> 1 tablespoon honey
> 1 dash vinegar

Combine all the ingredients and chill. Serve as a salad or tucked into pita bread pockets, which you can then cut into wedges.

GERMAN POTATO SALAD

> 12 new white (very small) or red potatoes
> 1 small onion, diced
> 1 stalk celery, diced
> 3 tablespoons wine vinegar
> 1/4 cup minced fresh parsley
> 2 tablespoons Dijon mustard (available "with
>   no salt added" in many health food stores)
> 1 drop "liquid smoke" flavoring stirred into mustard
> 1 tablespoon Parmesan cheese

Boil the potatoes in their skins. Drain and slice. Add remaining ingredients, toss, and chill before serving. As a variation, this may also be served hot.

RATATOUILLE

This is a delicious French eggplant dish. It is wonderful served with French garlic bread and a tossed salad.

1 large onion, chopped
2 medium zucchini, sliced
1 green pepper, chopped
8 large mushrooms, sliced
1 eggplant, skin on, diced into small cubes
3 medium tomatoes, cut into pieces
1/2 cup tomato paste, "no salt added"
1/2 cup red wine
1 tablespoon frozen apple juice concentrate
2 cloves garlic, minced
1/4 cup minced fresh parsley
2 teaspoons sweet basil
1 teaspoon oregano
1/2 teaspoon freshly ground black pepper

Combine all the ingredients in a large saucepan. Cook, stirring frequently, until vegetables are tender. Reduce heat, cover, and simmer 10 to 15 minutes. Remove cover and continue simmering until excess liquid has evaporated and mixture thickens. Let stand overnight in the refrigerator, if possible, since this really brings out the flavors.

Crock pot method: Use your crock pot and let this cook on low heat all day while you are at work.

CELEBRATION RICE

To me, wild rice is festive, and you've got plenty of reason to celebrate!

2 cups homemade, defatted chicken stock
1 red pepper, cut into strips, or 1 small jar pimientos
   rinsed with fresh water and drained
1 small onion, diced
1 clove garlic, minced
1 stalk celery, diced
1 cup fresh peas or 1 package frozen baby peas
1 teaspoon poultry seasoning (nonsalt variety)
1 cup raw wild rice or 1/2 cup brown rice and 1/2 cup wild rice
2 tablespoons chestnut or walnut pieces

Sauté vegetables and seasoning in small amount of stock until tender. Add remainder of stock and washed rice. Cover and simmer 30 to 45 minutes, until rice is tender and water is absorbed.

Remove from stove and let stand for 10 minutes. Place rice in serving dish and garnish with nuts.

MEATBALLS IN MIDDLE EASTERN SAUCE

1 pound ground turkey breast
1/2 cup toasted whole wheat bread, crumbed
3 egg whites, lightly beaten
1 onion, finely chopped
1 stalk celery, finely chopped
2 cloves garlic, pressed
2 tablespoons fresh minced sweet basil or oregano
  (use dried if necessary)
1 teaspoon fresh or dried minced mint leaves
1 teaspoon freshly ground black pepper
1 tablespoon Veg-It (low-sodium seasoning)

Combine all ingredients in bowl and mix thoroughly. Shape into meatballs and place on nonstick tray or cookie sheet. Bake at 375° for 25 minutes or until lightly browned.

Sauce

1/2 cup defatted unsalted chicken stock
1 cup nonfat yogurt
2 tablespoons cornstarch
1 small cucumber, peeled, seeded, and grated
1/2 teaspoon cumin

Heat stock. Add yogurt mixed with cornstarch. Stir over low heat until thickened. Remove from heat and blend in grated cucumber and cumin. Pour over meatballs in serving dish.

INDIAN CURRIED CHICKEN AND VEGETABLES

4 raw chicken breasts, boned, skinned, trimmed
  of fat, diced
1 box (16 ounces) frozen baby carrots
1 cup fresh cauliflower pieces
2 stalks celery, coarsely chopped
2 tablespoons raisins
1/4 cup diced dried apricots
2 tablespoons honey

1/2 teaspoon ground ginger
1 tablespoon or more (to taste) salt-free curry powder
dash cayenne pepper
1 cup defatted unsalted chicken stock
1 cup nonfat yogurt
3 tablespoons cornstarch
parsley or cilantro for garnish

Place all the ingredients except the yogurt, cornstarch, and parsley in a large skillet. Cook until the chicken is done and the vegetables are tender.

Stir the cornstarch into the yogurt. Over very low heat, add the yogurt mixture and cook until the sauce thickens slightly.

Garnish with fresh parsley or cilantro.

FRESH FRUIT SALAD

1 package frozen, unsweetened cherries or 2 cups
fresh, pitted cherries
3 bananas, peeled and sliced
1 cup seedless red or green grapes
2 oranges, peeled, seeded, cut into bite-sized pieces
1 small can crushed, unsweetened pineapple
1/2 teaspoon rum flavor extract, optional

Combine all in a large bowl. Serve chilled.

POACHED FRESH PEARS WITH RASPBERRY MINT SAUCE

6 medium fresh pears, ripe but firm
1 quart unsweetened pear nectar (or other
fruit juice) for poaching
6 strips lemon peel
1 package (10–12 ounces) frozen raspberries, thawed
(fresh if in season)
1/2 cup honey
1 tablespoon vanilla extract
3 tablespoons cornstarch dissolved in 1/4 cup water
6 fresh mint leaves

Peel pears and core from the bottom with an apple corer. Leave stem on. Place in saucepan with enough juice to cover. Add lemon strips. Bring to a gentle boil and poach until tender (about 15 minutes or until fork easily pierces to center).

Drain and set pears on a serving dish.

Place thawed raspberries in blender or food processor. Blend and strain to remove seeds. Place in a saucepan and bring to boil. Add honey, vanilla extract, and cornstarch in water. Stir until thickened. Remove from heat and pour raspberry sauce over pears, garnish with mint leaves next to the stems. Chill 1/2 hour before serving.

BANANA DATE BREAD PUDDING FLAMBÉ

This is the grand finale. Dim the lights and bring it out at the end for a spectacular display of fireworks. Get everyone to sing, "For he's (she's) a jolly good fellow."

> *1/4 cup unsweetened apple butter*
> *6 slices whole wheat bread*
> *4 egg whites, lightly beaten 5 to 10*
> *   seconds with a whisk*
> *1 can evaporated skim milk*
> *1/2 cup frozen apple juice concentrate*
> *1 tablespoon vanilla extract*
> *1 tablespoon coconut extract*
> *1 tablespoon cinnamon*
> *1/2 teaspoon nutmeg*
> *1 teaspoon grated lemon rind*
> *1/3 cup chopped dates*
> *2 ripe bananas, sliced*
> *rum or brandy, optional (must be*
> *   over 100 proof to flame)*

Spread the apple butter on the bread slices. Cut them into cubes and place in the bottom of an ovenproof casserole. Combine egg whites, evaporated milk, apple juice concentrate, vanilla and coconut extracts, spices, and lemon rind. Pour over bread cubes. Sprinkle with chopped dates and garnish with banana slices and a little more nutmeg.

Place the casserole dish in a baking dish filled with water. Bake at 300° for 1 hour, or until a knife inserted in the center comes out clean.

For a special effect, serve flaming with rum. The alcohol will burn off, leaving just the rum or brandy flavor. For easy flaming, heat rum or brandy in a pan with a strip of lemon peel. Hold a match over the edge of the pan and the liquid will ignite. Rock the pan gently from side to side to spread the flame, and pour over the pudding.

Have a wonderful party!

AND NOW WHAT?

After twelve weeks, your program is over. As the saying goes, today is the first day of the rest of your life. Your body probably feels a whole lot better than it has in a long time. So keep enjoying it. By now you've discovered a diet that works for you. You're well in stride with your regular exercise program. And you're getting much more agile at dodging stress. Your blood pressure's lower now, and your medicines have probably been cut way back, if not stopped altogether.

Fantastic.

In the process of following this program you've discovered a new way of living that works for you. You're going to want to keep it up. Because you feel great. You'll still want to check your blood pressure once a day, just to make sure things are going well. And weigh yourself once a week. If the diet you worked out has resulted in some pounds disappearing from here and there, you'll want to continue it until you hit the weight you'd like to have. And then level out.

Your exercise times will continue to improve. Just keep getting in those thirty to thirty-five minutes at Training Heart Rate with the stretching, the warm-up, and the cool-down: Your body will surprise you. A year from now it will be able to do nearly effortlessly what may have been almost impossible just twelve weeks ago.

By now you've spent enough time listening to the tape recordings you made that you may want to start phasing them out. You know what they say. Start to just "hear" them in your head when a stressful situation arises. If you want a refresher, go back and pop a tape in the machine. But you can do it, you can relax. Keep spending some time each day doing the muscle relaxation, or a little meditation, or reminding yourself of a couple of affirmations, or simply imagining yourself in a beautiful place.

You've been in training for twelve weeks: now just let the program be a normal part of your life. The results are going to keep happening. You may backslide a little here and there, but if you do, don't feel badly—and don't let go. You've worked hard for this. It's yours now.

One of the ways you may find to stay in touch with the ideas in this program is to tell other people about what you've done. If somebody you talk to gets excited and wants to do it, offer to be a buddy. You've been through it: you can really help someone else who wants to do it.

And keep in touch with your doctor.

I had thought about offering some specific advice about what to do over the coming months and years. There isn't a lot more I can tell you, really. You're a much different person now in many ways, not the least of which is that you know a lot more. So you can really tell me a few things: what worked for you and what didn't; and how you handle your new life style, once the program is over.

You're now educated, innovative, maybe even experimental. The old saying, "Necessity is the mother of invention," can work for you. How are you (the new you) going to relate to your doctor? Work it out. You're probably not cured yet, but you've learned to handle the blood pressure problem in a different, healthier way, and it's going to get better and better as time goes by.

Oh, your pressure may still go up and down sometimes, or even a lot. But if you're not eating salt, and have lost some weight, and are exercising regularly, your pressure going up and down is just an indicator of the old emergency nervous system turning on too much. Your pressure may still go up when you see your doctor, so be sure to take along your blood pressure records every time you see him.

It's a matter of attitude really. You and your doctor need to stop thinking of you as someone with a Chronic Illness and begin to look at it as something that can be handled. I'll give you an example.

Irma came in the other day to exercise on the track at our clinic. She's in her sixties and she's still on a diuretic and a blocker. She had run out of the diuretic four days before, her weight was up four pounds, and I guess she was pretty worried about what her pressure would be.

Our exercise leader called me over to check it, because she'd got a reading over 240! I took Irma's pressure and told her, in a calm and reassuring voice, "It's 280/126—that's up pretty high today, isn't it?" I asked her to walk slowly around the track for a while. Her pressure fell to 180/86 within twenty minutes. And I sent her out to refill her prescription.

I know some doctors would have given her medicine in the vein or swept her off to the hospital in an ambulance. A blood pressure of 280/126! It's a wonder that I didn't get any chest pains! But I trusted Irma and thought that, if what I was suggesting worked, it would be such a good lesson for her. It gives the control back to her—and then I'm just on the sidelines, coaching and cheering her on.

That's what I want you to get from your doctor—coaching, and lots of encouragement. That's what you need, and that's what you can get if you ask for it.

Once again, congratulations. And keep it up.

Readings

19

The White Lab Coat

*I got Hip on this Expedition that there
is a GREAT POWER WITHIN which
when used with Purity, Unselfishness
and Immaculate Thought can Cure,
Heal and Cause Miracles. When you
use it, it Spreads like a Magic Garden.
AND WHEN YOU DO NOT USE
IT, it recedes from you.*

Lord Buckley, *The Religious History
of Núñez Cabeza de Vaca*

I'd like you to sit on my side of the desk for a change. I'd like you to wear
my lab coat for a while and see what it feels like to be a doctor practicing
medicine in the 1980s. And I'd like to introduce myself. I want to tell you
a little of my own story, and I want to do this for three reasons.

First, I'd like to dispel some of the priestly aura that hangs around
doctors. Throughout this book I have tried to avoid talking in the secret
language of medicine and to speak to you in my own natural voice. I find
that, if you view doctors as near-almighty beings with a special knowledge

that you can never hope to match, you wind up taking less and less care of yourself, and your physician winds up relying more and more on technology and less and less on compassion and common sense to keep you well.

Second, I'd like you to be able to understand why I have come to the conclusions I have about high blood pressure and the practice of medicine in general. I would like you to know the experiences that have led me to put this particular kind of program together and to write this book.

And I would like you to know that I have done research in the best labs, taught in the finest schools, and worked in the most advanced medical clinics—so that you have confidence in me and know that I'm not some complete outsider coming into the field with a new and untested theory. I want to give you my credentials.

Third, I'd like you to know that I've been through some of the things I'll be asking you to go through. I've changed my diet, and quit smoking, and taken up jogging—and none of these things looked easy to begin with, but I learned how to do them, and I did them, and I know they can be done. I'd like to share some of my newfound confidence with you, and I'd like you to feel more confident in yourself.

Now for a little information about myself.

My grandfather was called Cleaves Bennett, and I was named for him. He was a family doctor, a general practitioner in downstate Illinois, and he was beloved by everyone. People trusted him. They felt better when he came over to see them, even though he didn't have a lot of tricks in his bag, the way doctors do nowadays. He didn't have a lot of modern diagnostic tests to perform, and he probably didn't use a lot of the tests that were available back then—but he had a good sense about people, he could understand what they needed and what they wanted. He really made a contribution to people's lives, and they loved him for it.

As soon as I could talk, people used to ask me, "Are you going to be a doctor when you grow up?" And even when I was a little kid I thought that was a great idea. I never really thought about being a fireman, or an engineer, or anything like that. I always knew I was going to grow up to be a doctor like my grandfather.

Ironically, my grandfather died of high blood pressure right after I was born, so I never got to know him. But I knew where I was headed from the time I was old enough to know there were things to be when you grew up. I had a goal in life.

It was a great advantage, knowing what I wanted to do. Going through the school system, I didn't really have to ask myself whether I like to study so hard, whether I enjoyed taking Latin and German and mathematics and physics and chemistry and zoology and biology—all the courses that you needed to take if you were going into medicine. Those were the things I needed to do, and I just didn't question them. A lot of people are run around by what they like and don't like. I didn't worry much about it. I just did what it took to reach my goal, which was to become a doctor.

I went to medical school at the University of Rochester in New York, an excellent school. While I was there I became close friends with two academicians, two men with the qualities most needed in modern medicine—a lot of compassion and a lot of smarts. One was the associate dean, the other was an assistant professor in medicine. I admired them both tremendously, and I sought to be like them. They were very knowledgeable, humanistic people—educated, articulate, and cultured. And through my friendship with these two men, I decided I wanted to become an academician.

I dropped out of medical school for a year and helped in some very sophisticated research on the heart. When I came back I wrote up my research as a thesis and was able to get my M.D. with honors.

Next I decided to come out to California. I'd been there before and liked it, and I thought I'd enjoy the sun, and meet some pretty girls, and that kind of thing. I had a fantasy about marrying a movie star. So I came out to California and really did marry a starlet. She was gorgeous, she'd been Miss California, she was in the movies, and we got married.

I did my internship and my residency at UCLA. Let me tell you how they teach you internal medicine at a first-rate teaching institution. You have a patient who has a problem or problems. You bring in a brain specialist and a heart specialist, a liver expert, a lung specialist, a back person, and so on—and you learn from all of them.

You are the general physician who has to take care of the whole person, and you bring in all these specialists, and then you have to negotiate, to mediate between the competing specialties. The specialists are all arguing about what to do with your patient, each from his own point of view. The treatment one specialist suggests for your patient's asthma may make his blood pressure worse, which another specialist is trying to avoid.

So, as a young doctor, you find yourself ending up with an enormous responsibility—you have to make really important choices between the sometimes conflicting suggestions offered by your various teachers. It's not a good system—but it was the only system I knew, and I stayed with it a long time. I was a student in that system, I was an intern in it, I was a resident in it—first at UCLA and then in New York—and along the way it became clear to me that I really liked to teach.

To teach—to become an academician—you have to do research. So when my formal training as a physician was over, when I'd completed my residency, I went to the National Institutes of Health in Bethesda, Maryland, and spent nearly four years learning how to do research.

I was lucky enough to work with one of the world's foremost kidney physiologists, Dr. Robert Berliner. His lab was the most prestigious kidney research lab in the world, and that's where I was. I was in the best place there was for learning how the kidney works—and that's what I wanted to do.

I learned about the scientific method. I learned how to take an idea like, "Gee, I wonder what that is and how it works," and go on from there to design an experiment, learn all the techniques I'd need to carry it out, then to carry it out, organize my results, analyze them, write them up, and get them published.

I was using the most sophisticated equipment and techniques—computers, calculus, microchemistry. We even had a biomedical engineering lab there.

We needed to learn how to measure the amount of potassium in a drop of urine that was so small you couldn't even see it. The drop was from one of the million or so tiny little tubes (called *nephrons)* which make up a mammalian kidney. The drop itself might be less than a micron wide, the volume would be down around 25 picoliters. Now a picoliter is one thousandth of a nanoliter, a nanoliter is one thousandth of a microliter, a microliter is one thousandth of a milliliter, and there are a thousand of those in a liter. We were trying to study the potassium content in a drop of liquid that weighed a little less than one ten-millionth of an ounce.

We designed an air-driven micropipette sharpener—and even the name should give you some idea of just how delicate an engineering job that was. We went beyond any existing technology. We tested out equipment to handle the drops of fluid so that they wouldn't evaporate. If they were exposed to the air for an instant they were gone—so we had to keep them under oil at all times. We even had to find the right kind of oil to use—because there are thousands of types of oil, and most of them would easily absorb that small a quantity of liquid. Then we had to put the drops into the machine we'd designed, and activate the sodium and potassium in each drop so they would emit a light, and then we measured the amount of light they emitted.

You can see that we went to very great lengths to get the most minor details just right, and if the project involved engineering and microchemistry and computer modeling, so be it. It was incredibly exciting.

From there I went on to Duke University for a couple of years to do further research. I would go off to scientific meetings, and our lab would tell them our results, and other people would tell us their results, and after a while—it took me several years to figure this out—I discovered that none of this was really helping anybody very much.

I was writing papers that cleverly disproved the papers that someone else had written the year before, and the next year someone would write a paper that cleverly disproved mine, and I would write another, and so on. It was a kind of intellectual sparring, and we were all doing it as if it was an end in itself.

What we were doing, of course, was advancing up the academic ladder —becoming assistant professors, and associate professors, and professors, and making our curricula vitae a little bulkier, a little more impressive each year.

In a sense I am exaggerating here, but it didn't seem to me that I was making much of a contribution to people's lives, and none of us were really asking ourselves, "How does this help anyone?"

Finally I came back out to UCLA, and I began to get interested in doing lab work that definitely made a contribution to people. I happened to get into a line of research in which I could actually see the mechanism of kidney disease, and this helped me. I could take the knowledge I was getting in my lab right to the bedside and use it to help my patients.

This also made me a more effective teacher. I could explain what was happening in the patient to the young doctors who were now my students —using my lab work as the basis of my explanation. I tried to make all my work—as a researcher, as a teacher, and principally as a physician—as helpful to the patient as possible.

I was a pretty controversial teacher. My students either loved me or hated me. I would come into the Intensive Care Unit and see some poor soul lying there with a tube in every orifice and a list of medications so long that no one doctor could tell you what they were all for. And I would say things like, "We have to take all these tubes out—this person has to sit up, look outside, and say 'I want to go there.' "

Once you get the patient to take an interest in being alive, then you've got it made. Then you can cut down on the medications. But if you don't do that you can give all the medicines you want and the patient's not going to get better—in fact is maybe going to die. The patient has got to want to get out of there *a lot* in order to make it. It doesn't matter what else you do—you have got to have the patient on your side.

Some of the young doctors liked that approach, but I guess some of them thought it was crazy. I don't know exactly what they were thinking, but maybe it ran something like this: "All we have to do is keep the blood gases right, and the blood sugar right, and the blood urea right, and make sure all the bleeps and squiggles and flashing lights are right, and look after all those medicines and tubes and fluids—we just have to take care of it all." And I'd come around as their professor and often find out they'd given the wrong amount of something. They were real amateur gods.

As I said before, the system involved a committee of specialists looking after the patients. There was the heart doctor, and the bone marrow doctor, and the brain doctor, and they sometimes didn't understand one another. If you were a kidney doctor you didn't know very much about bones or hearts—you were too busy keeping up on all the thousands and thousands of papers about kidney research, learning more and more all the time about less and less. Believe me, that's the trap I was in.

So I began to see that the patient didn't matter to the system. It was a little like veterinary medicine. The patient wasn't a participant at all. The technology had become so sophisticated, the computers and diagnostic tools were so incredibly complex, that even other doctors didn't understand what was going on, let alone the patient.

As a result we began not to talk to the patient. How are you going to explain the calculus, the chemistry, the computer program, the technical wizardry to your patient? You don't try. You just say, "Trust me, Mrs. Jones, we need to do this little test." Medicine in a large hospital was getting so heavily technological, it was becoming inhuman.

It took me five years of growing disenchantment with the whole system —and finally, one day, I just walked out on it. I didn't want to do it anymore. I didn't want to teach it anymore. I didn't even believe in it. It wasn't working. It seemed to make so little difference to people's lives.

Looking back now, I can see why I was so dissatisfied. I had become a doctor—but not the kind of doctor my grandfather was, beloved of his patients. No. I had become another kind of doctor completely—the sort of doctor who sits in an office, does a lot of reading and research, goes to all the meetings, and teaches young doctors—but who has somehow lost touch with people. Patients didn't get to know me, sick people didn't have a chance to trust me—and something was very wrong with what I was doing.

So I quit.

And I went off to Saudi Arabia. I went back to seeing patients, doing procedures, and staying up all night when I was on call. I wanted to make sure I hadn't forgotten how to do all those things, because I'd been a professor for so long and had students and interns and residents to do them for me. I found I hadn't forgotten, and I really got my confidence back in the seven months I spent in Saudi Arabia.

I came back with the idea that I had to do something other than the same old academic medicine game. I wanted to learn how to take care of myself, and then to teach patients how to take care of themselves.

At that point in my life I had already quit smoking, after agonizing about it for three or four years. But I wasn't exercising, my diet was abominable, and with my insatiable sweet tooth I was looking more and more like a Hostess Twinkie.

Over the last six years, what I have done is learn how to take care of myself and how to pass that knowledge on. My first step was to work with Nathan Pritikin, who has probably done more than any man I know to raise the consciousness of doctors and other people in this country about the importance of nutrition. Whether you agree with all his ideas or not, he has certainly put nutrition center stage and turned the floodlights on it. He preaches practical, preventive nutrition. He has a positive impact on the lives of many people, and it was a real privilege to work with him for two years.

At the time when I was beginning to work at the Pritikin Center, I was also taking care of some hemodialysis patients. I remember one of my patients very clearly. He was a very large man who used to weigh around three hundred pounds and was now in the low two hundreds. He had diabetes and high blood pressure. And the diabetes was causing blindness; he had kidney failure; and closure of the small blood vessels in his legs caused him recurrent infections, and poorly healing ulcers in his feet.

I took care of this man for about two years, and you know I could never persuade him to lose weight, never got him to understand what his diet was doing to him. I tried to explain it all but never could get through. I had to give him more and more medicine for his various ailments, and I watched him go slowly blind, lose one leg below the knee—and suffer endlessly.

At one point I told him his blood pressure was still too high and I was going to have to give him even more pills, and he asked me, "Isn't there anything else I could do?" I told him, "Sure—go on a diet, stop eating so much salt, and begin to take better care of yourself." Somewhere deep inside, I think he really wanted to do it—but he didn't think he could. He thought about it for a while. Then he told me, "Forget it; I guess I'd rather take the pills."

He was a brave man, with a lot of heart, and he was making what he thought was the best of a progressively deteriorating situation. But his lack of self-confidence when it came to changing his life around was more than he could handle.

I remember him vividly, because the people who came to me at the Pritikin Center were so different. They were willing to do something really fundamental to participate in their own care and to improve the quality of their lives. I saw people losing weight, lowering their blood pressure, exercising more, and feeling better. I saw people come off insulin, and blood pressure pills, and heart medicines. And I actually became very good at tapering people off medications, which is not something most internists know much about.

It turned my life around to see what happened to people who got on an excellent diet, started exercising, lost their stress, and gave up smoking and coffee habits. I didn't know people could feel that much better. I didn't know patients could be thrilled and pleased and satisfied.

By now I felt I really understood something about how to look after myself—but the question still bothered me: "How can I teach other people what I know, people who so often think, 'It's all very well that you did it, but I could never do that'—so that they will be able to make it a part of their own lives?"

About that time I had the good fortune to run into Tim Gallwey and to learn about the new system of teaching he was pioneering. Tim is the author of *The Inner Game of Tennis* and a number of other books, and I count our friendship as one of the most profound influences in my life. He taught me one of those simple truths that are so easily forgotten—that people really learn all the most important things by experience.

The first few times I sat and talked with Tim, I knew I'd found what I was looking for. Since I first tried to motivate people to change their diet or take up exercise, there had always been one thing I didn't know how to do—how to empower people to make the changes I was talking about, which they wanted to make, without the cloud of self-doubt and discouragement getting in their way.

Tim knew how to get people past their self-doubt better than anyone else I'd ever encountered. That was the skill I needed to really make an impact on my patients' lives. Let me give you an example of the kinds of barriers I am talking about. When I took up jogging some years ago, I had a lot of reservations before I started. I had resisted exercising completely for many years. I simply couldn't imagine myself going out to jog in the mornings—I used to be pretty defensive about it; I thought it was totally ridiculous, out of the question.

One day I went to a meeting to give a lecture on high blood pressure. I happened to stay around to hear the next speaker, who was president of the American College of Physicians, and he was telling us about the joys and beauty of jogging. He had some beautiful slides; he was in his fifties; he'd run in the Boston Marathon; he looked fit and trim. I was really impressed. I said to myself, "Dammit, I'm going to do that."

So I started. When I first began to run, after a few hundred feet my chest hurt, I was huffing and puffing, I felt faint, and I thought I was going to die. It took several months to get to the point where I could actually run a mile without stopping. And when I timed myself a month or so later, and found I was running a mile in twelve minutes, I didn't think that was all that bad.

Then a friend who was into jogging and hiking compared notes with me. He looked at me. "A twelve-minute mile?" He grinned. "That doesn't even qualify as running—that's a fast walk." I read Ken Cooper's book *Aerobics* and discovered that if you can run a mile in twelve minutes you're right on the border line between poor and very poor condition.

Over the next year I built myself up to the point where I could run a mile in eight minutes and began to increase my mileage from about one and a half miles a day until I could easily run five, and sometimes on weekends I ran ten or even fifteen miles. I enjoyed it. And now I can't really imagine not jogging.

I guess the point here is that my attitudes about jogging were the biggest hurdle I had to face—and they got in my way for the longest time. In my experience, it's almost always our attitudes and beliefs about ourselves—underestimating our power, abilities, and self-worth—that are the biggest barriers to our making positive changes in our lives.

What I've learned from Tim Gallwey is how to speed the whole process up, how to get people to move out into new territory without bringing all their old attitudes with them. He taught me a method of getting people past their hurdles; and for me the most exciting point is that, as you do so, you can not only be an effective student, you can become an effective teacher of his method too, by the same process.

I don't regret any of the stages that I went through. From Rochester to UCLA, to New York, to Dr. Berliner's lab, to Duke, back to UCLA, to

Saudi Arabia, and then to Pritikin and Gallwey, I have always gone to the best, studied with the best, and been pretty open to the best of new ideas.

I now feel completely competent to teach what I have learned about maintaining a human body. I have learned how to feel better than I used to believe possible. I have seen the lives of my patients transformed. And in this book I hope to show you, using the best that I have learned from all over, how you can transform your life and get away from those terrible pills.

And the most amazing part of it all for me is that I have discovered that I am now much closer to the kind of doctor my grandfather was. And I know very well, taking care of a large number of patients as I do, that my patients now know me, love me, admire me, and trust me.

I seem to have stumbled onto the path I always wanted to take.

20

Letter to a Physician

> *Each patient carries his own doctor inside him. They come to us not knowing that truth. We are at our best when we give the doctor who resides within each patient a chance to go to work.*
>
> Albert Schweitzer

Dear Doctor,

Your patient and I are grateful to you for taking time to read this letter. I will be brief and to the point.

By reading this book, your patient is expressing a desire to work in partnership with you on his or her own health care. Your patient will learn to attend to those aspects of life, such as diet, exercise, and stress management, that have traditionally been outside the purview of busy medical practitioners. Your patient will also help you make certain observations, such as home blood pressure measurements, that will make it easier for you to make decisions regarding appropriate medical treatment.

The premises upon which this program is based are derived in part from the current medical literature, as well as from my own experience in teaching and patient care. I have detailed these premises in the appended paper and bibliography that conclude this chapter.

In brief, my contention is that hypertension is not a disease per se but comes about principally because of the combined effects of

1. sodium intake and
2. stress
3. in susceptible individuals
4. over time.

How can we physicians influence this complex process? My own experience tells me that lifelong use of one or more medications to manage hypertension is not at all desirable, not if it can be avoided. My patients tell me the same thing, either to my face or by "dropping out" of any chronic drug treatment program I devise.

The approach I have used with considerable success is as follows:

1. Encourage the patient to understand his or her disease as completely as possible, and to participate in measurements of weight, blood pressure, etc., that will make the process more real and the patient more responsible for what is happening in his or her body.

2. Help the patient understand the nature of the risks involved in high blood pressure, smoking, obesity, etc., by constructing a Coronary Artery Disease Risk Profile.

3. Gradually introduce the patient over a twelve-week period to a progressively more impactful diet, exercise, and stress management program, all of it self-taught and practiced in the home.

4. Meet frequently with the patient to discuss progress, provide encouragement, and consider reduction in medications.

My experience with patients who are

      a making frequent measurements of blood pressure at home and work;

      b conscientiously reducing the intake of salt, fat, and, if appropriate, calories;

      c exercising regularly at some recommended level of intensity; and

      d practicing other techniques to produce a state of relaxation daily or at least several times a week,

is that *it is safe to taper antihypertensive medicines* to determine their need.

Home BP measurements are critical here. Blood pressure may rise considerably when the patient comes to your office to see if you approve of what he or she is doing, so I have found an experimental approach works best: "We'll try reducing the propranolol slowly over the next week or so and see what happens. If the pressure rises too much we'll assume that we were premature and we'll try again later." Under such controlled conditions, very little harm can come from this.

The current literature suggests that mild hypertension (diastolic less than 105; systolic less than 160–80, depending on age) need not be treated with drugs if other coronary risk factors can be reduced or eliminated. My aim is to help patients with this problem to be more physically active, give up cigarettes, eat less salt, animal fat, and cholesterol, lose weight, and learn to relax.

Sometimes elimination of diuretics and/or beta blockers will improve the lipid profile and carbohydrate tolerance. This may reduce coronary risk more than might have occurred from further blood pressure lowering with drugs.

In summary, mild hypertension in the absence of other risk factors is such a benign process that it need not be treated with medication; it is susceptible to hygienic management.

I hope this brief overview of the theory and practice of the program has been helpful. Please feel free to write to me, in care of the publisher, with questions, criticism, or comments. I want this book to make a contribution to your patients' overall medical care and quality of life. I value your input and will whenever possible respond to it.

Thank you for your time.

Sincerely,
Cleaves M. Bennett, M.D., F.A.C.P.

PREMISES CONCERNING THE CAUSES OF HYPERTENSION

The premises upon which this program is based are as follows:

1. Hypertension is not a disease, per se, but the *skewed* upper end of a normal distribution of a particular parameter, blood pressure.

2. The condition becomes increasingly more common with age. Using the liberal definition of hypertension (140/90 or above), the incidence is approximately 1 in 10 at age twenty-five to thirty-four, and 2 in 3 at age sixty-five to seventy-four years.

3. The hypertensive *diseases* come about because of the long-term harmful or destructive effects of high pressure on the vascular system (cerebral arteries and arterioles, retinal arterioles, coronary arteries, and renal arterioles and glomeruli) and on the left ventricular myocardium.

4. High blood pressure comes about principally because of the combined harmful effects of:

    a a high-sodium dietary intake and

    b prolonged sustained emotional/psychological/adrenergic nervous system arousal ("stress")

    c in susceptible individuals

    d over time.

SODIUM:

5. Lifelong habitual high sodium intake in most members of the population occurs because of the increasing dependence on processed foods in the home and the habit of frequent eating at restaurants and fast food establishments. Sodium in foods vastly enhances their marketability in terms of taste, texture, and shelf life, so that manufacturers are loath to remove it.

6. Adults on typical high-sodium diets *who are normal in every respect* carry five to ten pounds of excess extracellular fluid (ECF) compared to adults on a low- (approximately one gram) sodium diet.

7. Thus virtually all members of a salt-eating society are extracellular fluid volume expanded, and as a result are more sensitive to the blood-pressure-raising effects of adrenergic arousal. Indeed, sodium loading seems to produce adrenergic arousal.

STRESS:

8. Chronic sustained adrenergic arousal comes about because of

    a learned behavior at a very young age, in the family/neighborhood/school—(Type A personality is an example of this);

    b the complexity and fast pace of modern life—the rapid commu-
      nication, omnipresent dangers and opportunities, the obligatory
      responsibilities;

    c repeated ill fortune; and

    d frequent simulated danger and horror—at the movies, on TV,
      etc.

9. Adrenergic arousal may lead to:

    a reduced venous capacity, leading to high cardiac preload;

    b increased heart rate, strength of contraction and cardiac ejection
      fraction;

    c increased renal and peripheral vascular resistance (PVR);

    d a tendency for reduced renal blood flow and renal sodium excre-
      tion, for which rising blood pressure is compensatory in order to
      maintain renal sodium excretion constant and equal to intake.

SUSCEPTIBILITY:

10. Susceptibility to hypertension may involve either or both of these
two areas—sodium/ECF volume or stress/adrenergic arousal.

    a Sodium susceptibility may be an expression of a genetically
      transmitted renal factor, which in a salt-eating culture leads to
      greater extracellular fluid volume (ECF) expansion in those af-
      flicted than in those not afflicted. Thus the renal factor is a
      relative resistance to sodium excretion, which then requires a
      greater ECF volume and a higher blood pressure to assure a
      fractional sodium excretion commensurate with sodium intake.

    b Stress susceptibility may be an expression of an inherited and/or
      learned tendency to translate chronic adrenergic arousal into
      elevated blood pressure (rather than into asthma, peptic ulcer
      disease, skin rashes, colitis, etc.). The power of this factor to
      raise blood pressure is related to the product: stressful circum-
      stances $\times$ cardiovascular susceptibility. A very susceptible indi-
      vidual (whose target was cardiovascular) would raise blood pres-
      sure repeatedly over trivial matters, whereas a very resistant
      individual could weather almost any storm and never raise the
      blood pressure.

11. Susceptibility can be expressed in quantitative terms. Highly susceptible individuals (who eat salt) become hypertensive in childhood or
the teen years, whereas resistant individuals become hypertensive very late
in life if at all. Most of us are somewhere in between.

12. In any group of hypertensives one sees a broad spectrum, from
those in whom ECF volume expansion is relatively more important (low

renin hypertension) to those in whom ECF volume is normal or even low (high renin hypertension). In the latter group, adrenergic arousal is associated with increases in other vasopressor factors as well.

TIME:

13. As the patient ages, several factors appear in time which strongly influence this process:

    a Excessive calories/sedentary life style lead to obesity, which of itself elevates blood pressure
- by mechanical/hydraulic means (blood volume, cardiac output, etc.).
- by producing further adrenergic arousal.

    b High cholesterol/animal fat intake promotes atherosclerosis of aorta and its major branches, leading to systolic hypertension; hypertension and other risk factors such as smoking, obesity, stress, and lack of exercise in turn accelerate the further development of atherosclerosis—a self-perpetuating process.

    c Continued lifelong high protein/sodium intake produces a gradual reduction in the kidneys' ability to excrete sodium and increases resistance to the diuretic effect of high blood pressure; this converts less susceptible persons into more susceptible persons. This renal destruction is hastened by high blood pressure. The advanced stage of this process is called *nephrosclerosis*. The kidney by this stage is liable to be strongly sodium retaining.

    d Peripheral vascular (arteriolar) resistance rises because of
1 high sodium content and edema of arteriolar wall;
2 hypertrophy of its medial (muscular) wall layer;
3 fibrosis;
4 chronic myogenic reflex stimulation and continued adrenergic arousal;
5 loss of arterioles (rarefaction).

    e Under the influence of hypertension and continued repeated stimulation by the adrenergic nervous system, left ventricular hypertrophy occurs. This hypertrophy leads to a left ventricle that is more powerful and capable of generating higher systolic pressure and greater stroke work under the continued influence of adrenergic arousal and high cardiac preload.

    f Other dietary factors, such as low potassium, high fat, high meat, and low calcium, exert their additive effects on raising blood pressure; as do drugs such as nicotine, caffeine, alcohol,

birth control pills, and decongestants, any of which may be used
intermittently or continuously.

Thus at a later stage in essential hypertension the pathophysiology may
have changed considerably. Its continuance (as distinguished from the
originating factors) depends on:
1. high dietary sodium (few are successful in handling this);
2. prolonged sustained adrenergic nervous system arousal (fewer still
handle this);
3. in susceptible individuals whose susceptibility is inherited, learned,
or acquired through some pathologic process:
    a nephrosclerosis and enhanced sodium retention;
    b myocardial hypertrophy;
    c hyperactive adrenergic nervous system;
    d generalized arteriolarsclerosis;
    e generalized atherosclerosis;
    f obesity.
(As before, the importance of each of these "susceptibility" factors varies
among individuals.)

Thus hypertension is seen not as a disease caused by a contagious agent,
nor as an example of the spontaneous and unlucky breakdown of a physio-
logic system. Rather it is the result of the long-term, repeated, or continuous operation of a rather large number of different factors, each of which
tends to raise blood pressure.

Given the ubiquitous nature of many of these factors in a country such
as the United States, nearly one half of people over forty, and two thirds
of people over the age of sixty-five (in aggregate, some 60 million adults),
are hypertensive at least part of the time. Some authorities have even
inquired into the possibility that something has found its way accidentally
into the water supply.

In fact the causes have been found in the food that we all eat and in our
everyday lives. And even if we are lucky enough not to have been born
with a great sensitivity to these external factors, we soon enough begin to
acquire greater sensitivity to them by the gradual erosion of renal function
as a consequence of continued high sodium/protein intake and excretion
(13c, page 220).

Thus the changes that occur in time in the individual tend to worsen
and cause the persistence of the high blood pressure, so that, later on,
removal or reduction of some of these factors (e.g., the high sodium diet)

may not immediately produce much (or even any) beneficial effect. This is particularly true if the adrenergic arousal persists because of the psychosocial and/or pathophysiologic reasons enumerated above.

One final factor plays an important role in the persistence of or the gradual improvement in high blood pressure in older patients aged approximately sixty or above. As the myocardium ages in sedentary individuals, it tends to weaken and become less efficient, and cardiac output falls.

This may:

      a be due to a progressive sclerosis and loss of muscle mass, the result of atherosclerosis and the chronic muscle hypoxia associated with myocardial hypertrophy;

      b come about in part from the lessened adrenergic arousal that one would expect to occur in older, retired, more sedentary persons.

As the pump weakens its beat, the pressure *must* fall. This is a time when patients are especially sensitive to congestive heart failure, and so sodium restriction is vitally important in this group.

The potential for intervention here is very great and of utmost importance. If lifetime medication is to be avoided, a variety of strategies must be employed simultaneously. A "low-sodium" diet alone may not work if the renal lesion is pretty far along (even though the serum creatinine may not be raised), and the patient needs attention paid to heretofore unrecognized adrenergic arousal as well.

The program outlined in this book addresses all the etiologic factors in each individual (except, of course, the genetic ones), and so offers a high likelihood of success in most patients.

BIBLIOGRAPHY

Quill, T. E. "Partnerships in Patient Care: A Contractual Approach," *Ann. Int. Med.* 98: 228–34 (1983).

Maxwell, M., et al. "Nonpharmacologic Intervention," *Dialogues in Hypertension* 4:3:1–8 (1982).

Finnerty, F. A. "Step-Down Therapy in Hypertension," *JAMA* 246: 2593–96 (1981).

Pickering, T. G., et al. "Blood Pressure During Normal Daily Activities, Sleep and Exercise," *JAMA* 247: 992–96 (1982).

Kaplan, N. M. "Hypertension: Prevalence, Risks, and Effect of Therapy," *Ann. Int. Med.* 98 (Pt. 2): 705–9 (1983).

National Center for Health Statistics, M. Rowland, and J. Roberts. "Blood Pressure Levels and Hypertension in Persons Ages 6–74 Years: United States, 1976–80," *Advance Data from Vital and Health Statistics,* #84. DHHS Pub. No.(PHS) 82–1250. Hyattsville, Md.: Public Health Service (1982).

Kotchen, J. M., et al. "Blood Pressure Trends with Aging," *Hypertension* 4 (Supp. III): III-128–34 (1982).

Cruz-Coke, R. "Etiology of Essential Hypertension," *Hypertension* 3 (Supp. II): II-191–94 (1981).

Havlik, R. J., and M. Feinleib. "Epidemiology and Genetics of Hypertension," *Hypertension* 4 (Supp. III): III-121–27 (1982).

"Genetics, Environment, and Hypertension," *Lancet* 1: 681–82 (1983).

Iwai, J., ed. *Salt and Hypertension.* New York: Igaku-Shoin, 1982.

Tobian, L. "Dietary Salt (Sodium) and Hypertension," *Am. J. Clin. Nutr.* 32: 2659–62 (1979).

Battarbee, H. D., and G. R. Meneely. "The Toxicity of Salt," *CRC Critical Reviews in Toxicology,* September 1978, pp. 355–76.

Trevisan, M., et al. "Dietary Salt and Blood Pressure," *Preventive Med.* 12: 133–37 (1983).

Tobian, L. "The Relationship of Salt to Hypertension," *Am. J. Clin. Nutr.* 32: 2739–48 (1979).

Denton, D. "Hypertension: A Malady of Civilization?" in Sambhi, M. P., ed. *Systemic Effects of Antihypertensive Agents.* Chicago: Yearbook Medical Publishers, 1976.

Joossens, J. V., and J. Geboers. "Salt and Hypertension," *Preventive Med.* 12: 53–59 (1983).

Rose, G. "Epidemiology of Familial Factors and Salt Intake in Man," *Postgrad. Med. J.* 43 (Supp. 2): 139–43 (1977).

Porter, G. "Chronology of the Sodium Hypothesis and Hypertension," *Ann. Int. Med.* 98 (Pt. 2): 720–23 (1983).

Hunt, J. C. "Sodium Intake and Hypertension: A Cause for Concern," *Ann. Int. Med.* 98 (Pt. 2): 724–28 (1983).

Luft, F. C., et al. "Sodium Sensitivity in Normotensive Human Subjects," *Ann. Int. Med.* 98 (Pt. 2): 758–62 (1983).

————, and M. H. Weinberger. "Sodium Intake and Essential Hypertension," *Hypertension* 4 (Supp. III): III-14–29 (1982).

Weitzman, R. E., et al. "Effect of Opposing Osmolar and Volume Factors on Plasma Arginine Vasopressin in Man," *Mineral Electrolyte Metabol.* 1: 43–47 (1978).

Brown, W. J., et al. "Exchangeable Sodium and Blood Volume in Normotensive and Hypertensive Humans on High and Low Sodium Intake," *Circulation* 43: 508–19 (1971).

Fujita, T., et al. "Factors Influencing Blood Pressure in Salt-Sensitive Patients with Hypertension," *Am. J. Med.* 69: 334–44 (1980).

Campese, V. M. "Abnormal Relationship Between Sodium Intake and Sympathetic Nervous System Activity in Salt-Sensitive Patients with Essential Hypertension," *Kidney Intern.* 21: 371–78 (1982).

Surwit, R. S., R. B. Williams, and D. Shapiro. *Behavioral Approaches to Cardiovascular Disease.* New York: Academic Press, 1982, Chap. 6, pp. 132–38.

Haddy, F. J. "Mechanism, Prevention and Therapy of Sodium-Dependent Hypertension," *Am. J. Med.* 69: 746–58 (1980).

De Wardener, H. E., and G. A. MacGregor. "The Natriuretic Hormone and Essential Hypertension," *Lancet* 1: 1450–54 (1982).

Brown, M. J., and I. Macquin. "Is Adrenaline the Cause of Essential Hypertension?" *Lancet* 2: 1079–82 (1981).

"Stress, Hypertension, and the Heart: The Adrenaline Trilogy," Editorial, *Lancet* 2: 1440–41 (1982).

Laragh, J. H., et al. "Renin Profiling for Diagnosis and Treatment of Hypertension," *JAMA* 241: 151–56 (1979).

Campese, V. M., et al. "Neurogenic Factors in Low Renin Essential Hypertension," *Am. J. Med.* 69: 83–91 (1980).

Sims, E. A. H., and P. Berchtold. "Obesity and Hypertension," *JAMA* 247: 49–52 (1982).

Reisin, E., et al. "Cardiovascular Changes After Weight Reduction in Obesity Hypertension," *Ann. Int. Med.* 98: 315–19 (1983).

Sowers, J. R., et al. "Blood Pressure and Hormone Changes Associated with Weight Reduction in the Obese," *Hypertension* 4: 686–91 (1982).

Sims, E. A. H. "Mechanisms of Hypertension in the Overweight," *Hypertension* 4 (Supp. III): III-43–49 (1982).

Brenner, B. M., et al. "Dietary Protein Intake and the Progressive Nature of Kidney Disease: The Role of Hemodynamically Mediated Glomerular Injury in the Pathogenesis of Progressive Glomerular Sclerosis in Aging, Renal Ablation, and Intrinsic Renal Disease," *NEJM* 307: 652–59 (1982).

Webb, R. C., and D. F. Bohr. "Recent Advances in the Pathogenesis of Hypertension: Consideration of Structural, Functional, and Metabolic Vascular Abnormalities Resulting in Elevated Arterial Resistance," *Am. Heart J.* 102: 251–64 (1981).

Winquist, R. J., et al. "Vascular Smooth Muscle in Hypertension," *Federation Proc.* 41: 2387–93 (1982).

"Essential Hypertension—Another Defect," Editorial, *Lancet* 1: 1227–30 (1980).

Culpepper, W. S., et al. "Cardiac Status in Juvenile Borderline Hypertension," *Ann. Int. Med.* 98: 1–7 (1983).

Frohlich, E. D. "Hemodynamic Factors in the Pathogenesis and Maintenance of Hypertension," *Federation Proc.* 41: 2400–14 (1982).

Bartter, F. "Vasopressin and Blood Pressure," *NEJM* 304: 1097–98 (1981).

Davis, J. O. "Pathogenic Mechanisms in Hypertension," *Federation Proc.* 41: 2385–86 (1982).

Ophir, O., et al. "Low Blood Pressure in Vegetarians: the Possible Role of Potassium," *Am. J. Clin. Nutr.* 37: 755–62 (1983).

Meneely, G. R., and H. D. Battarbee. "High Sodium-Low Potassium Environment and Hypertension," *Am. J. Cardiol.* 38: 768–85 (1976).

Arkwright, P. D. "Effects of Alcohol Use and Other Aspects of Lifestyle on Blood Pressure Levels and Prevalence of Hypertension in a Working Population," *Circulation* 66: 60–66 (1982).

Major Symposia and an Overview

McCarron, D. A., et al. "Current Perspectives in Hypertension," Symposium, *Hypertension* 4 (Pt. 2): 1–183 (1982).

McCarron, D. A., et al. "Nutrition and Blood Pressure Control," Symposium, *Ann. Int. Med.* 98: 697–890 (1983).

Folkow, B. "Physiological Aspects of Primary Hypertension," *Physiol. Reviews* 62: 347–504 (1982).

21

The Diuretics

One of the first duties of the physician is to educate the masses not to take medicine.

Sir William Osler

You remember I talked about the conventional approach to the treatment of high blood pressure in Chapter 5, and ended the chapter as the doctor was taking out his prescription pad and telling you to take some pills?

The second part of the conventional approach to high blood pressure is *treatment with medications.* In the next three chapters we'll be taking a look at the different kinds of drugs a doctor may have prescribed for your high blood pressure. And we'll have one chapter that talks about other drugs you may be taking too.

You probably don't need to read all four of these chapters through from beginning to end. But I would like you to read carefully the chapters and sections that talk about the kinds of medications you are taking, so that you know something about them, their effects and side effects.

Let's suppose your doctor has just diagnosed high blood pressure in your case, and he's reaching for his prescription pad. For now, let's just say there are two kinds of medicines he may want to start you off on. Medicines in the first group, the water pills or *diuretics*, help you to excrete salt. And one of these drugs is likely to be your doctor's first choice.

The medicines in the second group, the *adrenergic* or *sympathetic blockers*, work by blocking your emergency nervous system. Some of these drugs may be used first by some doctors.

Let's take a look at the diuretics in this chapter, since they're not only usually the drugs of first choice but they also have a profound effect on the usefulness of the other drugs that are sometimes prescribed with them.

THE DIURETICS

To show you how these drugs work, I'm going to start by quickly reviewing some of the material we covered in Chapter 4.

The kidneys are designed to last maybe a hundred years or so before they wear out. One of their jobs is to get rid of the surplus minerals and salts we eat every day, such as sodium chloride, calcium, phosphorus, potassium, etc. But the amount of sodium chloride (salt) in our diet is so much greater than our kidneys were designed to handle—even before we add salt to our food at table—that many people develop high blood pressure as a way of helping the kidneys flush out that excess salt.

Let me explain.

By the time you're an adult with hypertension your kidneys have been so heavily overloaded with salt for so long that they have developed an abnormality, which we call "the kidney lesion." And this results in their being unable to excrete salt as fast as we eat it. So the salt slowly builds up or accumulates in our bodies.

Salt is so highly toxic that we retain water to dilute it—which, because of the excess fluid in our systems, makes us several pounds heavier than we need be. Obviously this fluid accumulation can't just go on getting worse and worse every year.

But as a result of the lesion our kidneys aren't doing such a good job by themselves any more, and so our blood pressure rises, to force the kidneys to excrete more water and salt and get us back into balance. High blood pressure is the ultimate "natural" diuretic, more powerful than most of the drugs we'll be talking about in this chapter.

The idea behind diuretic pills is to take over this function from your high blood pressure. If a "water pill" can help the kidneys get rid of the excess salt, your body won't need to keep your blood pressure up so high— so by taking a diuretic you can excrete the salt you eat every day at a lower body fluid volume and blood pressure (see chart below).

Relationship between kidney function, blood pressure, and body fluid volumes

Kidney function	Dietary salt	Urinary salt	Approx. blood pressure	Body fluids (approx.)
Normal	12 gm	12 gm	100/50	normal
Kidney lesion				
mild	12 gm	12 gm	140/90	+ 3%
moderate	12 gm	12 gm	170/105	+ 6%
severe	12 gm	12 gm	205/118	+10%

When you're overloaded with salt and water in this way, and you begin to take a diuretic, the *diuresis* (big loss of fluid and salt) will occur only for the first few days. After that your urine output will be equal to the amount of fluid you take in every day.

There are three major types of diuretics available today. The first is known as the *thiazides.* There are fourteen or so brands of thiazides on the market and, like toothpastes, they are all basically so similar to each other that manufacturers have a terribly hard time persuading doctors to order their particular brand. I've included some brand names in a chart at the end of this chapter.

The thiazide that most doctors use is *hydrochlorothiazide,* which you can order generically (not by brand name)—because it's very cheap, and it's really the best. It's pretty long acting, so you can take it either once or twice a day and have about the same effect either way.

Now when you have high blood pressure and you take a thiazide diuretic, one of several results will occur.

First, nothing may happen. And exactly that—nothing—does happen fairly often, more often than most people, or even most doctors, imagine. The patient gets no better and no worse. In fact the main effect the drug has is to cost the patient money. There may be a little stomachache now and then, or a skin rash, but nothing, absolutely nothing therapeutic, happens.

No diuresis. No weight loss. No fall in blood pressure.

When nothing happens—when the thiazide simply doesn't work—your doctor may decide you need more pills. High blood pressure is usually treated by a *step-care approach*, which means that when one level of treatment doesn't work we step up to another, until we finally come up with something that does.

Let's be clear about this. Most doctors don't change the medicine, they add another one to it. So the result of a thiazide not working will be that you need to take more medicines.

Most doctors have patients whose blood pressure is hard to control and doesn't respond to diuretics. Again, let me make myself clear. I don't mean the diuretics did their thing—diuresis—and the blood pressure stayed up anyway. I mean no diuresis, no weight loss, no drop in blood pressure—*nothing* happened!

If the patient's real trouble is that he has too much fluid in the body, and the thiazide doesn't work, then the other medicines probably won't work either, or won't work very well. They only work properly if you can get rid of that excess fluid (and salt) in the first place.

The second thing that can happen with a thiazide diuretic is that it does work. It can work a little (we'll call that a partial response), but because you eat so much salt, not much weight loss or fluid or pressure reduction occurs.

Or there can be a complete response. The diuretic produces a real diuresis, with weight loss and all that. Cutting back your dietary salt intake will help make sure you're in this last (complete response) group.

However, when a thiazide works, you not only excrete surplus fluids and salt, you also lose potassium. And the symptoms of potassium loss (which doctors call *hypokalemia)* may be anywhere from nothing to mild weakness to complete paralysis. Paralysis is rare, but mild weakness is a fairly common symptom.

In addition, potassium loss occasionally causes heart problems. These are particularly dangerous if you are also taking digitalis *(digoxin)*, a heart stimulant. If you take a thiazide diuretic and drop your potassium blood level, and you're taking digitalis, you'll be at high risk of developing a heart irregularity *(arrhythmia)*. On rare occasions this can be serious enough to require hospitalization.

Another thing that almost always happens when you take a thiazide (or any other kind of diuretic, for that matter) and it works is that the uric acid level in your blood will go up. Usually that's harmless enough—but it can sometimes cause an attack of gouty arthritis.

So the thiazides often need to be combined with other drugs to counteract these adverse effects. For the hypokalemia, you can use a potassium supplement, or your doctor can prescribe another drug that neutralizes the impact of the thiazide on your potassium levels. *Triamterene, spironolactone,* and *amiloride* are three drugs that can be taken with a thiazide to neutralize this potassium loss. They are known as potassium-sparing diuretics.

And you may well prefer taking one of them, because potassium supplements usually taste horrible and occasionally cause ulcers and intestinal bleeding. The potassium pills (potassium embedded in a waxy substance) don't taste bad, but they are devilishly expensive and sometimes not very effective.

Okay. So now, because you are taking one medicine (the thiazide), you may be taking another (potassium itself, or one of the potassium-sparing drugs). And your doctor may also have to put you on *allopurinol,* to lower your blood uric acid. Now you're taking two extra medicines to counteract the side effects of the original diuretic. And both those other drugs have side effects of their own.

But, Doctor, can't I just eat a banana or drink an extra glass of orange juice, and get my potassium that way?

My experience has led me to prescribe about 3 grams (40 millimoles) of potassium for every dose of diuretic I give. (Remember now, I use a diuretic dose that really *works.)* To get that much potassium in fresh or frozen produce, you'd need to eat about three to four hundred extra calories a day. That translates into thirty to forty extra pounds a year you'd gain, unless you exercised a lot more—by adding about a three-mile run every day to your schedule!

If the hydrochlorothiazide isn't strong enough to work in your case, the next step up is a diuretic drug called *metolazone.*

Metolazone does the same thing the thiazides do, and it has the same side effects. In fact it's really very similar in composition to the thiazides. But it's stronger. It will work even if you have a moderately severe kidney lesion, even if you keep on eating salt, or even if you have one of the more serious kidney diseases. In other words, it tends to work for the people the thiazides didn't work for. And there are a lot of them.

Metolazone is more powerful than the thiazides. It's more expensive and it's newer. Basically, it does the same thing—but it does it more predictably than the thiazides.

A lot of doctors don't know about metolazone, however, and they are likely to move on to the third group of diuretics when the thiazides don't work.

The third category of diuretics contains three drugs: *furosemide* (better known under its brand name, *Lasix*), *bumetamide (Bumex)*, and *ethacrynic acid (Edecrin)*. Again, furosemide is far better known in the United States than ethacrynic acid, although both drugs do about the same thing. Bumex is very new, just out in 1983.

Lasix, like metolazone, is more powerful than a thiazide and will work even if you have the kidney lesion, and even if you have more serious kidney diseases. But it has one serious drawback: it's very short acting—its effects only last for about an hour or two. When I'm describing its action to medical students, I tell them it's like a "punch" to the kidneys. A recent study showed that if you only take it once a day you will have diuresis for about an hour or so, and then intensely retain sodium the other twenty-three hours—so the net effect on your body's salt and water content is minimal.

That makes people who take it once a day *very* sensitive to salt eating— in fact they may be worse off and even retain more salt this way than they would if they had not been given a diuretic in the first place.

In fact, even though hydrochlorothiazide simply isn't as strong, dose for dose, as Lasix for many people, scientific double-blind studies over months and years have shown that thiazide works better on average than furosemide—perhaps because so many people have trouble taking their Lasix often enough to make it work for them. The studies were reported by Dr. J. Anderson and his colleagues in the *Quarterly Journal of Medicine* (1971).

If you use Lasix you'll have to take it at least twice a day and, depending on how much salt you eat, maybe even three times. And that's difficult, first because remembering to take any pill that often is a nuisance, and second because when you take Lasix and you need to go to the bathroom you have to go right away. There's no waiting around.

So a lot of people don't take their Lasix when they know they're going to be on a bus, or on a car trip, or out shopping somewhere downtown. Although it's a more powerful drug than hydrochlorothiazide if you take enough of it often enough, it doesn't always work as well as it should because patients don't take it correctly.

One other thing, while we're on the subject of diuretics. You may get the idea that, since you're now taking one of these drugs, you can eat anything you want to eat and that the problem with your salt intake is licked. It isn't.

Unfortunately, if your diuretic works well, and you go on eating a lot of salt, it tends to aggravate the potassium loss. So continuing to eat salt puts you on the horns of a dilemma. If the diuretic really works and you don't decrease your salt, you'll lose a lot of potassium and have a lot of other problems as a result. And if the diuretic doesn't work and you still eat lots of salt, your blood pressure will stay up, or even go up further.

So there's the choice: which is worse for you, to have low potassium or high blood pressure? It's virtually a lose-lose situation. That's why I don't like to use diuretics very much.

And that's why the approach of restricting salt intake makes much more sense. If I can get that across to you, and to the millions of other people who are having problems with diuretics—either because they're working or because they aren't—that will reduce an incredible amount of problems and suffering.

One of the things I hate about water pills is that, when I take them, I have to go to the bathroom a lot. I sometimes have to get up at night, sometimes two or three times, and in the daytime the urge hits me—and I mean, the URGE—*at the worst possible times. Isn't there some way to avoid this problem?*

Yes, there is. But before I tell you the answer, let me tell you a story about two of my patients who suffered from this problem.

I remember a surgeon friend who had hypertension. I prescribed some diuretics for him, but on days when he had surgeries to perform he simply didn't take them. There was no way he could "break scrub" (take off his gloves and gown and so on) in the middle of a delicate abdominal operation and run to the bathroom!

I had another patient, a lady who, years after several pregnancies, suffered from stress incontinence—that is, a tendency to leak a little urine at odd times, if her bladder got too full or if she got too harassed and stressed.

Wouldn't you know it, diuretics really caused this little weakness of hers to become an almost daily problem. To avoid embarrassment, she even resorted to wearing a pad. She skipped her pills some days when it was just too inconvenient for her to deal with the problem. And she was real reluctant to talk about it with me. I don't blame her. It's not the kind of thing you like to admit to, even to a doctor.

Well, the good news is that you can avoid the problem. And this program will help you to do just that. The cause of the frequent and excessive urination isn't the diuretic! Oh, I know it seems like it, sure enough. The real cause is simply that you drink too many fluids.

You see, if the diuretic really made you urinate more fluids than you drank each day for very many days, you'd get *dehydrated*, your skin would wrinkle, your mouth would get dry, you'd stop sweating completely, and your blood pressure would probably get low as well. And if this continued you'd go into shock within a few weeks. This does happen occasionally, generally with older people. It's rare, but it does happen from time to time. And doctors have to watch out for it.

So, however much you're urinating, that's how much you're drinking. Sometimes the diuretics start a complex process inside you, involving the hormone called renin that we talked about in Chapter 4, that actually stimulates your thirst. But it can be very subtle—you may not realize that you're drinking more fluids than usual.

But remember, what goes in must come out. That's Bennett's Fourth Law of Thermodynamics. And water can neither be created nor destroyed, at least not in any substantial amounts in your body. The corollary to this is, what comes out must have gone in.

If you're getting up at night to pass water, you drank it. So cut your fluid intake (water, milk, juices, tea, coffee, soda pop, etc.) in half, and see if this doesn't help. And keep your salt intake down, too (as if you needed an extra reason), because the diuretic is actually making you urinate salt, which then carries the water along with it.

If your intake of salt and water is low, no more getting up in the middle of the night. If it's lower still, you may not need the diuretic anymore!

Now that's what I'd like to see.

I've a question, Doctor. The pills I've been taking seem to be bringing my blood pressure down, so they must be good for me, right?

Not necessarily, by any means. It simply isn't true that anything that brings your blood pressure down must be okay. The *Journal of the American Medical Association* carried a recent report entitled "Multiple Risk

Factor Intervention Trial" (1982). The authors described their results as "ambiguous but disquieting." They found that the use of pharmacologic therapy—drugs—in the treatment of some hypertensives seemed to be associated with "an increased coronary heart disease mortality."

In simple English, they found that taking a diuretic for high blood pressure might lower the blood pressure while raising the overall risk of dying of heart disease.

Unfortunately most doctors can't possibly read all the articles in all the medical journals. In fact a recent study published in the *American Journal of Medicine* (1982) showed that many doctors are more influenced by the glossy four-color handouts that drug salesmen bring around than they are by articles in the medical journals. They're only human. And the drug companies make their advertising literature a whole lot easier to read than the scholarly journals, with their small print and extensive footnotes.

As a result, research that *encourages* the use of drugs is often more familiar to doctors than research that doesn't. After all, no one is going around from doctor to doctor promoting the fact that if you take care of yourself—if you learn to relax, and modify your diet, and exercise—you may not need any drugs. Because that approach doesn't really sell anything.

And I assure you that for every drug there's a drug company representative knocking on doctors' doors and showing them beautiful brochures with all the data to support the drug's use. Because if the drug company can sell your doctor on a drug, then he can sell hundreds or thousands of patients on it. And there are huge profits to be made.

I've included reports on a few of the adverse effects of diuretics in the bibliography for this chapter. It is the variety of hidden effects that they have on your metabolism that constitutes our main problem with the diuretics.

THIAZIDE DIURETICS

At this writing there are roughly nine *thiazide* diuretics, sold under fourteen brand names in the USA. Hydrochlorothiazide (HCTZ) is probably the most widely used, convenient, and inexpensive. It can be purchased in a generic form—less expensive than the brand-name varieties—for seven cents a tablet.

Generic (chemical) name:	Brand name:
hydrochlorothiazide	Hydrodiuril, Oretic, Esidrix
chlorothiazide	Diuril
cyclothiazide	Anhydron
methyclothiazide	Aquatensen, Enduron
hydroflumethiazide	Diucardin, Saluron
benzthiazide	Exna
trichlormethiazide	Metahydrin, Naqua
polythiazide	Renese
bendroflumethiazide	Naturetin

RELATED DIURETICS

There are three other diuretics that are closely related to the thiazide group in terms of chemical structure. Of these three, metolazone (sold only under the brand names Diulo and Zaroxolyn) is more predictable in its diuretic action in patients with high blood pressure than any of the thiazide group.

Generic name:	Brand name:
quinethazone	Hydromox
metolazone	Zaroxolyn, Diulo
chlorthalidone	Hygroton

POTASSIUM-SPARING DIURETICS

Generic name:	Brand name:
spironolactone	Aldactone
triamterene	Dyrenium
amiloride	Midamor

COMBINATION DIURETICS

The three potassium-sparing diuretics by themselves are not very effective in promoting sodium loss, and thus are not often used alone. But each has been combined with hydrochlorothiazide (HCTZ) and sold as a combination drug, and these are as effective as hydrochlorothiazide, without (or with much less of) the problem with potassium wasting.

Brand name:	Ingredients:
Aldactazide	HCTZ and spironolactone
Dyazide	HCTZ and triamterene
Moduretic	HCTZ and amiloride

STRONGER DIURETICS

Generic name:	Brand name:
furosemide	Lasix
ethacrynic acid	Edecrin
bumetanide	Bumex

22

The Blockers

It is the best Physician that knows the
Worthlessness of most Medicines.

Benjamin Franklin

The second group of drugs used in the step-care approach to the treatment of high blood pressure are those that block the emergency nervous system. They are seldom prescribed by themselves. And it's important that you know about them, because they can really affect the quality of your life.

Let's take a look at the way they work. There are two parts to the *autonomic* (automatic) *nervous system,* known as the *sympathetic* and *parasympathetic nervous systems* (SNS and PNS).

The parasympathetic nervous system looks after the smooth running and maintenance of the body under most circumstances—when we're eating or sleeping, for instance—but it is the sympathetic or *emergency nervous system* (ENS) that switches on in times of emergency or stress. For some people even a seemingly trivial activity, such as mental arithmetic or conversation, can turn it on.

This sensitivity or tendency to turn on the emergency nervous system easily may be inherited or learned or both. We don't really know for certain. It is this emergency nervous system that makes us energetic, active, and alert—and allows us to put forth our best efforts. It also comes on when we experience negative emotions, such as fear or anger, or worry a lot. (In the terminology of the movie *Star Wars*, this aspect of the emergency nervous system is "the dark side of the Force.")

One part of the emergency nervous system's job is to speed up the heart and raise the blood pressure, so that we will be more ready to do whatever is required to meet the challenge or stressful situation that is facing us.

The problem here is that this *preparedness response* is only intended to be used in times of real emergency—but the stresses of modern life are so frequent that many of us have emergency nervous systems that are almost constantly active.

Many people know that they are nervous and tense, and some are that way without really knowing it. But it's almost impossible to imagine someone who is suffering from hypertension who *doesn't* have excessive activity of the emergency nervous system as an essential component of the high blood pressure.

The blockers are drugs that dampen or block the emergency nervous system—thus tending to slow the heart and lower the blood pressure. Some of these drugs block the emergency nervous system up in the brain, some out at the nerve endings, and some in several different places. But in each case the problem with these drugs is pretty much the same.

They block the part of your nervous system that produces your energy and ambition and enthusiasm. It's your aliveness that's liable to be diminished. This is not a side effect, it's part of their action. They are designed to do this very thing: to diminish your vitality, your energy—your old get-up-and-go. They tend to block your ability to be excited or enthusiastic, and your ability to perform at your peak. Among other things, sexual excitement, interest, and performance may all suffer.

So when your doctor prescribes a blocker for you he may be asking you to give up some, or even a great deal, of your enjoyment of and enthusiasm for life.

Let's look at the different types of blockers.

Reserpine is a drug that interferes with your emergency nervous system's normal functioning by depleting the chemical messengers at *all the nerve endings* throughout your body. It's been one of the best-selling blood pressure pills worldwide—yet most people find it gives them side effects ranging from a dry mouth and stuffy nose to drowsiness and psychological depression.

Reserpine acts in the brain as well as elsewhere in your nervous system, and since it causes malfunctions in the *neurotransmitters* or chemical messengers in the brain, it can produce psychological depression and nightmares. It can also mix up the brain's signals to the stomach, so your stomach produces excessive acid, which can give you stomach or intestinal ulcers.

It's been years since I prescribed this drug for anyone. The last time I did, I remember the man had such misery from a stuffy nose that he overdosed himself on nose drops and decongestant pills, which then raised his blood pressure higher than before I began treating him. Because when you take reserpine, and some of the other blockers I'll be talking about, you become supersensitive to the stimulant in cold and allergy pills, nose drops and sprays that, in the words of the TV commercials, "shrink the inflamed tissues and open up your nasal passages."

The *beta blockers* are another group of drugs that slow down the heart and lower the blood pressure. They do this by blocking some specific sites in the emergency nervous system—the *beta-receptor* sites where adrenalin and other natural (hormonal) chemical stimulants attach themselves to produce their effects on the body.

Sometimes blocking beta stimulation of receptors produces a good response. But sometimes beta stimulation can be necessary to save your life, so blocking it with beta blockers is very harmful.

There are six beta blockers on the market in the United States at this writing, and perhaps a total of twenty or twenty-five available worldwide—and they all basically do about the same things. Some of them you need to take only once a day, and some of them twice; and some of them have more effect on the heart than on other parts of the body—but for dealing with high blood pressure there's not very much to choose between them. They just have different names (again, like toothpastes) and different prices, and the pills are different colors and shapes. I've listed them in the chart at the end of this chapter.

Medical Letter for Drugs and Therapeutics, a sort of no-nonsense consumer guide for doctors (which incidentally carries no advertising), recently reviewed the qualifications of the latest beta blockers on the market and found no evidence for their advantage over the more established ones.

The beta blockers block the ENS receptors in organs all over the body and lower the blood pressure in several different ways.

They slow the heart down and weaken its beat.

They block the receptors in the kidneys that release the hormone *renin*, and they also block the physical symptoms of emergency nervous system hyperactivity—but they don't actually turn it off. It's still cookin', you just don't feel it so much.

I feel pretty strongly that it's not a good idea to have your emergency nervous system turned on a lot of the time and be unable to *feel* it because of some drug you're taking. That's like having dinner burning on the stove and going around wearing a nose clip so you don't have to smell it— instead of taking it off the stove and turning off the fire.

I have a doctor friend, a professor of medicine at one of our major university hospitals, who's under a lot of stress all the time. He's in a highly responsible and demanding job, he's in competition with doctors all over the world for a shrinking supply of grant money to fund his research, on which his academic stature depends. He's also got his eye on the one or two bright young "movers," men who would no doubt like his job if he ever faltered.

You know what I'm talking about. The burden of being "top dog" is that too many people want your job. So you don't want to look back to see who's gaining on you. His nervous system is probably constantly at "survival"—his emergency nervous system is just about always on the go.

And so he's hooked on *propranolol*, one of the beta blockers, because, when he takes it, it allows him to avoid the symptoms of stress—the sweaty palms and rapid pulse and attacks of diarrhea. The fire is still raging inside him all the time—he just doesn't *feel* it when he takes propranolol. And that's the way he described it to me. He actually told me he was "hooked."

And I think both of us know, deep down, that that's not a very good idea.

A recent study in the *American Journal of Medicine* (1982) describes the use of propranolol to prevent stage fright in performers. In these short-term experiments, anxiety and upset decreased and performance actually improved. The doses were low and the problem short-lived—only a few hours. Ingenious! And probably not harmful. But using these drugs every day for the rest of your life? That's another matter.

It's the addictive potential, the dependence on the drug to function every day, that I worry about. Because if you depend on it strongly enough you'll overlook the cost. And I'm not just talking about the cost in terms of money. I'm talking about the bad things it's doing to you as well.

In fact patients can sometimes get just as "hooked" on their legal prescription drugs as junkies are on their illegal ones.

Let me give you an example.

A situation cropped up some years ago with patients who were suffering from certain forms of chronic destructive arthritis. Doctors found that if they gave these people *cortisone* (steroids) their patients felt so much better, it seemed as if a miracle had taken place. But what was really going on was that the patients just couldn't feel the effects of their arthritis anymore—yet it was still gnawing away and destroying their joints worse than ever.

Arthritis specialists don't use cortisone now in that situation. Too many people became dependent on it. And I think we'll come to understand that beta blockers can be dangerous in much the same way, for people who lead highly stressed lives.

On top of all that, the beta blockers have an effect on the brain that we don't fully understand yet. It's unpredictable. But it can be very real and very important.

And the brain is so important. You may remember Woody Allen's movie *Sleeper*. One of my favorite moments in the movie happens when Woody decides that he's not about to let some evil scientists tamper with his brain. "My brain," he exclaims, "that's my second favorite organ!"

And he's right. The brain is such a delicate and sensitive part of us that we'd do well to avoid tampering with it. Yet, like other emergency nervous system blockers, the beta blockers interfere with the normal functioning of the nervous system in a variety of ways, including "central" effects—effects in the brain itself.

In addition to lowering our vitality and general energy, the beta blockers, particularly in high doses, sometimes cause impotence.

Now that's something you'd imagine a lot of people just wouldn't put up with, no matter what their doctors said. And yet, over the last ten years, the beta blockers have become the most popular of the emergency nervous system blockers—witness the flurry of new ones on the market. And because they're so widely used now, unexpected problems are cropping up all over the place.

An article in *Emergency Medicine* (1982) entitled "The Beta-Blocker Blues," describes the potential for these drugs to cause psychological depression. Sometimes it's severe enough that it comes to a doctor's attention. But while a slight depression might be enough to depress your functioning, it might not be severe enough that you'd tell anyone about it. Or even suspect it was caused by the drugs you were taking. So we really don't know how widespread this specific side effect may be.

Propranolol has also been described as a cause of *dementia,* or premature senility. A recent article entitled "The Dementia Syndrome" in the English journal, the *Lancet* (1982), suggests that this type of senility or intellectual impairment (usually associated with advancing age and thought to be irreversible) can in fact be treated successfully in up to thirty percent of cases.

Many drugs, including antihypertensive drugs, are frequent culprits here, since hypertension is such a common problem in the elderly. If you have a relative or loved one who is suffering a noticeable decline in memory or intellectual powers, who is on *any* drugs, and especially the ones discussed in this chapter, you should ask your doctor to give him or her a trial period off the drugs, to see whether the mental function will improve.

The trouble with these drugs is that their action is sometimes extremely subtle. It can tax even the best doctor's abilities as a sleuth to track down the effects of these drugs on his patients' problems.

People who take beta blockers, like people who take reserpine, tend to be ultrasensitive to the stimulants that you'll find in most allergy medicines and "decongestants." They're even sensitive to the usual amounts of nose drops or nasal sprays.

I recently got a phone call from Cal, a fifty-five-year-old who's in the wrecking business with his brother. Cal was taking a diuretic and propranolol to keep his pressure under control, while he was deciding how hard (I guess "consistently" might be a better word) he wanted to work on his diet, weight, exercise and stress levels.

He knew what he had to do but he just hadn't gotten around to doing it all the time. So he'd come and see me once in a while—and in the meantime we used the drugs as a holding measure.

When he called me he said he'd noticed his pressure was going up quite a bit, so I asked him what was happening. He said he'd had a cold and was taking *Dristan,* so right away I knew what was wrong. I told him to stop the cold pills and try just a plain antihistamine, which is also available without prescription. It worked, his pressure came back down in a few days. And we were both relieved.

Let's talk about another "favorite" organ—the heart.

Beta blockers were originally developed to treat the pains and abnormal rhythms of some kinds of heart disease. Yet heart problems are another potential side effect of these same drugs.

When the heart is overloaded—both by the increased volume of blood to be pumped (due to excess salt and water retention), and by heightened blood pressure—it has to depend on the emergency nervous system to strengthen its action. The whole system is beautifully designed to regulate how hard the heart works. But if the emergency nervous system is *blocked*, the heart can't call on it and heart failure may result.

Let me try to explain what this is all about, so you can understand it a little better.

Having a problem with fluid retention in the body, and thus a high blood volume plus high blood pressure, makes your heart work extremely hard. So you need every bit of energy and strength that your heart can muster up.

Imagine this: if Roger Bannister had tried to push his heart as hard as he did when he ran the world's first four-minute mile, *while his emergency nervous system was blocked,* his heart just wouldn't have made it.

(He wouldn't have made it either. Someone else would have been the first to break the four-minute barrier.)

In the same way, when you ask *your* heart to cope with high blood volume *and* high blood pressure *and* you block your emergency nervous system's strengthening action, your heart may not make it.

But it's unpredictable, the effect on the heart. A few years ago I was working with a group of cardiologists at UCLA-Harbor General Hospital. We were studying the cardiovascular effect of a powerful vasodilator, minoxidil, combined with propranolol, the most popular of the beta blockers.

Our patient was in his fifties and had just started experiencing chest pains (angina) again, after being free of it for almost a year—a year during which his blood pressure had been under very good control.

We used a technique called "heart catheterization," which showed us that our patient's coronary arteries were not blocked, so we knew the problem wasn't atherosclerosis.

We turned to the next possibility. Some hypertensive patients with large, hypertrophied hearts may have a problem called Syndrome X, angina with open coronary arteries. This syndrome (or collection of symptoms) almost always occurs when the blood pressure is high and the heart muscle is working overly hard and needs a lot of oxygen. But our patient had a blood pressure of 120/80! It seemed unlikely that he was suffering from Syndrome X.

We then took some X-ray movies (not X-rated ones) of his beating heart—they are known as *cineventriculograms*—and met the next day to look over the results. Even though our patient was taking 800 mg of propranolol a day and was sitting at rest, his heart was beating rapidly and very forcefully—so forcefully that it was ejecting nearly ninety-eight percent of the blood in the chamber each time it beat.

That's a superhuman effort! I heard grunts of surprise from the cardiologists in the room. Even during maximum exercise, most people don't push more than eighty percent of the blood in the heart out with each beat. And at rest it's nearer fifty percent.

So we finally came to understand that underneath our patient's calm exterior and low blood pressure, hidden from our observation and even the patient's own inner feelings, the stresses that had originally sent his blood pressure up were still getting to him. Excesses of adrenalin and noradrenalin were raging through his system like a fire, driving his heart to get bigger and stronger and to empty more completely—as if they were acting as a sort of growth hormone for the heart itself.

We reported this and other similar cases at several meetings and published our findings in *Circulation* (1975).

Here are a few more problems caused by the beta blockers:

Poor circulation. The emergency nervous system stimulation of beta-receptors in the skin and muscles opens up those little arterioles to improve your blood flow—a good idea if you're ready for fight or flight. So the beta blockers (which block this response) actually increase the resistance to blood flow in your arms and legs. This tends to raise pressure a little bit in some people. Oh, the overall effect is to lower the pressure, I agree—but this part of the drug's action actually raises it!

This effect on the vessels can be a real problem for people who have poor circulation in their limbs, who sometimes feel numbness, tingling, or coolness, or notice a bluish discoloration of the hands and feet. Especially when people feel pain because of their poor circulation, beta blockers probably shouldn't be used. So if the circulation to your arms and legs is poor you had better find some other way to treat your blood pressure.

Asthma. People with asthma, and also many people with other kinds of lung disease such as bronchitis and emphysema, who wheeze or have difficulty breathing, need the emergency nervous system stimulation of their beta-receptors to keep their air tubes (bronchioles) open. So it doesn't make sense to shut down this lifesaving response with beta blockers.

Lipids. The beta blockers don't affect only the brain and the heart, they also affect the metabolism of most people who take them—tending to raise the blood sugar and lipid levels. If you already have a problem with your lipids (fats) or blood sugar, beta blockers are likely to make it worse.

They may bring your blood pressure down but turn you from a borderline to a full-fledged diabetic in the process. Or increase your heart risk by raising your lipid levels, while reducing it by lowering your blood pressure at the same time. The trade-offs don't always work out in your favor.

Angina. Propranolol and other beta blockers were originally developed to treat angina, the squeezing heart pain that people get if their coronary arteries are blocked and they try to walk or run too fast. But when you take these drugs for angina, two of the same problems occur that you'll find when you take them for hypertension. Once started on propranolol, people seem to take it indefinitely. And the drug certainly hides the symptoms—but it doesn't really do much of anything about the problem.

How much better it would be to tackle this angina problem head on, by

1. increasing the blood's capacity to carry oxygen to the heart, by eating less fat, and quitting smoking;

2. decreasing the metabolic demands you make on your heart (and thus its oxygen needs) by avoiding caffeine (in tea, coffee, and colas) and nicotine, learning to handle stress better, and lowering your blood pressure, if it's high;

3. improving the efficiency and strength of the heart and lungs by regular exercise;

4. promoting the growth of new blood vessels (called collaterals) in the heart muscle, to bring blood around the blocked areas, again by a program of regular exercise;

5. and clearing up the atherosclerotic, fatty, fibrous clotting sores and lesions which are blocking the coronary arteries, by eating less fat and cholesterol, and thus lowering the blood cholesterol level.

Common sense, isn't it?

The third category of emergency nervous system blockers is known as the *central acting drugs*—clonidine, methyldopa, and guanabenz. The pills come in three different colors and three different shapes, but there's not much else to distinguish them from each other.

These are drugs that shut down the emergency nervous system from within the brain. And because these drugs tend to concentrate in the brain, they produce a lot of other effects, too.

The opposite of being alert and vigorous is apathy, and these drugs do tend to make people apathetic. (Apathy is not caring about what's going on and not caring that you don't care; and that's the problem, because you don't even feel like doing anything about it.)

These drugs also tend to diminish your sexual excitability. They may interfere with a man's ability to get an erection. (I'd imagine they diminish a woman's interest in sex too—but we are so chauvinist in the medical profession that we haven't really looked into that yet, as far as I know.)

Like so many of these drugs that affect the emergency nervous system, the real problem with the central acting blockers is that they usually do too little or too much. Emergency nervous system activity is something that varies a great deal from one situation to another. So when you take a high enough dose of these drugs to control your most hyperactive moments, it will probably leave you apathetic the rest of the time. Not to mention dizzy and sleepy. And if you take a small enough dose not to leave you apathetic, it just won't be enough to control those frequent peaks—which is precisely when the blood pressure skyrockets.

I recently saw a woman in the hospital who had had a small stroke, her blood pressure was high, and she'd been given clonidine to bring it down. It worked—her pressure was very good—but she was so slowed down she was like a toy robot whose batteries are almost exhausted. You've seen them, the head . . . moves . . . ever . . . so . . . slowly . . . . and . . . . . the . . . . . . arms . . . . move . . . .

I asked her to sit up, and it took minutes, not because of her stroke but because it took a long time for her to hear, to understand, and then act. No wonder the FAA doesn't let you pilot a plane when you take these medicines. But you can drive a car, and work with machinery, and try to get your job done every day. There are no regulations against that.

I wonder about our cavalier acceptance of these things. Ours is a busy, complex, and fast-paced society. I shudder to think of the increasing numbers of people taking these drugs that slow them down, diminish their energy, perhaps even impair their ability to deal with problems. Can they function effectively and safely? Listen, it's a tough world out there, and we need to have our wits about us.

Sometimes I feel like Paul Revere, trying to awaken a sleeping populace and alert them to a danger, a very grave danger. The message doesn't always fall on receptive ears, you know. There are loyalists, even now. But I'm finding a lot of rebels, too. And their ranks are growing.

How about you? How do you feel taking these drugs? Really take a moment, and look, and find out how you feel. You may know something's wrong. Maybe you're too sleepy at the office or plant, or you fall asleep in front of the TV. Or maybe you're not very interested in sex or parties or dancing any more. And things you used to like to do, like driving to the beach or the desert, seem just too much trouble to be worth it.

You may not notice these things, or you may not make a connection between the way you feel and the drugs you take. It can happen insidiously, which just means these things can creep up on you. You may think you're just growing older and getting a little lazy—that apathy problem again.

But if you're reading this book I have to assume that you care that these things are happening to you. And you don't want them happening to you anymore.

When people get off these drugs they are usually surprised—I guess "shocked" is a better word—at how lazy they'd become. One man described it to me like this. He said that when he stopped taking methyldopa it was like having a gray veil removed from his head. He had so much more clarity—all of a sudden the whole world was in Technicolor again.

Listen, in large enough doses, these drugs can bring Superman down out of the sky. Turn the man of steel into a man of rubber. Oh, I know, some people still seem "wired" and hyperactive while taking them. But they're the exceptions. And I know that even they're not untouched. Something has happened to their thinking processes too.

Do you realize some people are excited by sleeping pills? Older people especially can have an unexpected or paradoxical response. And I'm sure that some people will have a paradoxical response to methyldopa or clonidine and actually get more rather than less hyperactive. But most of us will be slowed down and maybe not even know we've slowed down. At least, now you've read this chapter, you can be on the lookout for it.

The other day a friend and colleague stopped me in the hallway. He said, "You know, Cleaves, since you've been talking about these things— prevention, and stress, and so on—I've become more aware of what happens to my patients when I prescribe these medicines. Oh, I always used to ask my patients if they felt any side effects, but I did it in a sort of perfunctory manner. I guess I didn't really want them to say yes, because that would complicate matters. I was putting out that kind of message— 'Don't tell me about it.' You know?

"Now when I ask my patients the same question and they say, 'No, I don't have any side effects,' I don't stop there. I spend a little more time, and probe a little, and go into the whole question more carefully. That's the key, I guess. They get the *caring,* and so they open up and tell me about their sleepiness and lethargy, and problems with sex, and memory, and just getting things done every day.

"Boy, what an eye-opener! Everybody I see who's on drugs has some of those symptoms. And I'd never realized that before."

Isn't that beautiful? I'd like that to happen to everyone's doctor, all over the country, all over the world. We're a caring, helping profession, and we have that instinct, that natural desire to help—or at the very least to do no harm. That's the physician's cardinal rule: *Primum non nocere* (First, do no harm). I learned it in medical school. And now I'm trying to make it more and more a part of my daily practice.

I'd like to say a few words to my fellow doctors while we're on this point. As physicians, we ought to look behind the dry statistics in the medical journals. The side effects of drug X: 4 percent nasal stuffiness, 17 percent gastric distress, 7 percent skin rash, etc. *These are just the side effects that patients tell us about.* And there can be a vast difference between what people tell us and what's really going on.

Our patients don't always recognize their symptoms. Sometimes they don't even have the language in which to express them. So we need to be on the alert to recognize their humanity and understand what's happening to that humanity.

What does it mean to be a human being? What qualities of life do we as physicians need to protect? And what do these drugs do to those human qualities? I don't find the answers to these questions in my *Physicians' Desk Reference* or in most of the medical journals.

We need to develop a sensitivity to a quality in our patients that our brain scanners and panels of blood tests just can't pick up, no matter how sophisticated they are. It's kind of a radical idea, and I'm just learning about it myself, so I don't want to preach to or admonish anyone. I'm too vulnerable myself to get away with much of that.

But it's an exciting idea, though, to nurture and protect a patient's humanity. How do you measure it? And how can you tell when it's growing and when it's fading?

I'm slowly developing eyes to see and ears to listen.

There are two other types of blockers that I should mention.

Guanethidine is a powerful emergency nervous system blocker, but it can cause a variety of unpleasant side effects that tend to limit its usefulness. One particularly bizarre effect is known as "retrograde ejaculation" in men. Men who take this drug can get an erection and have intercourse, and even have an orgasm. But the semen, instead of being pushed out, backs up inside the man's body. And this whole experience is so strange and embarrassing, it often causes psychological potency problems.

Guanethidine can also cause an excessive drop in blood pressure and dizziness when you stand up—but because of the sexual and other problems described above, it's very seldom used anymore.

Prazosin is another type of blocker with a unique side effect. Your doctor will warn you to make sure you are lying down the first time you take it (and usually only the first time), because you may faint sometime during the next six hours.

And another problem with prazosin is that it takes about two or three weeks to determine whether you've been given the right dosage—so your doctor can only adjust the dosage upward every few weeks.

Prazosin seems to have less of an adverse effect on metabolism, but because it's relatively new, and not sold here very much, we don't yet know all the side effects that may crop up. But certainly it can cause dizziness or sleepiness and lack of energy in many people who take it.

All the various categories of blockers can be used alone. But there is a problem. They don't do anything to help the salt/volume question, and in fact most of them tend to make you retain even more salt—and thus more water—in your system.

Of all the different categories of blockers, the beta blockers are the ones that tend to produce the least sodium retention, so they are the most likely to be used alone.

Doctors usually follow the *step-care approach* when prescribing these drugs. This means they start by trying one category of drug, and if that doesn't work they move on to the next category. The diuretics are usually considered as *step-one drugs*, and the blockers are usually *step two*.

And remember, we don't replace step-one drugs with step-two drugs. We add them.

As we saw before, the diuretics don't work for everyone, and therefore many people progress to step two. But the blockers cause their own problems—their effects on the brain and emergency nervous system, and their side effects in terms of reducing your energy, enthusiasm, excitement, vitality, and ambition.

These drugs tend to simply squash your aliveness. It's that simple. It's unfortunate, but it's what they're designed to do.

The other problem with the blockers is that, if you're under a lot of stress, the stress can usually bust right through and send your blood pressure up anyway. None of these drugs is really strong enough to combat the stress you'll feel in the middle of a good, old-fashioned domestic quarrel with your spouse or teenager.

And if your doctor prescribes enough of a blocker to block the stress that comes about from a domestic quarrel, or the loss of a job, or some big upset, he'll probably have prescribed enough so that you'll spend most of your time walking around like a zombie, feeling completely squashed and useless.

And speaking of big upsets, there's another interesting problem I ran into the other day at the hospital. A woman in her fifties was admitted, having overdosed a little on insulin. (Her sister had been helping her with the dose, and together they overdid it a bit.) She was also taking a diuretic and a beta blocker for her blood pressure.

Now when you take insulin your blood sugar can drop. But because she was taking the blocker she didn't feel anything when her blood sugar dropped to dangerously low levels (under 40 mg/dl)! At levels like that, the brain is in such peril that the emergency nervous system goes crazy, pouring out adrenalin and other hormones in an attempt to raise the blood sugar quickly. If ever there's a time for alarms to go off and red lights to flash, this is it—a blood sugar of less than 40.

In situations like this, beta blockers actually increase the pressure-raising effects of these hormones, leading to a hypertensive crisis. Fortunately I had read an article describing this type of situation, so I recognized it right away and knew what to do.

There's a moral here, of course, and a lesson to be learned: if at all possible, you don't want to interfere with or alter the natural function of your emergency nervous system. You never know when you might need it. Why not add it to your list of rules to live by:

> Keep a spare key to the house hidden outside; you might get
>   locked out someday.
> Always keep air in your spare tire, and a jack that works;
>   because you may end up on the highway with a flat.
> Check the fire extinguishers in your home and office at least
>   every six months.
> Keep a little money set aside for a rainy day.

Common sense, don't you think?

And here's the big one.

Keep your body ready to respond to emergencies.

Don't live the rest of your life with your beautiful emergency
system drugged and ineffective.

All right. I've told you a lot about the blockers and their side effects. As
you can tell, I'd much rather find some other way of dealing with high
blood pressure.

But I'd like to give you a warning:

If you're the kind of person who takes the pills for a while and then runs
out, and figures, "That's a nuisance. I'll fill the prescription in a day or so
. . ." or if you're the sort of person who goes off on vacation and forgets
to pack your pills, and then thinks, "Oh well, my blood pressure has been
pretty good lately, it probably won't matter too much . . ."—this warning's for you.

If you've been taking some kind of blocker drug regularly, and your
blood pressure has been under control, and you suddenly stop taking the
pills, *your blood pressure may rebound.* This may happen rather quickly,
and (even more disturbingly) it may go up much higher than it was before
you started taking the pills. Some people have actually had blood pressure
crises in which their blood pressure went up to 300/150 and they had to
be hospitalized.

This kind of rebound effect was first reported in people taking
clonidine, but it's happened with other kinds of blockers too. Your body
gets used to the drug, and if you suddenly take it away the reaction can be
alarming.

With propranolol, it seems that people who suddenly stop taking it may
find their hearts are racing for a while, and there have even been cases
reported that may have resulted in heart attacks. It has an action on the
blood platelets which, when the drug is stopped, may make the blood clot
too easily. That can be dangerous if your arteries are badly clogged from
atherosclerosis.

So if you're taking any of these pills, make sure that you don't just by
accident stop taking them suddenly. Because something really dreadful
can happen to your cardiovascular system.

So that's the warning. And this doesn't mean that you can't ever stop
them—it just means that if you're going to do it you need to do it gradually, under the care of a doctor who knows how to do it.

You don't want to stop them by yourself.

THE BLOCKERS

Generic (chemical) name:	Brand name:
Reserpine-like drugs:	
reserpine	Serpasil
rauwolfia	Raudixin
deserpidine	Harmonyl

Rauwolfia (a less purified plant extract) and deserpidine have actions and side effects similar to those of reserpine.

CENTRAL BLOCKERS

Generic name:	Brand name:
clonidine	Catapres
guanabenz	Wytensin
methyldopa	Aldomet

GENERAL SNS (SYMPATHETIC NERVOUS SYSTEM) BLOCKER

Generic name:	Brand name:
guanethidine	Ismelin

BETA BLOCKERS

Generic name:	Brand name:
timolol	Blocadren
nadolol	Corgard
propranolol	Inderal
metoprolol	Lopressor
atenolol	Tenormin
pindolol	Visken

DIURETIC/BLOCKER COMBINATIONS

For the convenience of taking one pill rather than two, most of the blockers have been combined with a thiazide diuretic (either hydrochlorothiazide or the pharmaceutical firm's favored "in house" thiazide) and sold as a combination pill. If the dosages work out for the individual, this is an attractive alternative to taking two different medicines. But of course there's no flexibility in dosages, and if you get a rash you can't tell which medicine caused it. The following is a representative list of the more popular combinations.

Brand name:	*Ingredients*
Ser-Ap-Es	HCTZ, reserpine, and hydralazine
Minizide	prazosin and polythiazide
Aldoril	HCTZ and methyldopa
Inderide	HCTZ and propranolol
Combipres	chlorthalidone and clonidine

23

The Vasodilators and Other Antihypertensive Drugs

> *Medicine is a collection of uncertain prescriptions the results of which, taken collectively, are more fatal than useful to mankind. Water, air and cleanliness are the chief articles of my pharmacopeia.*
>
> Napoleon

The next category of drugs are those that act directly on the tiny blood vessels we discussed earlier—the arterioles. These drugs relax the muscles in the arterioles and thus open them up, allowing an increased blood flow to pass through them and the diastolic pressure to fall. They are called *vasodilators.*

There are four vasodilators on the market right now: *hydralazine* and *minoxidil*, which are taken as pills; and *dyazoxide* and *nitroprusside*, which have to be injected. Dyazoxide and nitroprusside, as a result, are usually only administered in hospitals, during emergencies, when the blood pressure is very, very high and something has to be done about it immediately.

Let's concentrate on hydralazine and minoxidil.

Minoxidil is probably significantly stronger than hydralazine. So there are some people who won't respond to maximum doses of hydralazine but will respond to minoxidil. That has been my experience, and it's generally the experience of most other experts in the field. But, basically, the two drugs work in the same way and have roughly the same side effects.

There is one specific side effect of minoxidil that I should probably warn you about—and it's quite common. It causes people to grow hair all over their bodies. Really what happens is the fine, short, invisible hairs that are normally present all over the body turn dark and coarse and long.

It's not a big problem for men but it can be a terrible problem for women and kids. Nobody wants to end up looking like Lon Chaney after he's turned into the wolfman. . . . I had one young patient, about nine years old, whose mother had to shave him with a razor every morning before he went to school, because the other kids would tease him otherwise. She had to shave his back, and his belly, and the whole of his face. The boy had been dying of high blood pressure and the drug saved his life —but the side effects were a nightmare.

It was one more reason for me to look for another way to deal with this whole problem.

When you have too much fluid in a system of elastic tubes and you want to lower the pressure in them, there are two things you can do. You can try to drain off some of the fluid, which is what the diuretics are supposed to do. Or you can make the elastic tubes bigger which is what the sympathetic blockers and vasodilators do.

But most people are put on vasodilators because their diuretic didn't work in the first place, and then their sympathetic blockers didn't either. And if there's enough fluid in the blood system and a high enough flow, changing the size of the arterioles may not help much either.

The number of people who really need a vasodilator is very, very small. If you've been given an effective diuretic and a program of sodium restriction, and then had some attention paid to your tendency to keep turning on the emergency nervous system—either using drugs that block it or by the nondrug means we have suggested in this program—you probably won't be needing a vasodilator. Very, very few people do.

Now let's look at the people who do. If the diuretic worked, and there's now a more normal, smaller amount of fluid in the circulation, and if the emergency nervous system blockers are reducing the stimulation of the heart and blood vessels to an acceptable level, some people may still have a pressure problem.

Those little arterioles which are supposed to open and close freely may be so stuck that they need more than just a reduction in emergency nervous system stimulation to allow them to open up again. And the vasodilators may be able to help them do just that.

Of course it's not always that simple. You know how things like that often are—more complex than you'd expect from first appearances.

When the doctor and his medicines come intruding into your body, your automatic nervous system is very likely to say, "Wait a minute, you can't come barging in telling us what to do. We've been running things in here for a long time now, and we're not about to change so quickly, just because you say so!"

Far from cooperating with the doctor when he's using this category of drugs, your body may be cleverly trying to outwit him and keep the blood pressure high. The outcome is unpredictable, and the side effects of the battle going on inside you may be unpleasant indeed.

The problem with the vasodilators is that they vasodilate all over the body indiscriminately, without regard to what is needed in different tissues and organs. And this can make the body as a whole think there is some kind of emergency going on.

What's the emergency?

Well, you probably know that if you were to lose a lot of blood—in an accident, say—you'd be risking not having enough blood to continue the functioning of your brain or heart, or the rest of your systems. Your body would treat the situation as a very serious emergency.

That's what your body may think is going on when you take a powerful vasodilator and it works. Suddenly there's not enough fluid to keep your blood vessels full. In this case it's not because you've lost any fluid, it's because you've increased the capacity of your blood vessels to hold the fluid. And your body is liable to treat it as an emergency, turn the emergency nervous system on vigorously, and raise your blood pressure back to where it was again, just as it would if you'd lost a lot of blood.

Now if you've taken enough of the emergency nervous system blockers, you'll not only be blocking out any symptoms of this "emergency" but you'll also prevent the rise in pressure again. Neat, isn't it? And powerful if used properly.

And if you haven't taken enough of the blockers to keep the symptoms blocked out you'll probably be feeling pretty terrible. Let me give you an example of what I mean. Not many readers will have had the experience of hemorrhaging, losing a lot of blood, and going into shock. But it doesn't feel pleasant.

You might feel cold and clammy; you'd have palpitations of the heart; and you'd feel nauseated. It's uncomfortable. It's scary. And that's what your reaction to sudden dilation of your arterioles may feel like, if the symptoms do manage to come through.

I remember Gerry, a writer in her fifties who came to me after trying hydralazine just once. Her pressure was out of control, and the doctor added this vasodilator to the other drugs she was already on. She described her reaction to it as "almost out of the body"—for her, a very terrifying experience.

She said, "That's it! No more! I've got to find a different way to handle this."

She found our program. She's doing great. She's off the drugs completely, and at home her pressure is normal. Oh, it still goes up a little when she comes to see me, but I look at her record of home blood pressures, they're just great, and I tell her not to worry. It goes up less now when she sees me than it did before. I guess I'm less intimidating as a friend and teacher than as the doctor in the white lab coat who hands out prescriptions and looks at her sternly over his glasses. But it's taken a long time to get rid of that aura.

OTHER ANTIHYPERTENSIVE DRUGS

Endocrine inhibitors block the formation of *angiotensin,* a hormone that can raise the blood pressure profoundly. There are two endocrine inhibitors in current use. *Saralasin* can only be given in the form of an injection and is not commonly used. But *captopril* can be taken orally, and it has recently been heavily advertised as a major breakthrough.

It isn't. Not all that many people have overactive renin-angiotensin systems in the first place. And besides, the drug is what's known as a "competitive inhibitor" in any case—which means that even when it works it only works for a while, and then the body learns to make a lot more of the hormone to counteract the effect of the drug. So you are quickly back where you started.

But by this time you're in a predicament. You're stuck with the drug now, because if you were to stop it your body would feel the effects of a much larger quantity of the hormone than before you started.

Competitive inhibitors basically set up a competition between themselves and the body. The body manufactures a hormone that has an effect on the pressure. The drug tries to interfere. The body works harder and makes more hormone. Increasing the dose of the drug steps up its interference. And so on.

It's a little like a kid who's losing a fight and calls in his older brother. So the other kid naturally calls in *his* big brother. So the first kid brings his father, and soon all their brothers and their great-aunts are involved in a colossal fight.

That's what you get when you use a competitive inhibitor. So they are far from ideal.

Pargyline is one of a group of drugs called the *MAO inhibitors*. It is a powerful drug that interferes with several brain and nervous system functions by inhibiting the production of certain important chemicals in the brain and nerves. As an accidental by-product of this, blood pressure is lowered. But, so far as I'm concerned, the side effects of dizziness and weakness, and the long list of warnings (for example, you're not supposed to eat cheese, bananas, or chocolate if you're taking this drug), have steered me away from ever using it.

The *calcium channel blockers* at the time of this writing have not yet been officially approved for use in hypertension but they probably soon will be. They are so powerful and interfere so drastically with the body's function that I would be loath to use them except in the most serious life-threatening situations.

And, new as they are, the severity of their side effects is not yet fully recognized. They will likely produce loss of energy and alertness in most people, and they very significantly weaken the heartbeat as well. These are "last resort" drugs, and even then their use should be temporary if at all possible.

I'm waiting for the medical profession to come up with a miracle drug that will make high blood pressure a thing of the past. How near are we to a breakthrough like that?

This is the "silver bullet" theory, and it suggests that every disease has a specific cause and a specific cure. This kind of approach works well with infectious and some other kinds of disease. The Salk and Sabin vaccines have eliminated polio. Penicillin cures pneumonia. Vitamin C cures scurvy. And smallpox has been relegated to the history books.

But, as I have said, high blood pressure has a number of different, interacting causes. It is what we call *multifactorial*. And, like the other degenerative diseases, it simply can't be dealt with this way.

The medical profession has had great success treating the infectious diseases with antibiotics or vaccines, and of course we all wish we could come up with similar solutions to the degenerative diseases, which are now the major causes of death in our society. But they don't have a single cause and there won't be any silver bullet that cures them.

It's as simple as that.

You can't afford to wait for a magic drug that will never be found.

Okay, okay, there's no pill that will actually cure my high blood pressure. But isn't there one drug that's good enough to bring everyone's blood pressure back to normal? Isn't there one drug that's the best?

I thought I'd found it a few years ago.

It was a powerful new drug, and it lowered everyone's blood pressure to normal in a few hours—even if the blood pressure was very high and hadn't responded well to lots of other drugs.

I quickly obtained the FDA's permission to study it—while it was still under investigation and not yet generally available to other physicians or in pharmacies.

I used to feel pretty good about myself when I'd bring my "magic medicine" to some poor soul in an Intensive Care Unit, in response to an urgent request from the doctor on the case. I would tell myself, "Boy, this is the way to do it, this is The Answer." I dreamed of the day when all my patients would be on it, when everyone I saw in the Hypertension Clinic would take it, and they would all have their blood pressure back to normal. Perfectly normal. Perfect.

I think that's what they call a pipe dream. It didn't work out that way. I discovered I had opened up a whole Pandora's box of troubles, of really disturbing, often puzzling side effects.

Sometimes large amounts of fluid collected in the sack around the heart —enough to compromise its function. Blood pressure fell in the major arteries—but it rose in the arteries of the lung. I found out about that particular side effect by accident and published my findings in *Circulation* (1975). And there were more and then more side effects that I kept finding: high blood sugar, high blood levels of the stress hormone adrenalin.

It was a real pharmacological nightmare—until finally I woke up and said, "Stop! That's enough already." I knew then that I would have to deal with this whole problem of blood pressure in some other way. That's why this program. That's why this book.

SUMMARY OF CHAPTERS 21-23:

Well, we've looked at the four major types of medication that are currently used in the treatment of high blood pressure: the diuretics, the blockers, the vasodilators, and the inhibitors.

Even when they work, the best the *diuretics* can do for you is cause you to get rid of some salt—and you could often manage that much more simply by just cutting down on the amount of salt you eat. But they often don't work if they're not used right. And when they don't work it is harder for the other drugs to work as well. Good diet would do what the diuretics do—and do it better.

The *blockers* leave you drowsy when they work, and when they don't leave you drowsy they can't control your blood pressure in a routine domestic crisis or a slow traffic jam. Stress management would do what the blockers do—and do it better.

The *vasodilators* diminish the pressure in the blood vessels by acting directly on the muscles of the arterioles. Salt reduction would do a better job of controlling the fluid content of the blood vessels, and stress management would relax the muscles in the arterioles more effectively.

And the *endocrine inhibitors* end up forcing your body to make more of the very substance whose effects they're trying to get rid of. You'd be better off just not taking them in the first place.

Those are the drugs that are commonly used in the current treatment of high blood pressure. I wanted to tell you a little about them so that you could understand a bit about what it actually was that you were taking. In the next chapter I'll be describing some common other drugs that you may be taking for other problems, and how they affect your blood pressure.

There is an alternative to the drug-based style of treatment, of course. And that's what this program presents. Because exercise, nutrition, and stress management have so much more than the drugs to offer.

And because, for most of you, the pills are simply not the way to go.

VASODILATORS

Generic (chemical) name:	Brand name:
minoxidil	Loniten
hydralazine	Apresoline
prazosin	Minipres

OTHER BLOOD-PRESSURE-LOWERING DRUGS

Generic name:	Brand name:
pargyline	Eutonyl
captopril	Capoten

CALCIUM CHANNEL BLOCKERS

Generic name:	Brand name:
verapamil	Calan, Isoptin
diltiazem	Cardizem
nifedipine	Procardia

24

Additional Drugs

> *I firmly believe that if the whole materia
> medica, as now used, could be sunk to
> the bottom of the sea it would be all the
> better for mankind—and all the worse
> for the fishes.*
>
> Oliver Wendell Holmes

This chapter is about a number of other medicines, food substances, and chemicals that you might already be taking or that you may take at some time in the future. These are not drugs prescribed for high blood pressure. But each one of them has an effect on your blood pressure, on your overall health, on the medicines your doctor gave you to lower your blood pressure, or on the treatment that this program recommends. So they are all relevant to what we're talking about in this program.

The best thing is for you to browse through this chapter, stop every time you see a heading that applies to you and read it. Okay? Let's start with some common drugs.

ALCOHOL

Alcohol is a central nervous system suppressant and a vasodilator. So several drinks can lower your blood pressure.

But there's a problem here.

If you've gotten yourself down to normal blood volume, with a low-sodium diet and/or the proper diuretics, and if you have managed to turn off or turn down the emergency nervous system with the exercises you've learned in this book, or with the use of blocking drugs, you will be very, very sensitive to the effects of alcohol. Particularly on a hot day. Or after getting heated up in a sauna or a hot tub. Because heat is also a vasodilator. So one of the dangers of alcohol is that it can lower your blood pressure too much—and you could even faint.

The other problem with alcohol that we have already mentioned here is that, when the effect of the alcohol wears off and the emergency nervous system (ENS) comes back to life, it may react in an exaggerated manner. In this case the blood pressure may rise quite a bit, depending on how sensitive you are to your ENS hyperactivity.

NICOTINE

Nicotine is a cardiovascular stimulant, so it may raise blood pressure. Combine it with the caffeine in your morning cups of coffee, or your afternoon Pepsi-Cola, and the two drugs together keep your blood pressure up for several hours. They may do a more effective job of it than a scary movie will!

It's difficult to imagine that you could care enough about yourself to read this book but not care enough to stop smoking.

Call the American Cancer Society. Ask for help. Do it now!

VITAMINS

A lot has been written about vitamins and, as far as I know, Americans take more of them than anyone else. Which makes a good deal of sense if you live off fast food and junk food and the typical American diet. If you do, you're getting so many calories that don't have any vitamins in them—all that fat and all that sugar make up about 60 percent of your calories—that you may need some supplementary vitamins.

But if your diet is full of vegetables, fruits, whole grains, and beans, they are so vitamin rich you probably don't have to supplement yourself. But it's your money! If you're going to take them, shop around and buy the least expensive ones.

The evidence that vitamins are useful as a food supplement for most Americans is marginal at best. But their use as drugs in very large doses (so called megavitamin therapy) is even less convincingly documented. There does seem to be a case to be made for high-dose vitamin C; but, to be honest with you, the evidence is pretty controversial and it's not at all clear that everyone will benefit from it.

LAXATIVES

There's an absolute mania in this country to have a bowel movement every day. There seems to be in each culture an organ of fixation. In France it's the liver. In America it's the colon. We expend hundreds of millions of dollars on laxatives, most of which, I'm sorry to say, make the problem worse.

The basic problem in constipation is that there's not enough waste material in the colon to fill it up. I know, it feels like it's too full, but it's really too empty. Our diet is so refined. And because of stress (which results in the excessive operation of the emergency nervous system on the colon) the colon goes into spasm and contracts erratically, not necessarily in a way that helps propel its contents in a forward motion down to the rectum to be eliminated. Most laxatives contribute to this problem by causing more forceful, but not necessarily useful, contractions.

For someone with hypertension, there's a particular danger here. The bowel stimulants may also promote the loss of potassium into the feces and thus aggravate a problem initially begun by the use of diuretics. In fact excessive laxative use *just by itself* can sometimes lead to a very severe hypokalemia (low blood potassium).

I remember an elderly man whom I saw in the hospital where I attend occasionally. He was in for prostate surgery, but this had been delayed because his blood potassium was so low, about 2.8 (normal is about 4.0), that the anesthesiologist wouldn't put him to sleep. He feared he might suffer a serious cardiac irregularity.

I saved him quite an expensive diagnostic workup by asking him a simple question: "Do you suffer from constipation?" The answer was, "Yes." "What do you take for it?" I asked. "Ex-Lax," he replied. "I suppose you take quite a bit of it, don't you, sometimes?" Again the answer was, "Yes. Four or five doses a day when the problem really gets bad." Problem solved. I earned my consultant's fee that day.

All right. So what do you do? The only laxative that makes any sense is a bulk-forming laxative. Make sure you don't get one that has a stimulant in it, even if it says it's a mild stimulant. You want to fill up the colon, then it's easy to empty.

I'll give you a little analogy. You know how easy it is to get toothpaste out of a full tube? You just have to touch it, and just the right amount comes out. And you know how hard it is to get toothpaste out of an empty tube? You have to practically step on it, right?

So the idea is to make your colon like a full tube of toothpaste, not an empty one. That will happen if you eat a diet that's rich in whole grains and bulky vegetables and fruits. If that's not enough, you can buy plain bran in any health food store and in many grocery stores now. Sprinkle it onto your soups, salads, and sauces.

A word of caution. If you have an irritable colon, because your emergency nervous system has been stimulating it wildly over the years, or you've been taking laxatives that stimulate it, you may have to work up to this gradually. You may not be able to take bran, or cereals that contain a lot of bran, at first.

There is a substitute bulk former, which I often suggest, called psyllium. It's derived from a plant called plantain. The three most popular preparations are called *Metamucil, Hydrocil,* and *Konsyl.* They are available in any drugstore without a prescription. Use them as directed on the label.

They are harmless, they even have a mild cholesterol-lowering effect, although you probably wouldn't take them in large enough amounts to make a difference. They tend to cool off the fire in the colon and are now the treatment of choice by specialists for spastic colitis (irritable colon syndrome)—this bowel problem that afflicts so many Americans.

SLEEPING PILLS

Another sign of stress is sleeplessness. A companion mania to having a bowel movement every day is getting a good eight hours of sleep every night. If we didn't worry about it so much we'd probably sleep more easily, and even find out we could get by just fine on fewer hours. There's no evidence, for example, that adults need eight hours of sleep. And the amount of money spent and suffering that goes into achieving that sometimes elusive goal is truly outrageous.

The stress reduction techniques that we discuss in this book may help you relax enough to begin to sleep more easily. Often just regular exercise will do the trick. Of course, cutting down on (or giving up) stimulants such as caffeine and nicotine will help too. You might be brave enough to try cutting down on sleeping pills as you begin to feel better. We'll talk more about this in later chapters. But don't push it, and don't get anxious about it—I think as you take care of yourself more and more your need for sleeping pills will just naturally decline.

TRANQUILIZERS, NERVE PILLS, MUSCLE RELAXANTS

I would say the same about these kinds of pills (of which there are many varieties) as I would about sleeping pills. As you learn more about stress—what it is, and what it does to you, and how to control it—your need for these medicines will just naturally fall away.

You've probably already noticed they don't do such a good job anyway, so it's not as if you're giving up anything very valuable in your life as you use them less and less.

In any one issue of a medical journal a doctor is likely to run across three ads for three top-selling drugs—*Valium (diazepam), Dalmane (flurazepam),* and *Librium (chlordiazepoxide).* Valium is promoted to reduce anxiety, Dalmane to encourage sleep, and Librium to relax muscles.

Advertising is marvelous! There's actually very little to distinguish these three drugs from one another except their advertisements. They all belong to the same large group of drugs (the benzodiazepines) and have virtually interchangeable actions. It's the toothpaste story, once again.

But I'd like to give you one warning about them. They all tend to be *long acting* and their active ingredients tend to *accumulate*—to build up in the body and bloodstream. This can lead to altered mentation (thought processes) or reduced alertness in most people, and especially in older people if they take one of these drugs every day.

Flurazepam in particular, according to a report in *Medical Letter* (1981), can build up to a blood level four to six times higher after seven consecutive nights of use.

Doctors and their nervous patients would like to believe there is a "happy pill"—one that will take away your troubles and make you feel better. Science fiction stories such as *Brave New World* may talk about such things, but I'm afraid we haven't reached that point yet in medicine. But we pretend we have as we write prescriptions for Valium and other such medications—and our patients go along with the pretense.

I don't want you to stop these kinds of pills abruptly if you really feel you need them. Ask your doctor, see what he says. Maybe you could cut back as you begin to learn to relax by using other techniques such as meditation.

DIGOXIN (DIGITALIS)

I saw a man today—this very day I'm writing this—who illustrates perfectly the ridiculousness, the absolute inappropriateness, of using digoxin in most people with hypertension.

What does digoxin (or any other preparation of digitalis, for that matter) do?

Mainly, it's used to strengthen the heartbeat. So here was a seventy-two-year-old black man, such a nice, kindly, cooperative gentleman, so anxious to please the doctors who saved his life only a few months ago, perfectly willing to take their medicines. Who was he to argue with these superheroes in white?

He had come into the hospital in congestive heart failure, which means there was so much fluid backed up in his lungs, he could hardly breathe. He was given diuretics to get rid of the fluid, and digoxin for his heart failure. If he has heart failure, he must have a weak heart, right? "Why were you in the hospital?" I asked him. "It's my heart, Doc," he said. "I've got a bad ticker."

I asked him to step up on the treadmill, and I started it up. Every few minutes I increased the speed and the inclination. I watched him carefully. At first his steps were a little wobbly, a little tentative. He wasn't used to walking on a machine—and it was pretty noisy. His heart rate slowly increased, 85, 95, 105 . . . His blood pressure was high to begin with—the excitement of it all and his fear of the test sent it up to 180/95.

As the treadmill rose and speeded up, his pressure inched upward to 210/100, 230/105, finally reaching 270/110. I almost never let people get over 240, that's the stop point in a treadmill test, but I could see he was okay.

And he felt fine. Not winded, no heart pain, no headaches—in fact no symptoms at all. I finally stopped the test and told him his heart was just wonderful, that he had a strong heart. In fact I said his heart was about as impressive as Arnold Schwarzenegger's biceps. He'd gone into heart failure because he ate salt and the fluid built up in his body and filled up his lungs—but his heart's not weak. Are you kidding me? Get to a pressure of 270 with a weak heart?

I told him he didn't need digoxin. He just needs to stay away from salt.

I don't think that many doctors see high blood pressure as a sign of a *strong* heart. But a world authority on stress testing, Dr. Myrvin Ellestad, considers a large rise in systolic pressure during the treadmill test a sign of very good heart muscle function indeed *(Cardiovascular Reviews and Reports,* 1983).

Now don't go throwing the digoxin pills away yet. Maybe they're used to slow your heart rate down if you have something called *atrial flutter-fibrillation* or some other form of abnormal, rapid heart rhythm.

But ask your doctor if you really need this pill. A recent article in the *American Journal of Medicine* (1982) described just how useless it usually is to strengthen the heartbeat. This is one pill most people with blood pressure problems can do without.

DIET PILLS

The pills people use to reduce appetite are mostly a rip-off. It's shocking but true. It's a multimillion-dollar industry, though, and the money to be made depends on how desperate many people are—and also on plain old hokum and marketing.

Pills that contain *sugar* are supposed to produce a quick rise in blood sugar and do, I'm certain, result in some trivial suppression of appetite, but the effect is mainly one of suggestion. Beware the rebound effect, however—the blood sugar dropping and the appetite increasing again.

Pills that *swell* and *expand* and are supposed to make you feel full are completely harmless but phony. Effectively, you're paying ninety dollars a pound for bulk when you take these pills—and you'd do better to eat lettuce and carrots and broccoli, which at least have some nutritional value and are cheaper.

The *stimulant* that's in over-the-counter, nonprescription diet pills produces a loss of appetite but may also cause your blood pressure to rise. The FDA describes phenylpropanolamine, the substance most commonly found in these pills, as safe and effective. That's to say that these drugs were found to produce greater weight loss than a placebo in scientific studies—but the difference was only about one to two pounds a month—which is an insignificant difference biologically.

I don't recommend that you use other, more powerful stimulants; the *amphetamines,* such as *Dexedrine,* will certainly raise your blood pressure, so watch out for them. The American Medical Association describes their effect for weight loss as "clinically insignificant" and their potential for abuse "considerable."

In any case you should talk with your doctor about all this, share your concerns with him, and ask his advice. My own knowledge of these pills suggests that they're not much use at all and can be more than a little dangerous for people with hypertension.

A medicine that's commonly prescribed to produce rapid weight loss is *thyroid hormone*, also known as *Synthroid*. The idea is that, if you're overweight and can't lose weight easily, your metabolism may be slow. So thyroid pills can speed up your metabolism.

It sounds reasonable, only it doesn't work.

I saw a woman recently, in her thirties, who was taking so much thyroid she was actually toxic—flushed, with moist, warm skin, rapid heartbeat, tremors. Her emergency nervous system was on, and it was driving her a little bit nutty, and she wasn't even losing weight—she was actually putting it on!

But she lost weight once we stopped the thyroid pills and taught her how to eat and exercise and take care of herself.

For most of you, thyroid isn't the answer. There's never been and never will be a scientific study showing thyroid is the answer to this problem. And *especially* if you have hypertension, don't try this approach, because thyroid turns on the emergency nervous system and makes your blood pressure go up.

Check with your doctor if you take thyroid, and make certain you really need it. There are tests that can show whether your thyroid gland is working properly or not, and whether you do really need thyroid pills.

PROTEIN POWDERS

The Cambridge diet and other vitamin-supplemented protein powders (Optifast, etc.) are a widely popular approach to the problem of weight control.

The Cambridge diet plan, originally developed by physicians to be dispensed by physicians, is now marketed by housewives and schoolboys, grocery clerks and bus drivers and anyone else who can scrimp up the entrance fee and get into this burgeoning pyramid sales scheme.

This is one of a variety of products and programs that come under the general heading of "protein-sparing modified fasts." The fast is based on the assumption that supplying a certain minimum number of calories as protein in the diet will prevent your own body from burning up important proteins from your heart, skeletal muscles, and other tissues.

This premise has never been adequately proved. Moreover, there is scant advantage in restricting calories this severely. The Cambridge diet plan (330–440 calories) plus a small salad can provide about 500 calories a day with virtually all known nutrients. The calories are consumed in the form of a protein drink made by adding one of several flavored powders to water.

By way of contrast, with carefully chosen normal foods, one can quite easily plan for about 1,000 calories a day, again with all nutrients provided.

The difference between 1,000 calories of normal food and a synthetic diet containing 330–500 calories is only one to one and a half pounds weight loss a week—hardly worth it. And that's an expensive 330–500 calories, too—not a bargain, at ten dollars a pound.

A second "advantage" of the diet is that it produces a state of *ketosis*. That is, the metabolism of your body is so disturbed by this restricted diet that large amounts of organic acids are produced by the breaking down of fat stores, which cannot be completely cleared out by the kidneys. As a result they build up in the blood and produce four effects—headaches, bad breath, euphoria, and loss of appetite.

Of course! You're starving, and nature naturally provides any starving animal with strength and optimism to continue to seek food, and a reduction in appetite and food craving, to make things go more smoothly. (I don't know the whys and wherefores of bad breath and headaches—unless it's to decrease your sex appeal and keep your attention on the urgent matter of finding some more food!)

The diet works. No food choices, no more going to the grocery store. You were supposed to see your doctor once or twice a month, and get some blood tests and a cardiogram (EKG) from time to time—but I think that's all gone to the four winds, now the diet is out of the hands of professionals. But the diet does produce weight loss.

I saw a man who lost a hundred pounds on Optifast, and I'm damned if he didn't gain it all back in six months! He rewarded himself for all those months of deprivation, I guess, and then rewarded himself again and again. He really hadn't learned anything from his fasting experience.

The answer to the problem of overweight isn't to starve yourself—it's to find out what your body really needs.

COLD AND ALLERGY MEDICATIONS

There are fifty-seven varieties of these patent medicines at least. Most of them contain the antihistamine *chlorpheniramine*, which reduces sneezing and other allergy symptoms—and makes you sleepy. They often contain a *decongestant* as well, which works like a spray or nose drops, except that when you take it in a pill it's absorbed into the bloodstream and goes from there to your nose.

There are two problems. You need to take a lot of it in pill form to equal the effect you'd get from applying a little directly to your nose by spray. And of course, when the drug is in your blood, it also goes to other tissues and organs besides your nose—notably your heart and blood vessels, where it acts as a stimulant and may raise your blood pressure.

People who have high blood pressure already may be very sensitive to oral decongestants, especially if they are also taking emergency nervous system blockers (see Chapter 22). The stimulants in common use are pseudoephedrine, phenylpropanolamine (the diet pill in a new guise), and phenylephrine. And many of the pills contain caffeine as well—to counteract the sleepiness caused by the antihistamines.

Read the labels—it's all there, and you need to know.

PAIN MEDICATIONS

As we get older, especially if we're sedentary, we start getting aches and pains—what they call "rheumatism" in the TV ads.

There's stiffness, too, especially in the early morning when you first get up, or after sitting for a long time in your car. And maybe you're sensitive to cold, wet weather. Lots of people have this problem. Mostly it's sort of a low-grade inflammation—it's called degenerative arthritis, and it's limited to the joints we use the most.

We used to take aspirin for this condition, until the drug manufacturers came up with a new generation of pain pills called the *nonsteroidal anti-inflammatory drugs.*

NONSTEROIDAL ANTI-INFLAMMATORY DRUGS

Generic (chemical) name:	*Brand names:*
ibuprofen	Motrin, Rufen
fenoprofen	Nalfon
indomethacin	Indocin
meclofenamate	Meclomen
mefenamic acid	Ponstel
naproxen	Naprosyn, Anaprox
sulindac	Clinoril
tolmetin	Tolectin
zomepirac	Zomax (recalled 1983)
phenylbutazone	Butazolidin
benoxaprofen	Oraflex (withdrawn 1982)
piroxicam[1]	Feldene
diflunisal[1]	Dolobid

[1]Unusually long acting; so if toxicity occurs the effects will take longer to wear off.

You need to be very careful about these drugs. They can be killers. There is a review article in *Medical Letter* (1983) that details the serious toxicity of these drugs. Lung toxicity, kidney injury (especially when these drugs are taken at the same time as a diuretic), intestinal bleeding, and blood cell disorders are a few of the many problems cropping up because so many people are taking these drugs.

They are liable to raise your blood pressure—and if you read the fine print on the packet insert you'll find that it tells you that too. These drugs inhibit one of your body's own natural blood-pressure-lowering hormones, prostaglandin, which can be very important to you.

So if you have arthritis or other kinds of chronic pain, and you're taking one of the drugs on this list, talk to your doctor. Your blood pressure may be easier to control, and you may get better results from this program, if you don't take this kind of pill for your pain.

BIRTH CONTROL PILLS, ESTROGENS, AND TREATMENTS FOR MENOPAUSAL SYMPTOMS

As a third-year medical student I had the "concession" to dispense free contraceptive devices and oral drugs to my classmates. I guess the pharmaceutical representatives wanted to establish brand-name recognition in future doctors as early as possible. And I was a willing dupe.

Two years later I watched helplessly for two weeks while one of my patients, a pretty, frightened young lady, died. She was one of the first cases of fatal pulmonary embolus (blood clotting in the lungs) associated with the use of oral contraceptives.

Since then I've never let any ladies I cared about take these drugs. And I haven't prescribed them, either. Just as I quit prescribing chloramphenicol (an antibiotic) after I cared for the young son of one of my professors in medical school and watched him die. He'd taken the drug for a cold, or something pretty trivial like that, and then developed aplastic anemia— his bone marrow stopped working—as a result of a side effect of the drugs. And he never recovered.

We learn important lessons from experiences like that. I turned into a "therapeutic nihilist"—which is just a fancy way of saying that I don't like to use medicines or surgery unless I really have to. And I mean, really.

The estrogen in Premarin and birth control pills stimulates the liver to make more of a certain protein that combines with renin (a protein made in the kidney) to make a hormone we've talked about a bit already, *angiotensin*—which raises blood pressure and decreases the blood flow to the kidneys.

If you take these drugs long enough your blood pressure will rise. If you're especially susceptible your pressure may rise quite a bit, giving you hypertension. This problem has recently been discussed in the *British Medical Journal* (1982) and in a review in the *New England Journal of Medicine* (1981).

If you already have hypertension, stop taking "the pill" for a while and see if your blood pressure drops.

And if you're not using the pill don't start it. Use some other technique —a diaphragm, an IUD, or something else.

If you're taking estrogen for menopausal symptoms, take the smallest possible dose that controls your complaints—this is often 0.3 mg. Taking a small dose will prevent your bones from thinning out, and the risks are very small at this level. There's a good review of this subject in the *Annals of Internal Medicine* (1983), pointing out the advantages of keeping the dose low.

CIMETIDINE (TAGAMET)

I definitely feel like David facing Goliath with this one. *Tagamet* is the most popular prescription drug in the world—it sold $750 million worth in 1981. And what's it for? Stomach ulcers, if you can believe it.

Are there *that* many people with ulcers who are willing to take tablets that cost thirty-five dollars a month and that they have to go to a doctor to get? Whatever happened to *Rolaids* or *Tums* or *Maalox*—or milk, for that matter? I lived on those things in college. I didn't go to a doctor for heartburn, for God's sake.

If cimetidine were used properly—as a short-term remedy only—it wouldn't be the number-one-selling drug of the year. But people are people and pain is pain, and the drug does relieve pain and prevent flare-ups, and doctors keep renewing the prescriptions—if they didn't their patients would just go get it from someone else.

Cimetidine reduces blood flow to the liver. And so any other drugs you are taking that are excreted by the liver tend to build up in your bloodstream if you take cimetidine too. Blood levels of the beta blocker propranolol increase if you take cimetidine, and so do levels of the xanthine drug theophylline, used in asthma.

Now I know that lots of people who have high blood pressure and are taking medications for it also have stomach ulcers or heartburn. So be very careful about cimetidine and see if you can do without it once your ulcer has had a chance to heal. And tell your doctor your concerns about this, too.

Be careful about *antacids*, too, as some of them have lots of sodium in them—*Alka-Seltzer* and *Bromo-Seltzer* because they contain sodium citrate, and others because they contain sodium bicarbonate. Don't be too innocent and trusting about these things. Be practical. Read the labels.

DIABETES MEDICINES

Many people with diabetes have high blood pressure, too, and may be reading this book. Most of them will have the kind of diabetes that comes on late in life and is associated with a rich, fatty diet, sedentary life style, overweight, and stress.

If you are taking medicine for your diabetes—either the pills or the insulin shots—you need to read this section and discuss it with your doctor. This is very important.

This program may improve your diabetes so much that you'll be able to stop taking these medicines, or at least reduce them substantially.

A diet that's low in fat and sugar, with less caffeine and alcohol, and plenty of fiber from whole grains, together with regular exercise, weight loss, and stress management—that's powerful medicine! Your body will breathe a sigh of relief and your overworked pancreas (which is where insulin is made) may at last be able to keep up with things on its own.

So check with your doctor, watch your urine and blood sugar, and reduce the diabetes drugs if you can. And remember, stopping or reducing the blood pressure pills may help the diabetes too.

One more thing. Insulin and the diabetes pills reduce blood sugar, which stimulates appetite, which of course sends you to the refrigerator or the doughnut shop—so watch out for this trap. I let people's blood sugar stay pretty high, even up to 200, during the early phases of the program—in the short term, it's harmless, and it does tend to promote weight loss if that's something you need.

POTASSIUM

The majority of people who are taking diuretics need to take a potassium supplement. This makes the diuretic work better, helps suppress the blood-pressure-raising hormone renin, and also maintains muscle strength and the regularity of the heart.

The cheapest form of potassium supplement is the bitter pink liquid, 10 percent KCl. Some people don't mind taking it. But most hate it and won't take it regularly—they'd rather lie, cheat, and steal! And they often don't tell their doctors they're not taking it, either.

There are several tablets or powders that dissolve in water or juice, which don't taste much better but cost a lot more. They make evil-looking bubbly orange or red concoctions that are difficult for anyone to down. Rather like your first martini.

And there are slow-release tablets or capsules that don't taste at all since they don't release the potassium in your mouth but instead release it slowly as they pass through your intestines. These are the most popular—but also the most expensive.

For the most part you'll find that it's cheaper to take these medicines than to obtain an equivalent amount of potassium by eating fresh fruits and vegetables, and of course you also avoid the 300–400 calories in food that accompany the standard dose of potassium, about 40 millimoles.

And if you need to lose weight it may be wisest to use the 10 percent KC1 solution—the pink liquid. It tastes so bad, it may even spoil your appetite!

How's that for killing two birds with one stone?

ANTIANGINAL DRUGS

Some people with high blood pressure and enlarged hearts suffer from angina pectoris. This is a tightness and/or discomfort, perhaps painful but not always described that way, that comes on with exertion or excitement and is located in the middle of the chest, just beneath the breastbone (sternum). It may also appear in the neck, jaw, left shoulder or arm.

It can usually be relieved by a few minutes' rest, or more quickly by popping a nitroglycerine tablet under the tongue. There are also longer-acting nitroglycerine-like medicines, and if you take them regularly they may prevent these attacks and lessen the need for under-the-tongue nitro tablets. However these long-acting nitros aren't usually all that effective, and if they haven't noticeably benefited you, you can ask your doctor if you can stop them.

The beta blockers (see Chapter 22) are used to treat angina, too. They act by decreasing the work the heart is doing and thus decreasing its need for oxygen. Angina occurs when the heart muscle isn't getting enough oxygen—either because the muscle has grown so big (hypertrophy) that it has outstripped its blood supply, or because one or more of the coronary arteries is blocked (atherosclerosis, or hardening of the arteries) by cholesterol, scarring, clots, or calcium.

Most people with angina have this second problem, and they're at risk of an artery totally closing and causing a heart attack. Beta blockers prevent the heart from doing too much work, so it doesn't have the problem of not getting enough oxygen anymore.

A new group of drugs, the calcium channel blockers we talked about a little in the last chapter (diltiazem, verapamil, and nifedipine), are getting lots of publicity these days. They also prevent the heart from working too hard and using up too much oxygen, and they have a nitroglycerine-like action too, to open up the coronary arteries.

The angina that people with hypertension have is often a different kettle of fish from the usual angina. For one thing the coronary arteries may not be blocked, and the risk of heart attack may not be as great. The problem is that the size and work load of the heart are too great for its blood supply. You need to reduce the blood pressure so your heart won't need to work so hard! So treatment can be dramatic and even curative. Here's one problem where life style change can make a big difference right away.

You may need medicines to begin with, but don't feel discouraged. And by all means keep in communication with your doctor, so he knows what's happening to you and can recognize when your need for medications is lessened.

MEDICINES TO LOWER URIC ACID OR PREVENT GOUT

If you take a diuretic, your blood uric acid level is very likely to be raised above normal. And there are other ways you may be raising your blood uric acid levels, too. If you eat a rich diet, especially heavy in meat, that can do it. If you have a genetic predisposition, that can do it. If your kidneys have been badly damaged by high blood pressure, so your blood filtering rate is noticeably reduced, this can be another contributing factor. And these four factors can work together additively.

The usual range for blood uric acid is about 4–7. Above 9, the risk of gout rises. (Gout is a severe pain in one or more joints, usually but not always the joint of the big toe.) With uric acid levels above 11 or 12, the risk of gout gets very great indeed.

Allopurinol is a drug that slows down (or halts) your body's production of so much uric acid. *Probenecid* and *sulphinpyrazone* are two drugs that increase the excretion of uric acid and lower the blood levels that way.

These three drugs are overused. Most people with elevated uric acid levels under 12 will never get gout in any case—and so we wind up with eight or nine people out of ten who take the medicines getting no actual benefit from them. All the drugs are doing is lowering a number they wouldn't even know about if their doctor hadn't told them.

Changing your rich meat diet and getting off diuretics seems a better way to handle the problem. But ask your doctor whether you really need these pills.

One more thing. If you do get, or have gotten, gout, and are taking pain medicine for it, be very careful about what else it's doing to you. *Indomethacin* and similar medicines will raise your blood pressure (see page 273 under Pain Medications). They may be useful in a severe, acute attack of gout, but not so good when taken indefinitely.

DRUGS THAT LOWER CHOLESTEROL

The overwhelming majority of scientists, researchers, physicians, and others interested in preventing heart attacks agree that diet, and in particular *dietary fat* and *cholesterol*, are very important risk factors for promoting hardening and blockage of the coronary arteries.

The American diet (indeed, the diet of any relatively industrialized country) is too high in calories from meat, fowl, seafood, and animal products such as dairy foods, eggs, lard, and organ meats. We add on average about 80–100mg of cholesterol for every 100ml of plasma by the diet we eat—in other words, our habitual diet increases our cholesterol count by 80 to 100 points. Our average cholesterol count is about 230, where ideally it could be 120–150.

There are a variety of drugs that lower blood cholesterol or blood fat levels or both. Most of these are not very effective in reducing deaths due to heart attacks, and many have side effects that are unacceptable or worse. These drugs are hardly ever prescribed unless the cholesterol level is above 300, since there are just too many of us with cholesterol levels between 220 and 300.

Some of these drugs, when their effects are compared with the effects of no treatment at all, actually turn out to *increase* the risk of death or illness.

The safest among them seem to be the resins, which bind cholesterol in the gut and speed its elimination from the body by excretion. Two of these are called *colestipol* and *cholestyramine*, and their side effects are seldom anything worse than upset stomach and a change of bowel habits in some patients. They do also tend to bind other drugs that are taken at the same time—so you need to watch out for this problem if you're taking other medicines.

Probucol is currently being promoted as a lipid (fat)-lowering drug, which should be used only after diet by itself has proved ineffective. Its actual action—how it works—is not certain. Nor are there scientific studies to prove that lowering cholesterol by the use of this drug prevents heart attacks.

And we should bear in mind that previous reports of five other kinds of cholesterol-lowering drugs showed that they were of no benefit or were actually harmful to the people who took them. These findings were reported by the Coronary Drug Project in the *Journal of the American Medical Association* (1972, 1973, and 1975).

The CDP's findings dashed our hopes that there was a pill we could take that would make up for (and undo) the harmful effects of decades of a rich diet, smoking, and other abusive practices.

Gemfibrozil is a new drug that lowers fat levels in the blood (the triglycerides) but not cholesterol. The value of this drug is completely unproven but, since it is similar to a drug called *clofibrate* that was used in the Coronary Drug Project and found to be harmful, I'm not too optimistic about its long-term value.

Clearly the best way for most people to handle the problem of cholesterol and fat is to change their diet and learn to handle stress better. Ask your doctor what specific measures are most important in your case. It's usually effective to lower the amount of red meat, shrimp, organ meats (liver, etc.), dairy foods and eggs, oils, lard, and butter in your diet. And you may also need to decrease your consumption of sugar, fruit, and alcohol.

DRUGS FOR THE TREATMENT OF ASTHMA

Asthma, or narrowing of the bronchi and bronchioles (large and small air tubes carrying air from the throat to the lungs), results when the tiny muscles that line the walls of these tubes go into spasm.

This spasm can come about because of allergy, infection, or a variety of complex psychological reactions that you could loosely describe as "stress." It's often the case that all three of these factors are at work in the same individual, though any one attack may be brought on by one specific factor—such as allergy to house dust or pollen.

The usual treatments for asthma include oral liquids and medicines that loosen up the sputum, so that it can be coughed out more easily, extra oxygen and moisture in the air we breathe, and antibiotics to help the body combat any infection that may have triggered the attack.

None of these treatments raise the blood pressure, although obviously the anxiety that accompanies acute asthma attacks can trigger the emergency nervous system, thus raising the blood pressure of most asthmatics. Some particularly susceptible people—by which I mean those who already have a problem with high blood pressure—may fare worse than others in this respect.

The other drugs that are commonly used *may* affect your blood pressure and are often overprescribed by doctors and overused by patients. In other words the potential for abuse is very great.

Drugs such as *metaproterenol* and *terbutaline* are beta stimulants. Just as we saw that beta blockers lower the blood pressure, beta stimulants are likely to raise it, and more so in susceptible people.

These drugs can be taken as pills, injected, or inhaled in a small hand-held nebulizer as needed. And that "as needed" on the label can lead many people to overuse of these drugs. It's a big problem.

Aminophylline and related *xanthine* drugs are available in a variety of forms. These drugs also work by relaxing the tightened muscles lining the air tubes. And they work together with the beta stimulants to produce a greater effect than either would by itself.

The problem with the xanthines (remember, the caffeine in coffee is a xanthine) is that they stimulate the body, turn on the emergency nervous system, and may contribute to high blood pressure—again, mostly in susceptible people.

These drugs can save lives in an asthmatic emergency. But if you're using them daily you'd do better to find out what can be done to prevent the asthma.

Avoid or somehow get rid of those allergens (you may even have to move—but your life may be at stake), get counseling on your emotional factors, and do what you can to avoid infections.

You must stop smoking—no ifs, ands, or buts.

Ask your doctor to help you get on the lowest possible dose of these drugs. And if he feels you can simplify things, and use only one medicine, you'd do much better with one of the xanthines (aminophylline) than with one of the beta stimulators.

Steroids or cortisone drugs are also sometimes prescribed for asthmatics. *Prednisone* is the commonest, but other steroids are also used.

Use these drugs very sparingly if possible—they raise the blood pressure in several different ways, and their effects last a long time. Their most significant blood-pressure-raising effect is to raise angiotensin levels, which we talked about when we were discussing birth control pills.

DRUGS FOR ABNORMAL HEART RHYTHMS OR PALPITATIONS

The commonest form of abnormal heart rhythm is the PVC, or *premature ventricular contraction,* in which the heart ventricle beats too early, before the heart has had a chance to fill completely. Sometimes the early beat originates from the atrium, and this type of abnormal rhythm is described as a *premature atrial contraction,* or PAC.

PVCs and PACs are usually harmless, though sensitive people may be alarmed or annoyed by them. They may occur in people who smoke, drink caffeinated beverages, worry (or show other signs of stress), are sedentary or out of shape, or who have high blood pressure. They may also occur for no apparent reason at all.

In people who have severe blockages of one or more coronary arteries, PVCs may point to a relative lack of oxygen in some part of the heart muscle. In such people the irritability of the heart muscle may be a sign of great danger—and doctors usually treat this quickly.

PVCs may happen to people who are taking digoxin (a heart-strengthening pill; see pages 268–69), especially if the blood potassium level is low. And low potassium by itself may do it.

The problem is whether or not to treat people with harmless but frequent PVCs. Many doctors bring out the old prescription pad whenever a patient has PVCs, and one stroke of a pen can give you an order to take medicine—maybe for the rest of your life.

There are a variety of drugs—*quinidine, procainamide, lidocaine, disopyramide,* and the beta blockers (see Chapter 22)—that are sometimes successful in suppressing these abnormal beats and allowing the heart to beat more normally.

Many of the people who take these drugs get little benefit from them. And, once again, we are talking about a tremendous potential for abuse and overuse. Ask your doctor if you really need these medicines. This is a situation in which a second opinion from a specialist might be very useful.

I have found that many people can rid themselves of this problem by eliminating smoking and coffee, reducing their dietary use of sugar and fat, managing stress more effectively, replacing their low potassium stores, and participating in regular aerobic exercises.

Your heart wants to be treated right. If it's irritated and twitching, maybe you should listen to it—it's the only heart you've got, and probably the only one you'll ever have.

The Wizard of Oz didn't have a spare heart to give the Tin Woodman, and the wizards of medicine aren't much ahead of him. And reading about the ordeal that Dr. Barney Clark, the dentist who received the first plastic heart, went through doesn't lead me to believe that this is now or ever will be a really viable alternative to the preventive practices discussed in this book.

Listen. I'm not advocating closing down all the drugstores—don't get me wrong. I'm just saying that we all, consumers and physicians and pharmacists, need to use drugs more wisely, more judiciously.

Dr. Joseph Cosentino, chief medical consultant to the Board of Medical Quality Assurance in California, remarked in a recent interview that he agreed with Oliver Wendell Holmes's comment: "If all the medicine in the United States was dumped into the sea, only the fish would be worse off."

Dr. Cosentino went on to say that, under the influence of "an enormous barrage" from the media, we have "become a culture of drug users." We are bombarded with commercials promoting drugs to cure everything from headaches and indigestion to hemorrhoids and depression. And as a result, not surprisingly, some of us "believe there is a drug to solve every problem we face."

Drugs do have a purpose, which is to help the body make corrections that need to be made and fight battles that need to be fought. But let's not overburden the body with unnecessary drugs and their side effects.

Let's use drugs when they'll really help. And remember, it's your body that's the ultimate healer.

25

Nutrition

An apple a day bugs the A.M.A.

Proverb

Nutrition, exercise, and stress management are the three keys to an effective alternative program to combat high blood pressure. And they work together. They're interrelated and *synergistic*—that is, their effect together is greater than the sum of their individual effects. A healthy exercise program helps you to reduce stress. Good stress management techniques will help with nutrition—so you won't eat so many "worry" foods. A good diet will take a load of stress off your body. And so on.

So I'd like you to have a clear understanding of each of these three areas as we move on into the program. Because the better you understand what's going on in your own body the easier it will be for you to change it —and to bring that blood pressure under control again, permanently!

Let me start out by saying that your body knows what it needs in the way of nourishment. So you don't have to be convinced by what I'm going to tell you about diet—you just need to be open to it.

I'm confident that if you will learn to pay attention to what your body tells you about different foods—not what you think is right, not what the TV tells you, not even what your mother taught you, but what your own experience now tells you—then you're going to end up on a good diet, a healthy diet.

You're going to end up on a diet that is appropriate for you. Your own personal diet. It's probably going to be fairly low in cholesterol and fat and sugar and salt. In fact it'll probably be pretty near the kind of diet I'd recommend for you. But you will do best to discover this for yourself. This chapter is meant to alert you to your own body's requirements in the way of nutrition—and to offer you some clues and some guidelines that may help along the way.

Let's start with salt.

SALT

The biggest single nutritional question that faces the hypertensive is salt use.

How much salt do you use on your food?

How much salt do you use in your food—salt that's added while the food is being cooked?

And how much salt have the manufacturers added to the food you eat —before you even begin to cook it? While it was being processed, or preserved, or packaged?

Most people with high blood pressure are aware of the effects of salt in their diet and don't add any salt to the food at the table. You may have thrown the salt shaker out already. I certainly hope so! Some people are already avoiding adding any salt to the food they cook. But that's usually less than half the problem. The real question isn't how much salt you add, it's *how much salt the food already has in it* when you pick it up in the grocery store.

Salt isn't added to food only as a seasoning, of course, it's also added as a preservative, a mixer, and a stabilizer. Manufacturers don't really know yet what to replace it with in every case.

Food that spoils on the shelf could cause botulism and other forms of food poisoning—and the specter of customers dying of food poisoning is something that makes food manufacturers very reluctant to stop using salt as a preservative until they can find a satisfactory substitute.

Some of the substances that have been suggested cause cancer; others don't work well as preservatives; some make the food taste bad; and some turn it a funny color.

We've gotten used to the pink coloration of bacon and ham; in fact now we even think it means the meat's in good condition. But that coloration comes from sodium nitrate and nitrite. You will find nitrates and nitrites in all the pink meats—hot dogs, luncheon meats, bologna, ham, bacon, and so on. And those nitrates and nitrites don't just change the color of the meat. They are *sodium based*. And there's also some concern that they may cause cancer.

We are so used to manufactured, processed convenience foods (and so dependent on them) that we are buying more and more of them. It's a real advantage to the manufacturers to be able to make food with a long shelf life, and if they don't use salt to preserve these foods, what are they going to do instead? At the moment, salt and other sodium products are the best they've come up with. *So even when you don't add salt to the food you eat, the manufacturers have almost certainly added it for you.*

Cutting out salt at table, and not adding salt while cooking, may be reducing only about 20 to 25 percent of the total salt in your diet. And once you have hypertension, that may not be enough to make much of a difference.

What's the problem with salt? As I've said before, our bodies simply aren't designed to cope with the amount of salt that's in our everyday diet. There are now plenty of studies available that show a direct correlation between the amount of salt a society consumes and the amount of hypertension in that society. In the few isolated cultures that still exist where there's virtually no salt in the diet there's also virtually no hypertension.

Our bodies have been around for millions of years, and they are best adapted to an environment in which salt is very hard to come by. Primitive man didn't have salt shakers or manufacturing companies that preserved his foods for him, and salt occurs naturally in foods *only in very small amounts*. So we're perfectly adapted to an environment where sodium is rare and the potassium content of food is very high.

What goes wrong today is our kidneys. They simply weren't designed to throw off the quantity of salt that we eat every day. At least, not for a lifetime. Oh, they may manage to do it for forty or fifty years before they begin to fail, but sometimes they give out when you're only twenty-nine years old. You suddenly find out from your doctor that you have high blood pressure. Then you *really* need to go on a diet!

Do you use any canned foods? Anything that comes from a jar, or a sack, or a box, or a bag? Anything frozen? (If it has been frozen, even if it's a dessert, it likely has salt in it.) Any kind of cheese? Any bakery goods? Any restaurant food? There's salt in virtually everything that's prepared by other people and marketed for you to eat.

Salt, of course, is *sodium chloride;* it's present in soy sauce, tamari, sea salt, garlic salt, seasoned salt . . . or under a dozen other names. Most kinds of seasonings in shaker bottles have salt in them. It's in most sauces and dressings. Cured and prepared meats are full of it. And the *sodium* part of sodium chloride is also toxic by itself; it is found in such things as baking powder, baking soda, Accent (monosodium glutamate).

With a high blood pressure problem, you need to watch all this very closely. You'll need to read the labels and know your way around foods. (In the Appendices to this book you'll find the names of some books that list the sodium content of foods.)

If you're on a diuretic and you're eating what you think is a low-sodium diet, but you're not responding, it may mean that you're still eating too much salt. The only way to find this out for sure is to have your doctor perform a twenty-four-hour urine sodium test. The amount of sodium you excrete every day is a very accurate indicator of the amount of sodium you're eating. So this test will let you know how low in sodium your "low sodium diet" really is.

The typical American eats about 180 to 200 millimoles of sodium a day (about 4.5 grams of sodium, or 11 grams of salt)—and we want you to try to get down to less than 50 millimoles (a little over 1 gram of sodium). You can get down to less than 50 millimoles and still enjoy your food, but you'll probably have to be more careful about it than you are at present.

Even then, you'll still be eating four or five times more sodium than the average Yanomamo tribesman!

I read in Newsweek *that the idea that salt causes hypertension is pretty controversial still, and that not all the experts agree. Apparently some of them feel the evidence isn't strong enough to warrant reducing the salt intake of the average person, or even restricting salt in the diet of everyone with hypertension.*

You're right, these are controversial issues. But not as controversial as some of the media would lead you to believe.

An article in *Nutrition Action,* published by the Center for Science in the Public Interest (1982), looked at some of the behind-the-scenes maneuvering that led to stories in both the New York *Times* and *Newsweek.*

One item they mentioned was that a Dr. David McCarron has been lobbying very hard to promote his own theory that calcium loss is the most important factor in the genesis of human hypertension. (Naturally, he's been an outspoken critic of the theory that links sodium with hypertension.) However, Dr. McCarron has received substantial financial support from the National Dairy Council, who would obviously love to see 60 million hypertensive Americans drinking a lot more milk to obtain extra calcium!

A symposium held in September 1982 led to headlines in some papers such as "Experts Challenge Low Sodium Diet." This symposium and its participating speakers received major support from . . . the Campbell Soup Company and the International Life Sciences Institute (an organization whose membership includes General Foods, Kellogg, Kraft, Nabisco, ITT-Continental Baking, Procter and Gamble, and others). These organizations would naturally be only too happy to take some of the heat off sodium, which is such an important constituent of many of their products.

There will always be experts who disagree—that's just the way we are. We're an argumentative species. And more than thirty years after the first research showed the link between cigarette smoking and cancer the American Tobacco Institute can still find "experts" who disagree. That's human nature.

But since it affects your health and well-being so directly, you shouldn't just throw up your hands as if to say, "Well, if the experts can't agree, I'm not going to change my eating habits." Talk to your doctor and see what he says. Read this book carefully and try out the program. If I'm right, it'll work for you—and that's the true test: what works for you.

The American Society for Clinical Nutrition considered the links between different dietary factors and human disease in 1979. On a scale of 0 to 100, they judged the strength of the relationship between salt and hypertension to be 74, which is especially significant when you consider how many other factors are involved that we already know about. Only two other factors (sugar and tooth decay at 87, and alcohol and liver disease at 84) received higher ratings.

Oh, the evidence is there, all right.

A very large-scale study of the effects of weight loss and salt restriction on literally thousands of hypertensives is being conducted now at the Universities of Minnesota, Alabama, Mississippi, and California. But the results won't be available until 1992.

Must we wait till then to know what to do?

Of course not! How ridiculous!

According to one of the principal scientists involved in this study, Dr. Ronald Prineas, "The best animal, epidemiological (population), human clinical and anthropological evidence says it is reasonable for everyone—even people with normal blood pressure—to cut down on sodium."

Addressing public health policymakers, Dr. Prineas says, "By not taking action, you're actually adopting a conscious policy . . . to let people at risk *go on being at risk*. I am not willing, given the current evidence, to make that decision." (My italics.) He says, in effect, that we *can* and *should* do something now.

Salt isn't the only factor causing hypertension in humans. But it's probably the most important one. Salt is not as dramatic or as predictable and immediate in its effects as cyanide. But its toxic effects in this country alone are like a mini-holocaust.

It's a major contributing factor in the more than 800,000 cardiovascular deaths we suffer each year. Without salt, the other factors—obesity, stress, sedentary life style, and other dietary influences such as fat, calcium, potassium, and alcohol—just wouldn't have the same effect, at least not on the grand scale that we see in this country today.

If it weren't for our excessive salt intake, hypertension would be a relatively rare problem, interesting to a few specialists—about like systemic lupus erythematosis or polycythemia vera—afflicting a few thousand, instead of 60 million Americans!

POTASSIUM

Our bodies are designed to function best on a low-sodium, high-potassium diet (this is the pattern of mineral content in natural, unrefined foods). But while we're processing foods we not only add a lot of sodium, we also leach out potassium. So the typical diet of Americans and other industrialized societies—most of whose food is grown, stored, processed, and even cooked by others—tends to leave us short of potassium.

Potassium, just by itself, promotes a loss of salt (sodium chloride) from the body. It acts like a diuretic and so can be an important factor in reducing blood pressure. Doctors at London's Charing Cross Hospital reported this effect in a recent issue of the *Lancet* (1982).

It's important for people with high blood pressure to eat foods that contain plenty of potassium—particularly when they're taking diuretic pills that may reduce the body's potassium level even further. Processed foods are high in sodium and low in potassium, but unprocessed fresh fruits, vegetables, and grains are the reverse and are wonderful sources of potassium.

You'll find your body is a lot happier if you eat more of a natural diet of fresh vegetables, fruits, and grains and cut back on those processed foods.

SUGAR

Sugar and sweeteners are also recent additions to the human diet.

There's not a lot of evidence that sugar directly affects the blood pressure, but it certainly can have an enormously adverse effect on psychological well-being—and thus on stress.

There was even a murder case recently in which the defense attorneys and their expert witnesses convinced a jury that the murderer of the mayor of San Francisco and a county supervisor was not responsible for his cold-blooded crime—because he was acting under the influence of sugary junk foods. The press whimsically called it "the Twinkie defense."

So there is evidence that sugar consumption can be harmful and can even cause bizarre and inappropriate behavior in some people. I certainly advise all my patients to begin to restrict their sugar intake. But in treating high blood pressure, sugar isn't nearly as dramatic an issue as salt. It's just something you'd probably feel better with less of.

PROTEIN

Being a nephrologist, or kidney specialist, this is one of my favorite topics, since there's so much misinformation about protein. People in this country have an absolute protein mania, a craziness that is manifested in an inappropriate concern about getting enough of it.

We Americans, on average, eat two to three times as much protein as we need. There's a current theory, reported in the *New England Journal of Medicine* (1982), which I feel makes a whole lot of sense; it suggests that our excessive protein intake is a major factor in wearing out the kidneys and in promoting the development of the kidney lesion at a much earlier age than it would otherwise occur.

Protein is not one of those things about which you can say, "A little of it is good for me, so a whole lot must be much better."

Along with the protein in meat, for example, we get lots of other things that are not so neat: hydrochloric and sulphuric acids—very toxic, you bet; phosphoric acid—it's weaker but still toxic; as is uric acid. So a large protein meal is like a large acid load as far as the body is concerned. And as the protein is metabolized it forms even more acids—the amino acids.

The body must protect itself against all this acid until the kidneys can get rid of it, so it buffers or stores it in the bones. As the acid is buffered, calcium is released. A high protein diet therefore slowly demineralizes your bones and makes them weaker. Over a lifetime, it will probably lead to brittle, easily broken bones. The scientific evidence has been published in the *American Journal of Clinical Nutrition* (1974, 1978, and 1979) and in "Symposium: Nutrition and Aging Bone Loss," *Federation Proceedings* (1981).

We just don't need that much protein to replace losses once we're adults. Any excess that we eat we either turn into sugar to use immediately as energy (as if we needed any more sources of sugar in the American diet!) or into fat to store.

And when we turn amino acids into sugar or fat we leave behind ammonia—also very toxic—which has to be detoxified right away or it will cause coma. So that's another big work load for the liver and kidneys.

Nutritionists who have investigated how much protein we actually need have come up with a minimum figure of about 40 grams a day. This is a generous minimum. Yet the average American eats in excess of 100 grams a day.

There's a lot of misunderstanding about what's the best source of protein too. Let's say we want to eat some protein to get some strength and energy. We usually head right for the steak, or cheese, or eggs. These foods have been on the training tables for years. A steak and egg breakfast on the day of the "big game" is still a tradition, although many coaches are wising up now and serving lighter meals that are high in carbohydrates.

Steak and cheese—indeed, all red meat and most dairy products—are really high fat foods! Really. Just think of what a cow or a pig goes through before it's butchered. Hormones are put in the food, and the animal is fed lots of corn, and gets no exercise. Just to make the meat tender, marbled with fat, easy to cut and chew and swallow. So we'll eat more of it, of course. Consume at any cost!

And the darker the meat the higher the fat. White meat chicken and fish contain less than twenty-five percent of their calories as fat. But the calories in a filet mignon with all the visible fat trimmed off are still more than fifty percent fat. Imagine!

In my view, we've wound up with a rather bizarre, upside-down set of values, in which the higher the fat content of the animal food (meat or dairy) the more expensive it is. The difference between flank steak at three to four dollars a pound and filet mignon at six to nine dollars a pound is *just fat*. The protein, the muscle fiber, is the same—so you're paying four to five dollars a pound for beef fat. And for the privilege of raising your own blood fat and cholesterol levels and risking a heart attack.

A particularly ridiculous supplement to your diet that is popular in some health circles is gelatin capsules. You're paying ten to twenty dollars a pound for ground-up horse hooves and chicken claws! For what? More protein? Which just weakens the bones, and . . . No. No more. We definitely don't need protein supplements—any of us!

If I eat less meat and dairy products and eggs, where am I going to get my protein from? I always heard that meat protein is the best for you and that other protein is incomplete.

The truth is that humans are omnivorous—both herbivorous and carnivorous—and we can survive on vegetables and grains, nuts, roots, seeds, and fruits just fine. And as long as we get enough calories we'll be getting enough protein and all the essential amino acids we need.

True, animal-source protein more closely resembles our own proteins in exact amino acid composition. But we break down the protein we eat into its building block amino acids anyway, so as long as there are enough of all the right amino acids in plant proteins (and there are in a mixed diet) we can build our own proteins out of them. No problem. Grains or beans will do just fine. Or skim milk and egg whites, if you have to have animal protein.

Hey, I'm not saying you have to give up all meat, fowl, fish, dairy products, and eggs—just eat less of them. But if you want to have vegetarian days or weeks or months, it's okay. And you'll do just fine on nonanimal-source protein.

There is even evidence that switching to a more vegetarian-type diet will lower your blood pressure! That is, according to studies published in the *Journal of the American Medical Association* (1981 and 1982) and the *Lancet* (1983), which suggest that eating meat raises your blood pressure and that this effect becomes more pronounced as you grow older.

If you don't believe me, would you believe the American Academy of Pediatrics? They appointed a Committee on Nutrition to look into the recent increase in unusual nutritional practices in our country that might be hazardous to the health of children. They concluded, in a report published in *Pediatrics* (1977), that all but the most extreme forms of pure vegetarianism not only are nutritionally adequate for growing children but also, in a way, advantageous—because of "the rarity of obesity and the tendency for lower serum levels of cholesterol" in people who don't eat meat. The Food and Nutrition Board of the National Academy of Sciences concurs. And so do I.

FAT

It's only recently in human history that we've been able to afford to fatten up the animals that everyone eats. I've already mentioned the two differences between flank steak and filet mignon—price and fat. Filet mignon is much more expensive because more grain has to be fed to the animal to put that fat in the meat. It takes fifteen pounds of grain to make one pound of edible beef (and fourteen pounds of cow manure?)—which is very, very wasteful, if you want my opinion. But it's what people seem to want.

One problem with fat—and particularly with animal fat—is that it also tends to promote a higher cholesterol level in the blood. And high cholesterol puts you at risk for heart attack and stroke, as you saw when you calculated your Coronary Artery Disease Risk Profile.

In addition fat has more than twice as many calories as carbohydrate or protein, so it's the principal factor in the widespread development of obesity or overweight.

A high-fat, high-protein diet isn't a good diet to mix with high blood pressure. It can increase the systolic pressure in the arteries by lining and hardening them with cholesterol; it can weaken the kidneys and give you the kidney lesion; and it adds more risk to your Coronary Artery Disease Risk Profile, which is already high because of the blood pressure factor.

Dr. J. M. Iacono of the U. S. Department of Agriculture has done some interesting studies that suggest that fat can raise the blood pressure in another way as well. It's a little too early to tell what it all means as yet, but his work shows that reducing animal fat in the diet reduces blood pressure. It's as simple as that.

He doesn't know yet which is most important here: reducing the total fat or lowering the ratio of saturated (animal) fats to polyunsaturated fats (vegetable oils). But his method works. He and his colleagues have presented their results in several forums, most recently in a special supplement to the medical journal *Hypertension* (1982), in the *Lancet* (1983), and in *Preventive Medicine* (1983).

His theory is that reducing saturated fat in the diet increases a natural blood-pressure-lowering hormone in the body. The hormone is called *prostaglandin.*

Animal fat as a cause of hypertension is becoming a hot issue, and other scientists are looking into it too. In my own view, sodium is the most important factor. But, by all means, check with your body and be open about this. I think you'll find that fatty meats and dairy products leave you feeling fatigued and sluggish—and that your body is trying to tell you something: stop eating so much of them!

Vegetable and grain fats, too, are things we've only recently learned how to make. Safflower oil, corn oil, palm oil, and all the other oils we eat are recent inventions, compared to the length of time the human body has been around.

It takes seven ears of corn, pressed at very high pressure and temperature, to make one tablespoon of corn oil. So you can imagine how many ears of corn go to make up a whole bottle.

Do you know that vegetable fats tend to linger in the bloodstream even longer than animal fats? It's as though we don't have a good system for processing them. Perhaps we can't metabolize them easily because we were never intended to eat them in this quantity. That makes sense to me.

One other thing, while we're on the subject of fats and meats. The amount of grain it takes to feed the cattle that feed ten meat eaters would have enough protein in it to feed a hundred people on a grains and vegetable diet. It's as though the diet that is healthiest for us is also healthiest for the planet. And that makes a lot of sense too.

I've read that hamburgers at fast food chains are really very wholesome and good for you—that they give you a balanced meal, with meat, vegetables, grains, and dairy.

Let me tell you one of my favorite stories about food. A friend of mine in the insurance business told it to me, so it's sort of an "in house" story, and we won't name any names.

A colleague of his was lamenting the loss of one of those huge, oceangoing freighters, on which a substantial claim was to be paid. My friend asked him what the cargo was.

"Fat," he replied.

"Fat?" my friend asked, a little surprised.

"That's right. Beef fat, from Australia, a whole shipload, if you can imagine that."

My friend asked what anyone would want with beef fat that would make them buy it by the shipload and bring it all the way over from Australia.

"Oh, they use it for hamburger filler in one of those fast food hamburger chains," his friend told him. "It's cheaper than bread crumbs or anything else they've come up with, and it allows them to advertise their hamburgers as a hundred percent pure beef."

What you don't know about food can hurt you—if you eat it. A fast food hamburger is really a gastronomic nightmare. High fat meat and cheese, loads of salt, more fat and sugar in the dressing, and a white flour bun with yet more salt and sugar!

We've pretty much solved the problem of *acute* food poisoning in America—the kind that results in vomiting and diarrhea within hours or minutes of eating the food. But we haven't solved the problem of *chronic* poisoning—the sort that builds over time and leads to heart disease, high blood pressure, and cancer, not to mention obesity and diabetes. It's ridiculous to point the finger at any one restaurant and say, "You did it, you're to blame. I'm going to sue you, because I got sick eating your food. Look at me, I've been crippled by a stroke, I'm disabled and can't work anymore —and it's all your fault." The jury just wouldn't believe it.

These diseases start when we're kids, when we learn to eat like our parents, and as the TV ads tell us to eat. And years of meals at home, with friends, at school, at work, and in all those restaurants slowly take their toll, and you can't sue anybody, you can't blame anyone. I don't even want you to blame yourself. I just want you to learn what food does to you and to be a lot more particular about what you put into your mouth.

And I don't want to blame the fast food chains, either. We who eat the food have a choice. So let's keep informed, stay committed to our own well-being, and make our choices wisely. Let people know what you want. It works. Fast food stands can serve healthy food, and movie theaters can, and so can football stadiums, and fancy restaurants, and your friends. As long as you know what you want . . . And let them know too.

CHOLESTEROL

Cholesterol is a substance that's essential to your bodily well-being. But your body can make all the cholesterol you need, so you don't really have to eat any—it's not at all like a vitamin.

The cholesterol in our diet comes from animal foods—especially red meats, organ meats, butter, shrimp and lobster, and egg yolks. When we eat these foods our bodies make less cholesterol; but they can't decrease production enough to make up for the amount that most of us eat. So our blood cholesterol levels rise with age, and we deposit the cholesterol in our tissues—notably in the walls of the arteries, causing hardening of the arteries or *atherosclerosis*. (You can sometimes actually see the cholesterol deposits forming a white ring around the *cornea* or clear part of the eyes.)

When we are born, our blood cholesterol level is about 80, and if we ate only small amounts of fish and no other animal foods (like most of the peoples of the Third World), our cholesterol levels would end up about 120–150.

Now Americans typically have a blood cholesterol level of about 220–250; so we are adding about 100 points to our levels by our rich diet. And we are also adding about 1.5 million heart attacks. People with cholesterol levels under 150 just *don't get heart attacks*.

I know, I know. I used to love scampi too, swimming in garlic butter. And rare roast beef and cheese omelets. But is it worth it? I don't think so. There's one ray of sunshine, though—the liver I never did like turns out not to be good for me either! In fact it's one of the highest sources of cholesterol. And I for one don't miss it at all.

CARBOHYDRATES

We need to distinguish here between simple carbohydrates (sugar) and complex carbohydrates (starch).

Starch is present in large amounts in most plant foods. The simple carbohydrate content of grains, fruits, and vegetables gives them a sweet, enjoyable taste.

The beauty of carbohydrates as a source of nutrition is that they are *clean*-burning—just what the body wants and needs. No pile-up of residual acids and ammonia after we use carbohydrates in our bodies. No work for the liver or kidneys to clean up the mess. When carbohydrates burn, they leave behind only water and carbon dioxide—which we eliminate in the lungs.

It's like burning natural gas or alcohol in the furnace or automobile, instead of high-sulfur crude oil or coal. We don't want to pollute the air—and we shouldn't want to pollute our bodies!

ALCOHOL

The problem with alcohol, from the point of view of high blood pressure, is that eventually its effects wear off. That may sound a little strange at first but it's true. Alcohol is a relaxant. It tends to suppress the nervous system, the cardiovascular system—and when you stop drinking the relaxant effect wears off and your blood pressure rises. And it may overshoot. It may rise distinctly above your baseline—in fact it often does.

The most extreme example of this occurs with the severe alcoholic withdrawal symptom called *delirium tremens* (or DTs), when the blood pressure may go very, very high.

So when you withdraw from alcohol, while you're sleeping it off, and when you're stumbling around the next morning looking for coffee, what's happening inside you is that your emergency nervous system is turning on. And the whole thing may backfire on you. If you drink quite a bit over the weekend, your blood pressure will be higher on Monday morning than it would have been if you hadn't been drinking. That's basically the problem.

I don't really want to go into the issue of whether or not you should be drinking at all. Obviously, drinking in excessive amounts is injurious to your heart as well as your liver and kidneys.

There is some interesting evidence, though, that people who drink in moderation, maybe one glass of wine or beer a day (or several times a week), develop less cardiovascular disease than complete teetotalers. And this may have something to do with the fact that alcohol stimulates the liver to make a protein called *high-density lipoprotein* (HDL), which grabs onto cholesterol in the arteries and brings it back to the liver to be flushed out of the body. So drinking in small, regular quantities may actually have some benefit for people with high Coronary Artery Disease Risk Profiles. Check with your doctor. I'm not recommending this. I just want you to be informed.

CAFFEINE

Caffeine is the most commonly used, naturally occurring nervous system stimulant. It's in coffee, it's in black tea, and cola drinks, and cocoa—as well as over-the-counter stimulants such as NoDoz tablets. And it's something we often use as a means of coping with stress or the chronic fatigue that often accompanies it.

Drinking coffee to handle stress is like trying to quench a fire with gasoline. A recent study in the *American Journal of Medicine* (1982) showed that caffeine raises the blood pressure. And if you really want to promote high blood pressure, smoke a cigarette while you're drinking your coffee. The effects of nicotine and caffeine mixed are even more powerful than the effects of either taken separately. After a cup of coffee and a cigarette the blood pressure stays up for hours.

I tend to encourage people to drink less and less caffeine. A lot of people are surprised and upset to find out how addicted to caffeine they are—and if you're a regular coffee drinker you may get headaches, or sick to your stomach, or depressed when you try to quit. These symptoms are the result of an actual physiological addiction; but they are very short lived and usually last only a day or two.

You may also have a psychological expectation and tell yourself, "I've got to have coffee, or I can't wake up." But reducing or giving up your coffee habit will actually leave you with more energy, not less.

CALCIUM

Recently evidence has been discovered linking inadequate intake of calcium with hypertension in adults (symposia headed by Dr. D. A. Mc-Carron in *Hypertension*, 1982, and *Annals of Internal Medicine*, 1983). The causal relationship here is unclear.

Other studies have shown that adults commonly have less than optimal amounts of calcium in their diets, since intake of dairy foods and leafy vegetables tends to fall as we grow older. Beer replaces milk and cookies in the evening, and our mothers aren't around anymore to make sure we eat all our vegetables! And Dr. J. M. Belizan and colleagues of Johns Hopkins have found that calcium supplements have a mild blood-pressure-lowering effect in adults *(Journal of the American Medical Association*, 1983).

CHANGING YOUR NUTRITIONAL HABITS

You've got to discover your own diet. That's the main thing. I'm not going to tell you what to do. If I just gave you a list of things not to eat and told you, "You'd better keep to these rules or you'll die," it wouldn't work. Your heart just wouldn't be in it. That's why there are so many diet books on the market—and why they don't work. Or at best they only work for a while.

If you're going to treat high blood pressure nutritionally, it's a lifetime thing. We can't afford to have you go on some crash diet, and get fed up with it, and come crashing back off the diet and onto some wild eating binge. It's no use. Because as soon as you got back to your old ways, *wham!* your blood pressure would rocket back up.

Good nutrition has to be something you choose—for yourself. Because you care enough about yourself to try it out. And the only way you'll stay on it is that you'll find out by your own experience that it's more satisfying, it's more enjoyable this way.

All that I'm asking from you is an openness, a willingness to try a few things you maybe haven't tried before. This is an educational effort, and the most important educator around here is you, the reader—because you're going to learn from your own experience what works best and feels best for you.

I won't bully you. I can tell you right away that if you have high blood pressure you're probably doing something about food that doesn't work for you, and your body is just trying to let you know about it.

During the course of the program I have suggested that you check out any number of my ideas. But you'll always be free to form your own opinions. So have your own opinions and be skeptical if you must. But also be observant and notice how your body responds to these things. I'm interested in evolution, not revolution. So learn at your own pace. Twelve weeks or twelve months, it's really up to you to decide how quickly you want to change things. It's been twelve years in my case, and I'm still learning!

Over the course of the program you'll discover your own diet can be both nutritious and delicious. And you'll be a lot happier with it. You'll be inspired by it, in fact. And inspiration, not deprivation, is what we learn the most from. I know you can learn what your body wants—and the fact that you're even reading this book means that you want to learn.

My job as a teacher is very simple. I want to show you how you can learn best.

Pat was a lawyer, a good one, who had a knack for winning at whatever he tried his hand at. He was so soft-spoken and gentlemanly, I would have thought he was a Virginian, had it not been for a faint trace of a New York Irish accent. But he had a tough side, and he was a survivor, too— including a big one, a nearly fatal battle trauma in the Korean War think he always felt just a little guilty about this, and very appreciative of his miraculous recovery so long ago. So he seemed to go through life always wanting to pay someone back for the favor.

We hit it off immediately. When I met him he wasn't winning against his blood pressure problem, though. He'd read about our program on a flight back from New York and stopped in at the Center on his way home from the airport. After talking to me for a while, he just threw away his pills and decided to go for it.

He was as successful at this as at everything else, which meant that he had the best weight loss, the best drop in blood cholesterol, the best rise in endurance and fitness—everything was the best.

After he'd graduated from the program, on sort of a dare he took me to Perrino's, a fashionable French restaurant in Los Angeles. He wanted to see how I'd handle myself when knee-deep in rich sauces, butter, soufflés, and pastries. . . . The waiters, always attentive, hovered nearby. Pat was a good customer, and a favorite, it seemed.

At my request the waiter brought some thin-sliced dark toast sans the usual garlic butter and cheese. It was delicious, with a subtle, nutty flavor. I looked over the multipage menu and, seeing nothing even remotely "healthy," said to the waiter somewhat optimistically, "I'll bet your chef could make an absolutely exquisite steamed vegetable plate, no salt, no butter, and no cheese—am I right?"

"But of course."

And, you know, he did. It was beautiful, to the eye as well as to the palate. And I'd taught Pat, the "old survivor," something about survival in the big city that day.

26

Exercise 1

By chase our long-liv'd fathers earned their food;
Toil strung the nerves and purified the blood;
But we, their sons, a pamper'd race of men,
Are dwindled down to threescore years and ten.
Better to hunt in fields for health unbought
Than fee the doctor for a nauseous draught.
The wise for cure on exercise depend;
God never made his work for man to mend.

Dryden

This is going to be a piece of cake for some of you, the easiest thing in the world.

And some of you are going to think the whole thing sounds impossible. Exercise? You can't even imagine yourself doing such a thing. It's out of the question.

Some of you know very well that you need to get some exercise. You've been thinking about it, planning to do it, and wishing you'd start. But somehow you just haven't gotten around to it.

And some of you have excuses. . . . I remember talking to a doctor friend of mine about jogging, and he told me he'd tried it once and decided it wasn't for him. He claimed it "jostled his brain around," and he was really worried about what that might do to him. Now you have to admit that's an original excuse!

I want you to know, right away, that there'll always be excuses. If we didn't have excuses we wouldn't be human. But we can always find a way around the excuses if we want to. If we are inspired to. So I'd like to talk a little about inspiration.

One of the things that makes me really want to exercise regularly and never give it up is my own work. Several times a week I administer tread-mill stress tests to patients who are about to enter a cardiac rehabilitation program. These are people who have either just had a heart attack or are at great risk of having one in the not too distant future. And the treadmill test is designed to tell us how much exercise these people can handle.

Just doing that inspires me to get up every morning and jog, because I see what bad shape people can get into. I see people who can barely walk slowly for three minutes before they're exhausted. I don't want to be in that bad shape, ever. It scares me.

Then I look at our human species, and I see just how wonderfully we are made. For millions of years humans have run and climbed and jumped and trekked and hauled. As a species, we are extraordinary. We have incredible physical capacity. If you look through all the different species of animals, we humans stand out in terms of our stamina and endurance.

There are some tribes where the test of a chief is that he can run down a deer in a good-sized box canyon and kill it. True, there are many animals that are capable of phenomenal bursts of speed, the deer among them. But a man with a lot of stamina can literally chase a deer to death.

Until recently we have been an incredibly physically active species, and our survival has depended on it. But with the coming of the Industrial Revolution a lot of that has changed. More and more of us can physically survive without even needing to walk from home to the grocery store, let alone chase down a deer. Instead of walking, we ride golf carts onto the golf course and no longer get the exercise we used to from our golf, or from other sports, for that matter. We become easily tired and unwilling to exercise. And we use our tiredness as the reason for not exercising. Somewhere along the line life becomes a lot less wonderful.

Studies have been made recently of astronauts and other people who, for one reason or another, spend periods of time in enforced inactivity.

Dr. W. M. Bortz II, writing in the *Journal of the American Medical Association* (1982), reviews the evidence that when these healthy young people are prevented from exercising their bodies go through all the changes that we associate with the aging process—the stiff joints, the thinned-out, weakened bones, the weakened muscles, the declining strength of the lungs and heart, the inappropriately large appetite, the sleep disorders, the loss of vigor and vitality.

It happens rapidly, too. In just the few weeks or months that they are in space, the astronauts' bodies age remarkably. The same thing happens when you have a cast on your leg for a month or two. When the cast comes off, it's as if your leg isn't your own any more but belongs to someone years older than you. It's stiff, withered, and weak.

In fact, the effects of exercise on the brain in preventing the usual degenerative changes have been studied in both humans and animals (Spirduso 1983).

Exercise is, in a sense, the antidote to aging. The fountain of youth that Ponce de Leon was looking for has been found! Millions of Americans know about it. Regular, physical exercise prevents the aging process. It's as simple as that! Yet we tend to forget how wonderful that fountain of youth is. We get out of touch. . . .

I've just read a remarkable article in *Runner's World* (1983) about five oldsters ages sixty-four to eighty-two who run, who are competitive, and who keep going because they want to stay active and feel young.

Dr. Paul Spangler, who is eighty-two, started running at age sixty-eight! He's now set more than a dozen world records in his age range, and even ran a marathon in under four hours at Avenue of the Giants in California in 1979. Ruth Rothfarb, also eighty-two, ran three marathons last year— and typically runs or walks between forty and fifty miles a week.

These people aren't superheroes, they're "ordinary" human beings, of the same species as you and I.

Take a moment, right now, put this book down, go outside, and take a look at some young kids playing. See how energetic they are, how much fun they are having. There's a kid inside you, right now, wanting to be enthusiastic and play. It doesn't matter whether you're eight or eighty.

A lot of us get turned off to exercise while we're still in school. I know I did. I had to tumble, and I felt so clumsy, I couldn't even turn a simple somersault. I had to wrestle, and I hated it—I didn't like being that close to a sweaty, half-dressed male who looked and acted as if he wanted to hurt and humiliate me. I guess I just wasn't that aggressive as a teenager

If you're not very athletic, if you're not very aggressive, you can wind up not enjoying gym and physical education in high school, and determined not to do any more of that stuff when you leave school.

I can understand that. High school PE classes can sometimes be uncomfortable, embarrassing experiences. And boring, too. Even if you won't admit to being embarrassed, you might admit to being bored. . . .

But look. Exercise doesn't have to be like that. It can be refreshing. You can start exercising gradually, in a way that's interesting and pleasant. And you'll quickly come to enjoy it for its own sake.

Why? Because it makes you feel wonderful.

That brings me to another point. The real inspiration now that keeps me exercising day in and day out is how good it makes me feel. I may have started exercising because I could see how foolish it is *not* to exercise, but I've kept on doing it because I enjoy it. I feel so much more alive. And that's the best kind of inspiration there is.

A lot of people I see feel tired, fatigued, and generally worn out. For them, it's no fun getting up in the morning, and they come home exhausted from their jobs and want nothing better than to rest. I've heard it time and time again. "When I get home from work, I like to take my shoes off, lie down, and take a little nap."

Taking a short nap can seem like the most natural thing in the world. If you feel tired, it's *reasonable* to lie down and rest. In fact it's so damn reasonable, I'll have a terrible time trying to talk you out of it.

"Listen," you'll say, "I know my body. I know when I need rest, when I need to slow down, and when I need more sleep." And I'm listening. I hear you. I know you believe that's true. But let me tell you something. In my experience most of us, when we feel a little tired and low on energy, need more exercise, not more rest.

When you sleep in late on the weekend, have you ever noticed how it makes you feel a little groggy and lethargic for the rest of the day? Sometimes when I want to sleep in, I remember how I used to feel a little dazed for most of the day when I did. So now, after a long night of it, if I want to wake up and feel energetic, what I do is go out and run.

And it works. It's so much better than "a hair of the dog that bit you." It charges my body up with my own natural hormones and wakes me up. It's a pick-me-up—and it works as well as three cups of strong coffee. Or any number of pep pills.

If you're the kind of person who feels tired a lot of the time—I under-

stand. I've been there myself, and I've found that exercise is the solution
—not more sleep.

Okay. So far I've been trying to let you know why exercise might be
wonderful for you. Let's assume now that you've decided to exercise—but
you're having some difficulty going about it. You'd really like to exercise,
but you notice you're not doing it, and you do have reasons to explain why
not.

What are your reasons? Are they really reasons, or excuses?

Some people feel they're too busy to exercise. Some people don't think
the environment is appropriate. It's snowing outside, or the city streets
downtown aren't safe, or there's so much smog you wouldn't want to
breathe it. Some people are worried because they can only exercise at
night. . . .

Sure, there are places where the streets aren't too healthy. But heart
attacks aren't too healthy either. Have you checked out whether there's a
YMCA or a health club nearby? Or an aerobic dance class? Or a high
school running track? Have you thought about getting in your car and
driving somewhere where you'd feel free to exercise?

There's usually a solution, if you're willing to look for it. And exercise
means so much to your health and well-being.

I have some pictures of myself jogging outdoors in Alaska in the dead of
winter. I brought them home with me to Southern California to remind
myself I'd really done it. The sun didn't rise until noon—which we'd only
know about on the rare days when there wasn't a thick cloud cover anyway
—so we ran in the dark, in the cold, and in the snow.

That's how strongly I'm committed to exercise—yet a few short years
ago I wouldn't have done that at gunpoint. You couldn't have paid me
enough to go run at the beach in California on a fine day, let alone in
Alaska in the snow. So there are excuses and excuses, and then there's your
word—doing what you say you'll do, because you want the results: no
more pills!

A lot of people who haven't exercised for a long time aren't sure they
know how to go about it. You may even be afraid to try, because you're
worried you might do yourself more harm than good.

Some people just don't like to try new things unless there's someone
there to encourage them and support them. Some people need support,
some people need encouragement, some people need advice or instruction. And support, encouragement, advice, and instruction are available.

Some people I talk to think they're getting a lot of exercise by walking.

And they may be. Then again, they may not. Many people who live fairly sedentary lives overestimate how much exercise they get.

I was talking to a woman the other day who was obviously very overweight, and I asked her if she got any exercise. "Oh yes," she said with absolute conviction, "I exercise a lot." She told me she sat on the edge of the bed several times a week, whenever the idea occurred to her, and swung her legs for three to four minutes at a time. To her, that was a lot of exercise!

So I guess it's a relative thing.

If you think you're getting enough exercise from walking, it might be a good idea to check. You could buy one of those little pedometers at a sports store and actually measure how far you walk in an average day. And if it's pretty low, if you find out you're walking only two or three miles a day or less, you'll know it's time for you to get in some more exercise.

What do you do when you want to start an exercise program?

If you're over the age of forty, or if you have any of the risk factors for developing heart disease (if you're anything above very low risk on your Coronary Artery Disease Risk Profile), then you should talk things over with a physician before you start in on a big exercise program.

Hopefully, you already did this in Week One. And your doctor may have recommended that you take a treadmill stress test or measured your blood pressure while you were exercising.

When you take a treadmill test (or some other type of exercise test) the doctor or technician can advise you about what level of exercise is safe and appropriate for you to do, and what level of exercise you will get the most benefit from.

They can actually give you an *exercise prescription,* just like the ones you take to the pharmacy—but this prescription you can follow at home, or in a health spa, or at your local high school track.

Your prescription will tell you what *Training Heart Rate* (THR—you can also think of it as your *Target Heart Rate)* to work at. And that's how fast your heart should be beating for safe, healthy exercise.

If you haven't got an exercise prescription you can estimate your THR by using this formula. First, you need to calculate your Predicted Maximum Heart Rate (PMHR—figured at 205 minus one half your age [men] or 220 minus your age [women]). Your Training Heart Rate is roughly eighty percent of your PMHR. In the example given above of a forty-year-old woman, the PMHR is 180 (i.e., 220 minus 40), and the THR (eighty percent of the PMHR) is 144.

Next, you need to divide your THR by 6 to find out how many heartbeats there are every ten seconds at your THR. If the THR is 144, you'd have a heart that was beating twenty-four times in ten seconds at THR. Now, exercise for a while, then stop suddenly and count your pulse for ten seconds. In the example above, if you're forty years old, and you counted twenty-four in ten seconds, then you are training at your Training Heart Rate—which is how it should be.

AEROBICS

What kind of exercise will we be doing in this program?
Aerobics.

Aerobic exercise is exercise that moves the larger muscles freely, generates heat in the body, and thus burns up oxygen. Aerobic exercise generally makes you breathe more heavily than you would at rest and causes you to work up a little bit of a sweat.

There's no great straining or grunting and groaning involved. It's not weight lifting, or doing push-ups and pull-ups. And unless you've been exercising a lot the level of aerobic exercise that's appropriate for you will be fairly easy. It's certainly not going to totally exhaust you and wipe you out. In fact the more you do of it the harder it will be to wipe you out.

Aerobic exercises include walking, jogging, running, skating, swimming, cycling (even on a stationary cycle), cross-country skiing, and even dancing. There are classes in most communities with names like Aerobic Dance, or Jazzercise, and you can get your exercise there. Check with the YMCA or a local health club. Usually there's music playing, and a leader in the room, and you can work up a sweat dancing and jumping around in time to the beat.

Most of these organized activities cost money, though—whereas walking and jogging are free. I personally prefer jogging and running, because I can go anywhere in the world, and all I need is a pair of shoes and some workout clothes, and I can exercise every day of the year. I don't need to be near a swimming pool or lug an Exercycle around with me wherever I go. I have everything I need.

If you want, you can get a treadmill for your house and keep it in the garage or basement. The motorized ones cost about two thousand dollars or more. But they're really nice! You can set them at a certain incline and speed and get your half hour in without even leaving your house. No dogs chasing you. No getting wet or cold. You can even watch TV or read the paper while you walk, and not worry about banging into anyone.

Stationary cycles offer the same advantages, and some other ones as well. They're much cheaper for starters—a few hundred instead of a few thousand dollars. No bouncing up and down, so if you have large breasts, or a beer belly, an Exercycle may be the way to go. They're easier on your knees and ankles, too. Ask your doctor and see what he says.

Mini-trampolines are the rage in California right now—and jogging in place on them is called "rebounding." This is also easier on the feet, ankles, knees, and hips—which is especially important if you are out of shape. But it's hard to get a good workout on one of these things—you usually don't get your heart rate high enough, unless your Training Heart Rate is very low.

START GRADUALLY

When you start an exercise program it's very important, if you haven't done much exercise recently, to get into it gradually.

There are lots of stories about people who got into trouble because they pushed too hard, too soon. Most of the people I know who are totally against jogging have some story they like to tell about George, or Mary, who was out jogging and dropped dead. And they tell me, "See what I mean? Jogging isn't good for you. And that's why I don't jog, and don't intend to."

Yes, it does sometimes happen—but it usually happens to people who haven't been exercising for a very long time and who have gone out suddenly, in a not very farsighted way, and tried to exercise a lot. Perhaps they just recently gave up smoking—or haven't quit yet. Perhaps they're overweight or have been under a lot of stress. Usually their diet is poor. But they get the foolish, macho notion that they're going to go out and set everything straight in a hurry. "I'm going to go out, and get my health act together, and really run hard. I'll show 'em."

People can get so competitive about how much they're going to exercise that they raise the level of adrenaline in the blood and irritate the heart. And if they then push real hard while they're exercising, the heart may not be able to get enough oxygen. The heart rhythm can become abnormal, and they can die quite suddenly.

That's why I want you to take a very gradual, steady approach to this whole thing—and if you have some of the heart risks I mentioned above, go see your doctor, get a treadmill test and an exercise prescription, and take care of yourself. I want you to be able to read the rest of this book!

Particularly when you are starting out, you want your exercise period to be a pleasant, fun time. You don't want to push too hard. The length of time you exercise is far more important than the intensity of the exercise. You don't want to get exhausted, and you don't want to get discouraged.

I listened to Dr. Ken Cooper, the man who wrote all those books on aerobics, give a lecture recently, and he described their program down in Dallas, Texas. About a thousand people run three or four miles every day on his tracks and are kept track of in his computer. And he's had no cardiac problems in his program since he opened in 1970! But then he tests every one of his patients, and he gives each of them an exercise prescription.

So exercise needn't be dangerous—and won't be, if you're careful.

CLOTHES AND EQUIPMENT

As we've seen, aerobic exercise is exercise that generates heat—and, because it does, I'd like to talk a little about what clothes to wear while you're exercising.

Don't wear plastic pants. I know a lot of stores sell plastic pants with the idea that they will promote weight loss. But it doesn't work that way. Your body will be generating heat if you're exercising the way you should —and it needs an opportunity to lose some of that heat.

If you get too hot, you'd better take some of your clothing off and let the heat out. And be sure to drink enough fluids, especially if it's dry and hot outside. You can easily underestimate your body fluid loss and become dehydrated.

If it's cold outside you should dress warmly—but not as warmly as you'd dress if you were just taking a casual stroll or standing around downtown doing some window-shopping. Wear enough clothes so you feel warm after you've run or walked for five or ten minutes at your THR, but not so much that you're sweating profusely. And be wary of frostbite—cover your ears, wear gloves, and pay special attention to your face.

Otherwise, what you wear is pretty much up to you. But wear clothes that are comfortable and that give you plenty of room to stretch. You can wear your favorite old baggy pants—or the latest sporting fashion. It's your choice.

Lots of joggers and skaters and bikers are wearing these little personal stereos now—the music really energizes them and may make the whole experience more fun. But be warned about the dangers of being out on the street and not being able to hear what's going on around you—dogs, cars, ambulances, muggers, whatever. One community has actually banned these things, as a result of a fatal accident involving a car and a jogger.

SHOES

The most important exercise item of all is your shoes. If you're walking or jogging or running, you want to make sure you have good shoes. Spend a little time, make sure the shoes you buy are comfortable and that they fit.

The technology of shoe design has advanced tremendously over the last few years. There are 27 million joggers in America, and there's a whole industry set up to serve them. Most communities now have podiatrists who specialize in sports medicine, and there are stores that sell jogging shoes everywhere.

Runner's World magazine has had a whole issue devoted to shoes every year the last few years. They tell you just about everything you might want to know about shoes—what to look for, what special characteristics of shoes are appropriate for any particular problems you might have, how to buy shoes that are right for you, and what the world's top runners wear.

If you're going to be out walking, jogging, or running, get yourself some good shoes. The best ones cost about forty to sixty dollars, and some are even more than that. These days, good shoes are lightweight. They protect the foot and support the ankle. If you wear good shoes you're much less likely to injure yourself. Good shoes are really good for your feet, and they make the whole walking experience much more pleasurable.

In fact there's only one problem: color. Running shoes often seem to come in the most outlandish colors. So you may need to be resigned to wearing purple and orange shoes. And good luck finding matching socks!

Apart from that, good shoes make good friends. Spend a little time, shop around, and get yourself some shoes.

27

Exercise 2

A garden gives the body the dignity of working in its own support. It is a way of rejoining the human race.

Wendell Berry

It's very important to have a regular sequence that you follow before you start to exercise—to prevent injury and to get the maximum benefit from your time. And this routine needs to include stretching, warm-up aerobics, the aerobic exercise itself, a cool-down period, and some final stretching.

STRETCHING

Before you exercise you need to stretch your muscles. You've probably seen joggers stretching. It looks as though they're leaning against a tree or a wall, trying to push it down. That kind of stretching (and there are various different stretching exercises) is very important, to prevent injury. So before you start to exercise, you should do some stretching for about five or ten minutes.

Gently, now. It doesn't need to hurt to be effective.

Dr. Richard H. Dominguez, a sports medicine orthopedist in Illinois, has gotten a certain amount of notoriety recently because of his outspoken criticism of excessive stretching in runners. He says, and I agree, "Take it easy when you stretch, and keep your joints from going much beyond their normal range of motion, their comfort zone."

You can do more harm than good if you stretch too much. Some people are naturally and easily more flexible than others. If you're one of the stiffer ones, and you try to be a limber one, you can hurt yourself.

There's an interview with Dr. Dominguez in *The Physician and Sports Medicine* (1982), which you can read if you want to find out more about his views.

WARMING UP

The next part of the sequence is warming up.

Warming up means doing a slower, quieter version of the type of exercise you've chosen. For example, if your exercise prescription is for walking briskly for thirty minutes, you should start out by walking slowly. It gets your muscles warmed up so they are more relaxed and less likely to get injured. And it gets you into the mood of the whole thing.

I generally advise people to warm up for about five minutes before beginning the actual aerobic exercise.

COMMON AEROBIC (OXYGEN-CONSUMING) EXERCISES

Walking	Stationary cycle	Aerobic workout classes
Jogging	Bicycle riding	Aerobic dancing
Running	Swimming	Cross-country skiing
Soccer	Basketball (full out)	Rope skipping
Rowing	Skating	Hiking
Rebounding (mini-trampoline)		

For an average adult weighing 170 pounds, the following exercises would use up about 300–350 calories (i.e., the calories contained in about three large servings of fruit):

Running 3 miles in 24 minutes (8-minute miles)
Walking 5 miles in an hour and a half (3.5 mph)
Swimming 1,200 yards in 24 minutes (50 yards per minute)
Cycling 10 miles in 45 minutes (about 13 mph)

(In each of the exercises, an individual who weighs more than 200 pounds would burn about 30 percent more calories. One who weighs less than 125 pounds would burn about 30 percent less.)

Any one of the above exercises will do for our program. I'm going to talk about walking/jogging because that's the easiest and I've had the most experience with it.

If your exercise is walking briskly, or jogging, I'd like to have you do it for about half an hour. Early on in your program, when you're just starting to exercise, you may not be able to last half an hour at a brisk walk or jog. So when you're tired, and can't keep on so briskly any more, just slow down for a while. But try to keep on walking, even at a reduced pace, for the whole of the half hour.

If you've received an exercise prescription you have probably been advised to do your aerobic exercise at a particular heart rate. If you haven't been given a Training Heart Rate (THR), you should calculate it, using our formula—your THR is eighty percent of your Predicted Maximum Heart Rate (see page 306).

If your exercise is keeping you at your Training Heart Rate, it's probably the right intensity for you—but here's another way to tell. It's called the *Talk Test.*

While you're walking briskly or jogging you should be able to carry on a conversation with someone who's jogging along with you. You may sound a little breathless, but you should be able to carry on a conversation.

If you're pushing too hard you'll be breathing too rapidly and deeply to be able to talk—and that means your muscles are building up lactic acid and releasing it into the bloodstream too fast, you aren't getting enough oxygen, and it's time to cut back.

Here's another test. If you're doing aerobic exercise you should be generating heat and working up a bit of a sweat.

One other thing: you may get a stitch (a pain in the side).

I remember, when I was a kid, I got a stitch in my side nearly every time I ran. When I got to medical school I asked my professors what caused these stitches, and they told me they didn't know. I was pretty disappointed. But there are a lot more runners around now, and we know more about the problems they come up with.

Dr. George Sheenan, who writes a column in *Runner's World* and has published a book on running, says that stitches in your side are the result of improper or inadequate movement of the abdominal muscles during exercise. This comes about when we breathe mainly with the chest instead of the abdomen.

Do you have a problem with stitches? You can find out for yourself whether you're a chest breather or a belly breather by standing up, with one hand on your abdomen and one on your chest, taking ten deep breaths, and seeing which hand moves. If you're breathing properly with your belly, when you take a deep breath in, the hand on your belly will move out, and when you breathe out again, your hand will move back in. The chest needn't move very much at all.

Abdominal, or belly breathing, is something that people in any occupation or endeavor in which breathing is important have to learn—singers, actors, public speakers, athletes, and others.

If you do the simple test I suggested, and find out that you're not breathing abdominally, it takes a little practice to learn it. But it's worth it. When you've learned abdominal breathing you'll never have to have a stitch in your side again. Or, if you do, you'll know what to do about it—breathe in an exaggerated manner with your belly as you continue exercising at a slower pace.

COOL DOWN

When you've finished your thirty minutes of aerobic exercise, the next thing you should do is cool down.

If you've been walking briskly or jogging, you should switch to a slow walk for about five minutes. This period of cooling down is important. It reduces muscle cramps and the possibility of muscle injury, and allows the muscles to get rid of any lactic acid that may have built up in your system if you were pushing too hard.

STRETCHING

And you should end up with another short period of stretching. You can use the same stretches that you started with. But again, don't hurt yourself. You should only stretch within your normal range of motion. Don't try to bend those joints much beyond where they usually go.

HOW OFTEN SHOULD I EXERCISE?

You probably need to exercise a minimum of three times a week, and ideally five times a week, with a lower level of exercise (some casual walking, perhaps) on the sixth day. And then it's important to get one day of rest, to allow your muscles, your bones, and your joints to heal up and toughen up.

Eventually, when you've been exercising for some time, you may wish to do it seven days a week. I do—but I've been at it for quite a few years. For now, let's take a gradual approach to this whole thing.

You'll probably find out after a short while that you're becoming physically fitter than you were. You'll find that a certain level of exercise that used to exhaust you—pushing your heart rate up, putting you into a sweat, and forcing you to breathe very deeply—just simply isn't a problem any more.

You're making progress.

I made a lot of progress, pretty fast. Back in the early '70s I was so physically out of shape, I had nowhere to go but up! After several months of vigorous training workouts, sore, stiff muscles, and tired lungs, I measured how long it took me to run one mile—twelve minutes.

A chart in one of Dr. Ken Cooper's books showed me that being able to run a mile in twelve minutes was right on the border between being in poor and very poor shape for someone of my age. That shows you how far I had to come!

I didn't come from zero up to thirty or forty minutes seven days a week overnight. It took awhile—years, actually, since I had no guidelines and no sense of urgency about improving.

If I can do it, anyone can. Short of patients with actual heart or lung disease, I've never met anyone who was in worse physical shape than I was before I started. So if you think you're in bad shape, take heart from my story—and go for it!

If you've been working with a doctor or the exercise physiologist at a health spa, and they've given you an exercise prescription, in a few months it may be time for you to go back to them and say, "Hey, I'm in much better shape now. And I'm ready for a higher level of exercise."

You might progress from a constant brisk walk to three quarters walking and a quarter jogging, then to half and half, and then to straight jogging.

And then again you might not. Sometimes you may stay at roughly the same level of exercise for a while. And that's where what we call *interval training* comes in.

The idea of interval training is to increase the level of exercise you're getting gradually. And you do it by exercising for a minute or two at a higher, more intense level during your regular aerobic exercise. If you're doing a brisk walk, you could find a tree that's maybe a block or two away and jog to the tree. Then go back to your regular brisk walk.

You can do this kind of thing several times in one exercise session, and begin to push your heart rate up a little higher, and prepare yourself for the next level of exercise. You'll find that after a few weeks or months you'll be able to exercise at a higher level—and still pass the talk test, still maintain your Training Heart Rate.

But once again—if you've got some of the risk factors for heart disease, you should check with your doctor before you start increasing the intensity of your exercise.

Another rule. Don't increase your distance or speed more than about 10 percent every week or every other week. That's a rule that helps to prevent injury.

I broke this rule once and got hurt. I'd been running a mile and a half a day for many months. A lady friend of mine who ran marathons sometimes was going to run ten miles along the beach one Saturday morning and I decided to go with her. At six miles I dropped out lame with a very painful knee. She had to run on and fetch the car. Boy, was I embarrassed!

As I walked along watching the other joggers sail past me, I wanted to tell each and every one of them, "I've just hurt my knee, that's why I'm walking." I set myself back six months that day, just because I pushed too hard and acted too macho.

Now don't use this story as an excuse not to exercise at all—the way every skier I see coming back on crutches allows me to put off learning to ski a little longer. You can learn to exercise safely if you'll just follow the guidelines. I want to reassure you of that.

While you are exercising, I'd like you to make sure you pay a lot of attention to your body. Listen to your body. You may find you have an ache here or a pain there. Maybe you'll feel some discomfort and stiffness at first. Those aches and pains and feelings of discomfort are your body's way of talking to you. You may be doing something that doesn't work. You may be exercising too intensely.

Ridiculous as this may sound, if you do pay attention to your body you'll learn a lot about walking and running. Your body will be learning, so it won't be an intellectual process. But you'll find that as you pay attention to your body it begins to change. You'll fall into a better stride. Your sense of balance will improve.

And, with practice, what was a little uncomfortable will begin to feel easier and more natural. My stride is now immeasurably stronger, more stable and self-confident.

When I started I was a little shaky—I actually thought I looked ridiculous, and I was quite self-conscious about it. Here was this pear-shaped, pale (by Southern California standards), middle-aged man, huffing and puffing and holding his side, trying to act like—what, like a kid again? A runner? But now I know I'm beautiful when I run—it's a whole different experience for me. It feels easy and natural and right.

WHAT EFFECT DOES EXERCISE HAVE ON HIGH BLOOD PRESSURE?

It lowers it!

Let me give you a word of warning here. Weight lifting will raise your blood pressure, not lower it. As I said earlier, aerobic exercise is the kind of exercise you should be doing, not lifting weights. The kinds of exercise that make you grunt and sweat and strain are not recommended. Particularly if you have high blood pressure already. That won't always be true, but it's probably true right now.

Even aerobic exercise may send your blood pressure up at first. That's why I recommend that if you have high blood pressure, particularly if it's moderate or severe, you should ask your doctor to give you a treadmill test and an exercise prescription before you start to exercise.

You may need to start out pretty slow. But, over time, regular exercise will become so easy and natural for you that it will help lower your blood pressure. It's real nice, once you've learned how to measure your own blood pressure, to check it before and after exercise—and see that the exercise has lowered it. Sometimes it will be dramatically lower. I have seen people at the program I work with come in with high blood pressure and watched it drop to 90/60 at the end of the hourlong exercise program.

Exercise opens up the little arterioles all over the body, and it also tends to burn up a lot of the hormones that are produced by the stress response, which raise the blood pressure. So the lowest blood pressure of your day may be in the fifteen minutes or half an hour after a good, exhausting exercise.

Pat, the lawyer friend and patient I told you about earlier, got a lot out of his exercise program. It appealed to him because it was something immediate and physical and real—he could do something—it was "manly" (in an old-fashioned sort of way) to sweat and breathe hard and get tired. I already told you his cholesterol fell a lot—he'd done a good job. And his blood pressure was pretty good too, considering how competitively he approached everything. Oh, it still bounced up sometimes, but on the average it was pretty good.

When it came to stress management, he was always a little skeptical about meditation and things like that. He did practice a little therapeutic avoidance, however. On his own initiative, he dropped out of trial law for a while and let his associates go into court for him instead. He took to wearing turtleneck sweaters and sports coats to the office, instead of the blue pin-striped three-piece suits he had always worn before. He looked happier and more relaxed, and the wrinkles in his forehead even started to soften a bit!

But he always thought he got the most out of exercise, and that's what he liked to talk about.

I laugh when I remember how he passed his FAA medical examination, to renew his pilot's license. He got pretty uptight about it and postponed it several times, because he was afraid he'd have a relapse and his blood pressure would go up, and he'd flunk it.

I told him to go right after his daily run, when we knew his pressure was at its lowest point of the day. He did, and it worked. He ran his usual four or five miles, and then another seven miles, and went right on without even stopping for a shower! His pressure was very low because he was so relaxed and so exhausted by his run that his worries about passing the test just couldn't affect him at all.

Oh, his pulse rate was a little high and the doctor made a comment about it. But I told Pat not to worry, it was high because his body still had heat to dissipate after that near marathon endurance run.

To celebrate his success, he took me out to lunch at a place where we both had to scramble a bit with the menu and special-order to stay on a healthy diet. Ah, that's America for you!

OTHER BENEFITS OF EXERCISE

Your skeleton is a wonderful system that adapts to whatever you do with your life. If you need strong bones because you're exercising regularly, your bones will become strong. And on the other hand, if you're not exercising at all, your bones will become weak. A regular exercise program tends to strengthen your bones. And perhaps prevent *osteoporosis*, the thinning out with aging that makes bones so brittle and easy to break.

Exercise also strengthens your muscles, particularly in your legs, back, and abdomen. It strengthens your breathing muscles so that you can breathe more easily, whatever you are doing.

It will tend to make the whole system that delivers oxygen to your lungs, your organs, and your tissues more efficient. It will help your tissues to receive more oxygen. It will stimulate the formation of enzymes in the muscles that facilitate the movement and use of oxygen.

It tends to make your heart stronger. You will notice that as you get physically fitter your resting heart rate will fall, usually to a figure below 60 a minute.

Exercise tends to have a beneficial effect on *arthritis,* and particularly on the degenerative arthritis and stiffness that often accompany old age. I have seen people who were crippled with arthritis in the ankles, knees, and hips, and who could barely get around—and I have watched them go through a careful, gradual exercise program. They felt as if a miracle had happened. They lost their pain, and they could go places again. But with arthritis, once again, it's important that you cooperate with your physician and start out your exercise program carefully and gradually.

Exercise tends to promote the normal functioning of the bowels. I always tell my patients that I've never known a constipated runner. Somehow, in the jostling and vigorous movement of the abdominal muscles when you run, food and waste products are moved through the bowels, and so running turns out to be a cure for constipation. (You'll notice that seasoned runners pick paths where there are toilets at regular intervals—they know from experience how important that is.)

If you're a pretty sedentary person when you begin your exercise program, you may be surprised and delighted to notice that your appetite actually decreases at first. And that as you keep up with the program your appetite will be more closely related to your body's needs.

You'll become more responsive to what your body actually needs in terms of food, and less likely to eat out of boredom, or because you're "starved," or it seems like a good idea, or it's lunchtime.

One of the components of "hunger" is low blood sugar. And a very effective way to lower blood sugar, paradoxical though it sounds, is to eat sugar. While you're actually eating sweets, and right afterward, your blood sugar rises rapidly—but later on it plummets. And then look out. Because, when it falls, that's when you feel hungry ("I'm starved!"), and you're likely to feel like snacking or eating a full meal.

Given the momentum of eating—that is, the likelihood that once we start eating we'll continue until all the food is finished—having your blood sugar drop can easily lead to an excessive intake of calories.

Here's the solution.

Exercise also raises blood sugar—by burning up stores of fat. So if, once or twice a day when you feel hungry, you were to walk briskly or jog—say at lunchtime for example—you'd reduce your intake of calories, use up stored fat, lose weight, and eliminate one of the main forces that leads to compulsive eating.

Exercise will tend to promote the development of larger arteries, particularly the arteries that supply your muscles, lungs, and heart. And in some cases (we don't yet know how to make it happen every time) exercise will actually promote the development of additional circulation *(collaterals)* around blocked arteries, in the heart for example.

Exercise is a wonderful cure for stress, for feeling frazzled and hassled and burned out, as Dr. William Whitmer points out in his book, *Whitmer's Guide to Total Wellness.*

You come home, you've had a struggle at the office, you fought the traffic all the way home, you're upset. Instead of sitting down with a beer and watching the bad news on TV, go out right now and exercise. Even if it's just a brisk walk, do something to burn up those stress chemicals in your blood.

If you find yourself getting hassled during the day, and you feel like having a drink at lunchtime, or you tend to overeat at lunch on days like this—take a brisk walk instead! Use part of your lunch break to burn up some of the nervous tension that's been building in you all morning! Try it. You'll have a happier afternoon.

Weight loss is another area in which exercise is important. You simply can't conquer obesity without a regular exercise program. Exercise is absolutely necessary in any program to produce permanent weight loss.

Over a long time, exercise will actually remodel your body. People who sit around all the time and eat a lot develop fat, which functions as a cushion; while people who walk or run a lot need to be more streamlined. So exercise streamlines the body. It will use up your bulky fat stores, and your muscles and your bones will get heavier—your body will actually reshape itself to be more in line with your new life style!

Exercise is also wonderful for dealing with sleep problems. Many people who have some form of insomnia are not regular exercisers, and most people who exercise regularly find it's much easier for them to get to sleep.

I find that now I'm on a regular exercise program I sleep more deeply and just don't need as much sleep as I used to.

And exercise is the only thing that will really do the trick for people who are feeling tired and run down. The tonics they advertise on TV don't do it. But a regular exercise program will.

Some people who smoke, or don't get much exercise, or have high blood pressure, find their hearts beat a little irregularly.

These slightly irregular heartbeats are called premature ventricular contractions or PVCs in medical terminology, though people often refer to them as "skipped beats." They may be harmless—but regular exercise will often clear them up in any case.

One other effect of exercise that you probably won't notice, but that will please your doctor very much, is that it tends to reduce the amount of cholesterol and fat in your blood and also raise the percentage of HDLs.

HDLs are *high-density lipoproteins*, which scavenge the cholesterol in your arteries and bring it back to the liver to be disposed of. Regular exercise actually helps clean up your arteries. And that means that, in any program that's designed to prevent heart attacks, regular exercise is essential.

What should I do on hot days when I perspire a lot? Should I take salt tablets or drink Gatorade?

First of all, you don't need salty water. The salt in your diet is already a problem, so don't add to it. And you don't need any extra sugar, either. Your fat stores are being converted to sugar. You just need to replace the water you've lost during exercise. That's all. Your body knows just what to do—so let it do it, naturally. Particularly if it's a hot day, or if you live in a very dry climate, just drink a few glasses of plain water, slowly and carefully. That'll do the trick.

Philip Felig and colleagues at Yale University have been working in this area and have published their results in a recent issue of the *New England Journal of Medicine* (1982). Their research showed that it takes several hours of endurance exercise (such as cycling or running) to use up stored fuel and drop the blood sugar level, even in a lean athlete. Even then, performance doesn't suffer—nor is it improved by drinking glucose and water.

And those of us with some fat stored around the tummy or hips needn't worry at all about running out of fuel!

I'm just beginning my exercise program, and I'm wondering what I should do if my muscles are sore a lot of the time?

I know how it can be. And for the moment, about all I can offer you is my sympathy. If you're really exercising and stretching the muscles, you may well be pretty stiff and sore from time to time. In fact it's one way to tell you're doing a pretty good job.

The test is that when you're stiff and sore, and you do your stretching and begin to exercise, it should get better. If it gets worse when you exercise, you should go see your doctor about it.

I've been thinking of jogging, but I'm concerned about the quality of the air. Does it make any difference where I jog?

Yes, it does. It's very important, if you're going to be exercising outdoors, to be very aware of the quality of the air. It's a mistake to exercise in smoggy conditions. When you exercise, your lungs take in more air—and if it's full of carbon monoxide and other pollutants, this can be really harmful. If it's smoggy, find somewhere else to exercise. Or stay inside.

I really enjoy relaxing in a hot tub after my workout. Is that okay for me to do?

Hot tubs and saunas are more designed to reduce muscle soreness and stiffness, particularly after weight lifting, stretching, or calisthenics.

Be very careful about getting into a hot tub while your body's still hot (and trying to lose heat) after a good aerobic workout. I don't recommend it. Wait for a while, until you've cooled down.

I'd also recommend that you be careful about hot tubs and saunas if you're on blood pressure pills—especially the central acting drugs, methyldopa, clonidine, and guanabenz. Ask your doctor what he thinks—I recommend extreme caution if you're on these pills, because the heat may cause you to dilate your blood vessels and faint.

I'm taking the beta blocker Tenormin and find it impossible to get my heart rate much higher than 120, even though my predicted THR is nearer 150. What should I do?

Your exercise prescription after a treadmill test should take into account the fact that your heart rate response to exercise is blocked by the drug. Beta blockers almost always do this.

If your own maximum heart rate (with the drug) is 120, you'll probably be able to exercise at pretty near ninety to a hundred percent of that figure, instead of eighty percent. But ask your doctor—he's the best judge, because he's seen your electrocardiogram.

Another test you could use is the talk test that we described earlier. You should be able to carry on a conversation while you walk (or run or cycle), if you're not overtaxing your body.

When you stop taking the beta blockers (or reduce the dose), you'll need a new exercise prescription, because your THR will change, sometimes dramatically. Again, your doctor or cardiologist is the one to talk to about this.

All right?

And here's one final piece of advice. If you need to lose weight, and you're just beginning a regular exercise program, *don't* use food as a reward system for exercising. You have a beautiful mechanism inside you that matches your caloric intake with how much you burn, and exercise will tend to make you more aware of it. But I've seen people jog every day for two years and not lose a pound—and all because they rewarded themselves with snacks every time they'd been good and done their exercise!

Exercise can really help you lose weight! So give it a chance.

28

What Is Stress?

The mind is its own place, and in itself
Can make a Heav'n of Hell and a Hell of Heav'n.

John Milton

Let's talk about cats.

We've probably all seen a cat lying around in the sun at some time or another, looking very relaxed, taking life easy. Those creatures can be so relaxed on a windowsill, you'd think they were in the Bahamas. And then a dog shows up.

Suddenly the cat is very, very alert. Its hair stands on end, maybe it begins to show its claws, its muscles are suddenly very tense, and it may even begin to hiss. A lot of changes take place in a very short time.

If we could somehow analyze those changes we'd have a pretty fair picture of what stress, and in particular what we call the *stress reaction*, is all about. So let's see what's going on inside that cat.

First of all the cat is just lying there, relaxed. Then there's an emergency—the dog. The cat's blood pressure shoots up, its pulse rate rises, its breathing speeds up, and its blood sugar and fat levels increase, to provide fuel so its muscles can do what they need to do—right away. All this is a completely automatic reaction.

The cat can't just sit there and tell itself, "So what, there's a new dog on the block." When it sees (or smells) that dog, its vacation is over. Instantly. Because this is a survival reaction. Any cat that didn't immediately alert itself when a strange animal appeared wouldn't last very long.

And what's going to happen? One of two things. Either the cat is going to fight or it's going to run.

THE FIGHT OR FLIGHT RESPONSE

Over the millions of years that these animals have been developing, this response has developed too. It's known, for obvious reasons, as the *fight or flight response*—and if you want to think of the nervous system as operating like a computer, you would say that this response has been hard-wired in. Whenever there's an emergency, this part of the nervous system turns on, and the rest is automatic. I like to call it the emergency nervous system, because that describes it.

That's what's going on when the cat smells a dog. And we have the same response hard-wired into us. We have our own *emergency nervous system*—and when trouble threatens, we too go into the fight or flight response.

THE RELAXATION PHASE

What happens when there isn't an emergency?

There's another part of the automatic nervous system that keeps everything running smoothly. We don't notice it, any more than we notice every spark that jumps across the plugs in our car, or the circulation of gas, or the constant movement of the pistons. And when that part of the automatic nervous system is working, our bodies relax, digest food, and heal themselves. We're relaxed. Just like the cat sunning itself on the windowsill

THE BALANCE

How do these two parts of the automatic nervous system work together?

Obviously, when there's an emergency, the emergency nervous system needs to know about it and to take over the running of the body. So it keeps watchful. It never entirely shuts down. On the other hand, when there's no emergency in sight there's no point in being all fired up and ready to go, so the emergency nervous system keeps a low profile, and the relaxation and maintenance system kicks in.

It's like a teeter-totter. At any time, one or other of these two systems will be more active and the other will be in reserve. It's a delicate balance. Both aspects are important.

If we were living in Africa three thousand years ago, we'd be pretty good at keeping that balance. We'd relax in the sun some of the time, but when we needed to become specially alert—because we were out hunting antelope, and a tiger suddenly showed up—we'd go into that same fight or flight response and be well prepared to handle the situation.

STRESS AND TODAY'S WORLD

But we're not living in the jungles and veldts of Africa, and tigers aren't the kind of trouble we run into.

The boss calls us onto the carpet. New, tougher production quotas are set. Traffic makes us late for a dinner party. Or our teenager plays the stereo way too loud. It's *stressful.* And we respond in exactly the way we would if we met a tiger! Our bodies prepare us for *fight or flight.*

I'd like to get one thing clear right now. When I talk about stress I'm not talking about the things that happen in our everyday lives that *cause* stress, such as the boss's carpet, the production quota, the traffic, the stereo. The snafus and problems and uncertainties in life, the decisions we have to make, the pressures we are all under, are problems we all face. I am talking about our own *reactions* to those pressures and problems.

Most everyone is under pressure of some kind or another. But it's the way we handle ourselves under pressure, not the pressure itself, that's important. We'll talk in a bit about the kinds of circumstances that often tend to trigger stress in us; but stress itself is something that happens *inside* us, and that's the important distinction to grasp here. Stress is the upset you feel, not the situations that upset you.

Even if you find that last statement a little hard to believe, bear with me and keep on reading anyway. . . . You see, it's important for you to realize that stress (not your boss) is your problem—because you probably can't do a thing about your boss, but you can do something about yourself!

Now let's talk about cats again. The cat and you both experience the same fight or flight response when there's an emergency—and you are both prepared to respond to the emergency by fighting or running, and then (when you'd taken one of those two strenuous physical actions) go back into the relaxed phase.

When the cat scents danger, the danger is always a very real physical threat. Right there in front of him. Whereas, when you and I get all warmed up and ready for fight or flight, the threat is seldom a physical one. The loud stereo, the new production quotas aren't things you can actually fight or run away from. But we get ourselves all steamed up anyway, just like the cat. Our muscles are primed for fight or flight, our blood pressure has shot up, and all the rest . . . but there's no dramatic physical action for us to perform, and no point at which we've taken action and can relax again. Even if our teenager turns off the stereo, we're likely to be fuming inside for quite a while.

Sound familiar?

And that leaves us with the emergency nervous system switched on, blood pressure going up, and a whole batch of angry chemicals swirling around in our bloodstreams.

ACUTE STRESS

Which brings me to my next point.

If some kind of emergency happens your stress response will automatically switch on and you'll take an appropriate action to deal with the danger. Once it's over, you'll relax again. You've experienced what we call *acute stress*. And there's nothing wrong with that.

If you turn a corner in town a couple of blocks from the zoo, and there's an escaped tiger padding toward you, with a bunch of guards and policemen running after it, trying to capture it—or even if you're on the freeway, and the drunk in the lane next to you decides to move his car right into yours—that acute stress response will take over. It isn't just appropriate, it's wonderful! You wouldn't be able to survive without it.

We've probably all seen movies or TV shows about animals in the Serengeti, or some of the other wildlife parks in Africa. You know how the zebras all run away when a lion comes by, and then, when the danger's over, they all start grazing again? If they were still upset they wouldn't be able to eat, right? When you're really upset and your survival is threatened, your appetite just isn't there either. It has to be that way, because if you were running from a lion, and you felt hungry before the danger was over, and you stopped to eat, you'd get eaten yourself. So not only is the stress response useful for getting away from danger—but the relaxation phase is important, because once the danger's over you need to be able to get back to business as usual.

If we all switched on the stress response in emergencies, and then switched it back off again when the danger was past—if we could relax afterward, the way the cat does, or those zebras do—there'd be nothing to worry about (and very little high blood pressure anywhere around).

But can you curl up on a windowsill in the sun, with one arm hanging down the wall, and just *bask?* Especially just after the boss has hauled you onto the carpet? Can you really relax—and I mean, relax like the cat? Most of us can't relax that completely even when we're on vacation—even when we're *in* the Bahamas! And yet that's the great secret.

If you could relax as readily as the cat, if you could turn your emergency nervous system on when you needed to, and switch it right back off again when you didn't need it anymore, stress wouldn't be a problem.

So that's the skill we need to acquire. We need to be able to turn the emergency nervous system on and off, according to the circumstances. If we're going to speak to an audience of fifty or a hundred people, or run to catch an airplane or a bus that we're late for—switch on the emergency nervous system.

And when we've caught the plane or finished that speech—switch it off. Relax.

CHRONIC STRESS

Our problems really begin when we start to experience *chronic stress*—when the stress response stays switched on more and more of the time, and we never reach the phase of relaxation.

How does that come about? One of the differences between us and the cat (or the zebra, the antelope, or the lion) is that we can think about the past and the future. We have very good imaginations. And when we start regretting or resenting the past, or worrying about the future, we experience the stress response—even though there's no real, physical danger to deal with.

We go over in our minds what we should have said or done, if only we'd thought of it in time. Or we're sure things won't work out tomorrow at that job interview we've scheduled. And while we're lamenting the past and trying to avoid the future at all costs, we're picturing disasters. And our bodies just react to these imaginary emergencies as though they were real. Listen. The emergency nervous system is dumb. It doesn't know whether we're imagining the whole thing or whether it's real.

So we may wind up spending a whole lot of time with the emergency nervous system switched on, when there's actually no real threat present.

If there's no threat present, there's nothing much we can do about it, is there? Yet even though there's nothing much we can do about it, we don't usually get to the point where it feels safe to relax again. And over the years, what tends to happen to many of us is that, once we get the emergency nervous system switched on, it never really goes off. So instead of going from 0 or 1 on a scale of 1 to 10, up to 7 or 8 when there's a real challenge, and then relaxing back down to 0 or 1, most of us begin to live around 4 or 5 or 6. It's where we live. It feels normal to us.

We wake up in the morning after a night's sleep, and what usually happens? We start thinking about our problems. We remember something that happened yesterday that we didn't handle real well, or we start thinking about problems that are going to crop up over the next few days.

Right?

I know. I'm human, so I can have fifty-seven varieties of wonderful things going on in my life, and one problem, and my mind will go right to the problem. I start thinking about it. The sun may be out, it may be a beautiful day, but there I am, "down in the dumps" and worrying. And I begin to get tense. If I was thinking about any of the other fifty-seven things, I'd be feeling fine. But I tend to pick on the one thing that's not going so well and concentrate on that. Dumb! And there's almost always that one thing.

I went to see my accountant a while back and found out that I'd mislaid a tax form I was supposed to have filed many months ago, and I hadn't filed it yet. I didn't have to send any money, just the damn form—and somehow it had gotten buried on my desk.

So what's the penalty? I found out they could actually fine me ten dollars a day for every day the form was overdue. It's much worse than having books out and overdue from the library. And you know, I got real upset. I was driving along, thinking "My God, that could come to fifteen hundred or two thousand dollars—for nothing!"

Now in fact the IRS would be most unlikely to penalize me that much. And in fact, even if they did, my getting upset now wouldn't improve things at all. So when I noticed I was worried and tense, I decided I'd better calm down. Look at the flowers, notice the sunset, listen to some music.

Isn't that what we all do sometimes? Get upset about the things that might possibly present problems and forget all about the things that are going well now?

I know we all have enough things happening in our lives one way or another that there's always room for improvement. There's always something that could have been done better. There are always plenty of things that could go wrong. And if those are the things we tend to focus on, we tend to react as though our lives were in danger—with the stress response —more and more of the time.

Then the emergency nervous system almost never gets to take a break. Now that's chronic stress—and it's a problem. It's a whole different kettle of fish from the acute stress we were speaking about earlier. Your body is perfectly able to tolerate your emergency nervous system being switched on and off, on and off, many times a day. That's how it's supposed to be. But when you keep it switched on continuously, all day long, day after day, that's a different thing completely.

That's chronic stress, and it's a killer. And I'll tell you why. Partly, it's because chronic stress is so damn near invisible. By the time stress has become nearly continuous we may not think of it as stress anymore. As I said before, it seems normal to us.

If we lived at 0 or 1 on the stress scale, and went up to 5, say, we'd really notice the difference. We'd think, "Wow, I'm really excited, I'm really enthusiastic," or "I'm really riled up about this, it makes me mad." But if we live at 4 or 5, that level of stress arousal just seems normal to us. Business as usual. And we may not think of it as stress.

In fact we may not admit to feeling stress until we get up to 8 or 9, when there's a big blowup of some kind, a big argument, or a traffic accident, or something like that. Then we know there's something going on. Then we'll admit we're feeling stressed, that we're upset.

But we just don't think 5 or 6 is anything special. We not only become so used to 4 or 5 or 6 that we hardly notice it anymore; we also actively avoid noticing it. It's not a very pleasant feeling, living at 5 or 6 on the Richter scale of stress—in fact it's so unpleasant that after a while we become less aware of it.

You know how we tend to shut out an irritating noise if it goes on for long enough—we just don't hear it anymore? Well, the same thing can happen with the unpleasant effects of a stress level of 4 or 5 or 6. We may pay less and less attention to it, until we just don't feel it anymore.

So lots of people, when I ask them if they have much stress, tell me, "No, I don't have any stress to speak of. Most of the time, I'm just fine." But I can tell from the kinds of diseases they have that they're suffering from chronic stress. They're under stress all the time. They just don't know it.

Afterward, when we've worked together and they've learned to relax, they just can't believe how tense they were feeling all along, without knowing it—or how much better they feel, now that they've learned to let go of their stress.

So part of the problem with chronic stress comes from the fact that it's almost invisible to us. And the other part of the problem—the other reason why it's such a killer—is because of the things it does.

We talked earlier about some of the things that happen when the stress response is activated. Let's look at it in a little more detail:

The blood pressure goes up, the pulse rate increases, we breathe faster, there's more sugar in the bloodstream, and more fat, and our blood is more ready to clot—in case we get scratched or bitten, and need to heal in a hurry.

The digestion (and some other systems) shut down, because they can wait until the emergency is over. Often the skin turns pale, because blood is being shunted to the muscles, and we say that we've blanched with terror or turned white as a sheet. Some people flush, because when you're running from danger your muscles generate a lot of heat, you need to get rid of it somehow, and one way is to send blood to the skin. And you may perspire, for the same reason.

This whole response is orchestrated by the nervous system and the glands of the endocrine system—and particularly by two hormones that come pouring out of your adrenal glands, named adrenalin and cortisone. Adrenalin is mainly responsible for the acute stress response, and cortisone has more to do with chronic stress.

What does all this lead to, when the stress response is on day in and day out? The answer is that it can lead to a number of different problems. What's your weak point? What's your "target organ"? Because that's where it'll get to you.

In some people, we might see what's known as an "acute anxiety attack" (or *hyperventilation syndrome*, to give it its medical name). Free-floating anxiety. You're scared to death—but you don't know why. The symptoms are palpitations, a pounding heart, sweaty palms, flushing, heavy breathing, and the blood pressure going up. It can happen again and again.

There was this beautiful scene in the movie *Starting Over*, with Burt Reynolds and Jill Clayburgh. I'll never forget it. Burt Reynolds was in

Bloomingdale's department store in New York City, and he had an acute anxiety attack with hyperventilation. It was perfectly done, very authentic.

If you saw the picture you may remember that the doctor who attended him finally looked up and saw a whole crowd of people staring down at Burt Reynolds as he was having his attack, and he said, "Does anyone have a Valium?" And of course everyone in the crowd had a Valium! That's America for you! A lot of people, and a whole lot of anxiety, and hypertension. It's very, very common.

An increase in blood pressure is a normal part of the stress response, and if you're under stress most of the time your blood pressure will be up most of the time too. And that in turn puts you at risk of heart attack and stroke.

Your blood sugar may be continuously up. So it can be a cause of diabetes. One day I was at UCLA-Harbor General, the hospital where I teach, and I told one of my students that a certain patient we had seen together was suffering from "worry diabetes." The student wrote this down and then looked up and said, "I've never seen that before. Is that a new kind of diabetes or something?"

Well, it is and it isn't. To be honest, I just made up the phrase on the spot. But the relationship between stress and diabetes has been around a long time.

I remember in medical school there were internists (or diagnosticians) who were medical doctors—and there were psychiatrists. And they were worlds apart in terms of interests and expertise. And then there were some *psychosomatic* doctors, doctors who believed that the mind somehow can cause or worsen disease. The students were always a little cautious, even skeptical of them, and I know for my part I kept my distance. My view of disease was much simpler and more automatic than that.

Well, you live and learn! I know I did. We doctors need to remember that people, *human beings*, get sick. It's not only their organs we need to know so much about, we need to know about their families, and their jobs, and the pressures they're under.

Stress can focus on your lungs and you can get asthma. It can make that particular weakness in your makeup much worse—in fact it can be really disabling. Maybe your lungs are a problem anyway—as a result of air pollution, or smoking now or in the past. Stress will attack you at your weakest point.

We've already seen that, when your emergency nervous system is on, your digestion doesn't work well. And that gets to be quite a problem. Lots of people have "nervous stomachs," and some researchers even talk about people who have peptic ulcer personalities.

Stress can lead to gastrointestinal problems, all the way from constipation and diarrhea to colitis and ulcers. It can even get to the point that the entire inside of your colon can peel off and you begin to bleed to death. You can perforate an ulcer and die from stress. That's how destructive chronic stress can be.

When people are very sick, when they've had a heart attack or stroke or some other serious illness, and they're very frightened—they can literally die from stress ulcers. Bleed to death. Right in the Intensive Care Unit. Stress can be a killer.

Women who have been through a really upsetting and stressful event such as the death of a child, or a divorce, or the loss of one of their parents, may destroy their thyroid glands. Just like that, zap! Destroy them. In fact, when a woman patient appears in my office with a destroyed thyroid (it's called *thydroiditis)*, I'll usually find that she suffered a catastrophic loss sometime in the year before.

Stress can cause or worsen arthritis, first of all because it causes chronic muscle tension, and the muscle tension hurts the joint between the muscles, just beats it up again and again.

And again, stress can hurt the body so much that the immune system (that's the system that's supposed to fight against foreign viruses and bacteria, and kill them) becomes abnormal. Then we say, "My resistance is down," and we may get a cold, or boils, or a bladder infection.

This weakening of the immune system can also lead to joint destruction and arthritis. That's called *autoimmunity*—the immune system destroys you instead of the foreign bodies.

Stress may also be the way that cancer gets its start. I was on a panel TV program recently, and the moderator was a doctor, a cancer specialist. We were talking about stress, and he pointed out that there's mounting evidence to suggest that cancer is certainly helped along by stress—if not actually caused by it in some instances.

And on and on. In fact it's fair to say that any weakness you may have —any tendency you've inherited, or any weakness that's left over from an old injury, anything—can be the place where stress hits you. If you put the wing of an aircraft under a lot of stress, and it has a hidden weakness, that's where it breaks. And it's the same way with us. That's where we break—at the weakest spot.

In the next two chapters we'll talk about techniques for reducing stress —some of the destructive stress management techniques we tend to choose without thought, such as smoking, overeating, and drinking, and some more constructive techniques, such as avoidance, biofeedback, awareness training, and meditation.

If chronic stress is a killer, good stress reduction techniques can save lives.

29

Stress Management 1

> Confidence, the ability to be joyously in-
> volved in the world around oneself and
> to savor the good things in life, can be
> as important as medical treatment and
> can actually enhance the value of that
> treatment.
>
> Omar Fareed, M.D.

How do we cope with stress? Do we curl up, like the cat, and simply relax? Or do we first check through the refrigerator, grab something, and then sit down in front of the television?

What do you do to unwind?

Most of us have our own ways of dealing with stress. We have to. We want to cope with it, we can feel the need to do something about it. We really try hard to cope with it. But the ways we choose often aren't really helpful, especially in the long run. And they may even be hurtful.

Let's take a look at some of the coping mechanisms we humans use:

Some people, when they're under a lot of stress, act out their anger and frustrations. We call that "letting off steam." They may yell, curse, stamp their feet, and lash out at people and things that are in their way. The upset they're feeling washes over, and upsets other people all around them, in much the same way that a speedboat can rock all the other boats tied up in a marina.

There's really a myth in our society that we shouldn't suppress anger and frustration—that we should express them, we should "let it all out." And yet scientific studies show it doesn't really help that much, and it may even hurt. If you're under a lot of stress and you unleash your anger on the people around you, then they usually get upset too. So it comes right back at you. And things tend to get quite heated—in fact it's like putting gasoline on a fire.

Besides, if you do let your anger out, you have to go back the next day and apologize. And then what's your monthly bill at the florist going to look like?

Repressing your anger doesn't work too well either. It builds up inside you, and festers, and builds up some more—and when it finally bursts out the bad effects can be dramatic. No. Hiding your stress from yourself and others, and pretending that everything's fine, that it's all under control, simply isn't the way to go. That's like renting a pressure cooker, furnishing it, and moving in.

In the next chapter we'll be looking at ways to cope with stress that don't involve either dumping your stress on someone else or going around with it continually on the boil inside you. For now, let's look at a few other things we do to cope with stress—the things we may like to think work but don't really do the job.

Some people deal with stress by drinking—beer, wine, martinis, whatever. If the stress is pretty constant, that means the drinking may need to be pretty constant too. The problem with alcohol is, if you feel good and happy and relaxed when you're drinking, you're not going to like it the next day when it's worn off. That simple fact can lead to morning drinking, and luncheon drinking, and secret drinking—a very costly habit.

It's not good for your liver, it's not good for your pocketbook, it's not good for your friendships and relationships—in fact almost the only thing you know it's good for (apart from the liquor store) is the IRS.

Some people use cigarettes, pipes, cigars, or chewing tobacco to deal with stress. I don't need to explain in much detail that none of these strategies are really good for you, do I?

A Japanese-American lady in our program who's trying to stop smoking told me she thought smoking reduced her stress, and it sure seemed to her that not smoking increased it. Now if she thinks that, she'll naturally continue to light up, fifty or sixty times a day. The truth is that nicotine is a stimulant. It doesn't relax you. It only adds to the problem of stress.

Some people use drugs—legal, prescription drugs, and illegal, social drugs. Wake-up drugs, slow-down drugs, mellow-out drugs, feel-good drugs. Tranquilizers, sleeping pills, cocaine, grass. The more you have to do to yourself along those lines, the more you have to take to try to feel okay, the worse things get. That's the simple truth of the matter.

Some people use coffee.

If your emergency nervous system is almost always on, if you're almost always a little worried, or stressed, or harassed, it's very likely that you don't sleep too well. You go to sleep with problems on your mind, and maybe your sleep is none too restful.

So during the day you may feel sleepy—and that can produce anxiety just by itself. Let's see, I'm searching for a good analogy. It's almost as if you'd been asked to guard a group of bandits, and you had to watch them day and night. Oh, they're tied up all right. But you know that if you ever fell asleep they'd somehow get you.

A lot of people walk around feeling like that. Something's going to get them. They drink coffee to stay awake, because if they fell asleep something bad might happen, they might lose out on something. And by the time they go to bed, maybe there's too much coffee in them for them to sleep well. So in the morning they feel sleepy again and have to drink more coffee. It's a vicious circle. Coffee is one common way that people deal with that anxiety—the worry that they may not be alert enough during the day.

Sleep is another way of coping with stress. Whenever I hear someone say, "My God, I'm sleeping nine or ten hours a day, and I don't know what's wrong, but I just don't feel rested"—that's stress. I know that, right away. It's always stress.

It works like this: when we're asleep we're unconscious—and we don't have to listen to our worries or our thoughts or our concerns any more. So some of us try to sleep more than we need, to avoid having to deal with our problems. We're not really deliberately escaping, you understand. But it works out that way. And there's this great excuse. "I'm tired, so I need more sleep."

But here's the problem. Using sleep this way may make you unconscious, but it's not necessarily restful to your body. As soon as you open your eyes in the morning, *wham*, you start worrying again. It's almost as if there was a little voice in there saying, "Good, I've been waiting for you to wake up," so it can start chewing on you again.

Eating is another way to cope with stress. It's a great way to distract yourself. And soothing, too. Milk and cookies. Ice cream. Pizza. What's your favorite snack? The problem here is that you're only distracted as long as you're actually eating—so you have to keep doing it, for it to work. The distraction doesn't last much beyond the last mouthful—so you have to keep putting stuff in. That means you may end up eating a whole lot more than you need—and a whole lot more than is good for you. Pretty soon your clothes are too tight and you can't see your shoes any more.

Work, work, and more work can be another way of coping with stress. In fact anything that offers us a distraction can be a way of handling stress —parties, vacations, loud music, even sex and conversation. People who have to be doing something all the time may well be trying to deal with stress—because if they ever sat down by themselves they'd worry. They'd fret. They'd stew. That's what workaholism is all about. And the party circuit, "life in the fast lane." And portable stereos—turn the music up loud enough and you can't hear yourself worry. But the worrying's still going on, whether you can hear it or not.

Ever notice how people can't stand to be bored? They'd rather be upset (or have almost any other negative feeling) than bored. Boredom is just being alone with our own thoughts—and that's no fun at all for most of us. Distractions can keep our minds from noticing what's bothering us, sure enough—but they don't usually manage to turn off the stress response. Of course a lot depends on the kinds of distractions you choose— horse racing or chamber music, roller coasters or a visit to the Botanical Gardens, *Halloween II* (the movie) or a picnic in the mountains, penny-a-point cribbage or a trip to Las Vegas to play the slots. Las Vegas is distracting all right—but it sure doesn't turn off the emergency nervous system!

So distraction may make us less aware of our suffering and our stress, but the process usually just keeps going on inside, beating us up: raising our blood pressure, or making our stomachs ache, or setting us up for an infection or a takeover by cancer cells.

That's the bad news. Let's face it. As human beings we usually don't come up with very effective coping strategies for stress. And certainly, what's for sale and what's promoted as likely to make us feel good isn't always very effective either. But there is an answer.

The problem that most people have with the emergency nervous system is that it really is automatic. You've probably been in situations that seem to crop up over and over again. You can tell yourself each time, "I'm not going to get upset this time," and damn it, you get in there, and it happens all over again.

Not only that, but when you find yourself reacting in the same old way you may react to the fact that you're reacting. Lots of people do. If you get upset, you get upset about being upset into the bargain. If you get angry, you're annoyed with yourself for getting angry, too.

Does this ring a bell? Sound like you?

Worse still, part of the anger we feel about being upset may express itself as indignation. "How dare they get me upset like this? I've got other things to do in my life. The last thing I need today is to feel this way. They're making me feel bad."

We feel as though our own feelings are an affront to us, and we put the blame out there, on the people we're upset with. We tell ourselves they *made* us angry. We don't want to take responsibility for our own feelings —and that leaves us pretty much powerless to change them. In effect we're behaving like machines. Someone presses one of our buttons and away we go. Look out! But there's a way out of this one, too.

We'll be talking in the next chapter about what we can do to avoid stress and to cope with it efficiently and healthfully. We'll be learning to switch the stress response off, right when it starts. And we'll be learning not to always react in an automatic, machinelike way when things aren't going the way we wish they would.

Over the course of the program we'll become a little more adaptable, a little less easily controlled by our situations. We'll begin to control circumstances that used to control us.

But before we start I'd like to say one last thing that's really important. I'd like to emphasize that although stress may be accompanied by emotions—I've been talking about anger and upsets and so on—it isn't always.

You may be the kind of person who has the stress response going off all the time, and your blood pressure shooting up—and still not perceive it, because you don't notice any emotional response or feeling. It's all buried deep inside.

There's some evidence *(Science,* 1979) that high blood pressure is a way to anesthetize yourself to these negative feelings and emotions. Hypertension can be a whole lot more silent and tolerable in the short run than a migraine or a temper tantrum.

Kids who have asthma attacks often don't realize they're responding to emotionally charged circumstances—they may not know there's any feeling involved—but if you ask their parents or their teachers the emotional nature of the response is often quite obvious to them.

A number of people with diabetes can have their blood sugar levels go way up, without feeling any emotions connected with the process. And people with hypertension can run their blood pressure up a hundred points in upsetting situations—and not necessarily be able to tell they're experiencing stress. Because they may not be aware of any emotional response whatsoever.

With a "calm" enough act, we can even fool ourselves!

This particular problem is one that biofeedback can really help with. With biofeedback training, you can literally watch your emergency nervous system turn on and off, on and off. You can see what's going on inside you, in terms of muscle tension, blood pressure, heart rate, skin temperature, galvanic skin response (how moist your skin is), and brain waves. And when you can see (or hear) what's going on you can learn to do something about it.

Joan was twenty-nine, a very pretty, slender, dark-haired girl who had it made. She had a good job, and ideal, supportive, loving circumstances—nothing amiss here. Yet she had hypertension—had had it since she was nineteen. And she'd driven all her doctors crazy because she wouldn't take any medicines. Sure enough, when I saw her in my office, she had a blood pressure of 180/110.

We tried diet. And on a very low sodium intake her blood pressure dropped some, to 155/105. So I told her the rest of it was a matter of stress. She gave me a look of disbelief. "Stress? Forget it," she said. "I don't have any stress. Do I look stressed? Do I have any reason to be stressed?" The answer to both these questions was no—and yet I knew the stress had to be there: her blood pressure was telling me so.

To cut a long story short, it turned out she had been a real nervous child and had even needed tranquilizers. Later her nervousness got buried. Then, years later, it surfaced again as hypertension, covered by a very good "calm act." When I gave her some biofeedback training she discovered how tense her muscles had been all along. The stress was there, sure enough, but she needed to know it.

Plenty of people simply don't know when they're under stress. It's a very, very common problem—and it's not something you should worry a lot about. But it's something you should know and learn to deal with

But how we can cope effectively with stress is another subject—and we'll be talking about it in the next chapter.

30

Stress Management 2

> But his eyes were beautiful and soft and
> immune from stress or excitement,
> beautiful and smiling lightly to her,
> smiling with her.
>
> D. H. Lawrence, *Women in Love*

Let me tell you some good news: you are already learning to use two of the most powerful methods of positive stress reduction—nutrition and exercise.

NUTRITION

Proper nutrition is very important in any successful stress management program. We've talked before about the fact that coffee excites your emergency nervous system. Drinking coffee to cope with stress is like pouring gasoline on a fire to put it out. And we've talked about sugar and how it often stimulates the brain. We've discussed salt and the role it plays in hypertension. And so on. Let's just say here that good nutrition is one of the cornerstones of successful stress management.

If you can avoid eating things that make you uptight or "wired," and things that make you sleepy (like rich, fatty meals) your emergency nervous system will be much better able to cope with stress. Okay? And remember that, when you overeat, that puts a strain on your body too.

One other thing. When the body is under stress it needs more vitamins. In general I don't recommend that people become dependent on vitamins —but I do recognize that we live in stressful times and that the food we eat isn't always as rich in vitamins as it would be if we were living in the middle of a forest or savanna or delta, and getting our food from natural sources. So I don't really quarrel with people who take regular doses of vitamins.

In general I think using vitamin supplements is pretty harmless, as long as you don't take too much vitamin A or D. So if you want to take some of the B vitamins and vitamin C, that's all right by me. It's your money, and the vitamins may be of some value to you, particularly if you're burning them up fast because you're under a lot of stress.

But I would like to warn you—if you are taking large doses of vitamins, be consistent about it. When you take a lot of vitamins your body becomes used to them. It metabolizes them faster. So you don't want to take a lot of vitamin C for a while and then stop—because then there's a chance you'll get scurvy.

EXERCISE

Exercise is the next most important part of a good stress management program—there's no getting around it. The reason that exercise is so important has to do with the fact that the stress response basically prepares your body for fight or flight. If you're suffering from chronic stress you are literally walking around with your body all prepared for physical action. And unless you take some strenuous physical action the arousal is going to stay around indefinitely.

When you exercise you burn up that excess energy and tension. You use up the arousal, so to speak. You allow the body to do what it was prepared for, and when you've done it your body can return to normal—to its regular physiological baseline condition. In other words, it can go into the recovery or relaxation phase.

That's what a good exercise program allows you to do. That's one reason why people who get regular exercise keep at it. And that's why I suggest you exercise four, five, or even six days a week.

You come back from a hard day at the office, with your stress level quite high, literally prepared for some extreme physical action. You go out and jog or swim or whatever, and use up that biological preparedness. You just burn it off. By the time you've taken your shower you're really calm. At that point you're probably more relaxed than many people ever get from one month's end to the next.

Thirty or forty minutes of working out, sweating, breathing hard, and getting all tired out is just wonderful. You'll usually find that your blood pressure is at its lowest for an hour or so after exercise. In fact it's a good idea to have some time right after you exercise just to sit and feel great. Enjoy it. Learn from it. The way to become relaxed more and more of the time is to experience the relaxation that's available to you right now.

When you're getting some exercise, and eating well, you know it. Deep down inside, you can feel that you're taking care of yourself, and that means you're loving yourself. And just knowing that can really feel good. You'd be amazed how much less anxious you can feel when you know you're taking good care of yourself. Because if you're not going to care for yourself, who is?

So take the time to look after yourself and don't feel selfish about it. There's nothing selfish about taking care of yourself—it's something we all need to do.

What other methods of stress management are there?

AVOIDANCE

Maybe the next technique you might think about is what we call *avoidance*. It's simple, really. It just means avoiding the unnecessary things that get you riled up in the first place!

Just take a look through your life and see what things you do that tend to upset you, that you just don't need to do—and then don't do them. I canceled my subscription to the newspaper. I discovered that when I read the newspaper in the morning I got upset. And I'd go off to work upset about the terrible things that I was reading in the paper.

Not anymore.

I don't read the paper, I don't watch the news on TV, in fact the only news I listen to any more is the news on National Public Radio. When it's Beethoven's birthday they'll do a story on it, and it's fun. I enjoy it. But even on NPR, when they start talking about the nuclear arms race, or Central America or the Middle East, I switch over to some classical music. And the music calms me down. And I go to work.

If you don't learn anything else from this chapter, I want you to get that we human beings are *sensitive*, all of us. Our machinery is delicate stuff. Oh, you may tell yourself, "Life's tough, but I'm tougher!" But that's not strictly true. You may be daring, you may be courageous, you may be self-sacrificing. You may endure hardships and suffering without complaint. But you're probably much more sensitive than you think you are.

A diet of bad news served up on a daily basis has a bad effect on us—and I'm speaking medically. Among other things, it raises our blood pressure. And that's true even if we don't think it's true, or don't think much about it at all. Even if we tell ourselves and our friends, "Oh, I read the paper every day and watch the six o'clock news, and it doesn't upset me."

Can you feel your blood pressure go up when you read about the nuclear buildup in Europe, or a gang rape, or an airline crash? Or can you feel your gut tighten? Do you know what happens inside your body every time you watch a violent, ugly scene in a movie or on TV?

You may need to know the news and you may not. But it's worth asking yourself what you don't need, that's always getting you upset. And then just not doing it so much anymore.

PLAY

Play is another excellent stress reduction technique. It's really a good idea to spend an hour or two every week, or even every day, just playing. Doing something you really like to do. I'm not talking about doing something competitive, where you have to best other people. I'm talking about playing in a way that's relaxing, enjoyable, fun, that makes you smile or laugh.

I know that golf can be enjoyable—but it often isn't. I'm always meeting people who are under stress at home and in the office, and what do they do on weekends? They go out and play golf for money—and they get stressed there too. So when I say play, I mean doing something that you're sure will be fun, *no matter how it turns out.*

I'm going to go play golf this weekend. I haven't played in years, but I used to play a lot, so I know my way around the course pretty well. I'm going to have fun no matter how it turns out. I'll be playing with a guy who'll only have fun if he wins—but I'm going to enjoy myself whether I win or lose.

I don't necessarily mean that you have to be playing a sport or a game— a hobby that you really enjoy, that's relaxing and interesting and noncompetitive, will do just as well. Just so long as you're spending some hours every week doing something you genuinely enjoy and that isn't stressful.

Baking in a sauna or a hot tub might be your way of relaxing, of giving yourself a treat. Or you could try a massage. Whatever. You remember there was a musical a few years back, *Stop the World, I Want to Get Off?* A hobby, game, or pastime is a way to do that—to get out from under all our usual pressures and frustrations for a bit and take a break.

We all need to do that once in a while—and that's why playing is so very, very important.

ASSERTIVENESS

A lot of people think that assertiveness means being pushy or demanding or manipulative—selfish or rude in one way or another. But that's not what it means at all. When people talk about assertiveness as a stress reduction technique, they mean telling the world what you need and what you want. Just some simple, straightforward communication. No more and no less.

Most of us are too timid for our own good some of the time, and then we feel so frustrated and terrible that we overreact and swing to the opposite extreme. We may swing from being a doormat to being a lion, then back to being a doormat again. We aren't very good doormats, and we certainly aren't very good lions either—and things don't work out too well for us when we behave as if we were.

Assertiveness is really just a matter of being able to communicate your real needs consistently, without those big swings. Because when your real needs aren't being met you tend to become resentful.

If you go to a restaurant and the waiter's rude to you and brings the wrong kind of food, and you *don't speak up* for yourself, you're going to sit there feeling resentful. With your blood pressure going up by the minute. Not to mention the tension in your stomach, and what that all does to your digestion.

But there's a way to communicate your problem and get the whole thing solved. And then your blood pressure comes down. You *need* to look after yourself and your blood pressure, by communicating to people what you need and what you want. And you can do it in a very gracious way, without yelling and screaming and getting angry.

That's what assertiveness training is about. It isn't about being selfish, it's just a matter of good communication.

POSITIVE IMAGERY

One of the real problems with stress is that the emergency nervous system isn't turned on only when there's someone right there threatening your peace and security or your life—it can also be turned on just by thinking about unpleasant things. We can just sit there in the office, and think about a lot of little things, and get all steamed up.

When you think about things ahead of time and imagine ways in which they might not work out for the best, that's *worry*. And when you think about things after they've happened and emphasize the ways in which they didn't work out the way you wanted, that's *regret* or *resentment*. Regret is telling yourself how you messed up, and resentment puts the blame on other people. They're equally damaging.

Your ability to worry, regret, and resent can turn on the emergency nervous system and get your body ready to fight or run when there's nothing you can do about it at the time—because whatever it is you're worrying or feeling resentful about or regretting happened a week ago—or isn't going to happen until next week.

We've all given a friend some good advice at one time or another, like "Why worry? There's no sense in worrying." Right? And we knew it was good advice. However, when we're the ones who are worrying we seldom give ourselves that advice, although we need to. And when we do give ourselves that advice we need to take it.

The things we worry about have a tremendous effect on our lives. Let's suppose that two weeks from now something bad might happen. If you spend the two weeks worrying about it, then you've spoiled two weeks of your life—even if it doesn't happen.

Why suffer every day for two weeks when you have a choice? And that's the point, isn't it? We do have a choice. We can worry and regret all the time and keep our minds stocked with images of things going wrong. Or we can take control and spend our time imagining positive things. It may seem hard to do at first but practice makes it easier.

Our bodies will know the difference. The body responds to thought in the same way that it responds to events around us. You know the way you can tap someone's knee and it jerks? The body responds as automatically as that. It just responds to whatever you're thinking. So when you think pleasant, unhurried, unworried thoughts, your body will relax and your blood pressure will come down.

AFFIRMATIONS

There are other methods you can use to quiet the worrying voices in your mind, and using *affirmations* is one of them. Affirmations are positive phrases that you hear or repeat to yourself over and over again. "I am wonderful," or "I am strong," or "I am beautiful," or "I am going to be successful." That kind of thing. And affirmations have a profound, positive, healing effect on the body.

Don't take my word for it—try it and see. See how you feel next time someone is critical of you or you're critical of yourself. And then see how you feel when someone compliments you or you acknowledge yourself, pat yourself on the back, that kind of thing.

It's an easy choice, isn't it? Do you think self-criticism helps you accomplish *anything?* Nonsense! You've got lots and lots to learn, and you need *encouragement,* not criticism, to help you learn it.

MEDITATION

Meditation means learning to pay attention to something calming. If your head is full of worries and concerns and regrets and plans and dreams and schemes—and you want to quiet them, you can learn to pay less attention to them.

I'm not saying you try to switch off your worries. That's like trying very hard *not* to think of elephants for thirty seconds. It just makes you think about them even more. But you can pay less attention to your worries and learn to pay attention to something else. That's called meditation.

You can meditate by watching a candle, or by paying attention to your breath, or by learning a mantra—a phrase or word that doesn't mean anything, that you can repeat to yourself without it summoning up any emotions. Or you can simply meditate on your own body, paying attention to it. When you find one of your muscles is tense, and quietly put your awareness there, you'll find the tension tends to evaporate all by itself. That's another type of meditation.

Meditation is a skill that anyone can learn. Again, it takes practice. And when you spend some time focusing on something completely harmless and inconsequential, the emergency nervous system shuts off.

Dr. Herbert Benson's book, *The Relaxation Response,* talks about the effects of simple meditation on the body. His studies at Harvard showed that when you meditate your blood pressure goes down, your pulse rate goes down, and you enter a calm, relaxed state with *alpha waves* in the brain; your parasympathetic nervous system is on and the emergency system is shut off.

If you can do that, consciously and deliberately, by your own choice, for twenty or thirty minutes a day, it won't only make those twenty or thirty minutes relaxed and calm—it actually has a positive effect for the rest of the day, too.

And if you do meditation on a daily basis—any kind of meditation—it actually has a very positive effect week after week, month after month. As far as the body is concerned, meditation is often more relaxing and restful than sleep. In fact you can actually treat high blood pressure just with meditation, and for some people it's enough.

Mary had the biggest smile on her face that I'd ever seen. She sat there, watching me read over her chart, with the kind of excited anticipation you might have if you were watching someone open the perfect present you just gave them. In her fifties, black, divorced, I knew Mary probably faced more stress in one day than I did in a whole week. Her blood pressure had proved to be very resistant to medication after medication.

A few weeks before, when she had tried to tell me how tense and worried she often was, my white middle-class self really couldn't relate to it very well at first. I remember starting to "advise" her about not letting things get to her so much. My mouth was full of reassurance—the kind that sounds wonderful but usually doesn't help too much.

After I had had my go at it she looked me in the eye and asked, "Have you ever seen a gang war—up close?"

I gulped and shook my head, "No."

"That's what was happening on my street last night," she told me. "A gang war. Hundreds of young men breaking and smashing everything in sight. And police cars, fire engines, helicopters—all right outside my window. I was so scared, I didn't know what to do."

At that moment I was pretty sure that my "helpful advice" wasn't going to be much help.

Yet here she was, coming into my office four weeks later, with this enormous smile on her face. Her blood pressure was down! She'd gone on the diet and even started meditating. That's right, meditating. She waved a well-worn copy of Herb Benson's book at me and said, "This is my new bible!" And she looked more calm and self-confident than I had ever seen her.

I looked at her numbers again, and it was true. Her blood pressure was way down. She told all the other patients in the waiting room what she had learned and what had happened to her. And you know, a lot of people got the message that day.

MUSCLE RELAXATION

Muscle relaxation is the final technique I want to describe for you here. I've already mentioned that we can carry muscle tension around for weeks or months, or even years, without feeling it. So how can we relax tense muscles—if we can't even feel the tension?

It's really easy. If you tense your muscles even more, they become momentarily exhausted and will then relax quite readily by themselves. So muscle relaxation involves progressively tensing, and then relaxing, every muscle in your body in turn, starting with your toes and working all the way up to your scalp. I know that sounds time-consuming, but it's actually very easy to do and only takes about ten or fifteen minutes. And it's so refreshing. As your muscles relax, the emergency nervous system turns off and your whole system cools down.

Meditation, muscle relaxation, and positive imagery are three ways to quiet the mind and switch off the emergency nervous system. And any human being can learn to do that, using one or another of these techniques. But you need to learn them by doing them—and by frequent practice. And you can ask other people for help in the beginning. At the back of the book you'll find some scripts for tapes that you (or a friend or family member with a calm, soothing voice) can record and play back to yourself and that will help you to learn these skills.

There's a wonderful moment when it all clicks and you've learned a new kind of balance—a balance that's not only very healthy for you but deeply satisfying and relaxing. In fact at the clinic people often tell me they enjoyed the exercises and the cooking program, and that the food was wonderful, but the best thing of all was the class in stress reduction and relaxation.

This is what can really affect the quality of your life, more than any thing else!

Appendices

Recording Your Relaxation Tapes

The following pages contain the scripts for four relaxation tapes—for Progressive Muscle Relaxation, Visualization, the Relaxation Response, and Affirmations.

It is best to record these tapes in a quiet room at a quiet time of day (maybe even at night), away from roads, traffic, rock music, etc. You may want to ask a friend who has a gentle reading voice to record these tapes for you.

Each tape script should be read very slowly and carefully, in a warm and encouraging voice, with pauses between the paragraphs. Roughly, one page of script might take two or three minutes to read. I know that's really slow—but we're not having a speed-reading contest here; the idea of these tapes is to let you relax deeply, and the real pauses between paragraphs are important.

Each of the first three tapes should run about fifteen to twenty minutes. The Affirmations tape can be shorter—but remember that all these tapes work best when you are in a relaxed and quiet state, both mentally and physically.

There are also a number of commercial relaxation tapes available on the market.

PROGRESSIVE MUSCLE RELAXATION TAPE: SCRIPT

Progressive muscle relaxation will work best if you are in a room where you won't be disturbed, sitting comfortably (or lying down, if that won't make you sleepy).

Make yourself comfortable. If you want to, you can adjust the light. Find yourself a comfortable chair. Sit back. You can loosen any tight clothing, so that you can breathe deeply and relax.

Rest your feet flat on the floor. Rest your hands on your thighs. Take a slow, deep, breath and straighten your back . . . and relax.

Relax. . . . Let your worries and thoughts drift away. You are breathing slowly in . . . and out. . . . Relax. . . .

Gently begin to pay attention to your left foot. . . . Feel your left foot . . . slowly tighten all the muscles in your left foot . . . and hold it . . . and relax them. Feel the tension melting. . . . Feel your foot relaxed, and heavy, and warm. . . .

And breathe deeply in . . . and relax. . . .

Now begin to pay attention to your left lower leg and calf . . . feel them . . . slowly tighten all the muscles in your left leg and calf . . . and hold it . . . and relax them. Feel the tension melting. . . . Feel your lower leg relaxed, and heavy, and warm. . . .

And breathe deeply in . . . and relax. . . .

Bring your attention to your left thigh . . . feel it . . . slowly tighten the muscles in your left thigh . . . and hold it . . . and relax them. You can feel the tension melt away. . . . Feel your thigh relaxed, and heavy, and warm. . . .

Breathe deeply in . . . and relax. . . .

Take another slow, deep breath and feel the air as it comes into your lungs . . . and goes out again. . . . Let worries and thoughts and concerns drift away. . . . Just relax and watch your breath coming in . . . and going out. Coming in . . . and going out. . . .

Gently begin to pay attention to your right foot. . . . Feel your right foot . . . slowly tighten all the muscles in your right foot . . . and hold it . . . and relax them. Feel the tension melting. . . . Feel your foot relaxed, and heavy, and warm. . . .

And breathe deeply in . . . and relax. . . .

Now begin to pay attention to your right lower leg and calf . . . feel them . . . slowly tighten all the muscles in your right leg and calf . . . and hold it . . . and relax them. Feel the tension melting. . . . Feel your lower leg relaxed, and heavy, and warm. . . .

And breathe deeply in . . . and relax. . . .

Bring your attention to your right thigh . . . feel it . . . slowly tighten the muscles in your right thigh . . . and hold it . . . and relax them. You can feel the tension melt away. . . . Feel your thigh relaxed, and heavy, and warm. . . .

Breathe deeply in . . . and relax. . . .

Now move your attention to your hips and buttocks . . . feel the muscles . . . slowly tighten the muscles in your hips and buttocks and pelvis . . . hold it . . . and relax them. Feel the tension melting away . . . feel your weight settling comfortably into the chair. . . . You can feel the chair supporting you, and your hips and buttocks and pelvis relaxed, and heavy, and warm. . . .

Breathe deeply . . . and relax. . . .

Bring your attention to your stomach. . . . Feel all the muscles in your abdomen . . . slowly tighten the muscles in your stomach . . . and hold it . . . and relax them. Feel the tension draining away.

And breathe deeply . . . and relax. . . .

Bring your attention to your chest. Feel your chest, feel your ribs slowly moving up and down as you breathe in . . . and out. . . . Slowly tighten the muscles in your chest . . . and hold it . . . and relax. . . .

And breathe deeply . . . and relax. . . .

Feel your back . . . tighten the muscles of your back . . . and hold it . . . and relax them. Feel the tension melting away. . . .

Breathe deeply . . . and relax. . . .

Now bring your attention to your left arm . . . and hand . . . tighten the muscles in your arm and hand . . . and hold it . . . and relax them . . . feel the tension melting away . . . feel your arm heavy and warm, your hand relaxed . . . and heavy . . . and warm. . . .

Breathe deeply . . . and relax. . . .

Now bring your attention to your right arm . . . and hand . . . tighten the muscles in your arm and hand . . . and hold it . . . and relax them . . . feel the tension melting away . . . feel your arm heavy and warm, your hand relaxed . . . and heavy . . . and warm. . . .

Breathe deeply . . . and relax. . . .

Now bring your attention to your neck and shoulders . . . tense the muscles in your neck and shoulders . . and hold it . . . and relax. . . . Let the tension drain away. .

Breathe deeply . . . and relax. .

Turn your attention to your forehead, and the muscles around your eyes, and your jaw muscles . . . tense these muscles   and hold it . . . and relax . . . let the tension drain away

Breathe deeply . . . and relax. .

Slowly scan your whole body, and if you feel any tension, relax and let it go. . . .

Now your whole body is relaxed . . . and at ease . . . and at peace.
. . . Enjoy your quiet breathing . . . breathe in . . . and hold it . . .
and breathe out. . . . Now your muscles are relaxed . . . your whole
body is relaxed . . . and calm . . . and at peace. . . .

Enjoy this calm, peaceful sensation of deep relaxation . . . as you
breathe in . . . and out . . . and in . . . and out. . . .

Feel how soft and relaxed your muscles are . . . enjoy this calm sensation. . . . This is what it feels like when your body is relaxed . . . and at
peace. . . . Whenever you feel tense, you can return to this refreshing,
calm state of relaxation. . . .

Breathe deeply . . . and relax. . . .

Your body feels refreshed and energized. . . . Take one more deep
breath in . . . and relax. . . . You feel refreshed and ready . . . ready
to bring this relaxed, energized feeling back with you into your everyday
life. . . .

One more deep breath . . . and you're ready. . . .

Open your eyes gently, and stretch. . . .

Take a deep breath. . .

VISUALIZATION OR IMAGING TAPE: SCRIPT

This visualization or imaging tape will work best if you are in a room
where you won't be disturbed, sitting comfortably (or lying down, if that
won't make you sleepy).

Make yourself comfortable. If you want to, you can adjust the light.
Find yourself a comfortable chair. Sit back. You can loosen any tight
clothing so that you can breathe deeply and relax.
Rest your feet flat on the floor. Rest your hands on your thighs. Take a
slow, deep, breath and straighten your back . . . and relax.

Relax. . . . Close your eyes. . . . Let your worries and thoughts drift away. You are breathing slowly in . . . and out. . . . Relax. . . .

You are going to use your ability to daydream . . . to visualize . . . to make pictures in your mind's eye. . . . Some people visualize in color, some people visualize in black and white, and some people just have a vague sense of the places or people or things they are visualizing. Whichever way you visualize, your body responds to those images. . . .

Let your worries and thoughts drift away. Your imaging will be clearest when your mind is free of thoughts and worries and concerns. . . . If distracting thoughts and doubts about this process come up in your mind, just let them float away like small clouds in a blue sky. . . .

Relax. . . . You are breathing slowly in . . . and out. . . . Relax. . . .

Imagine yourself someplace that you love . . . or where you'd like to be . . . somewhere outdoors, that feels quiet and personal . . . a calm place, a quiet beach, or a wood, or a valley. . . . Take a deep breath, imagine the beautiful, clear air . . . and the warmth of sunlight . . . and a cool breeze. . . .

Imagine yourself sitting down . . . and breathing deeply in . . . and out . . . so calm . . . and so peaceful. . . .

Perhaps you can hear the birds . or waves lapping on the sand . . . or a river running nearby perhaps you can smell the flowers. . . .

Take another deep breath and relax.

Look around you . what do you see? This beautiful place . . . the calm weather . . . trees, perhaps their leaves moving in the breeze . . or the waves gently breaking a few small clouds . . . a flight of geese high overhead the deep blue of the sky . . . the rich browns and wonderful fresh greens of the earth. . . .

Imagine closing your eyes and just listening . . . feeling the peacefulness . . . the restfulness of the place. . . .

You can imagine yourself lying down in a comfortable position . . . and letting go of your worries and tensions . . . and relaxing. . . .

Imagine the warmth of the sun . . . and the cool breeze playing on your face . . . as you relax . . . and breathe quietly in . . . and out. . . .

Listen to the quiet sounds around you . . . feel the sun on your skin, warming you, soothing away all tensions and cares . . . feel the breeze playing on your skin . . . this place is so restful, so full of peace. . . .

Let the faint smells and sounds of this marvelous place gently relax you. . . .

And breathe in . . . and out. . . .

You can hear water in the distance . . . the weather is just perfect . . . as you relax . . . and breathe in . . . and out. . . .

Relax . . . and let the sun warm you . . . and the breeze cool and soothe you . . . breathe in . . . and out . . . and relax. . . .

Just be aware of your breathing, gently in . . . and out . . . in . . . and out. . . .

Your mind is still . . . if you have any last thoughts or worries, watch them float away like small clouds in a calm, blue sky . . . you are at peace. . . .

You are completely at peace. . . .

Relax, and enjoy the sunlight. . . .

Relax, and enjoy the breeze. . . .

Relax. . . .

Breathe gently and deeply . . . and relax. . . .

Your body is rested and at peace. . . .

You are drawing strength and energy from the sunlight. . . . As you breathe in, the energy fills you . . . your lungs are filled with oxygen . . . nourishing and healing energy . . . and peace. . . .

Your body feels refreshed and energized. . . .

Take one more deep breath in . . . and relax. . . .

You feel refreshed and ready . . . ready to bring this relaxed, energized feeling back with you into your everyday life. . . . One more deep breath . . . and you're ready. . . .

Open your eyes gently, and stretch. . . .

Take a deep breath. . . .

RELAXATION RESPONSE TAPE: SCRIPT

The Relaxation Response will work best if you are in a room where you won't be disturbed, sitting comfortably (or lying down, if that won't make you sleepy).

Make yourself comfortable. If you want to, you can adjust the light. Find yourself a comfortable chair. Sit back. You can loosen any tight clothing so that you can breathe deeply and relax.

Rest your feet flat on the floor. Rest your hands on your thighs. Take a slow, deep, breath and straighten your back . . . and relax.

Relax. . . . Let your worries and thoughts drift away. You are breathing slowly in . . . and out. . . . Relax. . . .

The Relaxation Response will bring your mind and body into a calm, deeply relaxed and healing state. To enjoy the Relaxation Response, you will need a place where you can focus your attention, inside your body. We recommend that you close your eyes now and begin to follow your breath.

You will also need to help the Relaxation Response to occur, by letting your thoughts and worries drift away like bubbles in a glass of soda water.

Research has shown that this kind of quiet, internal focus is deeply healing and relaxing. As thoughts occur, just disregard them and bring your attention back to your breathing.

Take a deep breath . . . and relax. . . .

Breathe in . . . and breathe out. . . .

Just allow your thoughts to drift away like bubbles . . . and bring your attention back to your breathing. . . .

Breathe gently in . . . and out. . . .

In . . . and out . . .

Just be aware of your breathing. . . . Follow the flow of your breath as it comes in . . . and goes out. . . .

Let go of your thoughts as you breathe in . . . and out. . . .

In . . . and out . . .

Let your body relax. . . .

Let all your muscles relax. . . .

Just allow your thoughts to drift away like bubbles . . . and bring your attention back to your breathing. . . .

Breathe gently in . . . and out. . . .

In . . . and out . . .

Just be aware of your breathing. . . . Follow the flow of your breath as it comes in . . . and goes out. . . .

Let go of your thoughts as you breathe in . . and out. . . .

In . . . and out . .

Let your muscles relax. . . .

Let your whole body feel relaxed, and calm, and at peace.

Your breath is slower, deeper, and gentler now. . . .

Quietly watch your breath coming in . . . and going out. . . .

Let your thoughts drift away . . . and bring your attention back to your breathing. . . .

Breathe gently in . . . and out. . . .

In . . . and out . . .

Just be aware of your breathing. . . . Follow the flow of your breath as it comes in . . . and goes out. . . .

Let go of your thoughts. . . .

Breathe in . . . and out. . . .

In . . . and out . . .

Let your muscles relax. . . .

Let your whole body feel relaxed, and calm, and at peace.

Your breath is slower, deeper, and gentler now. . . .

Quietly watch your breath coming in . . . and going out. . . .

Let your thoughts drift away . . . and bring your attention back to your breathing. . . .

Breathe in . . . and out. . . .

In . . . and out . . .

In . . . and out . . .

Just be aware of your breathing. . . .

In . . . and out . . .

No thoughts . . . no worries . . .

Your breathing . . .

In . . . and out . . .

In . . . and out . . .

In . . . and gently out . . .

In . . . and out . . . and in . . . and out . . .

Like a river . . .

Your breathing . . .

Just let go to your breathing . . .

In . . . and out . . .

Flowing gently along like a river . . .

So peaceful . . .

In . . . and out . . .

So calming . . .

In . . . and out . . .

In . . . and out . . .

Breathe in . . . and out . . .

In . . . and out . . .

In . . . and out . . .

Just stay aware of your breathing . . .

In . . . and out . . .

Let go of thoughts. . . .

Stay with your breathing . . .

In . . . and out . . .

In . . . and out . . .

In . . . and gently out . . .

In . . . and out . . . and in . . . and out . . .

Your breathing . . .

So relaxed . . . and at peace. . .

Your whole body is relaxed . . . and calm . . . and at peace . . .
and refreshed. . . .

Take one more breath in . . . and relax. . . .

You feel refreshed and ready . . . ready to bring this relaxed, energized
feeling back with you into your everyday life . . . One more deep breath
. . . and you're ready. .

Open your eyes gently, and stretch

Take a deep breath. .

AFFIRMATIONS TAPE: SCRIPT

These affirmations will work best if you are in a room where you won't be disturbed, sitting comfortably (or lying down, if that won't make you sleepy).

Make yourself comfortable. If you want to, you can adjust the light. Find yourself a comfortable chair. Sit back. You can loosen any tight clothing so that you can breathe deeply and relax.

Rest your feet flat on the floor. Rest your hands on your thighs. Take a slow, deep, breath and straighten your back . . . and relax.

Relax. . . . Close your eyes. . . . Let your worries and thoughts drift away. You are breathing slowly in . . . and out. . . . Relax. . . .

Take one more breath in . . . and relax. . . .

I am relaxed. . . .

I am refreshed and alert. . . .

I accept myself. . . .

I am whole and complete, perfect the way I am. . . .

I contain the seeds of my own health. . . .

I accept the wisdom of my body. . . .

The wisdom of my body is a source of health and well-being. . . .

I am growing in health. . . .

I am wonderfully able to heal myself. . . .

I accept my life. . . .

I am willing to learn. . . .

My life is perfect the way it is. . . .

I accept the wisdom that will allow my life to grow and to flourish. . . .

I accept the energy of life that is within me. . . .

I am a source of energy and warmth to myself and those around me. . . .

I now forgive everyone for anything that was ever done to me. . . .

I forgive myself. . . .

I love myself. . . .

I accept the clarity that is in me. . . .

I am a source of clarity and understanding for myself and others. . . .

I am relaxed and confident. . . .

I am able to listen to others. . . .

I express myself fully and clearly. . . .

I am a source of abundance. . . .

My life is full of abundance because I am provided with whatever I need. . . .

I am rich when I receive. . . .

I am rich when I give. . . .

I make my peace with the world. . . .

I accept the peace that is within me. . . .

I am a source of radiant peace to myself and others.

I express the peace that is within me.

I am relaxed. . . .

I am refreshed. . . .

I am ready. . . .

You feel refreshed and ready . . . ready to bring this relaxed, energized feeling back with you into your everyday life. . . . One more deep breath . . . and you're ready. . . .

Open your eyes gently, and stretch. . . .

Take a deep breath. . . .

Sources Listing the Sodium Content in Foods

Kraus, Barbara. *The Barbara Kraus Guide to Sodium*. New York: Signet Books, 1983.

Marsh, Anne, Ruth Klippstein, and Sybil Kaplan. *The Sodium Content of Your Food*. USDA Home and Garden Bulletin #233.

White, Philip, and Stephanie Crocco, eds. *Sodium and Potassium in Foods and Drugs*. Chicago: American Medical Association, 1980.

Related materials:

Brody, Jane. *Jane Brody's The New York Times Guide to Personal Health*. New York: Times Books, 1982.

————. *Jane Brody's Nutrition Book*. New York: Norton, 1981.

Cooking Without Your Salt Shaker. Dallas: American Heart Association, 1978.

Kraus, Barbara. *The Dictionary of Sodium, Fats, and Cholesterol*. New York: Grosset & Dunlap, 1979.

Bibliography

CHAPTER 1: MYTHS ABOUT HYPERTENSION

Chagnon, N. A. *Yanomamo: The Fierce People.* New York: Holt, Rinehart & Winston, 1968.

Oliver, W. J., et al. "Blood Pressure, Sodium Intake and Sodium Related Hormones in the Yanomamo Indians, a 'No Salt' Culture," *Circulation* 52, 146–51 (1975).

Kesteloot, H., and J. V. Joossens, eds. *Epidemiology of Arterial Blood Pressure.* The Hague: Nijhoff, 1980.

Page, L. B., et al. "Antecedents of Cardiovascular Disease in Six Solomon Islands Societies," *Circulation* 43, 1132–46 (1974).

Rose, G. "Epidemiology of Familial Factors and Salt Intake in Man," *Postgrad. Med. J.* 43 Supp. 2: 139–43 (1977).

Freis, E. D. "Salt, Volume and the Prevention of Hypertension," *Circulation* 53, 589–95 (1976).

"Salt, a New Villain?" *Time,* March 15, 1982.

Dawber, T. R. *The Framingham Study: The Epidemiology of Atherosclerotic Disease.* Cambridge, Mass.: Harvard University Press, 1980.

The 1980 Report of the Joint National Committee on Detection, Evaluation, and Treatment of High Blood Pressure. Bethesda, Md.: National Heart, Lung and Blood Institute, National Institutes of Health Publication No. 81–1088, 1980.

Gifford, R. W., et al. "Guidelines for Detection, Diagnosis and Management of Hypertensive Populations," *Circulation* 64, 1079A–89A
(1981).

Oliver, M. F. "Risks of Correcting the Risks of Coronary Disease and
Stroke with Drugs," *NEJM* 306: 297–98 (1982).

Cabot, R. C., and R. L. Dicks. *The Art of Ministering to the Sick.* New
York: Macmillan, 1936.

Oyle, I. *The New American Medicine Show.* Santa Cruz: Unity Press,
1979.

Cousins, N. "Listening to Your Doctor—and Your Own Body," New York
Times, September 15, 1979.

CHAPTER 2: FURTHER MYTHS

Grady, D. "The Selling of Oraflex," *Discover*, October 1982, pp. 86–90.

"Benoxaprofen," editorial. *BMJ* 285: 459–60 (1982).

Rossi, A. C., et al. "Discovery of Adverse Drug Reactions," *JAMA* 249:
2226–28 (1983).

"AMA Backs Proposal on Drug Approval," *Amer. Med. News*, January 28,
1983.

"Why the Rx Upsurge? New Drugs, Easier Regs, and More Oldsters,"
Medical World News 23:19: 18 (1982).

Farquhar, J. W. *The American Way of Life Need Not Be Hazardous to
Your Health.* New York: Norton, 1979.

Glueck, C. J., et al. "Diet and Coronary Heart Disease," *NEJM* 298:
1471–74 (1978).

Franceschi, M., et al. "Cognitive Processes in Hypertension," *Hypertension* 4: 226–29 (1982).

Shapiro, A. P., et al. "Behavioral Consequences of Mild Hypertension,"
Hypertension 4: 355–60 (1982).

Luft, F. C., et al. "Sodium Sensitivity and Resistance in Normotensive
Humans," *Am. J. Med.* 72: 726–36 (1982).

Laragh, J. H. *Topics in Hypertension.* New York: Yorke Medical Books,
1980.

————, et al. "Renin Profiling for Diagnosis and Treatment of Hypertension," *JAMA* 241: 151–56 (1979).

————, et al. "The Vasoconstriction-Volume Spectrum in Normotension and in the Pathogenesis of Hypertension," *Federation Proc.* 41: 2415–23 (1982).

Carter, A. B. "Hypotensive Therapy in Stroke Survivors," *Lancet* 1: 485–89 (1970).

Kannel, W. B., et al. "Systolic Blood Pressure, Arterial Rigidity, and Risk of Stroke," *JAMA* 245: 1225–29 (1981).

Friedman, M., et al. "Feasibility of Altering Type A Behavior Pattern after Myocardial Infarction," *Circulation* 66: 83–92 (1982).

CHAPTER 3: WHAT IS BLOOD PRESSURE?

Korotkoff, N. C. "On Methods of Studying Blood Pressure," *Bull. Imperial Military Med. Acad. [St. Petersburg]* 11: 365 (1905).

CHAPTER 4: WHAT IS HIGH BLOOD PRESSURE?

Guyton, A. C., et al. "Salt Balance and Long-Term Blood Pressure Control," *Ann. Rev. Med.* 31: 15–27 (1980).

Friedman, R., and J. Iwai. "Genetic Predisposition and Stress-Induced Hypertension," *Science* 193: 161–62 (1976).

Sowers, J. R., et al. "Blood Pressure and Hormone Changes Associated with Weight Reduction in the Obese," *Hypertension* 4: 686–91 (1982).

Hollenberg, N. K., et al. "Renal Blood Flow and Its Response to Angiotensin II," *Circ. Res.* 38: 35–40 (1976).

Kaplan, N. M. "Cardiovascular Complications of Oral Contraceptives," *Ann. Rev. Med.* 29: 31–40 (1978).

Fisch, I. R., and J. Frank. "Oral Contraceptives and Blood Pressure," *JAMA* 237: 2499–503 (1977).

Kannel, W. B., editorial. "Possible Hazards of Oral Contraceptive Use," *Circulation* 60: 490–91 (1979).

Kaplan, N. M. "Therapy for Mild Hypertension," *JAMA* 249: 365–67 (1983).

McAlister, N. H. "Should We Treat 'Mild' Hypertension?" *JAMA* 249: 379–82 (1983).

Kaplan, N. M. "Mild Hypertension—When and How to Treat," *Arch. Intern. Med.* 143: 255–59 (1983).

Weber, M. A., et al. "A Representative Value for Whole-Day BP Monitoring," *JAMA* 248: 1626–28 (1982).

Perloff, D., et al. "The Prognostic Value of Ambulatory Blood Pressures," *JAMA* 249: 2792–98 (1983).

Floras, J. S., et al. "Cuff and Ambulatory Blood Pressure in Subjects with Essential Hypertension," *Lancet* 2: 107–9 (1981).

CHAPTER 5: THE CONVENTIONAL TREATMENT

Evelyn, K. A., et al. "Effect of Sympathectomy on Blood Pressure in Hypertension," *JAMA* 140: 592–601 (1949).

CHAPTER 6: THE PROGRAM THAT WORKS

Levy, R. I. "The National Heart, Lung, and Blood Institute Overview 1980," *Circulation* 65: 217–25 (1982).

Freis, E. D. "Treatment of Hypertension in 1981," *Hypertension* 3 (Supp. II): II-230–2 (1981).

Oliver, M. F. "Risks of Correcting the Risks of Coronary Disease and Stroke with Drugs," *NEJM* 306, 297–98 (1982).

Korcok, M. "Do Antihypertensive Drugs Increase Coronary Risk?" *JAMA* 246: 2008, 2013 (1981).

Ames, R. P., and P. Hill. "Improvement of Glucose Tolerance and Lowering of Glycohemoglobin and Serum Lipid Concentrations After Discontinuation of Antihypertensive Drug Therapy," *Circulation* 65: 899–904 (1982).

Magnet, M. "The Scramble for the Next Superdrug," *Fortune* 104: 94–112 (1981).

Laughlin, K. D., et al. "Blood Pressure Reductions During Self-recording of Home Blood Pressure," *Am. Heart J.* 98: 629–34 (1979).

Cottier, C., et al. "Usefulness of Home BP Determination in Treating Borderline Hypertension," *JAMA* 248: 555–58 (1982).

"Hypertension—Salt Poisoning?" *Lancet* 1: 1136–37 (1978).

"Salt Restriction to Prevent Hypertension," *Medical Letter* 22: 14–15 (1980).

"Low-Sodium Diet Lauded in Curbing Hypertension," *Amer. Med. News,* August 13, 1982.

"AMA, FDA Act to Limit Sodium in Foods," *Amer. Med. News,* July 16, 1982.

Hayes, A. H. "Advances in Cardiovascular Pharmacology," *JAMA* 248: 537–44 (1982).

Council on Scientific Affairs. "Sodium in Processed Foods," *JAMA* 249: 784–89 (1983).

Reisin, E., et al. "Effect of Weight Loss Without Salt Restriction on the Reduction of Blood Pressure in Overweight Hypertensive Patients," *NEJM* 298: 1–6 (1978).

Tuck, M. L., et al. "The Effect of Weight Reduction on Blood Pressure, Plasma Renin Activity and Plasma Aldosterone Levels in Obese Patients," *NEJM* 304: 930–33 (1981).

Mazer, E. "12 Ways to Lower Your Blood Pressure Naturally," *Prevention,* July 1982.

Kristt, D. A., and B. T. Engel. "Learned Control of Blood Pressure in Patients with High Blood Pressure," *Circulation* 51: 370–78 (1975).

"Meditation or Methyldopa?" *BMJ* 1: 1421–22 (1976).

"Lowering Blood Pressure Without Drugs," *Lancet* 2: 459–61 (1980).

Stammler, J., et al. "Prevention and Control of Hypertension by Nutritional-Hygienic Means," *JAMA* 243: 1819–23 (1980).

Friedman, M., et al. "Feasibility of Altering Type A Behavior Pattern after Myocardial Infarction," *Circulation* 66: 83 (1982).

CHAPTER 9: THE FIRST WEEK

Hakki, A. H., et al. "Prediction of Maximal Heart Rates in Men and Women," *Cardiovascular Reviews & Reports* 4: 997–99 (1983).

CHAPTER 10: THE SECOND WEEK

Graedon, J. *The People's Pharmacy*. New York: Avon Books, 1976.

————. *The People's Pharmacy–Two*. New York: Avon Books, 1980.

Cooper, K. H. *The Aerobics Way*. New York: Bantam Books, 1978.

Farquhar, J. W. *The American Way of Life Need Not Be Hazardous to Your Health*. New York: Norton, 1978.

CHAPTER 13: THE FIFTH WEEK

Ellis, A., and R. Harper. *A Guide to Rational Living*. North Hollywood: Wilshire Books, 1975.

Goodman, D. S. *Emotional Well-Being Through Rational Behavior*. Springfield, Ill.: Charles C. Thomas, 1974.

Danaher, B., and E. Lichtenstein. *Becoming an Ex-Smoker*. New York: Prentice-Hall, 1978.

CHAPTER 14: THE SIXTH AND SEVENTH WEEKS

Gibb, W. T., quoted in Galton, L. *Coping with Executive Stress*. New York: McGraw-Hill, 1983.

CHAPTER 15: THE EIGHTH AND NINTH WEEKS

Cousins, N. *Anatomy of an Illness*. New York: Norton, 1979.

Beauchamp, G. K., et al. "Modification of Salt Taste," *Ann. Int. Med.* 98 (Pt. 2): 763–69 (1983).

Joossens, J. V., and J. Geboers. "Salt and Hypertension," *Preventive Medicine* 12: 53–59 (1983).

Patel, C., et al. "Controlled Trial of Biofeedback-Aided Behavioural Methods in Reducing Mild Hypertension," *BMJ* 282: 2005–8 (1981).

Kangilaski, J. "Dialogue: a Link to Psychosomatic Illnesses," *JAMA* 247: 2760–73 (1982).

Bibliography

CHAPTER 16: THE TENTH AND ELEVENTH WEEKS

Kempner, W. "Treatment of Hypertensive Vascular Disease with Rice Diet," *Am. J. Med.* 4: 545–77 (1948).

Schroeder, H. A., et al. "Low Sodium Chloride Diets in Hypertension," *JAMA* 140: 458–63 (1949).

Benson, H. *The Relaxation Response.* New York: Morrow, 1975.

CHAPTER 17: WEEK TWELVE—THE FINAL WEEK

Reps, P. *Zen Flesh, Zen Bones.* Garden City, N.Y.: Doubleday/Anchor, n.d.

CHAPTER 19: THE WHITE LAB COAT

Gallwey, W. T. *Inner Tennis: Playing the Game.* New York: Random House, 1976.

———. *The Inner Game of Tennis.* New York: Random House, 1974.

Cooper, Kenneth. *Aerobics.* New York: Bantam Books, 1968.

CHAPTER 21: THE DIURETICS

Avorn, J., et al. "Scientific versus Commercial Sources of Influence on the Prescribing Behavior of Physicians," *Am. J. Med.* 73: 4–8 (1982).

Kaplan, N. M. "Hypokalemia: What Does It Mean for Cardiac Patients?" *J. Cardiovasc. Med.* 8: 366–68, March 1983.

Anderson, J. "A Comparison of the Effects of Hydrochlorothiazide and of Frusemide in the Treatment of Hypertensive Patients," *Quart. J. Med.* 40: 541–60 (1971).

MRFIT Research Group. "Multiple Risk Factor Intervention Trial: Risk Factor Changes and Mortality Results," *JAMA* 248: 1465–77 (1982).

Ram, C. V. S., et al. "Moderate Sodium Restriction and Various Diuretics in the Treatment of Hypertension," *Arch. Intern. Med.* 141: 1015–19 (1981).

Lewis, P. J., et al. "Deterioration of Glucose Tolerance in Hypertensive Patients on Prolonged Diuretic Treatment," *Lancet* 1: 564–66 (1976).

Murphy, M. B., et al. "Glucose Intolerance in Hypertensive Patients Treated with Diuretics; a Fourteen-Year Follow-up," *Lancet* 2: 1293–95 (1982).

Helderman, J. H., et al. "Prevention of the Glucose Intolerance of Thiazide Diuretics by Maintenance of Body Potassium," *Diabetes* 32: 106–11 (1983).

Ashraf, N., et al. "Thiazide-Induced Hyponatremia Associated with Death or Neurologic Damage in Outpatients," *Am. J. Med.* 70: 1163–68 (1981).

"Medical Research Council Working Party on Mild to Moderate Hypertension, Adverse Reactions to Bendrofluazide and Propranolol for the Treatment of Hypertension," *Lancet* 8246: 539–43 (1981).

McMahon, F. G., et al. "Upper Gastrointestinal Lesions after Potassium Chloride Supplements: a Controlled Clinical Trial," *Lancet* 2: 1059–61 (1982).

CHAPTER 22: THE BLOCKERS

"Pindolol," *Medical Letter* 25: 13–14 (1983).

Brantigan, C. O., et al. "Effect of Beta Blockade and Beta Stimulation on Stage Fright," *Am. J. Med.* 72: 88–94 (1982).

"The Beta-Blocker Blues," *Emergency Med.* 14: 182, 188 (1982).

Small, G. W., and L. F. Jarvik. "The Dementia Syndrome," *Lancet* 2: 1443–46 (1982).

Wilburn, R. L., et al. "Long Term Treatment of Severe Hypertension with Minoxidil, Propranolol and Furosemide," *Circulation* 52: 706–13 (1975).

Day, J. L., et al. "Metabolic Consequences of Atenolol and Propranolol in Treatment of Essential Hypertension," *BMJ* 1: 77–80 (1979).

———. "Adrenergic Mechanisms in Control of Plasma Lipid Concentrations," *BMJ* 284: 1145–48 (1982).

Leren, P., et al. "Effect of Propranolol and Prazosin on Blood Lipids," *Lancet* 2: 4–6 (1980).

"Guanabenz Receives FDA Approval for the Control of Hypertension," *Med. Sci. Bulletin* 5: 1–2 (1982).

Wright, A. D., et al. "Beta-Adrenoceptor-Blocking Drugs and Blood Sugar Control in Diabetes Mellitus," *BMJ* 1: 159–61 (1979).

Myers, M. G., and H. F. Hope-Gill. "Effect of D- and Dl-propranolol on Glucose-Stimulated Insulin Release," *Clin. Pharmacol. Ther.* 25: 303–8 (1979).

Clark, M., et al. "Overdosing the Elderly," *Newsweek,* August 30, 1982.

Wilbur, R., et al. "Acute Organic Brain Syndrome from Nadolol Therapy," letter, *Arch. Intern. Med.* 141: 1723 (1981).

Fleminger, R. "Visual Hallucinations and Illusions with Propranolol," *BMJ* 1: 1182 (1978).

Houston, M. C. "Abrupt Cessation of Treatment in Hypertension: Consideration of Clinical Features, Mechanisms, Prevention and Management of the Discontinuation Syndrome," *Am. Heart J.* 102: 415–30 (1981).

CHAPTER 23: THE VASODILATORS AND OTHER ANTIHYPERTENSIVE DRUGS

Wilbur, R., et al. "Acute Organic Brain Syndrome from Nadolol Therapy," letter, *Arch. Intern. Med.* 141: 1723 (1981).

CHAPTER 24: ADDITIONAL DRUGS

"Choice of Benzodiazepines," *Medical Letter* 23: 41–43 (1981).

Betts, T. A., and J. Birtle. "Effect of Two Hypnotic Drugs on Actual Driving Performance Next Morning," *BMJ* 285: 852 (1982).

Schrager, B. R., and M. Ellestad. "The Importance of Blood Pressure Measurement During Exercise Testing," *Cardiovasc. Rev. & Rep.* 4: 381–93 (1983).

Fleg, J. L., et al. "Is Digoxin Really Important in Treatment of Compensated Heart Failure?" *Am. J. Med.* 73: 244–50 (1982).

Calesnick, B. "Nonprescription Anorexiants," *Am. Fam. Phys.* 26: 206–8 (1982).

Sours, H. E., et al. "Sudden Death Associated with Very Low Calorie Weight Reduction Regimens," *Am. J. Clin. Nutr.* 34: 453–61 (1981).

"A Joint Statement by the Board of Medical Quality Assurance and the California Medical Association on the Prescribing of Schedule II Non-narcotic Controlled Substances," *Action Report* #23: 5–6 (1983).

"Toxicity of Nonsteroidal Anti-Inflammatory Drugs," *Medical Letter* 25: 15–16 (1983).

Khaw, K.-T., and W. S. Peart. "Blood Pressure and Contraceptive Use," *BMJ* 285: 403–7 (1982).

Stadel, B. V. "Oral Contraceptives and Cardiovascular Disease," *NEJM* 305: 612–18 and 672–77 (1981).

UCLA Conference. "Estrogen Replacement Therapy: Indications and Complications," *Ann. Int. Med.* 98: 195–205 (1983).

Beral, V., and C. Kay. "The Pill and Circulatory Disease," *Am. Heart J.* 97: 263–64 (1979).

Kannel, W. B. "Possible Hazards of Oral Contraceptive Use," editorial, *Circulation* 60: 490–91 (1979).

Newmark, S. R., and B. Williamson. "Survey of Very-Low-Calorie Weight Reduction Diets (I and II)," *Arch. Intern. Med.* 143: 1195–98, 1423–27 (1983).

The Coronary Drug Project Research Group. "The Coronary Drug Project," *JAMA* 220: 996–1008 (1972); 226: 652–57 (1973); 231: 360–81 (1975).

DePaulo, J. R. "Psychiatric Morbidity from Long-term Medications," *JAMA* 247: 1867 (1982).

Young, B. B. "Bitter Pills: The Little-Known Behavioral Effects of Common Drugs," *Medical Self-Care* 38–42, Fall 1982.

"Drug Prescribing—How to Avoid Problems with BMQA," interview with J. P. Cosentino, *Action Report* 22: 1–7 (1982).

CHAPTER 25: NUTRITION

Liebman, B. "The Sodium-Hypertension Connection," *Nutrition Action* 9: 5–11 (1982).

Newman, L. "More 'Salt' Talks: Diet and Hypertension," *JAMA* 248: 2949–51 (1982).

"Nutrition and Blood Pressure Control: Current Status of Dietary Factors and Hypertension," symposium, *Ann. Int. Med.* 98 (Supp. Pt. 2): 697–890 (1983).

MacGregor, G. A. "Dietary Sodium and Potassium Intake and Blood Pressure," *Lancet* 1: 750–53 (1983).

——, et al. "Moderate Potassium Supplementation in Essential Hypertension," *Lancet* 2: 567–70 (1982).

Kaplan, N. M. "Hypokalemia: Real and Potential Hazards," *Primary Cardiology* 9:5: 133–41 (1983).

Langford, H. G. "Potassium in Hypertension," *Postgrad. Med. J.* 73: 227–33 (1983).

Bunag, R. D., et al. "Chronic Sucrose Ingestion Induces Mild Hypertension and Tachycardia in Rats," *Hypertension* 5: 218–25 (1983).

Brenner, B. M., et al. "Dietary Protein Intake and the Progressive Nature of Kidney Disease: The Role of Hemodynamically Mediated Glomerular Injury in the Pathogenesis of Progressive Glomerular Sclerosis in Aging, Renal Ablation, and Intrinsic Renal Disease," *NEJM* 307: 652–59 (1982).

American Institute of Nutrition. "Symposium: Nutrition and Aging Bone Loss," *Fed. Proc.* 40: 2417–38 (1981).

Margen, S., et al. "Studies in Calcium Metabolism I. The Calciuretic Effect of Dietary Protein," *Am. J. Clin. Nutr.* 27: 584–89 (1974).

Spencer, H., et al. "Effect of a High Protein (Meat) Intake on Calcium Metabolism in Man," *Am. J. Clin. Nutr.* 31: 2167–80 (1978).

Allen, L. H., et al. "Protein-Induced Hypercalciuria: A Longer Term Study," *Am. J. Clin. Nutr.* 32: 741–49 (1979).

Sacks, F. M., et al. "Effect of Ingestion of Meat on Plasma Cholesterol of Vegetarians," *JAMA* 246: 640–44 (1981).

Burstyn, P. "Effect of Meat on BP," letter, *JAMA* 248: 29–30 (1982).

Rouse, I., et al. "Blood-Pressure-Lowering Effect of a Vegetarian Diet: Controlled Trial in Normotensive Subjects," *Lancet* 1: 5–10 (1983).

Committee on Nutrition, American Academy of Pediatrics. "Nutritional Aspects of Vegetarianism, Health Foods, and Fad Diets," *Pediatrics* 59: 460–64 (1977).

Puska, P., et al. "Controlled, Randomized Trial of the Effect of Dietary Fat on Blood Pressure," *Lancet* 1: 1–5 (1983).

Iacono, J. M., et al. "Reduction of Blood Pressure Associated with Dietary Polyunsaturated Fat," *Hypertension* 4 (Supp. III): III-34–42 (1982).

————— and R. M. Dougherty. "The Role of Dietary Polyunsaturated Fatty Acids and Prostaglandins in Reducing Blood Pressure and Improving Thrombogenic Indices," *Preventive Med.* 12: 60–69 (1983).

Connor, W. E., and D. S. Lin. "The Effect of Shellfish in the Diet Upon the Plasma Lipid Levels in Humans," *Metabolism* 31: 1046–51 (1982).

Kannel, W. B., et al. "Cholesterol in the Prediction of Atherosclerotic Disease," *Ann. Int. Med.* 90: 85–91 (1979).

Freestone, S., and L. E. Ramsay. "Effect of Coffee and Cigarette Smoking on the Blood Pressure of Untreated and Diuretic-Treated Hypertensive Patients," *Am. J. Med.* 73: 348–53 (1982).

McCarron, D. A., et al. "Current Perspectives in Hypertension," symposium, *Hypertension* 4 (pt. 2): 1–183 (1982).

—————. "Nutrition and Blood Pressure Control," symposium, *Ann. Int. Med.* 98: 697–890 (1983).

Belizan, J. M., et al. "Reduction of Blood Pressure With Calcium Supplementation in Young Adults," *JAMA* 249: 1161–65 (1983).

Galton, L. *Executive Nutrition and Diet.* New York: McGraw-Hill, 1983.

CHAPTER 26: EXERCISE 1

Bortz, W. M. "Disuse and Aging," *JAMA* 248: 1203–8 (1982).

Spirduso, W. W. "Exercise and the Aging Brain," *Research Quarterly for Exercise and Sport* 54: 208–18 (1983).

Burfoot, A. "A Masters Plan: Turning Back the Calendar by Running," *Runner's World,* January 1983, pp. 40–68.

Cooper, K. H. *The Aerobics Way.* New York: Bantam, 1978.

CHAPTER 27: EXERCISE 2

Shyne, K. "Richard H. Dominguez, MD: To Stretch or Not to Stretch?" *The Physician and Sportsmedicine* 10: 137–40 (1982).

Woo, R., et al. "Effect of Exercise on Spontaneous Calorie Intake in Obesity," *Am. J. Clin. Nutr.* 36: 470–77 (1982).

————. "Voluntary Food Intake During Prolonged Exercise in Obese Women," *Am. J. Clin. Nutr.* 36: 478–84 (1982).

Whitmer, R. W. *Whitmer's Guide to Total Wellness.* Garden City, N.Y.: Doubleday, 1982, p. 83.

Williams, P. T. "The Effects of Running Mileage and Duration on Plasma Lipoprotein Levels," *JAMA* 247: 2674–79 (1982).

Kramsch, D. M. "Reduction of Coronary Atherosclerosis by Moderate Conditioning Exercise in Monkeys on an Atherogenic Diet," *NEJM* 305: 1483–89 (1981).

Felig, P., et al. "Hypoglycemia During Prolonged Exercise in Normal Men," *NEJM* 306: 895–900 (1982).

Barnes, L. "Electrolyte Replacement: Salt Pills to Bananas," *Anabolism* 1: 5 (1982).

McMurray, R. G., et al. "The Effects of Fructose and Glucose On High Intensity Endurance Performance." *Research Quarterly for Exercise and Sport* 54: 156–62 (1983).

Nicholson, J. P., and D. B. Case. "Carboxyhemoglobin Levels in New York City Runners," *The Physician and Sportsmedicine* 11:3: 135–38 (1983).

Leepson, M. *Executive Fitness.* New York: McGraw-Hill, 1983.

CHAPTER 28: WHAT IS STRESS?

Eliot, R. S. *Stress and the Major Cardiovascular Disorders.* Mount Kisco, N.Y.: Futura, 1979.

Resnekov, L. "Noise, Radio Frequency Radiation and the Cardiovascular System," *Circulation* 63: 264A–66A (1981).

Peterson, E. A., et al. "Noise Raises Blood Pressure Without Impairing Auditory Sensitivity," *Science* 211: 1450–52 (1981).

Jonsson, A., and L. Hansson. "Prolonged Exposure to a Stressful Stimulus (Noise) as a Cause of Raised Blood-Pressure in Man," *Lancet* 1: 86–87 (1977).

CHAPTER 29: STRESS MANAGEMENT 1

Dworkin, B. R., et al. "Baroreceptor Activation Reduces Reactivity to Noxious Stimulation: Implications for Hypertension," *Science* 205: 1299–1301 (1979).

CHAPTER 30: STRESS MANAGEMENT 2

Benson, H. *The Relaxation Response.* New York: Morrow, 1975.

———. "Systemic Hypertension and the Relaxation Response," *NEJM* 296: 1152–56 (1977).

———, et al. "Stress and Hypertension: Interrelations and Management," in G. Onesti and A. M. Brest, eds., *Hypertension: Mechanisms, Diagnosis and Treatment.* New York: Grune & Stratton, 1983, pp. 113–24.

Kangilaski, J. "Dialogue: a Link to Psychosomatic Illness," *JAMA* 247: 2760–73 (1982).

Patel, C., et al. "Controlled Trial of Biofeedback-Aided Behavioural Methods in Reducing Mild Hypertension," *BMJ* 282: 2005–8 (1981).

Index

Index

Saturated fats, 293
Saunas, 322
Sea salt, 94
Selacryn, 14
Senility, propranolol as cause of, 243
Serpasil. *See* Reserpine
Sexuality, effect of blockers on, 242, 247, 250
Shapiro, A. P., 16
Sheenan, George, 313
Shoes, for exercise, 310
Shortness of breath, 20
Side effects of drugs, 10, 14, 52, 248–49
  blockers, emergency nervous system, 242–51
  calcium channel blockers, 259
  diuretics, 230–31, 235
  estrogen, 274
  pain medications, 273
  pargyline, 259
  reserpine, 239–40
  vasodilators, 256–57
  See also specific drugs
Sleep
  coping with stress by, 337
  exercise as control for problems, 320–21
Sleeping pills, 266–67
Smoking, 7, 264, 281
  abnormal heartbeat caused by, 282
  quitting, 135, 176
  to reduce stress, 336–37
Snacks, sodium content of, 118
SNS. *See* Sympathetic (emergency) nervous system
Sodium, 6–7, 36–37, 218–21, 286–87
  in antacids, 275
  average intake by Americans, 287
  excretion test, 144–45
  food labels, 94
  foods with high content, list of, 116–18
  restriction, in phase one of nutritional program, 115
  sources listing sodium content in foods, 368
  See also Salt
Sodium bicarbonate, 94
Sodium chloride. *See* Salt
Sodium nitrate, 94, 286
Sodium nitrite, 94, 286
Spangler, Paul, 303
Sphygmomanometer (blood pressure cuff), 29, 63–64, 88–89
Spironolactone, 231

Stammler, Jeremiah, 57
Starch, 296
Stationary cycle, 307–8, 312
Step-care approach, in drug therapy, 230, 250
Steroids, 281
Stitch in the side, when exercising, 313–14
Stomach cancer, 162
Stress, 21, 32–35, 218–19, 324–34
  abnormal heartbeat caused by, 282
  acute, 327–28
  caffeine and, 297–98
  causes, 129–31
  chronic, 328–33
  colon, effect on, 265
  definition, 33
  job-related, 100–1
  physical symptoms, 101–2
  recording of, in blood pressure control program diary, 83–84
Stress analysis, 97
  tests, 98–107, 127
Stress management, 56–57, 183–84, 335–49
  affirmations, 347
  assertiveness, 345
  avoidance, 128–31, 343–44
  awareness training, 134–35
  in blood pressure control program, 62–63
    week one, 83–84
    week two, 97–107
    week five, 127–36
    week eight, 152–60
    week nine, 164
    week eleven, 174–76
    week twelve, 179–84
  destructive techniques, 182–83
  exercise, 320, 342–43
  forgiveness, 179–81
  laughing, 156
  looking on the bright side, 152–53
  meditation, 347–49
  muscle relaxation, 135–36, 349
  nutrition, 341–42
  play and recreation, 153–55, 344–45
  positive imagery, 346
  Rational Emotive Therapy, 131–34
  visualization, 156–57
  worrying on purpose, 155–56
Stress reaction, 324–25
Stress scale, 164